Angel Creek

Gail Porter Mandell

Angel Creek
where the river meets the sea

THE UNIVERSITY OF THE WEST INDIES PRESS
Jamaica • Barbados • Trinidad and Tobago

University of the West Indies Press
7A Gibraltar Hall Road, Mona
Kingston 7, Jamaica
www.uwipress.com

© 2014 by Gail Porter Mandell

All rights reserved. Published 2014

A catalogue record of this book is available from
the National Library of Jamaica.

ISBN: 978-976-640-461-1 (print)
978-976-640-467-3 (Kindle)
978-976-640-475-8 (ePub)

Front cover photograph: Cecropia tree, by Ken Jameson, 2014.
Back cover photograph: Street scene, Dangriga, Belize, by Gail Porter Mandell, 2004.
Cover and book design by Robert Harris
Set in Dante 11/14 x 24
Printed in the United States of America

For my "Angel Creek" family and friends, especially Charlie Woods, Malilee Zimmers Elis and Kathy Fridgen O'Connell, and for my brothers and sisters: Dennis, Tim, Lynn, Patrick, Colleen, Brian, and Jim (1944–2013), the first of us to reach the sea.

CONTENTS

Prologue	The Vow	1
Chapter 1	Crossing Borders	3
Chapter 2	Listening to Hattie	9
Chapter 3	Angel Creek	20
Chapter 4	Caught in the Middle	33
Chapter 5	The Eye of the Blackbird	47
Chapter 6	Priests and Virgins	55
Chapter 7	Yellow Bird	73
Chapter 8	Dark Moods	92
Chapter 9	Sherry, Sissy and Jean	104
Chapter 10	The Jesus Tree	119
Chapter 11	Dying for Ice Cream	129
Chapter 12	The Game	146
Chapter 13	A Busy Week	167
Chapter 14	Three Fires and a Disappearance	192
Chapter 15	Going Back	206

Chapter 16	Welcoming the Dawn	*217*
Chapter 17	Local Crises	*228*
Chapter 18	Betrayals	*235*
Chapter 19	Tiger	*247*
Chapter 20	Celebration	*261*
Chapter 21	Gifts	*273*
Chapter 22	Sleepless Nights	*284*
Chapter 23	Absence	*296*
Chapter 24	Revelations	*307*
Chapter 25	Leaving Angel Creek	*318*
Chapter 26	The River of Time	*321*
Epilogue	Where the River Meets the Sea	*327*

Author's Note *355*

Acknowledgements *357*

"For all at last return to the sea – to Oceanus, the ocean river, like the everflowing stream of time, the beginning and the end."

—Rachel Carson, *The Sea Around Us*

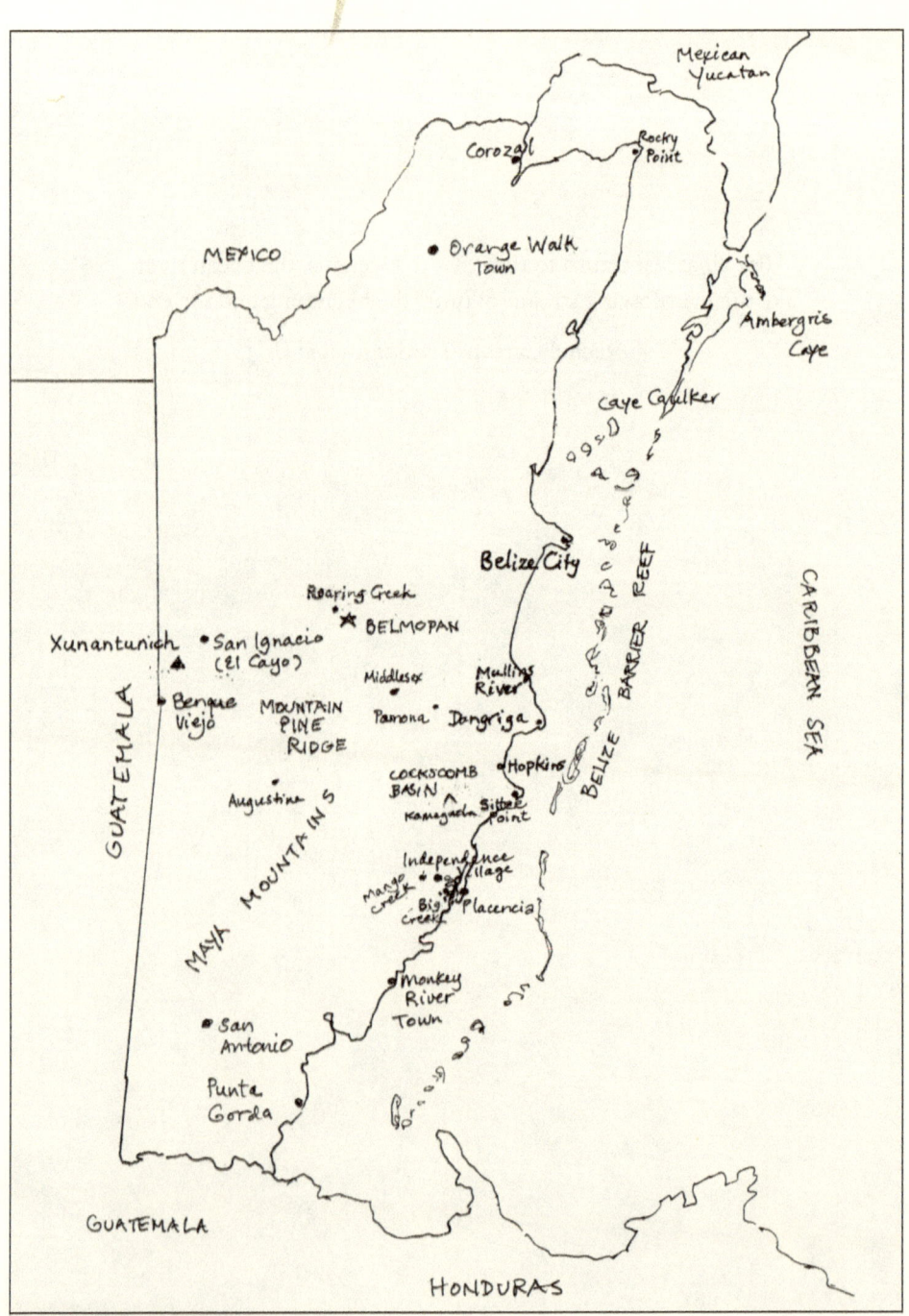

Figure 1. Map of Belize, 2004.

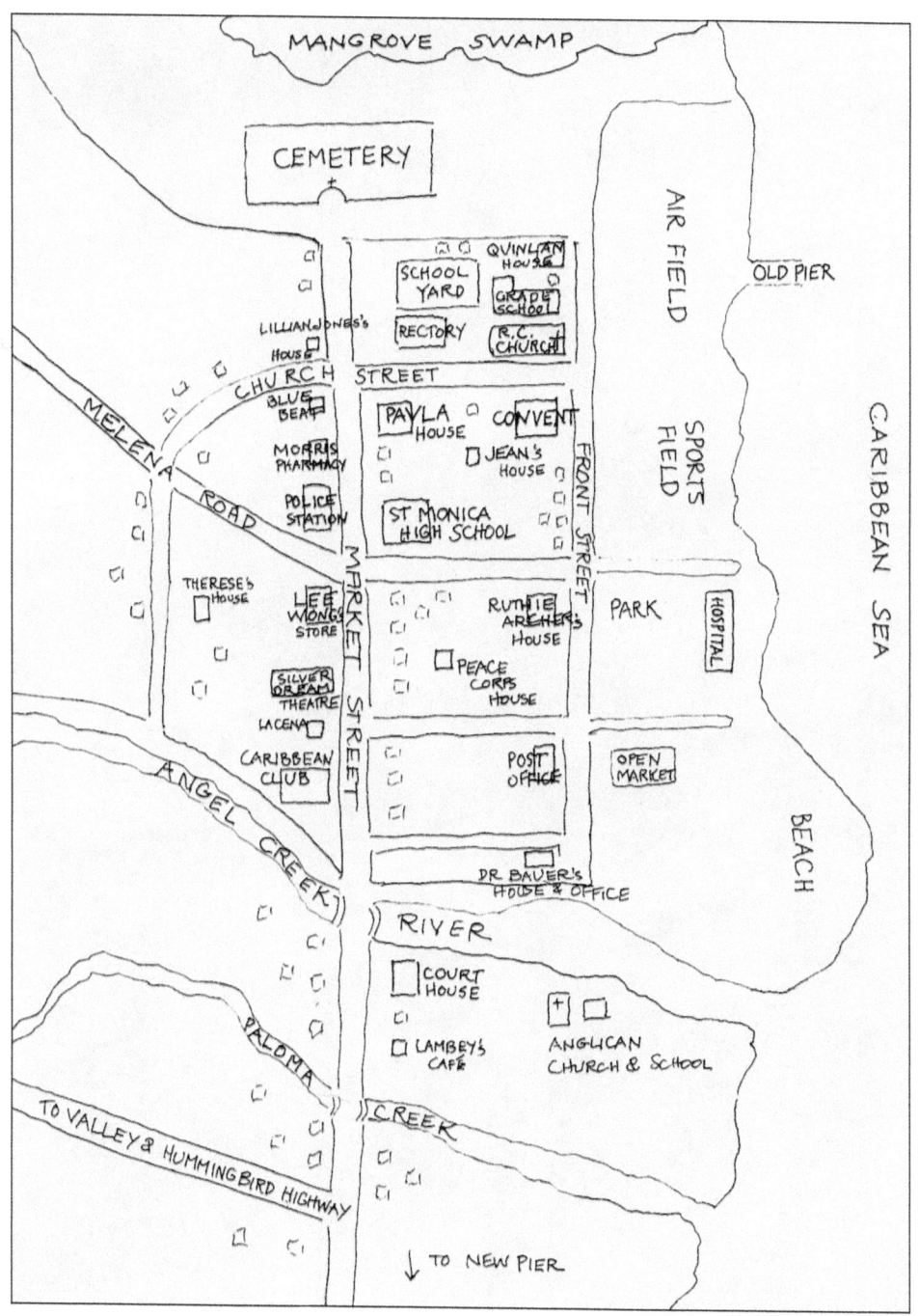

Figure 2. Map of "Angel Creek", 1962

Prologue

THE VOW

WE MADE OUR VOW on a windy night in 1962, by the light of a full moon, three young women, with a priest as our companion. In the distance, the liquid curve of the Caribbean, tarnished silver against the darkened sky, defined the eastern horizon.

Earlier that day, one of our last together in Angel Creek, Father Bosque had burst through our front door without knocking. He told us to bring some warm clothes and said we'd be out late. "I'm taking you someplace special," he announced.

Around three-thirty, we set off in his blue Jeep, the colour of a robin's egg, and it took us over an hour to arrive at the base of one of the mountains in the Coxscomb Range. It took us another hour to follow on foot the rough trail that wound its way to the top.

This was the highest mountain around, but the climb was easy for us, young and fit in those days. Like all the mountains in the part of the world then called British Honduras, our mountain was ancient, not new; rounded, not craggy; a hill, not a peak. Loose stones skittered away from us as we circled to the top. Wild orchids hid in crevices. While the sun was up, we were hot, even though it was winter up north, where Molly, Kate and I were from. When the sun went down, the air was chilly, and when the wind rose, we pulled on our sweaters and coats and huddled together, biting into the chocolate and oranges we carried with us.

As we watched the moon rise over the sea, a small cloud formed above it. Gradually it took the shape of a hovering dove.

"Look at that cloud," Kate said. "And the moon looks just like a communion host, doesn't it?"

Father Bosque had his rifle with him, as he always did on our trips into the bush. I felt uneasy around it, afraid it would go off accidentally. Now, on a whim, I asked if he'd let me fire it. It was the same gun he had used to kill the tiger.

He knew I'd never used a firearm before. "You're in a strange mood," he said as he showed me how to hold it.

"Where should I aim?"

"Anywhere but at us."

Holding the butt against my right shoulder, as he instructed me, I took aim at the cloud dove.

"Not the dove," Molly cried out in mock horror.

Deliberately, slowly I squeezed the trigger. The violent kick of the rifle knocked me backward. Father Bosque caught hold of me and kept me from falling. I staggered upright with a giddy feeling of release – and relief. Unimpeded, the moon continued its serene rise and the grey dove continued to brood, undisturbed.

Just before midnight, Father Bosque chanted compline, the last office of the day. By then, we had named the mountain "Kamagacha", combining parts of our names. With our hands piled on top of each other's, we swore someday to return together to this place we shared as home.

Chapter 1

CROSSING BORDERS

MY FIRST IMPRESSION OF British Honduras ("BH" as I soon learned to call it) was of walking under water. The atmosphere, dense, tropical, pressed against me as I moved. Everything slowed down. I took a deep breath and felt as if I were drinking the air. I began to like the feeling. In my memory, St Louis humidity, my native environment, seemed claustrophobic compared with this. There, nothing moved.

Leaving the airport lobby, cooled by open windows and overhead fans, I realized the difference. A current of air flowed around me, lifting my skirt and tangling my hair. Here, there was a constant breeze. And on it, I smelled the sea.

A warped poster near the door greeted arriving passengers: "Welcome to Belize City!" It pictured a blue canal bordered by white colonial mansions whose balconies overflowed with flowers.

"Yes, there are some canals in Belize City, as you'll see," Father Weaver said as he drove three of his new teachers – Peg, Sue Ella and me – along the potholed road from the airport into town. "Once, all this area was mangrove swamp. Long before white people arrived, the Maya built the canals to drain the swamp."

Father Weaver was the forty-something Jesuit with large, watery green eyes who'd recruited us to teach in a country none of us knew existed before we met him. On our left, briefly, lay the hazy sea, and on our right, the dark waters of the Belize River. My imagination generated images of a tropical paradise. Scenes from the movie version of *South Pacific* merged with memories of Xochimilco, where not two days earlier, during a layover in Mexico

City, Peg, Sue Ella and I had drifted on limpid water through sun and shadow, the scent of gardenias in the air.

"Why are so many of the buildings on stilts?" I asked, noticing that almost all the houses we passed sat at least ten feet off the ground on wooden or concrete posts.

"To catch the sea breeze. And in case of floods."

They reminded me of cottages along the Meramec River, just south of St Louis, where I'd spent occasional summer weekends as a child. Looking more closely, I saw that more than a few of these cottages looked unsteady on their perches, sagging and tilting at odd angles. The most dilapidated had been abandoned. All that remained of some was rubble among the pilings.

Not only on the outskirts but also approaching the centre of the town, I saw one vacant lot after another. On them, squatters had constructed shanties out of whatever came to hand: mismatched lengths of wood, salvaged pieces of rusty tin and cardboard packing crates. Brown-skinned children crouched on the shady side of shacks, out of the blistering sun. A few waved as we drove by in our Land Rover. Their greeting felt like a welcome, and I stuck my hand out the window to wave back.

As we crossed one small bridge after another, I saw for myself that a network of canals did indeed criss-cross the city. Their water was neither clear nor blue. Flowers did not festoon their banks. Instead, shops and tenements backed on what were in reality wide and dirty ditches. As we passed over one of them, I watched in disbelief as a woman tossed a bucketful of garbage out her window into the murky water. We'd gone by before I could be sure that what I'd seen scrabbling along the slimy bank were rats.

In the back of my mind, I heard my grandmother's sensible voice: "What have you got yourself into this time, Abigail Porter?" She often accused me of leaping before I looked, a reputation I'd established at age eight by running away from home and trekking nine miles over busy city streets to her house. What my grandmother didn't know was that I hadn't leaped at all that first time. I'd spent months memorizing the route every time we drove it, planning my escape from unpredictable parents and too many squalling babies.

This time, though, I feared she might be right. Accustomed as I was to the modern conveniences of the United States and fresh from the ancient beauties of Mexico, the city I came to that June afternoon in 1962 looked impoverished and insubstantial, improvised and temporary. It was hard to tell whether the city was coming into being or going out of existence. Even the nicer neighbourhoods looked besieged, with palm trees snapped off and hibiscus bushes ragged and misshapen, like beggars clinging to life.

"What happened here?" Peg asked. A native St Louisan like me, Peg was a large blonde with a decisive manner who'd quickly assumed leadership of our band of three as we explored Mexico City. Hers were the guidebooks, the sense of direction, the Spanish phrase book, and the handbag bulging with Bayer Aspirin, Pepto-Bismol, Band-Aids and Coppertone.

Father Weaver replied that Hattie had happened.

"Hattie? Whoever is Hattie?" asked Sue Ella. She was born and spent her childhood in Arkansas. Her twang perfectly complemented her auburn hair and narrow eyes, an earthier green than Father Weaver's. In Mexico City, men had turned on the street to watch her go by.

"Surely I mentioned Hattie when I interviewed you. She was our Halloween surprise last October – a Category 5 hurricane. The worst there is."

He told us Hattie's eye had passed directly over Belize City. The combined winds and floods had killed hundreds of people ("God rest their souls; we'll never know the exact number," he said) and left more than three-quarters of the population of British Honduras homeless. The cayes – islands just offshore – and all the towns and villages along the coast had been ravaged.

So nature itself was responsible for this sorry state of affairs. Those dark-skinned people among the ruins, throwing garbage from windows – not their fault.

As we drove into the city centre, Father Weaver pointed out a few new buildings that had gone up since Hattie, their tin roofs and fresh white paint glinting in the sun. Scaffolds encased many buildings, including one he identified as Holy Redeemer, the Catholic cathedral. The image of the massive cathedral in Mexico City – we'd visited it only two days before – flashed into my mind. It, too, had been encased in scaffolding – sinking under its weight, we were told, falling back into the ruins of the Aztec temple the conquistadors had demolished to build it.

Hattie had blown out all the stained glass windows in the church, Father Weaver explained, and the steeple was damaged too. But, he added, "We're still able to offer Mass there, thank God." Most of the shops along the main streets had reopened within a few months of the hurricane, he said, but rebuilding and repair were slow because, as he put it, "We have the time but not the money."

Our vehicle was one of only a few on the road, but we moved slowly through the narrow city streets, thronged at midday with pedestrians and bicyclists. We passed dozens of tiny, stall-like shops that displayed an assortment of goods, from straw hats and baskets to plastic sandals and buckets.

"What in the world are those birds?" Peg asked. She was in the front seat, leaning forward and looking up.

Sticking my head out the open back window, I saw dozens of prehistoric-looking birds circling overhead. He said they were frigatebirds, a type of marine bird. The wharf was close by, he added, but warehouses hid any clear view of the waterfront. The closer we came to it, the less we saw of the sea's mercurial expanse.

Father Weaver told us that cargo ships from all over the world docked offshore. Almost everything except citrus, mahogany, bananas and sugar cane had to be imported, making the cost of living in the city very high. He said that in the villages, people grew food and caught fish. They had most of what they needed just outside their doors. Life in the city was harder, especially for the poor. "And that means almost everybody."

Before we reached the harbour, where a branch of the Belize River emptied into the sea, Father Weaver turned to the left. This was the Fort George District, he told us, the nicest part of the city before the hurricane.

He soon stopped in front of a smaller version of the white mansion pictured on the airport poster. This was PAVLA House, where we'd be staying until we received our assignments. It was in the process of being repainted, and dark green shutters leaned against the railings of the upper balconies, waiting to be reattached. It was once the Dutch Embassy, he said, and pointed out the US Embassy, located down the street within a large, gated compound.

Papal Volunteers to Latin America – PAVLA for short – was the Catholic equivalent of the Peace Corps. Both were in their second year of existence, the Peace Corps founded by newly elected President Kennedy as a goodwill initiative and PAVLA by Pope John XXIII in response to the needs of the church in Latin America. That was almost all I knew about the organization I'd committed a year of my life to, but I knew a lot about the Society of Jesus – the Jesuits – an order of Catholic priests as notorious for subtle casuistry as they were respected for their top-notch educational institutions and worldwide missionary efforts. Many of my friends had attended St Louis U., one of their universities, and Jesuit scholars had often lectured at my college.

All along the winding street, surely one of the most impressive in Belize City before Hattie, we saw signs of construction, even though no workers were anywhere in sight. Several large houses were boarded up, with "Keep Out" signs posted on the doors. Father Weaver said that it takes a long time to come back from a hurricane like Hattie.

Sue Ella, Peg and I helped the priest unload our suitcases from the back of the Land Rover. As we stood on the pavement, our matching sets of luggage piled around us – mine was three-piece white Tourister, a graduation present – Father Weaver shook his head. "You girls could start a department store with all that stuff!"

I was taken aback. Except for a box of books and another of winter clothes stored in my mother's basement, everything I had in the world fit into those two suitcases, one smaller than the other, and a tiny overnight case. I'd just been thinking how little I had to get me through an entire year. Half the clothes I'd brought needed laundering after only three days in Mexico City.

It was Peg's idea to stop over in Mexico City on our way to British Honduras. Peg and Sue Ella, who'd been classmates at Fontbonne College, already knew each other, though not well. I'd gone to Maryville, another Catholic women's college in St Louis. We had met only once before we left for British Honduras, at Father Weaver's suggestion, to make travel plans. The plane ticket, paid for by our local bishop, wouldn't cost any more with a layover, Peg assured us, and Luisa, a college friend of hers from Mexico City, had offered to show us around. With an exchange rate of twelve pesos to the US dollar, she thought we could get by on less than ten dollars a day. After all, she pointed out, people went to Europe on five dollars a day.

I'd never been out of the continental United States and didn't need much persuading. Sue Ella hesitated – she was on a tight budget, she said. So was I, but if I was careful, I was sure what was left of my graduation money would cover the cost of a shared hotel room and food.

In fact, it wouldn't have if Peg's friend Luisa and her cousin Ramón, who met us at the airport, hadn't insisted on paying for almost everything. "But you are our guests," one or the other of them would say when we tried to pay our share of entrance fees or the cost of meals. I'd never before experienced such generosity outside of family.

Both of them and most of their friends had studied for a year or more in the States and could speak excellent English. They were in love with America and Americans. They told us that President Kennedy and Jackie were due to arrive for a state visit. We'd miss them by days only, Luisa said. Such a pity we couldn't stay until they came!

Luisa, Ramón and their friends introduced me to a world far away from the one I had left: Crystal City, Missouri, a sleepy Mississippi River town just south of St Louis. My mother lived there with her new husband and their one-year-old son – my infant half-brother. I had six other siblings, four boys and two girls, scattered here and there.

When I told my mother that I was heading off to Central America, she made me show her British Honduras on the map. There it was, a bite of land about the size of New Hampshire, with Mexico to the north, Guatemala to the west and Honduras to the south – all poised to devour the tiny country.

"I thought it was an island," she said. "Are you sure it's safe? Aren't all those countries down there always having revolutions?"

"Not British Honduras, Mother. It's a British colony. And I'll be working with American Jesuits. They wouldn't send me there if it wasn't safe."

"Can't you find a teaching job here, now that you have your degree? I know there's not much in Crystal City, but what about St Louis, or even Chicago?"

"I want to see another part of the world. Someplace different from here."

"Have you told your father?"

"I haven't seen him in months," I said with a shrug.

Chapter 2

LISTENING TO HATTIE

FATHER WEAVER WELCOMED THE newly arrived volunteers over supper that first night at PAVLA House. He regretted the condition of the house, he said. Because of the extensive damage caused by Hattie, the renovation was weeks behind schedule.

To make a table we had set up planks on sawhorses left by the workmen – most of the furniture hadn't yet been delivered – and covered these with a sheet. On it, Sue Ella, a home economics major, set the big pot of spaghetti she'd concocted in the half-finished kitchen from the ingredients Father Weaver provided. He also supplied a case of cold Heineken and a colourful array of soda pop, called "lemonade" here.

He blessed the food and then, lifting his beer bottle, said, "To the new Papal Volunteers."

I looked around the improvised table at those who'd be my cohort during the coming year, still not able to recall all their names. There were twelve of us from the States, ten single men and women just out of college and a married couple who were a few years older. There were also three young English women sent by Voluntary Services Overseas, a European organization not directly connected to the Church. We heard that several more PAVLA volunteers were scheduled to join us in September. Twenty members of the Peace Corps would also arrive then.

Peg, Sue Ella and I had already been dubbed collectively the "St Louis Women", and when someone, invariably male, wanted to tease us, they hummed the opening bars of "Saint Louis Blues". Three of the male volunteers had been classmates at St Benedict's College in Kansas. They were all about the same height, shorter than Peg by an inch or two, with boyish faces. They became the "St Ben's Men". Another two guys were best friends who'd driven down together from Milwaukee in an old Ford V-8 they referred to as "Carlos the Car". "He started out Carl," they said, "but we re-baptized him in the Rio Grande." They were tall and lanky, with lots of hair in an era of crew cuts, easy to distinguish from the St Ben's Men. The married couple, Ken and Judy Ritter, sat together at the other end of the table, near Father Weaver, as did a pale, quiet girl named Maureen Bone from a small town near Kansas City.

A dark-haired young woman I hadn't met earlier came in a few minutes after me. She was extraordinarily pretty, with glowing skin and a dimpled smile. She slid into the chair next to mine and introduced herself as Molly Ann Eliot from Racine, Wisconsin, adding, "Just call me Molly." She'd graduated from Marquette, she said, with a major in English and a minor in French. She wore simple clothes, a sleeveless white blouse and black cotton skirt, but the way she wore them made me wish that I, too, had on a sleeveless white blouse and black cotton skirt. I discovered that while I'd been upstairs writing in my journal, she had been walking around town, taking photographs with her Kodak Brownie.

Molly asked me if I'd seen the swing bridge. When I said I hadn't, she described it as an "amazing" bridge over the mouth of the Belize River, near the wharf. In the entire world, it was the only bridge like it, she said. Twice a day, once early in the morning and again late in the afternoon, the bridge was manually rotated ninety degrees to let sailboats and other small craft through, to or from the sea. It was the only bridge across the river for miles, and she'd found herself on the wrong side just as the bridge started turning. The rotation took about half an hour, and even if she'd almost missed supper, she was glad she'd seen it.

"I adore that whole area," she said. "Especially the wharf. The fishermen come in from the islands in their dugout canoes – they're called 'dories' – to sell their catch. It's the most colourful thing you've ever seen. Unfortunately, I only have black and white film. Who can afford colour?"

Molly said that she'd arrived in British Honduras almost a week earlier and been sent south to Punta Gorda, an Indian village close to the Honduras border, to settle in. But the flies and mosquitoes were bad there, and she was so allergic to them – she showed me her legs, covered with inflamed bites – that the priest in Punta Gorda had reassigned her to Angel Creek, a bigger town farther up the coast. She'd left her things there and come north to meet the rest of the volunteers.

"The mosquitoes in BH are as big as hummingbirds," she said. "This part of the Caribbean isn't called the 'Mosquito Coast' for nothing. But there's something even worse that you can't see called 'sandflies'." She said that at first the sandfly bites looked like a tiny speck of blood, but they soon became infected and swelled up because it was impossible not to scratch them. As if to demonstrate, she reached down and scratched one ankle until it bled.

"Disgusting, I know," she said. "I'm sorry, but I really can't help myself. I find myself fantasizing about cutting them out one by one. I think it would be less painful."

After she paused to try some of her spaghetti, she asked me if I had any idea where I was being sent. I answered that Father Weaver told me when I signed up that I'd probably teach in Belize City.

Diana Jones, one of the British volunteers who'd returned for a second year, leaned close and said in a low voice, "You'll be lucky if you're sent elsewhere. The nuns here keep us under lock and key."

"Why do you put up with it?" I asked.

"They'd send us home if we didn't," she answered matter-of-factly.

After supper, conversation circled back to Hattie. We were amazed that not one of us had heard a thing about it in the States, but Father Weaver said he wasn't surprised. Hattie changed directions – and names – three times before she blew herself out. She never reached the United States. Most likely she got a paragraph or two in the local newspapers and maybe ten seconds, if that, on radio and television news programmes.

"What goes on down here is probably the best-kept secret in the world. I guess you could call this one of the earth's forgotten places, except you have to know about a place before you can forget it. Most of the world doesn't even know we exist." He looked over at Diana. "You were here for the hurricane, weren't you, Diana?"

"Yes, I was here," Diana said, but added that she hadn't seen much of the storm itself. The hurricane hit around midnight and lasted till dawn. She'd been boarded up inside the convent through the worst of it. "Mostly, I listened to Hattie," she said. "And in a way, that was worse than seeing Hattie happen."

When we pressed for details, she told us that just after supper on the night of the storm – ironically the very last day of the official hurricane season –

most of the neighbourhood had gathered in the convent, a designated shelter. All the female volunteers in Belize City were living there at the time. Until that afternoon, it had seemed as though the storm was travelling northwest, towards the Yucatán peninsula of Mexico. Instead, it veered due west, towards the Belize coast. Evacuation was impossible. Most people had nowhere outside the city to go and no way to get there.

People were pretty calm, she added. Belizeans were used to hurricanes because as many as two or three could strike in a single season. Many of the older people had lived through the terrible hurricane of 1931, thirty years before, in the days before hurricanes had names. It had demolished the city. A thousand people died in that hurricane because there was no warning system and no one knew how bad the storm would be. People said that Hattie couldn't possibly be worse.

"In a way, they were right," Diana commented. "Only about a third as many died in Hattie. But they were wrong too. Hattie devastated almost the entire country, not just Belize City."

According to Diana, Hattie hit the city a little before midnight. The electricity had gone out hours before – it was never reliable, she warned us, even in good weather – and all the windows were boarded up. That made the sounds even more terrifying.

"The wind screamed like a banshee," she said, "and the rain pelted the building with a sound like stones being thrown. We could hear the metal roofs ripping off nearby buildings. I could imagine them slicing through the air like machetes. All manner of debris smashed into us, one explosion right after another – just like war."

In the middle of the night, there was a lull. The rain and wind died down, and it seemed like the storm was over. As people began to move, a man's voice called out, warning everyone that the silence was most likely the eye of the hurricane passing over. "That silence was almost worse than the noise had been," Diana said. "As though the eye was searching for whatever was left standing and whoever was still hiding. And then all hell broke loose, worse than before. It wasn't just the rain and the wind but now the sea, too, heaving itself onto the city."

Diana said she'd heard that in the 1931 hurricane, people went out after they thought the storm had ended. Word got around that the sea had pulled back beyond the barrier reef offshore and there was no water at all in the harbour. Hundreds went down to see for themselves. Without warning, the water came rushing back into the city, drowning most of them.

"I was just there, at the waterfront!" Molly gasped, as though she'd been in imminent danger. Diana looked at her quizzically, but I knew how Molly felt. It was as though Hattie and that earlier hurricane were happening now, outside our half-painted walls.

Diana told another story from the 1931 hurricane: a man out on the cayes was washed into Belize Harbour on a tidal wave, and lived to tell the tale. "That's perhaps twenty miles!"

Father Weaver added that during Hattie, the cayes took the brunt of the storm. A village on Calabash Caye simply disappeared, and almost all of its three hundred inhabitants vanished with it. On Caye Caulker, all the buildings were destroyed. Hattie lifted up a schoolhouse where people had taken shelter and dashed it against the rocks. A dozen people died there, most of them children.

When someone asked how many died in Hattie, he answered that estimates went as high as five hundred, but there was no way to know for sure. "We do know that in all of BH, with a population well under a hundred thousand, about sixty-five thousand lost their homes."

Just then, the electricity in the house flickered and went out. For a moment, I was once again ten years old, listening to my grandfather's ghost stories. Father Weaver told us to sit tight. He pulled out a small flashlight and found and lit a kerosene lamp. By its wavering light, Diana returned to her story.

"As I said, all the windows in the convent were shuttered and boarded up during the storm. At dawn, once the worst of it had passed, we opened up and looked outside. We were on the top storey, and the water was up to the second-storey windows. Tidal waves – some of them up to fifteen feet high, we learned – had swept in during the storm and, of course, all the rivers and creeks were flooded. I recall seeing parts of houses and all sorts of other things floating by. Rather like a watery version of *The Wizard of Oz*, if you can imagine.

"In the midst of it all, a man in a dory – one of those dugout canoes the local fishermen use – paddled by as fast as he could go. The dory was filled with the oddest thing: bicycles, piled every which way. 'Now why would he want so many bicycles?' I asked myself. What could this chap hope to do with them? There wasn't any solid ground to ride on! I thought the poor man must be mad. Then someone said, 'The looters are already out, robbing the shops.' Four of the looters were hanged publicly a couple of days later. It was ghastly, like the Dark Ages. The worst of it was that it took days for help to get to us. All the lines were down – no phones, no electricity, no means to call for help – "

Father Weaver added that the only way word got out was through Father Peck, one of the priests in Belize City, who had a ham radio. Hattie convinced Father Weaver that the Maya civilization, which had vanished mysteriously about a thousand years earlier, was destroyed by just such a storm and its after-effects: polluted drinking water, contagious disease and famine.

Diana said a foot of muck covered everything once the water went down. All over the city, swarms of people pawed through the slime and rubble, looking for something to eat or drink. If the British and Americans – she called them "Yanks" – hadn't come in a few days later with food, medicine and clean water, no one would have survived.

We asked why she had come back after such an experience.

"Actually, I did go home to London for six weeks after the spring term – the end of our school year here," Diana said. "But I didn't have anything to do there. I didn't have a place at university – in Britain, a person can wait years and still not get a place, even though they're theoretically accepted – and it's hard to find any sort of decent job without the degree. So I signed on again for BH. In fact, I surprised myself. I couldn't wait to get back here. Frankly, I felt totally unnecessary at home. After Hattie, it seemed deadly dull there!"

She looked around the circle. "Why did all of you choose to come?"

The owner of Carlos the Car answered: "In my case, I think it's President Kennedy's influence. You know: 'Ask not what your country can do for you, ask what you can do for your country.'"

"And for the Church, of course," somebody added. "And the world."

That explanation would do as well as any. We had grown up hearing that ours was a pampered, self-centred, apathetic generation from elders who'd lived through two world wars and the Great Depression. Organizations like the Peace Corps and PAVLA tapped into our idealism and also our latent desire for sacrifice and service.

Diana's account of Hattie both chilled and thrilled me. Later that night, I recorded details of her account in my journal with the aid of a borrowed flashlight. It was the stuff of legends. Hearing her tell her story, her voice vibrant and filled with emotion, I envied her. I longed to be tested as she had been.

The following morning began with Mass in the cathedral we'd passed on our way from the airport. It was an imposing brick structure, even minus its steeple and stained-glass windows, but it looked out of place among all the white, wooden colonial buildings with their dark green shutters.

Father Weaver told us that the cathedral was modelled on a church in Rome designed by Saint Ignatius Loyola himself, founder of the Jesuits. The Belize cathedral had been built by slaves over a century earlier from bricks brought as ballast in ships that came out empty from England and carried home logwood, in those days the colony's chief export. Inside, the church had once been entirely mahogany, although some of the panelling was now painted over and the mahogany floor, destroyed by Hattie, had been replaced by tile. All of the wood was from the rain forests that spread over the interior of British Honduras.

After Mass, Bishop Robert Hodapp, also a Jesuit from the States, formally welcomed the PAVLA volunteers. He told us that he would leave for Rome in early October to attend the opening session of the Second Vatican Council. It had been three years in the planning and would be the first Council in almost a century. The bishop described it as a bold step towards greater Christian unity in a time of enormous challenge to the Church.

"The threat of Communism alone is fearsome, as we can see in our near neighbour, Cuba," the bishop said. "Nuns and priests driven out by Castro and his hooligans, Catholic schools closed. It's a godless regime." He commended us for committing our "young lives", as he put it, to such a worthy cause. The PAVLA programme, he said, was one in spirit with the coming Council, and it was no accident that Pope John XXIII announced both at almost the same time. They represented a new spirit in the Church, with a strong emphasis on the role of the laity. He concluded: "You are a sign of the Church that is coming into being: lay men and women working side by side with priests and nuns across the globe to strengthen and spread the faith!"

The Second Vatican Council had been a constant topic in my required college theology courses, and I felt privileged to be in the presence of someone who would soon be part of such a momentous event. My teachers, most of them nuns, had described the Council as Pope John XXIII's desire to bring the Church into dialogue with the modern world. In his own metaphor, he wanted to open a window on the Church and let in fresh air.

Listening to the bishop, I returned to Diana's question about why each of us had joined the PAVLA programme. In my case, it certainly had something to do with religious faith and a desire to put that faith into action. Baptized Catholic two weeks after my birth, I'd spent a few years in parish grade schools, but in my family, no one went to church unless for a baptism, wedding or funeral. Only when I won a scholarship to a Catholic college did I discover the brilliant intellectual tradition of Roman Catholicism and fall in love with Christian culture, especially the art, literature and music of medieval Europe. In a sense, Giotto, Dante and Gregorian chant brought me back to the Church.

To be honest, though, joining PAVLA had more to do with my desire for adventure than dedication to any particular form of institutional religion. How disappointed the bishop would be if I told him the truth: that I wanted to do more than just read about exotic places and people. I wanted to experience a world beyond familiar boundaries. I wanted an unconventional life, one different from the sort of life that my mother with her new house and new husband and baby was trying for the second time to live.

The orientation we volunteers received that day was a brief, sobering assortment of cautionary tales and warnings. The presumption seemed to be that once we'd been given a few rules, experience would be our best teacher.

Father Weaver started by telling us that not long before, a priest in a village near the Guatemala border had been murdered in the rectory. He was sure we'd hear about it, if we hadn't already, and he wanted to assure us that we were in no danger. (Hacked to pieces with a machete, the English volunteers had already told us, supplying all the details Father Weaver left out.) One of the villagers had been convicted of the crime, a Mayan Indian who worked for the parish. He was already in jail. It had been a personal quarrel, not an attack on the Church itself.

Priests and nuns and those who worked with them were a respected presence in a country more than seventy-five per cent Catholic, he said. In partnership with the colonial government, Roman Catholic missionaries administered the entire British Honduran school system and were an essential part of the status quo. The system was British, with students following the curriculum of British schools and taking the Cambridge O-level (Ordinary) and A-level (Advanced) exams. At the same time, most of the schools were Catholic, observing all the holy days. For the most part, courses in the curriculum, and that included religion classes, were taught by members of the Catholic faith. It was an unusual mixture, maybe, especially in comparison with public education in the United States, but it provided an excellent education, he said, combining all the strengths of public and private schools. The select high schools where we would be teaching (he called them "colleges", as in Britain) educated the future leaders of a society that would someday rule itself within the British Commonwealth.

The people of the country the Spanish called "Belicé" were deeply religious and peace loving, Father Weaver said. They were a diverse people, many races and ethnic groups living harmoniously. He assured us that we'd be accepted with goodwill and tolerance – Americans were generally well liked and respected – but asked us to keep in mind that Belize was much more conservative than the States, especially in its attitudes to women.

Father Weaver then set forth three "PAVLA Commandments". He called them supplements to the "Ten Big Ones". They were the code we were expected to live by.

"Behave prudently," he told us. We were to avoid any behaviour that might give scandal or cause misunderstanding. We must be careful how we dressed. No shorts for anyone, no trousers or revealing dresses for women. We must cover up bathing suits on the way to and from the beach. And we must watch our language, never using swear words or telling off-colour jokes. When we socialized, it must be in groups. "People here don't 'date'," he warned us, "not like back home."

"Live simply," he said, reminding us that we were not tourists. We must not carry cameras or wear expensive watches or other jewellery. He suggested we leave all such things with the rector at St John's College, the boys' high school in Belize City, or with the priests or sisters in the missions where we were assigned. (Next to me, Molly slipped her camera into her bag, put her finger over her lips and mouthed, *Shh*.) He added that we should not carry large amounts of cash with us or keep it in our houses. (A big laugh from all of us. I, for one, had maybe five US dollars left in my coin purse.)

"Think communally" was the third commandment. We should always remember that we were not in British Honduras as private individuals; we represented the Church and also the United States. We should do our jobs and keep a low profile – no political involvement of any sort. Everyone would be watching us, especially in the towns and villages. "If you lose respect," he said, "you won't get it back. And you'll damage far more than your own reputation."

Next came "The Warnings", apocalyptic in their implications but delivered in Father Weaver's low-key, matter-of-fact way.

"In the States," he began, "we tend to take survival for granted. Here, people don't because they can't. As stories of Hattie surely have warned you, as well as all the inoculations you received before you left home, nature here can be more extreme and deadly than you are used to." My arms still ached from the tetanus, typhoid, typhus, hepatitis, cholera and yellow fever shots pumped into them over the past six weeks.

He made clear the dangers around us. Most obvious were tropical storms like Hattie. They could strike without warning and wipe out entire towns. There were less obvious dangers too. Murderous microbes multiplied in tap water, and mosquitoes randomly transmitted deadly fevers. Tarantulas and scorpions crawled into the toes of shoes in the night, rattlesnakes coiled in the marsh grass outside back doors and sharks and stingrays slipped silently close to shore, ready to strike unwary newcomers like PAVLA volunteers.

"I tell you this not to frighten but to forewarn you. Here, an ounce of prevention is worth far more than a pound of cure."

He cautioned us always to boil water before we drank it and never to wander into swamp or jungle or swim in the sea or river alone. Still white-skinned from the northern climate and with tender flesh on our bones, we should avoid prolonged exposure to the sun and overexertion in the heat of the day. We had to learn, and learn quickly, to watch where we walked, to listen for unaccustomed sounds and to smell strangeness in the air.

My heart beats hard as I wait for my assignment. I can't get the scene in that rectory out of my mind. A middle-aged priest who looks a lot like Father Weaver is just finishing his breakfast after daily Mass when the door bursts open and a man with the broad, bronze face of a Mayan Indian rushes at him, the arc of his machete glinting in the early morning sun. The priest instinctively raises his hands, knocking over his coffee cup. A stain spreads on the white cloth, first brown and then –

Father Weaver interrupts the movie in my head. I hear him say that Maureen Bone, the pale, quiet girl and the only one of us who speaks fluent Spanish, will go to El Cayo near the Guatemalan border. (Close to where the priest was macheted to death, I add silently.) Maureen looks unperturbed. Reassured by her composure, my heart slows down.

All of the St Ben's Men, whom I now know to be Dick, Jerry and Bill (he plays a Gibson guitar that he wraps in a baby diaper inside its case), will be sent north together, to a town near the Mexican border. They prod and soft-punch each other to show their delight.

Nick, Dave and Carlos the Car are also headed north, to a place called Orange Walk. A "walk", we are told, is another word for "plantation". I imagine groves of fragrant orange trees and envy them their assignment. I'm sure I'll be under lock and key in PAVLA House, reduced to watching the swing bridge for recreation.

But no. Peg and Sue Ella will stay in Belize City without me and live with the English volunteers in PAVLA House.

The Ritters will go to Punta Gorda, where Molly was first assigned.

Last of all, Father Weaver reads Molly's name and then mine. The two of us, he says, will go to Angel Creek, a town on the Caribbean Sea of about seven thousand souls (as he puts it) and a centre of black culture.

"I'm glad we'll be together," Molly whispers.

"Me, too," I say, entirely satisfied with this unexpected turn of events.

I dream that, without knowing it, I've spent my whole life in the eye of a hurricane. The light fades and I'm caught up in hectic blackness, swirled helplessly in sucking winds and rain. I'm carried out to sea. The only way to safety I realize, terrified, is through the storm and the sea.

I wake up before dawn, cold and gulping for air, even though it's already in the seventies and so humid that my hair hangs damp on my neck. I wrap around my shoulders the homespun shawl I'd bought for a few pesos from a street vendor in Mexico and go out on the third-floor balcony to watch the sun rise over the sea. The shawl has become my "Linus blanket", a comfort and a cocoon.

Molly soon joins me, carrying two mugs of coffee sweetened with condensed milk. We're to leave later that day for Angel Creek, forty miles by boat down the coast. "I'm homesick," she says. "I miss my family, especially my two younger brothers."

My eyes smart, and the lump in my throat makes it hard to swallow the coffee. Even though I haven't called anyplace home for years – not since my parents' divorce when I was twelve – I nod agreement. "Homesickness" is as good a name as any for my sudden yearning for the places and people I've left behind.

Chapter 3

ANGEL CREEK

AT FIRST SIGHT, ANGEL CREEK was a disappointment. From the deck of the *Heron H*, the mail boat that carried Molly and me from Belize City, I saw only a squalid assemblage of shacks jumbled together in no particular order along a mile or so of coastline. No bay, no white sand, only a few ragged palms and coconut trees uneven against the evening sky like pieces of a discarded jigsaw puzzle. My dismay must have shown on my face.

"Hattie did a lot of damage here," Molly said. "Not as bad as Belize City, but bad enough." She pointed out the convent and the church. "They escaped without much damage. Everyone took it as a sign. Of course, the church is solid concrete." At the far end of the street between them, she identified a little house she said was ours. It sat up high, on stilts, with a big water vat attached. "It's brand new," she said.

A few minutes later, she pointed to a cluster of large white buildings with predictable green shutters and dark red roofs. It was the centre of town, where the courthouse, police station and most of the stores were located. "And over there," she said, "is the mouth of the Angel Creek River, where it flows into the sea. People say it's the best place to swim."

Molly, reading my thoughts, gave me a sympathetic smile. "I know," she said. "I felt the same way at first. But you get used to it."

Riding into town from the new pier, built after Hattie, I saw one warped wooden house after another, most linked not by streets or alleys but by footpaths that zigzagged between them. Mangy dogs ran free and lifted their legs to pee on scraggly trees and bushes. Near-naked children darted in and out of the spaces under the raised houses, and women and old people sat on straight-backed chairs outside their doors to catch the breeze. Men in loose shirts congregated on corners, idling away the time after supper. Without exception, everyone I saw had dark skin.

Before arriving, I had known that Angel Creek was a centre of what the British at the time referred to as Black Carib life and culture, now known as Garifuna or Garinagu. I'd been told that they were the descendants of Africans brought as slaves to the West Indies. Their African language and culture had mixed with that of the Caribbean Amerindians, though I wasn't at all clear on how or why. In my interview for PAVLA, I'd naively assured Father Weaver that I wasn't prejudiced against "Negroes", the name we used back then for blacks when we wanted to show respect (it superseded "coloureds", the term most of my family still used). I'd read Harper Lee's *To Kill a Mockingbird* and despised the racists in that novel. Nor in my opinion was I like the whites in Lorraine Hansberry's *A Raisin in the Sun*. I was eager to know blacks and welcome them into my world. But that first evening in Angel Creek, I realized that nothing in my experience had prepared me to live in a black world.

It's a new feeling to be in the minority, I wrote to a friend a few days after my arrival. *Looking in the mirror is quite a shock. You can never believe you haven't turned dark too.*

"Do you pass foh wite in de Stay-uhts?" one of our neighbours asked, after looking Molly and me over carefully. She spoke pidgin English, a compromise between the standard English taught in the schools and the Creole patois most native British Hondurans spoke with each other. At first, Creole sounded as much like a foreign language to Molly and me as the Garifuna language. Until we got used to it, we found even pidgin English almost incomprehensible. Our neighbour repeated her question.

I swallowed my first thought: "But we *are* white!"

Molly and I looked at each other. As if for the first time, I noticed Molly's curly black hair, frizzy in the humid air, and she scrutinized mine, wavy, wild and almost as dark. Her eyes were the colour of milk chocolate; mine, I knew, were hazelnut brown, with glints of yellow and green in them. A few days in the Caribbean sun had burnished our dull, northern skin and given us the beginning of great tans.

"I guess you could say that," Molly said.

"Yes," I added, choosing my words carefully. "People call us white."

The young woman smiled. "Dat lucky foh you." She shifted her baby from one hip to the other. "Dey say it easiah up dere if you cahn pass. Yah, one drop ah wite blood mek you wite, but dere, one drop ah black blood mek you black." She added that in her opinion, there were no "blacks" in the United States. "Evrybady bahn dere gat some wite in dem by now."

I'd never heard the "one drop" rule before. Although the woman looked black to me, she called herself "Creole", which meant that she had her drop of white blood, possibly generations earlier from European conquerors. Could such a thing as race be arbitrary and not a fact of nature? I had not been raised to think so or even to ask such questions. The woman's observations made me queasy, as though the ground under my feet had shifted.

As our neighbours made clear to us from the beginning, Molly and I did not fit most British Hondurans' stereotype of white American women. They were thought to be blond and blue-eyed like Grace Kelly and Marilyn Monroe.

At the same time, Molly and I struggled to overcome our own misperceptions of British Hondurans. Their diversity came as the biggest surprise. Far more than the States, British Honduras was a melting pot. In those days, Creoles – those of mixed heritage, primarily European and African – were the majority. They themselves were a diverse group, not only in ethnic origin but also in appearance. Some Creoles were as dark-skinned as the Garifuna and a few were as blond as the fairest North American.

In our small town of seven thousand, Garifuna outnumbered Creoles, but by only a small margin. There was also an array of minorities, most of them immigrants from other parts of Central America or the remnants of the British Colonial Empire. Indigenous Amerindians lived beside Mestizos from Mexico, Guatemala and El Salvador; West Indians from Jamaica and other Caribbean islands; East Indians from Bombay, Delhi, Calcutta and East Africa; Middle Easterners, most of them Christians, from Syria, Lebanon and Palestine; and Chinese from Hong Kong, Taiwan and Mainland China. There were also quite a few British subjects, most of whom lived and worked in Paloma Valley, ten miles outside town, and even an occasional Canadian, Australian and New Zealander. Add to this mix a few other nationalities, like our German doctor and a fairly large contingent of nuns, priests and volunteers from Europe and the United States (some of them African American), and British Honduras was almost as diverse as the human race itself.

One of the things Molly and I learned almost immediately was that dark-skinned British Hondurans did not necessarily have much in common. The Garifuna, Creoles, Mestizos, Mayans and East Indians, for the most part "dark-skinned", had entirely different cultural identities, even though they all spoke at least a little English and lived in the same country. I realized for the first time that in the States, blacks were lumped together by many white people, whatever differences might exist in reality.

Molly and I also pieced together that although "whiteness" and "blackness" might be defined differently and carry different social implications than we were used to, British Honduras was not a colour-blind society. In part because of British rule and the influence of US culture, especially movies, fair skin carried a measure of privilege, even if it was much more subtle – and far less institutionalized – than in the United States. In general, fairer-skinned Creoles in Angel Creek, as in British Honduras as a whole, had more money and status than darker-skinned Creoles, but intermarriage among light- and dark-skinned Creoles was not uncommon. Nor, with the exception of the Garifuna and the Chinese, was intermarriage among different ethnic groups all that rare, as the unpredictable surnames indicated. Colour, along with class and ethnicity, was one of many factors in BH society, not everything as in the United States.

Trying to understand the world around us, Molly and I fell back on Josie, an outgoing, unselfconscious sixteen-year-old. She worked for the nuns who ran and staffed the school system in Angel Creek. Part of her job was to be our "house girl". She did our laundry, helped us clean, and delivered our meals – along with any gossip she had picked up – three times a day.

Josie became one of our chief interpreters of Angel Creek life and culture. Often, when she should have been working, we bombarded her with questions, and she soon dropped her dust rag or put her mop aside to sit and talk with us. Afterward, we would help her finish the housecleaning or do it on our own.

At first, she objected: "Oh, no, Miss Abby and Miss Molly. You be teachahs!" She soon grew used to our informality, and then, of course, we had trouble getting her to do any work at all. She was a big girl and moved slowly even when she was in a hurry, but her mind and tongue were quick. In spite of having left school as soon as she could – education was compulsory in the colony between ages six and fourteen – she impressed me as extremely perceptive. She had high spirits and a lively sense of humour that, once she got used to us, tended towards teasing and joking around.

After the first few days, she rarely referred to us by our proper names. I became "Miss Tempest" because a hurricane named Abby had ripped through Angel Creek the year before Hattie, and Molly was "Miss Dimples" because of her dimpled smile.

Josie informed us that she intended to find the perfect men for us so we would never leave Angel Creek. They would be light-skinned Creoles, she promised, tall and soft haired, with many gold teeth. A young man named Winston Taylor was her eventual choice for me, and from then on, she called me either "Miz Taylor" or "Miz Mommy", because she was sure Winston and I would have many fine children together. Although she promised to introduce us, she never got around to it.

I realized only later that it never occurred to me to ask why she'd ruled out all the good-looking young Garifuna men who watched Molly and me from a distance. Was it because I'd subconsciously ruled them out for myself?

Josie herself was Garifuna, profoundly dark, with the large-boned body characteristic of the Garifuna people. They are a handsome people, and she had characteristic Garifuna features: ears shaped like walnut halves, high cheekbones, a small, bridgeless nose, and straight, white teeth. Most beautiful of all were her almond-shaped brown eyes. Josie was our tutor in Garifuna ways, a resource we counted on once we began teaching our mostly Garifuna students at the girls' high school. Before we met the Garifuna girls, however, we would meet the Garifuna boys.

Not long after we arrived, Sister Veronica, our principal, told us that the opening of school would be delayed. Hurricane Hattie had demolished the high school, and the building recently leased as its temporary replacement still wasn't ready.

"It probably is just as well that we can't start until July," she told us. "The rains come then, and while it's muggy and messy, it's also a bit cooler."

Molly and I asked if we could help in any way.

"You wouldn't mind?"

She showed us through the building, a large colonial-style house that once belonged to the mayor of Angel Creek. The rooms were entirely unsuitable for classes. They led one into another, many through open arches. And they were a mess, windows broken, plaster falling from the high ceilings, wallpaper hanging in shreds, and wooden floors black and sometimes rotten with water damage.

For an entire week, Molly and I spent most of each day scrubbing floors and woodwork and stripping ruined wallpaper off the walls. The nuns worked right beside us with the sleeves of their long, black habits rolled up and their veils tied back like curtains. We rested after the midday meal, in Latin fashion the main meal of the day, and then went back to work most of the afternoon.

From the beginning, Molly and I fell into an easy rapport as housemates and companions. "What luck we ended up together," we often told each other. In many ways, we were alike, especially in our energy, enthusiasm and curiosity. She was interested in everything and everyone, intelligent and perceptive without being – like me – bookish. In our differences, we complemented each other. While I tended to be inward and self-conscious, she was typically outgoing and spontaneous. I could be impractical and dreamy. She was alert to present realities, focused and decisive. With her fresh-faced good looks and vivacity, Molly was a people magnet. Not only did she draw others to us, she drew me out of myself. Through a process of transference, I often energized her with my questions and intensity, and she activated me with her opinions and easy-going charm.

Usually about four-thirty each afternoon, when smoke began to rise from the sheds where the village women cooked the evening meal, Molly and I would change into our bathing suits, cover them with a loose dress and, filthy and exhausted after our day's work, head down Front Street, along the sea, to the mouth of the Angel Creek River.

At sunup, the river was the busiest place in town, with children bathing and women washing the clothes they then spread across the rocks to bleach and later carried home in baskets balanced on their heads. They also hauled home their drinking water from the river that way, in five-gallon tin cans. Around suppertime, though, the beach and the riverbank were usually deserted.

We'd swim in the sea, its salty astringency a tonic for body and spirit, and afterward wash off in the fresh river water, sweet and cold. If we had time, we'd sit for a while on the warm sand or lie back against the smooth driftwood that reminded me of the tusks and horns of prehistoric animals. At that time of day, the sea turned silver, as if a magic cloak had been flung over it, and as we watched, the sea disappeared into the sky.

For the first few days, we enjoyed our walk to and from the beach in solitude. Then the village boys caught onto our routine. Sometimes two, some-

Figure 3. One of the "Camelot Boys", mounted and ready to ride. (Typical post-Hattie houses in the background.) Photo courtesy of Malilee Zimmers.

times ten of them would appear suddenly and dance around us until we reached our destination.

"Gud eevnin', Miss!" they'd call out from a polite distance.

If we encouraged them, they'd move closer and egg each other on to tease us. Soon we learned the names of some of them and could pick them out of the crowd.

Their names revealed a people who still believed in heroes and saints. There was a core I came to think of as the "Camelot Boys" because of their legendary names. Arthur, soft-spoken and shy, and Roy, wise beyond his ten years, lived up to their royal names. Lancelot of the beautiful face, his classic Garifuna features as sculpted as an African carving, was at eleven already a head taller than Molly or me. Percival, nicknamed "Percy", appeared to be from a different tribe altogether. He was short and roly-poly, the clown of the group.

Quite a few had names that came straight out of the plays of Shakespeare: a Horatio, a Ferdinand and a couple of Sebastians. The Sebastians could also be classified with the "Saints", chief among them Alban, who made himself memorable by stripping naked to swim with us, and Valentine, a precocious twelve-year-old who delighted in passing on to us the town gossip.

"Be only careful, Miss Abby and Miss Molly, and wach out," Valentine warned us. "Dose ole ladies dey only loquacious! Dey talk 'bout de priests and de nons and say dose nons go an' have babies an' kill dem. Wach out foh weh you go, and don' you waak down de street wid any mon, or dey gone say, 'Dose American gals, I tought dey cohn down yah foh teach, no foh run loose wid de bwayz.'"

"Tell us who talks about us, and we'll go visit them on Sunday afternoons!" Molly said. "If they get to know us, maybe they'll trust us."

"No so," he said. "Dey say you too sweet foh stay outta trouble, and dey wach you, foh true."

Thanks to the boys, we learned the local definition of "sweet". Even though they spoke the Creole patois around town, the Garifuna had their own language. The boys taught us a song that they said was a Garifuna love song. They laughed uncontrollably when we sang it. That alone should have roused our suspicions.

We sang it for Josie, doing a shuffling little dance with it as the boys had done when they sang it:

"Higabu nárigi nati miragua
Nihein katei bímati ya
Ayé, nati miragua
Anihein katei bimeti ya!"

Josie almost dropped our supper tray. "Oh, Miss Abby and Miss Molly, why you sing dat song?"

"The boys taught it to us," I said. "What in the world have we been singing?"

"Cho!" Josie "kissed" her teeth, a sign of pure disdain. "Dose bwayz only mischievous! Dey teach you a song mo worse in our language dan English: 'Cohn yah, bruddah, Ah gat sohnting sweet.' Dis song de no-gud womon sing."

"Do you mean prostitutes?" Molly asked. "Do you mean we've been singing like whores all over town?"

Josie put down the tray and covered her face with her apron. "Oh, Miss Molly!" she squealed. "How you talk!"

Another interpreter of Garifuna ways was Josie's counterpart, Gilly, the priest's houseboy. He lived in the closed-in space under our house, where he also had a photography studio: "Portraits by Gilbert". Inside, he had a camera on a tripod and a couple of backdrops, one painted to look like a colonial mansion and another like lush jungle, with toucans flying in a bright blue sky. There was also a satin curtain hanging against one wall and in front of it an elegant chair and a pedestal with plastic flowers in a vase on it for those who preferred an interior setting.

Unlike most Garifuna men, Gilly was short, pudgy and always in a hurry. He usually wore a hat of some sort, often a baseball cap, a spotless white shirt tucked into khaki trousers and hard leather shoes, not the plastic sandals most townspeople wore.

Father O'Dea, the pastor, sent Gilly to pick us up at the new pier the evening Molly returned and I arrived from Belize City. Gilly drove a robin's-egg blue Jeep with a canvas cover.

"Hello, Miss Molly," he said. "Welcome bahk. You tek gud pikchas in Belize City?"

"I hope so, Gilly. Can you develop them for me?"

"You bet," he said. "I mek gud price foh you." He looked me over. "You Miss Molly sistah?"

"No," I said. "I'm another teacher. I'm Abby Porter. Molly and I just met each other in Belize City."

He shook his head. "People gone mix you up."

Even though we didn't really look alike, Gilly was right. For weeks, people asked us if we were related. Some even thought we were twins. To them, especially to the Garifuna, we looked alike, two young women of approximately the same height and weight, with dark hair and eyes and light skin. Local people were always calling me "Miss Molly" and her "Miss Abby". When either of us stopped in one of the stores on Market Street, the first question from the clerk was, "Now, wich teachah you be?"

Then, almost overnight, people began to call us by our right names.

"How did people finally figure out the difference?" I asked Gilly.

"You no straynjahs no mo," he said.

About the same time, I began to recognize the distinctive features of Angel Creek. I knew which shop on Market Street, the main street in town, belonged to Lee Wong and his wife and which belonged to the Morrises, some of whose children lived in the States. I knew that a Syrian, Emmanuel Zacharias, who was the richest man in town, owned the Caribbean Club, on the corner of Market and River streets. He was said to be the father of at least

Figure 4. Gilly, who worked for the priests and whose photography studio was under our house. Photo courtesy of Malilee Zimmers.

eleven children by different women, one of them his wife, who now lived in El Salvador. The woman who lived with him in a huge apartment above the club was his mistress, Josie told us. I knew that the Happy Time Café, run by a Garifuna family, the Lambeys, served Coca-Cola, even though it was warm, and that if I was in the mood, I could see a Hollywood movie at the Silver Dream Theatre, run by Oscar Ramirez, a Salvadoran. Seats on the main floor cost ten cents each and those on a raised platform at the back were five cents more.

To the south of our house lay the official centre of town, with its courthouse, police station, post office, hospital, stores, open meat and fish markets and a small park with benches and swings. In that direction were the two rivers that flowed through town and into the sea, the Angel Creek River and the smaller Paloma Creek.

To the west lay Paloma Valley, with its fragrant acres of citrus groves, called "walks", just visible from the balcony outside our front door. The Beaumont Citrus Factory was out there, I now knew, as was the British Forestry Station. Also in the valley were the tiny plantations farmed by the Garifuna families from town. When Molly and I wanted to take a long walk, we headed in that direction, usually along the unpaved Melena Road, the "back way" out to the valley. In the far distance ranged the Maya Mountains, bright in the morning and shadowy in the evening as they waited to swallow in a single gulp another setting sun.

Across the street from us to the north were the rectory, the church and the elementary school, and beyond them, the cemetery, overgrown with weeds. The bush, no more than a ten-minute walk away, darkened the northern horizon. There, tall coconut trees and massive mangroves felled by Hattie lay rotting in fetid pools. I came back from my only walk in that direction covered with sandfly bites. Like Molly's, they began to fester.

Filling up the east were the sea and sky, as alike and as different as a face and a mirror. An old pier of broken boards stretched twenty-five yards into the sea, and small boats tied up there, loaded with bananas, plantains, pineapples, oranges and grapefruit. When we saw them, Molly and I ran out to pay a few pennies for a pineapple or a grapefruit and to talk with the crew, usually Garifuna men from small villages down the coast towards Honduras.

A grassy field ran along the edge of the sea, almost to the centre of town. At its north end, an orange windsock blew like a banner. Once or twice a week, a Piper Cub landed there, bringing an occasional visitor or urgent mail from far away. Like everyone else in earshot, if we could we dropped what we were doing to watch it land. When school was in session, the field served as a playground. In the evenings and on weekends, teams from town and the surrounding area played soccer (they called it "futbal") and baseball. The city park marked the southern end of the field. After dark Molly and I would sometimes go there to swing on the swings and "kick de stars," as the boys put it.

Without a doubt, night was the best time in Angel Creek. No matter how hot the day had been, a breeze usually blew from the sea and the whole town came out to sit in yards, stroll along the streets, and wander in and out of the shops and clubs, all reopened after supper. Molly and I would walk down one side of Market Street, stopping along the way to greet and chat with people. When we came to the bridge over the Angel Creek River, we paused to watch the reflected lights from the clubs and the movie house run red, yellow and green in the black water. We'd wander on down to the bridge over Paloma Creek at the south end of town, and double back up the other side of the street to our house at its north end. In my journal I wrote,

> *I never knew the moon before. In British Honduras, it is the only thing to fill and light the dark sky. Even the stars, showers and showers of them, are unable to light a moonless sky. But when she is full, the moon poises yellow on the sea's horizon, then rises as the fountainhead of uncontainable light. When I rise at a quarter to six, her ghost still lingers above the mountains. The mountains are twelve miles inland by road. Citrus grows there all year long; the hills seem imbued with the smell of orange blossom. I think that it would stay, even if the trees were all spirited away some night. From the mountains, innumerable streams gush downward to the sea. The mouth of Angel Creek River is a five-minute walk from our house; it is the main artery of the town. Morning and night, the women and children crowd its banks, filling their tins with water, bathing, scrubbing their clothes. The bar mouth is never the same. Some days, the sand stretches far into the heart of the river; another, the river has broken bounds and invaded the sea. Silently, the seabirds circle, searching the waters for flying fish. Sandpipers swirl in shifting wreaths up the sandy beach, rolling horizontally on the salt air.*

Even after I knew my way around Angel Creek, its name continued to puzzle me. There were as many different accounts of the origin of the name "Angel Creek" as of its meaning.

The British regarded as fact that the name came from the surname – or it may have been the nickname – of an English pirate, one of many who in the seventeenth century hid out in the creeks along the coast. Eventually, so the story went, this particular pirate liked the area around one of the creeks so much that he settled there, founding the town first known as "Angel's Creek" but simplified over time to "Angel Creek".

Some of the Creoles, however, maintained that "Angel" referred not to the pirate's surname but to his pale skin. It looked white as an angel's to the dark-skinned natives, they said. But others said no, it came from the sails of the pirate ships, which looked like angels' wings.

The Mestizos had a different story. They were sure that the name reflected a Christianized version of the Mayan belief that the river, which originated high in the Maya Mountains, was the gift of the spirits of the ancestors – or angels – who lived there among the clouds.

I asked Gilly what he thought of the different interpretations. He shook his head. "Dey ahl wrong!" The name, he told me, referred to an actual angel, the one who had guided the dories of the Garifuna people from the island of St Vincent, where they were slaves, to freedom in their new home along the Caribbean coast.

"In de language of our people," Gilly said, "dis town be *Áhari duna*. Dat she true name, foh dose wan know."

First I missed home. Terribly! Then I resigned myself to living here, I wrote after a few weeks in Angel Creek. *Now I like it. I like the people, who really are the town, after all, and I begin to like the place too. It's possible I may even come to love it here.*

Áhari duna: a beautiful name for a place whose beauty daily became more apparent to me.

Only many years later did I discover that *Áhari duna* is simply a translation of "Angel Creek" into the Garifuna language. By then, British Honduras, renamed after independence, had become Belize and Angel Creek was officially "Ahariduna".

Chapter 4

CAUGHT IN THE MIDDLE

THE MORNING AFTER WE arrived in Angel Creek, a welcoming committee of nuns had appeared on our doorstep. They introduced themselves as Mother Eugenie, the superior of the convent, Sister Veronica, the principal of the high school where we would teach, and Sister Marietta, her assistant. Under their black veils, they wore stiff white coifs and starched collars that crackled when they moved. Pearls of perspiration oiled Mother Eugenie's moon-like face. Her skin was yellowish and stippled, like lemon peel, and her round cheeks were flushed from the heat.

The faces of the other two nuns were like polished mahogany. The Sisters of the Holy Family belonged to one of the congregations of black nuns and priests that were a visible sign of the segregation that still existed in most areas in the States. Until I met the Holy Family sisters, I had no idea such congregations existed.

At the end of a pleasant visit, Mother Eugenie said in her languid Louisiana drawl, as though it were an afterthought, "By the way, we have one piece of advice for you." She smiled but looked down at her hands, folded on her lap. "Please understand this in the right way. We speak from experience. It's best not to socialize with the native people."

I stared at her, sure I had heard wrong. "Why ever not?"

"Because it's best to keep one's distance, so as not to be taken advantage of."

"Or held cheap," Sister Veronica added. Her intonation betrayed a hint of the Creole patois, but was she Creole or Garifuna? I couldn't tell the difference. "To teach well requires respect. Respect depends upon authority. Authority requires distance."

Sister Marietta nodded.

Molly's colour rose. "Sisters, I have to say that I didn't come here to stay in my room. I'm not a nun, and I don't intend to live like one. I'm going to see as much of this country and meet as many people I can."

I could almost see the lock and key in Mother Elaine's pocket. "Won't we be better teachers if we get to know our students and their families?" I asked.

"Of course we will," Molly said. "I really don't understand this policy, Mother Eugenie, and I – "

"Don't worry, Sisters," I interrupted, afraid they'd send us home the day after we had arrived. "We'll be careful."

Mother Eugenie said in her soothing voice, "I'm sure that you are both good, Catholic girls. We were so happy to see you at Mass this morning, and we hope you'll be there daily. The personal example you set is very important. Everything you do will be watched and judged, you know. You wouldn't want to cause gossip or give the Church a bad name."

Father Weaver had said something along the same lines, I recalled, but he certainly hadn't warned us against getting to know our new neighbours.

Sister Veronica had the last word: "Be cautious, for your own good. You don't know these people or this place."

I wanted to ask, *How can we, if we listen to you?* but I bit my tongue.

"De nons say you and Miss Molly only frenly," Josie told us a few days later.

I suspected that what sounded like a compliment was just the opposite. "Didn't the volunteers last year visit with the townspeople?" I asked. "Or go out much?"

"No much, Miss," Josie said. "Dey lib in de convent wid de nons, and dey be jes like nons, excep dey no wayah de habit."

"They're going to be a tough act to follow," I said to Molly after Josie had gone.

"It's an act *I* don't intend to follow," Molly said. "And I don't care how many warnings the nuns send through Josie!"

When one of our Garifuna neighbours, Therese, invited us to her house for tea, Molly and I didn't hesitate to accept. It was our first invitation to someone's home, and we were excited to go. We dressed in our nicest clothes and were glad we had, because Therese wore what must have been hers, a dress of lime-green sateen with a leafy pattern on the bodice, and on her feet, black leather flats. Her three-year-old son and her baby, less than a year, were dressed up too, as were a woman she introduced as her sister, and her sister's daughter, about twelve, and son, four or five. She led us into a small, stifling parlour, where we sat on straight-backed chairs of different sizes and shapes.

Therese seemed to be the talker in the family. For the most part, her sister sat smilingly silent, taking her cues from Therese. The children had greeted us politely when we arrived, but after we sat down, the two boys retreated behind Therese's chair, peering at us around her sturdy body. Every now and then, one of them would venture out, stare at us intently, and dash back to safety. Without success, we tried to entice them to come closer, but they only held more tightly to Therese.

She clicked her tongue. "Terrible chiles," she said and laughed. Her sister nodded.

I was taken aback when Therese referred to her infant as "De Ugly Baby". When we asked why she called him that, she said, "Because he ugly! Evrybady say so." Again, her sister nodded agreement. The baby did look a little like a shrivelled-up grandfather, but I resisted the idea of anybody, especially its mother, calling a baby "ugly". Besides, I guess I expected Therese to be proud of the child's skin, a shade or two lighter than the other children's.

Therese laughed when she called the baby "ugly" as she had when she called the children "terrible", and she hugged him close to her. The baby scrunched up his face as if to cry but no sound came out. I had to laugh too, at the funny face he made.

Therese handed off Ugly Baby to her niece and served us cups of Twining's tea, the teabags still in the cups, a visible sign of prosperity. As we drank our tea, she told us that her husband and several other members of the extended family were in the States.

"Why would they leave all of you?" Molly asked.

"Dey gone to de Stay-uhts foh werk."

"Will they come back soon? It must be so lonely for all of you."

"No wile dey gat dey visa!" Therese explained that the money they sent home helped support the entire family. After Hattie, it had enabled them to rebuild the house where she and her extended family now lived.

Unlike most of the houses in Angel Creek, it had a new zinc roof over concrete walls, more than one room, and a wooden floor. The walls were decorated with a couple of portraits, obviously taken in Gilly's studio, and a calendar from the Morris pharmacy.

"Why you cohn to Angel Creek?" she wanted to know. "You wahn be non?"

"No! Not nuns," Molly said. "We came to teach in the girls' high school."

"Why, wen you have evryting in de Stay-uhts?"

"To see how the rest of the world lives," I answered.

Therese chuckled and shook her head. "Me hozban, he wait lang time foh he visa. An' you say, 'Bye-bye, America' and cohn to Angel Creek. Nobady satisfy wey dey be."

We sat in the parlour until we finished our tea. Finally, Therese said, "Now, cohn outside, pets, afoe we ahl ded!"

Pulling our skirts away from our sweaty legs, we followed her outside and into the shade of one of the large hibiscus bushes behind the house. A delicious breeze blew off the sea. Most of the time, Therese confessed, the family lived outdoors. Like most of the townspeople, she did her cooking in a shed in the backyard. The latrine was back there too. She had a vat on the side of her house to catch and store rainwater. Otherwise she, like most of the women in Angel Creek, would have to fetch drinking water from the river, and carry her dirty laundry there on her head to wash it.

As we sat in the yard, the little boys relaxed and inched closer to us. Soon they were climbing all over us, hanging on our necks, touching our hair and stroking our cheeks. One by one, some of the neighbours gathered to view Therese's exotic guests, the new teachers from America. As Therese introduced us to them and also to her sister's husband, who had been elsewhere while we drank our tea, the women nodded, smiling broadly, often giggling, but looking at us aslant, not meeting our eyes. The men took our hands, not to shake them but to bow over them with a gallantry that seemed to come from the distant past.

"Gud eevnen, Teachahs," they said. "You lak it yah?"

"Very much!"

"Dey eyes no blue," one old man announced to the group after coming close and squinting at us. "But dey sweet tings, foh true."

Our nearest neighbour was Father Jack O'Dea, our pastor, who lived in the rectory across the street from us. He stopped by at least once a day, usually carrying his toolbox. He was still putting the finishing touches on our house, installing the moulding in the living room and bedrooms, sanding down the doors that were sticking now that the rainy season had begun and caulking the washbasin and tub in the bathroom.

"These are the easy jobs," he said, "but time consuming. The hard part was putting up the frame. I had someone else help me with that and with the roof. I don't like heights. But I did most of the rest myself."

The little balcony outside our front door and the long flight of stairs leading up to it were a source of special pride. Their fancy railing he'd designed himself.

The rectory looked as though it could have used some of his carpentry skills. Hattie had taken off the roof and shaken the foundations. The roof was back, but the building itself looked off-kilter. The front porch had collapsed, and the front door was boarded up; the only entrance was through the kitchen. Debris from the hurricane still littered the yard, and inside, several rooms were unusable because of the clutter – broken furniture and box upon box of water-damaged books and papers. Father O'Dea seemed oblivious to the conditions in which he himself lived, but he constantly found some new thing in our house needing his attention.

Almost every time he came, he brought us something: mosquito netting for our beds, kerosene for the stove, and candles and matches for when the power went out. Occasionally, he would bring a treat, a bunch of ripe bananas or a half dozen juicy mangoes or oranges. These he would invariably hand over to Molly.

"How kind of you!" she'd say with her "Miss Dimples" smile. "You take such good care of us, Father O'Dea!"

He'd respond with a silly half-grin.

While he worked around the house, Molly would sit chatting with him, handing him a hammer or nails when he needed them. Mostly, he'd talk and she'd listen, laughing at his stories and corny jokes. "I think he's lonely," she said to me.

Father O'Dea took special pleasure in doctoring us. He said the only local doctor, a German immigrant, was a quack. Why else would he have left a practice in Germany to come to Angel Creek? (The idea that he may have been a Jew escaping the Nazi regime never occurred to any of us at the time.) He made clear that he himself would take care of us. He dosed both of us regularly with salt pills and stood by while we choked down big, bitter anti-malaria pills. With this new medicine, chloroquin, he promised that we could avoid the fever, though he said that the pills were a far less pleasant preventive than gin and tonic had been in his day. Not that the gin and tonic had been all that effective, he added. He'd come down with malaria when he was a young man and still suffered from recurring fever and chills.

"I don't want that to happen to you," he said.

The first time we took the chloroquin, we spent most of the day in bed, nauseated, dizzy and weak. He assured us we'd build up tolerance, and we did.

Molly's bug bites were no less a problem in Angel Creek than they had been in Punta Gorda. Father O'Dea fretted and fumed over them, bringing her various lotions and repellents. "Sometimes I'm afraid this country will eat you alive," he said. He didn't seem to notice that the bugs had also started biting me.

During one of our afternoon trips to the beach, Molly stepped on a sea urchin. I ran ahead to find Father O'Dea while she limped home, leaning on some of the neighbourhood boys.

"You're sure it was a sea urchin?" he asked me, grabbing a first-aid kit from a shelf in the rectory kitchen and running after me. "Not a jellyfish or a man-of-war?"

"I don't know the difference," I said. "The boys said it was a sea urchin. They saw it on the rocks and yelled, but it was too late."

"Urchin, foh sure, Fahdah," the boys told him.

Father O'Dea sat Molly down on the side of the road and examined her instep. It looked red and a little swollen, with black spines just under the skin.

"Oh God," she said, her voice trembling. "Am I poisoned?"

"It's nothing serious," he assured her. "There's a simple remedy. We need some wee-wee, boys." Molly looked up from her foot, alarmed. "To dissolve the spines. Vinegar will work, but urine is best. I know what I'm talking about."

One of the boys obliged, going off and wetting some gauze. Father treated her foot right there. Then he slathered it with salve and wrapped it. "This could get infected, and infections are extremely dangerous here," he said. "You'd better spend the rest of the day in bed."

Father O'Dea and I supported Molly the rest of the way home, he on one side and I on the other, and once she was in bed, he sat down beside her to take her temperature and feel her pulse. Several times that evening and the next morning, he came back to check on his patient, brushing off my assurance that I could take care of her.

"He has quite a soft spot for you, Miss Dimples," I said after one of his visits.

She didn't deny it. "I don't know why, but I get along well with older men." In fact, she added, she usually got along better with her boyfriends' fathers than with her boyfriends.

I could see why as I watched her with Father O'Dea. Not only did she charm him with her pretty face and playful manner but she also expertly buttered him up. "Thank you for all the house calls, Father," I overheard her telling him. "I hope you don't charge extra." He laughed, and she added, "Seriously, I don't know what Abby and I would do without you."

When Molly and I mentioned to Father O'Dea that the nuns had warned us not to socialize with the local people, he said, "Don't pay any attention to them."

"But why would they say something like that?" I asked.

"Prejudice," he said.

"How could that be?"

"These nuns have culture, don't you know. Doesn't matter they're the same colour, they think they're better than the people down here." He paused a moment before he went on. "Now the British are a different matter, and I'll tell you why. They are arrogant and corrupt. They'll be after you with their invitations to dinners and parties. Turn them down, politely but firmly."

"But we'd like to get to know everybody," I said.

"You don't want to hobnob with them. That's not why you're here."

"Oh, Father, you're such a dear to be concerned about us," Molly said. "We'll be careful."

When that conversation occurred, Molly and I knew that we'd just accepted an invitation from Andrew and Julie Todd, a young British couple who lived at the government Forestry Station in Paloma Valley, where Andrew was a forest ranger. We'd met them in Lee Wong's, the largest store on Market Street.

"You must be the new American teachers," Andrew said, holding out his hand as he introduced himself and his wife. "We heard you'd be arriving any day."

After we talked for a while, Julie invited us for supper that Saturday evening. "I'm past my morning sickness now and eager for company," she said, smoothing her hand over her belly, just beginning to bulge. She was built like a boy and wore her thick, reddish-blond hair in a full bob that suited her long face. Andrew was a tad shorter than Julie, and as round as she was angular.

"We'd love to," Molly said, "but we don't have a way to get out to the valley."

"Not a problem," said Andrew. "I'll pick you up about six."

"I've invited an eligible bachelor for the evening," Andrew announced as we drove along the Hummingbird Highway towards the Forestry Station. "But Julie is afraid you're going to be nuns."

"Good heavens, no!" Molly protested.

"That's what I told her," Andrew said. "You're too attractive."

"I know some very attractive nuns," I said.

"What a waste. I don't get it. Unless they're frigid." He didn't use the word *lesbian*, but I suspected that's what he meant.

"Maybe they have a different kind of passion," I said, thinking of some of the young nuns who'd taught me.

Andrew wanted to know what kind of passion that might be. "I only know one kind myself," he said. "And it requires an attractive female. I mean my wife, of course."

"I don't know. But I guess a passion for God. For goodness. For ideals and causes."

"We need to find this young woman a boyfriend fast," Andrew teased.

The eligible bachelor was a tall young man whose sandy hair was thinning, although he wasn't much older than we were. He wasn't exactly handsome; his features were pleasant but nondescript. His accent, we later discovered, originated in the Midlands, around Birmingham. He stooped slightly as he came through the doorway to the veranda, where we sat with gin and tonics sweating in our hands.

He saw me first and smiled. His face said, *This could work*, as clearly as if he'd spoken the words out loud.

"Abby Porter, David Lewis," Andrew said.

David shook my hand; he then turned to Molly, who sat across from me, and it was as if what he had thought would be a pleasant dinner had turned into a Christmas feast. He didn't know where to begin with her, and watching his loss of composure I forgave him immediately for dumping me two seconds after we'd met. Molly did that to people – discombobulated them – especially men.

Over the course of the evening, Molly told David that she had a serious boyfriend back home whom she intended to marry someday, but by then it was too late for him to come through that door again and sit by me. I felt sorry for him, so obviously smitten, but by then it was too late for me too. He'd fixed on Molly, and I realized I felt relieved.

We moved from the veranda to the living room, and I turned my full attention to the Todds' personal library. It filled floor to ceiling bookcases on both sides of the stone fireplace.

"Books!" I gasped when I first saw them. "Just look at all these books!"

By far my keenest disappointment with life in Angel Creek was the absence of the public library, which had been destroyed by Hattie. Hattie had also devastated the school library. How could I make it through an entire year without a steady supply of books? I'd asked myself that question over and over during the past week.

When the Todds offered to lend Molly and me our choice of books, as many as we wanted, all my doubts about living in Angel Creek vanished. Molly quickly chose Françoise Sagan's *Bonjour Tristesse*, a bestseller we both wanted to read. I took my time deciding what to take, changing my mind several times before I finally settled on Isak Dinesen's *Out of Africa*.

I'd never heard of the book or the author but picked it when Andrew said that even though she was a woman, the author's colonial experience of Kenya reminded him of his experience of British Honduras. I opened to the first page and felt chills as I read, "I had a farm in Africa, at the foot of the Ngong hills." Not "My father had a farm in Africa" or "My husband had a farm in Africa", but "*I* had a farm in Africa". Who was this woman with a man's name who had a farm in Africa? I had to force myself to stop reading, even though my stomach was rumbling. The fragrant smell of Julie's curried chicken and rice made me suddenly ravenous.

We ate by candlelight in a corner of the book-filled room. I had my first mouthful of mango chutney, made by Julie herself with fruit from the tree outside her door, and drank the first wine I'd tasted since leaving the States. The Todds' life, as I imagined it, seemed magical, and their house, a dream. Compared with most of the houses in Angel Creek, the long, low bungalow, covered with bougainvillea, was palatial. It lay within the gates of the Forestry

Station in a grove of trees, apart from the administrative buildings. The furniture, handcrafted from local mahogany, had come with the house. Julie had hung Guatemalan textiles on the white walls and scattered bright rugs on the floor.

David said that he had a similar but smaller bungalow a few blocks away, with two bedrooms instead of three. When we asked him what he did with so much space, he said that his mother had been out to visit him several times, and besides, all the British nationals who worked for government agencies in the colonies had access to such housing, separate from the native population.

"Who would ever come out here if we had to live in town?" Julie's question was actually a statement.

I drew in my breath. It was as if she'd thrown a glass of ice water in my face. "We like our neighbours," I said.

"She only means the living conditions in town are horrible," Andrew said, pouring more wine.

David invited us to his place the following weekend, and Molly seemed happy to accept, in spite of Paul Herman, her "serious boyfriend". I'd heard all about Paul, the brilliant son of Molly's favourite professor at Marquette. In the fall, Paul would begin the first year of a master's programme in history at Harvard and would no doubt go on for a PhD. Molly said that when she returned from her year in British Honduras, they intended to marry. She would find a teaching job to support them until he finished his degree.

"Molly, it's pretty clear that David really likes you," I said as we prepared for bed that night. "Is it fair to keep seeing him, even if I'm there to play chaperone? A role I don't relish, by the way."

"Of course it's fair!" Molly plopped down in the comfortable corner chair in our living room, as if ready for a long talk. "Paul and I aren't officially engaged yet. Besides, David is very nice, don't you think?"

"Very. You'll break his heart."

"Don't be silly."

"Then you'll break Paul's heart."

"That's even sillier."

"If you want to go, go alone next weekend. I'll just be in the way."

"No, you won't. David likes you too. He has a car, and he's offered to show us as much of the country as we want to see. We'll all just have a good time together as friends. Say you'll come."

We talked until I finally gave in.

In Angel Creek, no private house or office had a telephone. There was a pay phone for emergency use at the post office that worked occasionally, a phone for official government business at the police station and another phone at the Forestry Station in the valley. Those were the only three telephones in the entire district. Messages were delivered in person. Mail had to be collected at the post office and could take a week to make its way from one city to the next.

Returning home from a swim a few afternoons after our dinner with the Todds, we found a note stuck in our door. It was from David Lewis: *Back at eight!*

He arrived at eight with a bottle of gin in a bag under his arm. "Couldn't wait till the weekend to see you," he said. "Do you have anything to mix with this, or shall we have it straight?"

We used some tinned orange juice to dilute the gin and sat in our living room, sipping our drinks without ice. Golden light poured like syrup through the louvered windows until, without warning, it was dark. No twilight. At best, electric power was available only between nightfall and dawn. Around nine, the electricity flickered on, went off, came on again half-heartedly, and then died for good. We lit a kerosene lantern that cast long shadows around the room.

David told us his story. He grew up outside Birmingham in what he described as a boringly ordinary family: father in business, mother at home, one younger brother. He couldn't wait to get away. This was his second year in Angel Creek. He'd studied engineering at university and decided to go into colonial service – translation: he had a yen to see the world. The British Forestry Service provided the opportunity. It wasn't a bad life, really, he said, especially for a bachelor. Hurricanes aside, of course. At his age, just turned twenty-six, he was already a boss, with sixty men under him. His crews built and repaired roads and bridges on government land. What they did was crucial to the logging industry. He could transfer into another branch of the civil service when he finished his tour in Belize, he said. To his parents' delight, his future seemed secure.

"They think I'm ready for marriage, but they're terrified I'm going to fall in love with a native girl. My mother would adore it that I'm here with not one but two unmarried young ladies, even though you aren't British."

Molly told him her less-ordinary story, which I'd heard before: her parents and two younger brothers lived in a duplex with her father's parents. Her paternal grandparents lived on the ground floor, and Molly's family lived upstairs. Her father was very strict with Molly, especially about her dating. The only reason he had consented to her leaving home for British Honduras, she said, was that he wanted to get her as far away as possible from her boyfriend Paul. She'd never had a boyfriend he liked.

I tidied up my family story. My parents had divorced when I was twelve, I told David, repeating what I'd already told Molly. My mother had recently remarried, and I had a baby brother in addition to two other brothers. All true. But I left out the four middle children, two boys and two girls, who'd been adopted after first my father and then my mother deserted us. We'd lived apart since I was fifteen, when my maternal grandmother, newly widowed and ill, could no longer care for all of us. They now had a different last name from mine, and since going off to college on a scholarship, I had rarely seen them.

"Don't talk about it," my grandmother told my two oldest brothers and me after the adoption. "It's no one else's business. And it will only hold you back." People heard about it, of course, but never from my oldest brothers or me. We didn't even talk about it with each other or with my mother, once we were reunited after her remarriage. Divorce itself was hush-hush in that era of *Leave It to Beaver* and *Father Knows Best*. Even in 1979, almost twenty-five years after my mother left us, a runaway mom like Meryl Streep in *Kramer vs Kramer* shocked audiences. And Meryl Streep's character deserted only one child, not seven.

I knew I should be honest with Molly, whom I now thought of as a friend, but I told myself I'd already left out too much, and I certainly didn't want to fill in the gaps in front of David, who was still a stranger.

When I came back from the kitchen with a second tin of orange juice, Molly and David had moved closer to each other. She was laughing at something he'd said.

"It's bedtime for me," I said, putting the tinned juice on the table next to the half-empty bottle of gin.

In my room, I changed into my nightgown, crawled into bed, and for what seemed like hours, lay awake in the dark. The low drone of their conversation in the next room finally lulled me to sleep.

In church the next morning, Molly slipped into the pew beside me as daily Mass began, her eyes swollen from lack of sleep and too much gin. She pulled her lace mantilla forward so that it half covered her face.

"He stayed till two," she whispered. "I'd love to go back to bed. I feel kind of rocky."

After Mass, as we were sitting down to breakfast, Father O'Dea appeared at our door. "Whose Simca was parked outside your house last night?" he asked after we had greeted him and asked him to sit down.

"I really don't feel well," Molly said. She pushed back her chair and headed for the bathroom. Under the sound of running water, I thought I heard her throwing up.

"What's wrong with her?" Father O'Dea asked.

I poured him some coffee from our breakfast tray. "I'm sure it's nothing serious. I'll check on her in a minute."

"Do you know whose car that was?" he pressed.

"It belongs to a friend of ours," I said.

"What friend?"

"Someone we just met. The person dropped in and then stayed and stayed."

"British and male, I suppose?"

"Does it matter?"

"Don't you remember what I told you about hobnobbing with the British, Abby?"

"But Father," I said, pausing to sip my coffee and gather my thoughts. "We're not nuns, you know."

"I know that very well," he said. "But I also know you are not here to have a good time. Once you get a reputation for hanging out with the British, the local people will write you off."

"Not if we make friends with them too."

"I have to answer for you to the bishop," he said. "And also to the nuns, who already think you're a handful." In a gentler voice, he added, "But that's not the real reason I'm concerned. I want what's best for you. Don't you see that?"

"Please, let us decide what's best for us," I said, voicing what I imagined Molly would have said were she out of the bathroom and sitting in my place. "We're grown-ups."

"Don't give me that. You're both so naive, anyone could take advantage of you."

"I don't want to lie to you, Father O'Dea," I said. "We're going to have dinner with David this weekend."

"Where?"

"His house. It will be all three of us."

"What?" He sounded angry again. Furious, in fact. "If you have to see him, do it anywhere but alone at the house of a single man. Nice girls don't do that here. And you tell him, no more late-night visits."

"That sounds reasonable," I said.

Molly was upset when I told her about my conversation with Father O'Dea. "You shouldn't have given in."

"I didn't give in. I compromised."

"It doesn't make sense,' Molly insisted. "On the one hand, he doesn't want us to be seen with anyone British, but on the other hand, he doesn't want us to be where no one will see us."

David laughed when we told him about Father O'Dea's concerns. "That old fellow is jealous," he said.

"But he's a priest," Molly said.

"He's a man before he's a priest. I think he's trying to keep you all to himself."

"Maybe Molly, but not me!" I said. "I'm just caught in the middle."

"No," Molly protested. "We both are."

Chapter 5

THE EYE OF THE BLACKBIRD

"DO YOU HAVE ANY PAINT?" I asked Sister Veronica. We'd just finished stripping the last of the wallpaper off the classroom walls, and they looked worse than before we started.

Sister Veronica shook her head. "We'd have to go to Belize City for it, or maybe send to the States, and it would be expensive. We don't even have blackboards in all the rooms. In fact, we don't have enough textbooks for all the girls. They'll have to share."

Textbooks and blackboards were obviously beyond our reach, but I was convinced that somewhere in Angel Creek there must be a few cans of paint that we could buy or beg. Molly and I decided to find them.

Our search led us to the Beaumonts and the Olivers, the two most prominent families in the district. Both were British and owned vast tracts of land in Paloma Valley, where they grew citrus crops and sugar cane. The Beaumonts also operated a citrus factory that exported tins of orange and grapefruit juice to other parts of the Commonwealth.

With Molly doing most of the talking, we convinced Father O'Dea to act as a go-between. Not only did he manage to talk Mr Beaumont into seeing us but also he arranged for Gilly to drive us out to the Valley.

Once Sister Veronica heard what we were up to, she insisted on sending along Sister Marietta and another nun to help us plead our cause, even though Gilly shook his head, implying that we wouldn't all fit in the Jeep.

"We'll manage," said Sister Marietta. She sat in the front seat next to Gilly while the companion nun sat in the back next to Molly, who held me on her lap.

Figure 5. Molly, Abby and a Holy Family sister on the robin's-egg blue Jeep. Photo courtesy of Malilee Zimmers.

We met Mr Beaumont, a taciturn, middle-aged man, in his office at the citrus factory. He listened without comment to our request, and, still without replying, called his overseer into the office. The distinguished-looking, silver-haired man he addressed as Mr De Santos looked as though *he* should have been the boss.

"De Santos, find these young women some paint," Mr Beaumont ordered in his high-pitched, nasal voice. "They've come all the way from the US to teach here, and it's the least we can do." In fact, he added, he would be pleased to provide us with anything else we needed to redecorate the school. Just send Mr De Santos a list. He shook our hands, wished us good day, and was back at work before we left his office.

Mr De Santos took us to a storehouse, where he loaded seven gallons of paint into the back of the Jeep. "A couple of the gallons are rather bright blue and the rest are orange, I believe, with perhaps a couple of cream. I'm afraid it's all we have at the moment."

Before we left, he offered us a tour of the canning factory. The entire operation, both processing and packaging, was housed in a building that resembled an aircraft hangar, open at both ends. A total of twenty workers or so, all several shades darker than the foreman, produced the canned juices.

"How much are the workers paid?" I asked.

"Twenty-five cents an hour BH," Mr De Santos said.

That was about fifteen US cents. Molly and I both gasped.

"It's a decent wage here," he said. "If they had more, they would, sad to say, just drink it away."

I thought of Cuba to the northeast, and of the revolution Fidel Castro had successfully led there not even three years before. "Aren't you afraid of Communism?"

Mr De Santos's loud laugh took me by surprise; it had been a serious question. "The workers aren't discontented, my dear young lady. Most have their little plantation of land in the bush where they grow cassava and mangoes. They have a good enough life." He led us outside, into the bright sunshine. "Besides, ask anyone. Mr Beaumont is known to take good care of his workers. We always have more men wanting jobs than we can use."

As if to prove his point, he led us past the company-owned housing where many of the workers lived. We saw a cluster of small, unpainted wooden houses, shacks to an American eye, especially compared with the housing provided to the British at the Forestry Station nearby.

Mr De Santos seemed proud of the houses, no more than twelve feet square and raised about two feet off the ground so that air could circulate under them. Without question, they were an improvement over some of the houses in town, many of which were little better than scrap heaps salvaged from the hurricane.

"But they're so small," I said. Shutters stood open to catch the late-afternoon breeze, and a few inhabitants looked out at us from the interior shadows, mostly women, old people, and small children.

"Give them more space, and unfortunately, they just have more children," he said.

Before we left, Mr De Santos piled several cases of orange and grapefruit juice on top of the paint cans. "With the compliments of Beaumont and Sons," he said. "Good day to you, Sisters, greetings to Father O'Dea, and my best wishes to you, young women, for a happy stay in our country."

Our begging had not produced enough paint to cover the walls of all the classrooms in the temporary St Monica High. Molly and I decided it would make the most sense to commit ourselves to one wall at a time, alternating colours.

Later, surveying the psychedelic blue and orange rooms that resulted from our outing, Sister Veronica laughed out loud.

"Miss?" The big-eyed girl in the front row raised her hand. I had almost made it through my first class, English IA, a first-form composition class. I'd been telling the students, the equivalent of high school freshmen in the States, that to write well they had to take time to observe the world around them.

"Let nothing be lost on you!" I said. "You'll see beauty and find strangeness you never imagined. The English writer D.H. Lawrence called his poems 'acts of attention'. That's what I want you to do for homework. Pay attention to things. Remember, tomorrow I'm going to ask you to tell me what you saw that was most interesting or beautiful or unusual in some way – "

"Miss!"

I stopped. "Yes? What is it?"

"Please, Miss, what you name?"

"What *is* you name!" whispered the girl next to her. The students were required to speak standard English in school instead of the Creole of the streets.

I realized that in my nervousness, I'd neither told the students my name nor asked theirs. I took a deep breath. "My name is Miss Porter, Miss Abigail Porter, but people call me either 'Abby' or 'Gail' for short. I'm from the middle of the United States, from a city along the Mississippi River."

They nodded, as though I'd finally told them something worth knowing. I asked them their names, and for the first time, following my own advice, really looked at them.

The question-asker was Cassie, I noted, and Edna was the corrector. Both were Garifuna girls. I estimated that half of the twelve girls in the class were Garifuna and the rest were either Creole or Latina. In my other classes, I found the same mix of ethnicity in roughly the same proportions, with the addition of a Chinese girl in one and an East Indian in another.

"G'mahnin', Miss Abigail Portah," the class said in unison as I walked in the next day.

"Good morning," I said, emphasizing the final consonants. "Let's start with your assignment. Remember, I asked you to pay attention to things. What did you notice yesterday?"

A long pause.

"You must have noticed something. This was your homework!"

Finally, a Garifuna girl named Mavis slowly raised her hand. "I see – I mean, I saw – a girl sitting in a chair?"

"Why are you asking me, Mavis? Tell me what you saw."

"A girl standing next to a chair?"

"First, let's talk about this girl sitting in a chair. How exactly did she sit?"

"Like anybody who sit – sits – in chairs, Miss."

"Was her back straight or did she slouch?"

"Yes, Miss."

"Well, which one?"

"I don't recall, Miss."

"Did the way she sat remind you of anything?"

"Of ahl de people who sit in chairs, Miss."

"Try to be more specific, Mavis, so all of us can imagine the girl. Try a comparison. Did she look like the letter *S* as she sat there? Or like a cat curled up?"

"Yes, Miss."

Edna raised her hand. "Miss, you tell us de ansah, and we write it down."

"What I want you to do is describe the way things look to you. You have to do that for yourself."

"Even if we ahl see de same ting?"

"Well, let's try it!"

What could I use? I rummaged in my bag and pulled out a compact my mother had given me. I opened it so that the mirror and cream-coloured powder with its little puff were visible. "Pass this around," I said. "I won't tell you what it is or what it's for. Look at it carefully, touch it, feel it."

The students erupted with excitement and spontaneously encircled Mavis, to whom I had handed the compact. Apparently, even those who recognized it from movies or magazines had never handled such a thing before.

Responding to the noise, Sister Veronica, the principal, came to the door of my classroom. It was once a bedroom and opened onto the former sunporch where she taught math. "What is happening here?" she asked in a chilly voice.

The students immediately returned to their desks and sat in silence, eyes downcast and hands folded with fingers interlaced on their desktops.

"It's a writing exercise, Sister," I said. "I'm sorry if we disturbed you. It won't happen again."

"I should hope not," she said, glaring at the students before turning to leave.

One by one, the students silently gazed at themselves in the little round mirror. Some smelled the powder, others tried a taste of it, a few hesitantly patted some on their hands, noses, cheeks and hair.

"Now open your notebooks and write for ten minutes, describing that object in any way you want," I told them. "Just two rules. Think of a title for your essay. And try to notice details and use them when you describe."

When they finished, they read aloud their responses.

Although most students were able to write English closer to the standard than to speak it, the titles were usually the best part of the essays. One student entitled hers, "How White People Get Whiter." Another described her own reflection in a paragraph called "Mirror, Mirror in My Hand". The titles revealed that my students had a keen sense of humour and a knack for analogy and metaphor that indicated lively imaginations. I was satisfied, because by the end of class the students agreed that no two of them had seen the same thing in the same way.

Not long after, I decided to introduce the class to Wallace Stevens's poem "Thirteen Ways of Looking at a Blackbird". Since childhood, I'd made a project of learning many of my favourite poems by heart. One of my teachers had encouraged the practice, if for no other reason, she said, than as a preparation for the time in our lives when we would be "alone, blind, and in our rocking chairs." No need to wait till then, in my case. We had almost no books to teach from or refer to. Thanks to Hattie, we had at most one textbook for every three or four students and only the warped remnants of a library. Memory, I realized then, is the lifeblood of learning, and books are its lifelines.

I recited Stevens's poem to the class several times. They were excellent listeners with well-trained memories and could quote back to me some of the shorter stanzas after hearing them just once or twice. They knew blackbirds, they said – the "Christmas birds" that passed through Angel Creek each year on their journey south. Like the birds, most of the poem flew right over their heads, but because they liked poetry, they each caught a bit of it and felt its power. When I asked them to, they eagerly wrote down their own way of looking at a blackbird.

The poems, the first fruits of our labour, enchanted me. One from Jessie Nunez, a sombre child, convinced me I had found a poet in our midst. It was elegant and sad:

> Solitude like a blackbird is lonesome,
> where ever it may be.
> So when one is in solitude,
> He is out of the sight and mind of everyone.

Jessie, I discovered, was from Hopkins, a tiny Garifuna fishing village about ten miles by dory from Angel Creek, named for a British priest who had drowned there during the 1931 hurricane. The few survivors rebuilt because they didn't want to live anywhere else. Hattie, too, had hit her village hard, she said, and one of her brothers died in the storm. She had four sisters still at home and one brother also, and she missed them "like in death."

When I asked her why she had left home to come to Angel Creek, she said she had asked her father to send her. There was no high school in her village, and she wanted to continue her education. He was surprised, Jessie said, because few villagers left. When she promised to work hard, he agreed. "He say men have many ways to make dey fortune, but gals need a boost."

Maybe I read too much into Emma's poem, especially after I found out that she was the darkest child in a Creole family. One of her sisters, a third-former at St Monica's, was famous for her hazel eyes, and an older sister for her auburn hair. Emma wrote: "Outside, the blackbird be black. / Inside, he no colour at all."

Sherry's poem, she later told me, derived from a Creole proverb. She broke it into three lines:

> Every blackbird
> think her baby bird
> white.

Sherry had mothers on her mind, I subsequently learned. Her own mother died when she was eleven, and her stepmother had given birth not long before to a baby boy.

In her poem, Cassie, who had been the first to ask my name, betrayed her characteristic curiosity: "I do not see the blackbird at night. / Do he see me?"

(I came across Cassie one evening after dark, sitting on the curb outside Lee Wong's store, reading by the light from the open door.

"Cassie, why are you reading here?" I asked her. "This light is terrible."

"Dey no lights atahl at home," she said.)

"Dis my poem, Teachah," said Mavis, whose family had lost everything, house included, in the floods that followed Hattie. Her parents and their eight children were staying with relatives in a three-room house on Front Street. "I rewrite Mr Stevens's poem foh yah."

"The blackbird whirled in the autumn winds," Stevens had written. "It was a small part of the pantomime."

I have to admit that Mavis's plagiarized poem was my favourite: "The blackbird whirled in Hattie's winds. / It was a small part of the hurricane."

In my steamy classroom that July, in our own thirteen ways of looking, Stevens's snow and icicles melted away. His New England autumn became the season of rain and hurricanes. His innuendoes, his bawds of euphony, his Connecticut and his glass equipages disappeared except as indecipherable sound. What remained was the eye of the blackbird, returning an awakened gaze.

Chapter 6

PRIESTS AND VIRGINS

"WE'VE HEARD SOME GOSSIP about you," Molly told Father O'Dea. We had joined him in the rectory kitchen after supper, as we sometimes did.

"Oh, yes?" His tone was non-committal.

"The boys were talking. They said some people say you – well, that maybe you like to drink a little more than you should. And worse. But they didn't say what 'worse' was. We thought we should let you know."

"Let's not disappoint them," he said. "Would you like a beer?"

He took three Coronas from his gas refrigerator. Electric power in Angel Creek was so erratic that no one relied on it. "Let me tell you about the 'worse', or at least what I think it must be." He opened the beer bottles, offered us glasses, and sat back down. "About six months ago, not long after Hattie, I gave a woman a ride home in the Jeep – a rather beautiful woman with a definitely bad reputation. It was late, and she was drunk. More than a little drunk. I knew I shouldn't drive with her alone, but there was no one to drive with us. I almost had to carry her to her door, and she thanked me by throwing her arms around me and giving me a kiss."

He twisted his mouth into a smile. "It took me by surprise. I'm not used to being kissed." He took a long drink of his beer. "I doubt she even remembers what happened." His voice sounded weary. "I don't know who saw us, but someone's always watching. By now it's old gossip, not worth repeating except to newcomers like you."

"Will people talk if we go to the missions with you?" Molly asked. Father O'Dea had promised to take us with him when he visited some of the remote villages in the district. "We don't want to make things harder for you."

"I don't care if people talk," he said. "It's their suspicious minds that are the problem. Don't worry about it."

It was Molly, of course, who had convinced Father O'Dea to take us with him into the bush. A few weeks earlier, he'd mentioned that the bishop was ready to appoint an assistant priest to Angel Creek. As soon as the choice was made and the new man arrived, Father O'Dea said, he would be able to visit remote parts of the district more often.

Molly and I had listened spellbound to accounts from our friends and neighbours of picturesque villages scattered along the southern coast and others hidden away in the Mountain Pine Ridge. We wanted to see them for ourselves.

"People keep telling us about the villages," Molly said, her face aglow with anticipation. "They say we really can't understand this place and its people unless we visit them. If only we could come with you!"

"Travelling to these remote areas isn't easy," Father O'Dea warned. "And it's often dangerous. The roads, if they exist at all, can be hazardous. Sinkholes. Washouts. Flash floods. Some places can be reached only by boat or dugout canoe. And conditions in the villages are pretty primitive. No indoor plumbing, no electricity or other modern conveniences. You eat whatever the villagers have to give you, like it or not, and sleep wherever they put you. It's no picnic."

"We wouldn't expect it to be easy," Molly said. "And of course, we wouldn't expect you to take us unless we could be of some help to you and the villagers. It would be a wonderful experience for us, to travel with you and share your work. That's why we're here, isn't it? Won't you please consider it, Father O'Dea?

Before he answered, I could tell by his giddy smile that she'd won him over.

After that, Father O'Dea began to take us with him to places we could never have gone on our own. We went with him to a reception for a Garifuna priest who had recently been ordained in the States. Father Melvyn had come home to Angel Creek to celebrate with his family before going back to the United States to his permanent assignment.

Father O'Dea ushered us into a room behind a storefront on Market Street owned by one of the relatives of the priest. The three of us were the only foreigners there; the rest were Garifuna, with a few Creoles mixed in. The women sat on benches along one wall, and the men sat or stood along the opposite wall. One of the men rushed to bring us chairs, seating Molly and me on the women's side, high up, above most of the older women.

As soon as we arrived, the speeches started. The first was by the master of ceremonies, intoned in a powerful voice. The crowd immediately quieted down, and for almost ten minutes, the leader praised the man, introduced as Mr James, who was in turn to give a speech in praise of the young priest. Mr James, I gathered, was the young priest's maternal uncle.

As the first speaker delivered his praise, the crowd called out its approval and affirmation. Later, I learned their behaviour was part of an ancient Garifuna tradition of "call and response". A leader set the theme and the listeners chanted their reply. I loved it without understanding most of what I heard. It was strange music to me.

Mr James rose to his great height and for the next half hour, addressed us extemporaneously in a voice as deep as God's in *The Ten Commandments*. References to the Bible and Shakespeare, quoted from memory, studded his rambling but eloquent speech. Every time he cited a familiar passage, the crowd murmured in agreement and nodded their heads, so that there was constant motion and humming in the room while he spoke. Not once did he stumble or search for words as he described at length how even as a boy, the future priest had realized that "the price of wisdom is above rubies". There followed perhaps a five-minute digression on the nature of wisdom. Everyone applauded when he asserted that true wisdom comes from the spirit of God and the ancestors.

From a young age, Mr James continued, returning to his main theme, his nephew knew that "unto whomsoever much is given, of him much shall be required". The assembly hummed loudly at this quotation, and again at the assertion that the young student did not disdain to "burn the midnight oil". Dedicated to his search for knowledge, we were told, he excelled at school. God rewarded his labour; he won a full scholarship to St John's College in Belize City.

"Mmm-hmm!" the crowd sang. "Gahd gud!"

The uncle raised his hands, as if in prayer, saying that there, like Samuel, his nephew heard the call of God and his faith grew strong. His faith, we heard, was as "a 'lamp unto he feet and a light unto he path', along the narrow way to the priesthood."

"Praise de Lord!" several called. "Mmm-hmm!" the assembly responded.

"But He yoke easy and He burden light!" Nods and hums as heads bobbed.

Another digression followed on the special nature of priests, who are, he said – if I understood him correctly – our link to the spirit world. Drawing his remarks to a close, the speaker left us with thoughts prompted by a passage from one of Shakespeare's sonnets, recited from memory:

> As a decrepit father takes delight
> To see his active child do deeds of youth,
> So we take comfort of thy worth and truth.

"We de fahdahs and de muddahs of dis yong mon," he concluded. "We follow de ole ways and stay in de ole places. He go into de wide world we nevah see, to learn tings we nevah know. But we glad to see him go, because we know he follow de will a de Fahdah in Hebban and do deeds dat make us proud."

This occasion was my introduction to the speechmaking of the Garifuna people and to their vibrant oral tradition, expressed in oratory, storytelling and song: chants, poetry and other vocal renditions. Never before had I witnessed such delight in and reverence for human speech on the part of both speakers and listeners. Neither of the speakers had been long to school, Father O'Dea told us later. He doubted most of those in attendance could read or write much English. And Garifuna was not at the time a written language.

Father Melvyn himself at last rose and thanked the speakers and all who had gathered there. His accent had faded in his years away and his remarks were brief, but like those of the other speakers, his words were eloquent and delivered in a thrillingly deep voice.

"You brought my flesh to life, good people," he told them, "but God raised me up, even though He knows as you know that I am still a child in the life of the spirit. God's call has taken me far from my earthly home, but wherever I go, however far from you here, we meet each day in the communion cup. We truly are one in the Spirit and also in the body and blood we share. We are truly and ever one, not only in family but far, far more, in Christ, whose love for us and obedience to the Father brings us to our true and eternal home."

During the tears and the applause that followed his remarks, a mangy dog trotted in a side door, promenaded around the room, and without deigning to stop or sniff, trotted out. No one except Molly and me seemed to notice.

Men with bottles of whisky and wine went round the room filling glasses, and the toasts began, all delivered by men, all well-spoken. Then the women served "fry fish" with rice and beans cooked with coconut milk, followed by pudding a little like tapioca, made from the cassava root. It was our first taste of Garifuna food.

After the meal, Molly and I went up to congratulate the young priest. He shook our hands and said, "I'd still be swinging in the trees if it weren't for the Jesuits."

I was taken aback by his metaphor, unsure how to respond. "Are you a Jesuit, then?" I asked.

"Oh, no," he said. "I joined a Negro order in the States. Jesuits were my parish priests in Angel Creek, and they taught me at St John's in Belize City." He went on to explain that he was one of a growing number of young men and women educated in mission schools who had found vocations and been sent to the States for training. The irony, I discovered, questioning him, was that their choice of vocations was still limited by attitudes that segregated even religious communities. He told me that congregations like his, and like that of the nuns who ran our high school, had been founded in the previous century because most European and American orders refused to accept people of colour.

"Would the Jesuits have accepted Father Melvyn if he'd applied?" I asked Father O'Dea on the way home.

"He didn't apply to the Jesuits," he said. "And in my opinion, he's better off where he is." He paused, then added, "As a matter of fact, we've ordained a couple of native priests in the past year or two. One is a Creole from Belize City. He's been in the States until recently. You'll soon meet him. I just had word today that he's been temporarily assigned to this parish as assistant pastor, and he's due to arrive any day now."

Even though Father O'Dea complained, rightly, that the town and district were too big for one man to handle, he didn't seem particularly pleased with the appointment.

"Strike two!"

I was at bat for the girls' team. The Camelot boys and a few other boys from standard six – the same as eighth grade in the United States – had challenged some of the first-form girls along with Molly and me to a baseball game. It was the top of the ninth, and the game was tied at three all. I smacked a pop fly into left field, just the sort of hit the boys had been missing because of the sun in their eyes. I thought for sure I had a homer, but the boys screamed with glee and the girls with outrage as I headed for first base. Our new assistant pastor had loped onto the field, and he caught the fly barehanded.

"No fair, Father!" I yelled.

"Just as fair as you playing for the girls, Teacher!" he yelled back. "I'm just balancing things out."

It took us another inning to lose by one run – the priest's.

"You are not making a good impression on me!" I said as we walked back towards the rectory after the game.

"Don' be sore loosah, Teachah," he said in pidgin English.

"Well, den, don' cheat, Fahdah!" I said, doing my best imitation.

"Okay, Okay. Peace offering! Follow me."

Molly caught up with us, and Father Bosque led us into the rectory and opened a bottle of lemonade for each of us. As we sat around the kitchen table, I thought he was more handsome than I remembered from our first meeting.

A new Jesuit came today, Father Charles Bosque, I'd written the evening before in a letter home, still in my desk drawer. *He's from Belize City, fair-skinned, with brown-almost-black hair and blue eyes with laugh lines cobwebbing out from them. He's also young, unlike most of the priests down here.* At the time, any priest over forty seemed old to me.

The man who sat before me now had the fair skin I had described, but his eyes were in fact more green than blue. He had crisp, curly hair, a shade more black than brown, and a compact, muscular body. His most distinctive feature, I decided, was his expressive voice, a bit breathy, with a hint of huskiness that reminded me of singer Harry Belafonte, who was raised in Jamaica. As with Belafonte, the Creole intonation was all that remained of his native speech.

"Where did you learn to play baseball?" he asked me.

"From my brothers and my father," I said. "They love the St Louis Cardinals. And I always played in school, in gym classes."

It turned out that he'd spent several years at the Jesuit seminary in Florissant, Missouri, a suburb of St Louis not far from where I'd grown up, and we reminded each other of familiar places and mentioned names the other might know.

"How long were you in the States?" Molly asked him.

"On and off, I spent about eight years there, starting when I was eighteen. I came back to Belize City as a seminarian for a few years to teach at St John's, and then went back to Kansas to finish my training. It takes a long time to become a Jesuit."

"And your family lives in Belize City?" she asked.

"Most of them, but I have a sister and her husband here, and some nieces and nephews. You were playing ball with one of them just now. Sissy Quinlan."

"She's one of our best players!" I said. "And she's in two of my classes, composition and history."

"I teach her too," Molly said. "She's in my lit class. I also teach an Alma Quinlan, who's a sophomore. Is she your niece too?"

"Yes, they're sisters, though you'd never know it to look at them. Sissy is blond like the Quinlans and Alma with her black hair looks more like the Bosques. You know what we British Hondurans say about ourselves, don't you? 'We ahl mix up!'"

He laughed. "I'm taking my 'mix-up' nieces and nephews swimming tomorrow afternoon out in the valley. Do you want to come?"

"Yes!" Molly and I said at once. "When?"

"Around three-thirty, after classes. You can drive with Gilly and me in the Jeep. Lydie, my sister, will bring the kids. They have a farm out there, along the river."

As we rose to leave, Father O'Dea walked in. "Getting acquainted?" he asked, glancing at the empty pop bottles.

"Father Bosque is taking us swimming tomorrow afternoon!" Molly said. "Isn't that nice of him?"

"You don't have anything else to do?" I wasn't sure whether Father O'Dea was talking to us or to Father Bosque.

"Not a thing," Father Bosque said. "You're welcome to join us, Father O'Dea."

"I'm not a swimmer," he said and went into the back room, shutting the door behind him.

Swimming with the Quinlans meant defending yourself against a five-year-old who wouldn't let go of your neck as you swam, an eight-year-old with a lizard in a can, a ten-year-old who swam open-eyed under water, and an Uncle

Charlie who loved practical jokes, like pushing you off the bank into the water the minute you turned your back on him.

On shore, Lydie Quinlan sat in the shade of a tree along the riverbank, smoking Benson & Hedges, pointing at this or that child or her younger brother with the two fingers clamped on her cigarette, and calling out invectives and ultimatums as ashes flew. "Too rough!" she cried. "Charlie, you're worst of all. Get a nice game going, or I'm taking all you kiddos home!"

Charlie found a big rubber ball in Lydie's Land Rover and made up some rules for a game of water polo, girls against boys. When the girls fell far behind, he switched sides, but when we started winning, he switched back again.

"How do we know which side you're on?" I panted, swatting the ball over his head. On the last play, I'd sent it straight to him, and he'd passed it to one of the boys. "You're a double agent!"

"Not true," he said. "I just like to even the score."

"'Vengeance is mine, sayeth the Lord'," I quoted.

"And behold! The day of that vengeance is at hand!" He made as if to lunge for me, and I dove deep and away.

Later, I sat next to Lydie on the bank of the river, which pooled under the wide mangrove trees. She offered me a cigarette, and I shook my head.

"He likes you girls," she said, lighting up. "I'm glad. He needs friends."

The next weekend, around four in the morning, Molly and I left with Father O'Dea for Sand Bight, one of the most remote missions in the Angel Creek District. No roads went there. Gilly drove us down to the new pier, and we boarded the *Madre B*, one of several mail boats that travelled up and down the coast. Along with the canvas mail pouch, the crew took on board dozens of cases of tinned juice from the Beaumont Factory in the valley and a couple of crates of live chickens. We were the only passengers.

Father O'Dea greeted the crew like old friends. He introduced us as "lay missionaries" from the States and then led us into the cabin on deck, where the captain joined us after the boat pulled away from shore. He put his left hand on my shoulder as he pumped my right hand with his, then he did the same with Molly.

Moving a stack of Spanish language newspapers to the floor, he seated us at the bolted-down table and served us hot coffee in bowl-sized mugs with steaming milk and lots of sugar. I answered his friendly questions in a daze.

The dim light in the cabin took the edge off reality, and the pulsing sound of the boat engine beat out other sounds. My body vibrated to its rhythm.

"What time will we get to the village?" I asked.

"About nine a.m.," Father O'Dea said. "It's usually about a five-hour trip from Angel Creek."

"How many miles?"

"About twenty-five or thirty by sea."

I shook my head. Time and space no longer had their familiar relationship. Like Alice down the rabbit hole, I tried to accustom myself to new dimensions in the world around me.

After we finished our coffee, Molly and I went out to wait for sunrise, which came about half past five. As if to emphasize disproportion, the dawn revealed a huge sea turtle on deck, its shell as big as a doghouse. We walked over to where it lay trapped under a heavy rope net. Every now and then a sailor threw a bucket of water over it. Mesmerized, we watched the sinuous motion of its emerging head and wing-like legs.

I bent over to see its snub-nosed face better. Molly poked me.

"Watch out," she said. "We're being watched."

I looked over my shoulder. The crew, the captain and Father O'Dea had their eyes fixed on us.

"They were looking up our skirts!" Molly said. "All of them!"

I shrugged but tucked my skirt between my knees, wishing for my outlawed khaki pants, still in my suitcase back in Angel Creek.

"What would humans want with a reptile that big?" I wondered out loud. Obviously, it was being shipped somewhere.

"Mek feast foh ahl de villij," said one of the sailors. He laughed and added, "Gud foh mek babies!"

When we later asked what the sailor had meant, both the captain and Father O'Dea had a good laugh. The captain explained that many people considered turtles and their eggs to be aphrodisiacs.

"You yong ladies – and you too, Padre – bettah be careful wha' you eat in dat village you gone to!"

At that moment I had no desire to eat anything, ever. The plowing of the boat and the heavy smell of diesel fuel turned my stomach. At breakfast the sight of the fried eggs and thick slabs of tinned meat, oozing orange grease, that the captain offered us, and the appetite with which he and the priest ate them, sent Molly and me back outside to the railing. It was one of the days

Figure 6. A Sand Bight boy climbing a coconut tree, with the sea in the background. Photo courtesy of Malilee Zimmers.

when I felt not so much intrigued as overwhelmed by difference, and I longed for a place to curl up and fall asleep in the rising sun. I felt as if I were travelling to a place even farther away from Angel Creek than Angel Creek was from the States.

As the *Madre B* approached the pier at Sand Bight, villagers came running from their thatched-roofed huts along the shore and gathered on the beach. Father O'Dea told us that most of the men were out fishing in their dories or off working at their plantations, but scores of women and children and a few old men celebrated our arrival. Taking our bags, they led us into the village in a noisy procession, word spreading fast that "Fahdah and two teachahs from America" had come. Many of the children had never seen a white woman before. Not knowing whether to run towards us or away from us, they raced in circles around us as we walked.

"Look, Teachahs!" a boy of about ten shouted, and shinnied up a fifteen-foot tall coconut tree. He brought down a hairy coconut and ran to us, offering us his gift. Everyone applauded when we took it.

I had never seen a place so beautiful: the sheltered, half-moon bay and its dazzling white beach; the coconuts and palms, less ravaged by Hattie than those farther north; the cluster of simple dwellings; and the stately, black-skinned Garifuna women and children dressed in faded fabrics of pink, orange and blue-check, as though the same three bolts of cotton had supplied all the village clothing.

"It's the prettiest of all the villages," Father O'Dea told us.

Accompanied by scores of children and many of the village elders, he gave us a walking tour, showing us the dilapidated church, the tiny town hall, the one-room schoolhouse, and, the pride of the village, a new hospital, the only painted building in town. We met the two staff nurses, both in stiff white uniforms, one of whom turned on a faucet to demonstrate the most amazing feature of the hospital, indoor plumbing. As with our plumbing in Angel Creek, water flowed from a vat attached to the building that caught and stored rainwater.

While Father O'Dea visited the sick and dying, Molly and I went from house to house to greet people and tell them when Father would hear confessions in the church and offer Mass. Thanks to the school, almost everyone spoke English as well as Creole and their native Garifuna language, and most villagers eagerly chatted with us. A few invited us into their homes, where it was common for seven or eight people to live in a single room, no bigger than my bedroom in Angel Creek.

One grandmother sat us down on the two chairs in her house and opened a dusty bottle of Mexican lemonade for us, poured it out into cups as though it were the rarest wine, and insisted we drink the warm, sweet liquid while she and her daughters and grandchildren watched. Others offered us orange sections spiced with hot pepper seeds, cups of freshly drained coconut milk, or slices of ripe papaya and mango. As we chewed and swallowed, they stared at us intently. A few brave ones ventured to touch our hair, our skin or our clothing with a tentative finger or two.

At one house, a young mother who introduced herself as Annie Boyd greeted us outside the door. She held a baby of about nine months in her arms and struggled with a two-year-old toddler who clung to her legs, terrified of us. Like many of the young women we visited that day, she was pregnant. She couldn't have been much older than seventeen.

"Please, Teachahs, you tell Faddah he mos talk to Joseph Losey," she said to us. "Fahdah know Joseph. Fahdah mos tell Joseph it time we gat marry. Dese chiles need gat baptize."

"Are these Joseph's children?" Molly asked.

"Oh, yes, Miss. He my only mon. He say he my mon an' I belang wid him, but he have more womon dan me. You tell Fahdah."

"We'll tell Father," I promised.

When we did, Father O'Dea shook his head. "These black bastards live just to make more black bastards."

His tone and his language shocked me. "Isn't that what the Church insists on?" I asked. "Have all the babies you can?"

"Not outside the holy sacrament of marriage," Father O'Dea said. "It's about time Joseph settled down and married Annie Boyd and made her an honest woman."

"An honest woman? Why won't marrying her make him an honest man?"

"Stop your questioning, Abby, and you'll be happier." He put his hand on the top of my head to ruffle my hair. I pulled away. "You think too much," he said, his tone darkening. "All I mean is that a woman ought to wait for marriage before sex, or sex and illegitimate children are likely to be all she'll get. Once they're married in the Church, I'll happily baptize as many kids as God wants to give them."

I thought of one of my college classmates who'd been dating the same guy since high school. They planned to get married right after graduation. Over Christmas vacation our senior year, they slipped up. While her parents were out, they went all the way on the couch in front of the fireplace. Distraught, she told a few of her closest friends, and we all joined in saying novenas and offering up masses for her.

We understood her anxiety. The fear of pregnancy and the shame that went with it were as much a concern as the threat of mortal sin associated with any illicit sexual act. Then as now, the Catholic Church condemned any reliable form of birth control. Abortion, which at the time was illegal in the States, wasn't even a consideration. We all felt relieved when our friend assured us she'd confessed her sin to her parish priest and received absolution. And thank God! Her period came on schedule. Still, she was inconsolable.

"I'll feel like a liar and a cheat, wearing a white dress on my wedding day," she said in tears.Behind her guilt lay another, unspoken fear, shared vicariously by all of us: that her boyfriend would lose respect for her and maybe even dump her before the wedding as damaged goods. After all, it was the female's responsibility to set the limits. Didn't everyone know that after a certain point, any male worth his salt was incapable of self-restraint?

"Watch yourself," my grandmother would routinely caution me before I'd go on a date. "Men don't buy cows when the price of milk is cheap."

How I hated that saying! But I believed she was right.

"Things here ripen so fast," I said to Molly. It was siesta time, and we were lying on cots that had been set up for us in the house where one of the nurses lived. "People do too. Like Annie. She's probably five years younger than we are. That means she was only fourteen or maybe even younger when she first got pregnant."

"And here I am, almost twenty-two and still a virgin!" Molly said.

"Well, so am I," I said. "Do you ever feel like there's something unnatural about that? Like we've been in cold storage for the past ten years?"

"Would you want to have two or three kids and no husband? And even if you had a husband, would you want two or three kids at our age?"

"No, of course not, at least not back home. But here, a couple of twenty-two-year-old virgins seems a whole lot weirder than a seventeen-year-old with three kids and no husband. I don't know what to think."

"Take a nap, Abby. We've been up since three-thirty this morning."

"When I saw that girl, so young, surrounded by babies, I felt sorry for her. Like she'd wasted her life." Too many children too fast and too young were a large part of my parents' problem, and I'd never wanted that for myself. But now it crossed my mind that from Annie Boyd's perspective, I might be the one with the wasted life. "I know I have an education, and I would never give that up, but – "

Molly was already asleep.

"Fahdah say he done wid confession," one of the village boys said. "He say you cohn to de choch for you suppah."

We were down by the shore, where we were telling Bible stories to a group of young children. With the sound of the sea as accompaniment, we told them the story of the creation of the world.

"First God created the heavens and the earth, and it was very good. But it was dark and windy."

"Lak Hattie?" one of the children asked.

"Yes, just like Hattie, only there was nothing there to be blown away. Then God made light. And that was good, too, even if there wasn't anything to see.

So God made the sky and the sea. You see how the wind is moving across the water right now? Well, the Bible tells us that's how God's spirit moved across the water right after he made it. That's how much he loved and enjoyed it."

A breathed "Oh!" from the children.

"Next, God made the dry land. That's when Sand Bight came to be. And it was very beautiful and also very good, and he loved that too. But what was missing?"

They sat waiting for the answer.

"Figure it out," we said.

"Us!" one of them shouted.

"You're right! There was no life anywhere, no fish in the sea and no animals or people to live in this beautiful place. So what did God do?"

"Gahd mek ahl dem tings!"

"Yes, that's just what God did! And they were good too; very good. So think of one of the creatures God made, like a dolphin or a toucan or a dog. But don't tell anybody. We want each of you to act it out, and all the rest of us will guess which of God's creatures you are."

As in my high school classroom, the children went wild when they were given the least bit of freedom. Not waiting for their turns, they splashed and slithered and crawled and screeched and snarled and squawked and clawed. They were the new creation, as fresh and innocent as morning but perilously close to chaos. Father's messenger came just in time to save us, and them, as things spiralled out of control.

Someone had set up a small table outside the church, where a cool breeze was blowing from the sea. I expected that we would eat with others from the village, but they served us separately and left us to ourselves, disappearing into their own houses and yards, where dim lights bloomed in the darkness.

Father O'Dea pulled an extra bottle of altar wine, unconsecrated, from his satchel, and we drank it with red snapper caught only a few hours earlier and grilled over an open fire. The fish was crispy on the outside and soft as butter on the inside. With it we had starchy bread made from the root of the cassava plant and fried plantains and avocado pears. We lingered over the wonderful food and then carried the rest of the wine down to the shore to watch the moon rise over the sea.

Shoes off, Father O'Dea lay back against a piece of driftwood. "It's good to be here," he said. "I wanted you to see this. It's the most perfect place on earth – that I know of, anyway. I'm glad to be able to show it to you. It was worth all the hell Mother Eugenie gave me for bringing you along."

"Oh-oh," Molly said. "What did she say?"

He imitated her drawl. "I quote: 'The two volunteers last year didn't travel with you; why should these two? They're here to teach, not sightsee. People will talk. Priests and girls don't mix.' And about a dozen other objections. I reminded her you don't teach on weekends, and I could use your help, which is true. We obviously don't have enough priests or nuns to do the work that needs to be done, which is why PAVLA sent you here. Plus, it's good for these villagers to see that Americans are their friends. And for you to see what the Church and a priest mean for a place like Sand Bight."

"That's what I'm trying to figure out," I said. "In some ways, I almost feel like we're the snake in the Garden, telling people that their natural urges are sinful and making Annie think that there's something wrong with her and her children unless Joseph marries her with a priest there to bless them."

"Well, there *is* something wrong there, even if he does marry her. They both need the help of the sacraments – which is just another way of talking about the presence of Christ in their lives – to raise them above their selfish appetites and desires. And their children need that too. It's a lifelong struggle."

Father Melvyn's words came back to me: without the priests, he'd still be swinging in the trees. Is that what Father O'Dea meant? That religion transforms people from animals into humans? But what about all the crusades and inquisitions?

"I'm sure you're right, Father," Molly said. "Yet everything seems so simple and peaceful here. No struggle at all."

"Beneath the surface, out of sight, it's there. The beast inside. Working against us."

As if to refute him, the breeze shushed his words, and while the bush held back the darkness, the sand and waves caught and held the moonlight.

"Thank God for forgiveness," he said.

After a while, Molly asked Father O'Dea why he had become a priest. He poured himself the last of the wine and drank it in silence before he answered.

"I've asked myself that many times. I grew up on a farm. It's a brutal life. We grew wheat but had enough livestock to feed ourselves. I was just a stupid kid, and I made one of the pigs my pet. I must have been eight or nine. One day, my father gives me a butcher knife and sends me out to kill that pig. I knew then that I couldn't be a farmer."

"Oh no, Father O'Dea," Molly said softly. "Did your father actually make you kill it?"

"What do you think?" He didn't wait for an answer. "When it came time for high school, he sent me off to the Jesuits in Kansas City. That shapes you, bends you in a certain direction, even if you don't really like it all that much. Then war breaks out, and you get called up, sent to the South Pacific. You really like the place, even if you pick up malaria while you're there. You like the military, too, the order, the clarity of it, even if you hate what's going on. It's a short step into the Jesuits when you get back – you know, it's a lot like the military, without the killing. Saint Ignatius Loyola, who founded the Jesuits, was a soldier, so the resemblance isn't accidental."

I asked him how he'd ended up in Angel Creek.

"Your superiors in the Order get to know you better than you know yourself," he said. "One of my superiors decided on the missions for me, and that made a lot of sense. I came here as a scholastic – one of the stages before final vows – and I've been here on and off for almost ten years now. First in Belize City, which I didn't much like. I'm better off on my own. This is my fourth year in Angel Creek. Hattie was bad – all those funerals! It's not perfect, but it's not a bad life. Times like tonight, I think it's a great life."

If my own celibate life bothered me, his confounded me – the *how* of it rather than the *why*. The ideal seemed noble, selfless, especially when motivated by love of God, but the reality close to unattainable. I really didn't see how any ordinary human being could swear to give up intimacy with another person for life. "Have you ever regretted not being able to marry or have a family?" I asked him.

"I wouldn't be human if I didn't sometimes wish for that," he said. "Even the greatest saints had such longings. And I'm no saint. But in the end the grace of God and the example of Christ and the Blessed Mother have seen me through."

Almost the entire village turned up for Mass before dawn the next morning. The village lived according to the rhythms of nature, going to bed soon after dark and rising before the sun. Most of the men were fishermen, and would be heading out early with their nets. The women, who cared for the children and the old folks and often maintained the plantations, were up even before the men. The old folks and women with young babies took the pews, while most others stood in the side aisles or at the back of the church, spilling out the door onto the sand.

Dressed in his bright green vestments, Father O'Dea celebrated the Mass for the Fourth Sunday after Pentecost. The Gospel that morning was Luke 5: 1–11. When he read the passage where Jesus tells Simon Peter and the other fishermen, "Stand out into the deep water, and let down your nets for a catch," everyone drew a deep breath. They moaned at Peter's objection, "Master, we have toiled all the night, and caught nothing," and sighed with relief when he at last agreed: "At thy word, I will let down the net." And when they heard that the fishermen took in so many fish that their net was near breaking and they had to call their partners in another boat to come and help them, and that both boats were so full they were ready to sink, many sounded their delight. The end of the story, however, caused murmurs and puzzled frowns. What did Christ mean when he promised to make Simon a fisher of men? And why did Simon and the others leave everything behind – their boats, their nets and all those fish?

In his sermon, Father O'Dea did his best to explain. "Our earthly ties bind us. Our worries and our fears, our desires and our sins keep us from accepting God's grace, his many gifts to us. We must put our trust in the Lord. Only then can we realize that true abundance is spiritual. Even though our minds and our wills resist, we must ask God to bend them to His service."

That's lovely, but so abstract, I thought. What does it mean: "true abundance is spiritual"? I accepted the truism that happiness does not lie in wealth or possessions or prestige. But I could not accept that happiness could be detached from human love. And I could not see how human love could be detached from the spirit's habitation, a breathing, sensing body. Yet Molly and I were typical of many unmarried young women of our time, our sexuality locked away, with marriage the only acceptable key.

By the time we boarded the *Madre B* on its return journey up the coast, Father O'Dea had administered last rites to four in the village who were close to death, heard scores of confessions, led a community rosary, and celebrated the Eucharist. He baptized half a dozen babies and read the banns for three engaged couples, married two others, and blessed the unions of several who'd already had children together, including Annie Boyd and Joseph Losey.

After Mass that morning, Annie and Joseph stood together hand in hand before the priest as the village witnessed the sanctification of their union by Father O'Dea, who told them that they were no longer separate but one in the eyes of God and the community. Annie's mother, still a young woman herself, held Annie's baby and another of her own. Joseph's mother had charge of the toddler as well as several young brothers and sisters of the bride and groom, who themselves were little more than children.

Outside the church, Annie brought Joseph over to meet Molly and me. "Teachahs," she said with great pride, "dis me mon, Joseph. Fahdah say we a family now."

"You like de bush?" the captain asked us on our return trip as he once again served us steaming mugs of coffee.

"I've never in my life seen anyplace like it," Molly answered.

"It's another world," I agreed.

Chapter 7

YELLOW BIRD

FATHER BOSQUE CLIMBED OUR stairs, two at a time. I stood on our porch, waiting for him. Cupped in his hands he carried a bird.

"It's a yellow-tailed oriole, and it took me half an hour to catch it." He said it had flown through an open window into his attic room at the rectory. "It's so beautiful, I had to show it to someone."

He opened his hands a crack, and the brilliance of the bird's feathers escaped like morning sunshine. I drew in my breath at its beauty, but saw, too, its throbbing breast and terrified eye.

"It looks scared to death," I said. "Let it go. Please!"

"Impatient, isn't she?" He lifted the bird into the air. "Back to your nest, Yellow Bird!"

As the bird found its wings and streaked away from us, Father Bosque hummed a few bars of the calypso song "Yellow Bird" and then sang in his husky baritone, *"You can fly away, in de sky away. You mo lucky dan me!"* Passersby on the street below looked up, and seeing the young priest, they waved, and he waved back.

"Do you mind if I come in for few minutes?" he asked as I opened our front door. It was ten in the morning, my free period, and I'd just arrived home from school. We didn't have faculty offices, so I usually came home for the hour between my classes to mark papers or go over my lesson plans.

Please do," I said. "I'll make us some tea."

When I lifted the lid on the sugar bowl, it was crawling with ants.

"Don't worry," he said. He blithely spooned some of the raw sugar, ants and all, into his cup. "The hot tea kills them."

"No, none for me, thanks," I said when he offered me the bowl.

"After you're here a while, you won't even notice. Ants always go with sugar. You can use your teeth to strain them if you're pernickety."

"Already today you've caught a bird and eaten ants. What will you do for a third act, I wonder?"

He laughed his throaty laugh. "That's enough for one day, as a rule." He settled back in the armchair. "Tell me what you're teaching this term."

"*Jane Eyre* to the juniors, *Pride and Prejudice* to the freshmen. Two of my favourite books. No problem there, but I'm teaching a religion class to the freshmen, and I have no idea what I'm doing."

I explained that the book we were using, a basic catechism, started with a question. For example, "What was the result of Adam and Eve's disobedience?" It then gave a definite answer, in that case: "That we all share in their sin and punishment, which resulted in the loss of paradise, suffering and death." But the problem, I said, was the answers didn't explain *why*. "God is good, everything God creates is good, and suddenly there's evil. The students and I always seem to end up with questions the book doesn't answer. Even if Adam and Eve were disobedient, even if they chose freely – and I don't see how they could choose freely because they didn't have all the information – why couldn't God save them and himself a lot of trouble by forgiving them right off the bat and making everything good again? And why does everybody else have to suffer because of what they did?"

"Maybe it would help if we talked over some of the material you have to teach beforehand," he offered.

"Do you have time?"

"I'll make the time."

Thus began our daily conversations.

At ten every morning, I would hurry home from school and within a matter of minutes, I'd hear his knock on the door. I'd make him tea and during the next forty minutes we'd discuss whatever I or the students had found most puzzling.

That first day as he rose to leave, he said, "I'm going to Hawkens Creek on Sunday to celebrate Mass, and I was wondering whether you and Molly would like to come along." Hawkens Creek was a lumber camp about fifteen miles from Angel Creek over rough roads. "We'll have to leave around six in the morning. Are you up for another trip into the bush?"

"I'll check with Molly, but I'm pretty sure I can say yes for both of us."

"Great," he said. "Let's plan on it."

When Molly and I mentioned our proposed trip with Father Bosque to Father O'Dea, he frowned but didn't object. I wondered why he would disapprove. After all, he'd taken us on a far longer trip just a few weeks earlier.

During that week, the Jeep developed engine trouble, and Gilly and Father Bosque spent an entire afternoon working on it. On my way home from class that Friday, I saw them in the rectory yard with the hood open and the engine running. I stopped to see how things were going. Father O'Dea came out of the rectory just as I arrived.

"It's been overheating," Father Bosque said. "But I think we've fixed it."

Father O'Dea went over and put his hand on the engine casing.

"Don't touch it! It's too hot!" Father Bosque grabbed Father O'Dea's hand. For a fraction of a second, Father O'Dea strained against him, keeping his hand on the hot metal. Then he jerked his hand away with a curse and headed back into the rectory.

Father Bosque, Gilly and I stared after him.

"What was that all about?" Father Bosque muttered.

Gilly shook his head. "He strahnje sonetime."

"We're just about to take it out for a test drive," Father Bosque said, putting down the hood. "Climb in."

We headed out along the Melena Road, more picturesque and less populated than the Paloma Highway. Horses grazed in some of the fields, and the road crossed many small creeks that fed into the Angel Creek River. The best swimming holes were along the Melena Road.

"The Jeep seems to be running okay now," Father Bosque said, stopping at the pool where we swam with the Quinlans. "What say we take a quick dip? Gilly and I need to wash off after rolling around in the dirt all afternoon."

"I'd love to, but I don't have a swimsuit," I said.

"Take my shirt," Father Bosque offered. "It's rolled up in the back. You can wear it over your underwear."

With Father O'Dea, Gilly stood at attention, but with Father Bosque, he was at ease. "Don' worry, Miss Abby," he said. "Fahdah shirt mo modest dan you USA swimsuit. We no look no how."

No one in Belize wore a swimsuit. Most of my students, I'd noticed, swam in their cotton petticoats, and in mixed company the boys usually swam in their shorts. Behind one of the mangrove trees, I changed from my school uniform, a prim white blouse and navy blue skirt, into Father Bosque's short-sleeved sport shirt that hung halfway down my thighs. I decided to keep my half-slip on, knowing that I was nevertheless breaking at least one if not all three PAVLA Commandments.

I took a running jump into the deep pool, where Father and Gilly were already swimming. At first, the shirt ballooned out, but once it was wet it clung to me. Through the clear water I saw that Father and Gilly were in their boxer shorts and T-shirts, and I dove under water to cover my embarrassment and quench my laughter. I knew they'd be swimming naked if I weren't along.

After the swim, we drove around until our clothes, damp from our wet underwear, dried out, joking and laughing the whole time. We were like three kids out joyriding.

Hawkens Creek comprised a dozen houses in a clearing in a pine forest at the end of a rutted, muddy back road. The daily July afternoon downpours had washed some of the road away. We had to dig out twice on the way there and were so splattered with mud that before we arrived, we stopped to wash off in a creek on the edge of town. Father said the settlement was new, established after Hattie to meet the increased demand for lumber.

In the village Molly and I went from door to door to tell people that the priest had come and there would be confessions starting in fifteen minutes and Mass in an hour. Most of the families were Mestizo. I didn't see any Garifuna, who preferred fishing or teaching to the logging and factory jobs, though the latter were better paying.

At Mass, Father Bosque delivered two sermons, the first in English and the second, shorter, in Spanish. We understood why when we shared the midday meal with the Salazar family, whose turn it was to feed the priest. They were refugees from the political turmoil in Guatemala and had been in Hawkens Creek for only a few months. Señor Salazar and the older children understood enough English for a simple conversation, but Señora Salazar didn't. She nevertheless bombarded Molly and me with questions, counting on Father Bosque and her family to translate.

"She wants to know why you don't wear a habit," Father Bosque told us. "I explained to her that you aren't nuns."

"She ask why you don' has husband then," Señor Salazar said.

Molly answered, "We're not ready to get married yet."

When this was translated, Señora looked surprised and replied in Spanish.

"She says you're certainly old enough," Father Bosque translated. "And she will pray to St Anne that you find good husbands soon and have many healthy children. But she doesn't understand what you are doing here. Why you are so far from your families."

"Tell Señora we're teaching here and helping the nuns and priests," I said. "And that in the US, many unmarried women our age are independent of their families."

Señora registered dismay.

"Why do Americans want such a thing?" Señor asked for his wife. "She say independence very – how you say *sola*?"

"Lonely," Father Bosque translated. "She says independence fills people with loneliness."

"But it gives us freedom," I said.

"*Para que?*" Señora asked. For what?

"To live our own lives," Molly answered.

"She asks how being lonely can help you do that," Father Bosque said, adding, "Remember, I'm only translating."

"But we're not lonely!" Molly objected. "Can you help Señora understand that?"

"I don't think so," Father Bosque said.

On the way home, Molly said, "I didn't realize how odd it must seem to people in this country to see two unattached women all on our own."

"In this part of the world, like many other places, women are still walled up and protected from birth to death," Father Bosque said. "They don't exist apart from their families."

"When you think about it, Papal Volunteers and the Peace Corps are breaking a lot of new ground," Molly said. "It's really revolutionary, sending young men and women out together around the globe."

I agreed. "Our mothers couldn't have done something like this when they were our age."

"I wonder what our daughters will be able to do that we can't," Molly mused.

"Drive an automobile, in my case," I said.

"You can't drive?" said Molly. They both looked surprised.

"I once had a learner's permit, but I never actually got my licence. Nobody wanted to teach me." I grew up in the days before driver education in schools, in a family where men drove the cars and women rode in them. Neither of my grandmothers learned to drive. My mother passed her driver's exam only after her divorce from my father.

Father Bosque stopped the car. "Do you want to learn?"

"If you're willing to teach me," I said.

My driving lessons started that afternoon. From then on, anytime we had a free half hour, Father Bosque or Gilly took me out along the Melena Road or on the road south of town that ended in the new pier, where there was never much traffic.

During one lesson, I backed into a ditch, and Gilly never let me forget it. "Once she in gear and gone straight ahead, she A-okay," he reported later to Father Bosque, his eye glinting. "Too bad ain't but one straight road in ahl Angel Creek. In reverse, luk out, mon! She only danjrus!"

My lessons were often an occasion for fun. Molly or some of Father's nieces and nephews would come along, and we sometimes swam afterward, then sat on the rocks to dry. After that first day, I kept my bathing suit with me, rolled up in my bag. When I wore it, Father Bosque never failed to offer me his shirt as a "modest alternative".

The day that Father O'Dea turned over the salt and malaria pills to us, I realized how distant Molly and I had grown from him.

"I'm sure you'd rather do this yourself," he said, handing us the bottles. "Just be sure you don't forget."

After Father Bosque came, Father O'Dea's humour had grown caustic, even cruel at times, and his behaviour increasingly erratic. He mocked my driving lessons, saying that he'd rather teach a dog to tap dance than a female to drive; and he even began calling Molly "Miss Measles," because of her bug bites. We sometimes heard what sounded like arguments coming from the open windows of the rectory. One night after an angry exchange, we heard the door slam and the Jeep roar out of the yard.

After supper one evening, when we knew Father Bosque was out, we decided to drop by the rectory for a visit with Father O'Dea. It was almost dark, but there was no light in the kitchen. At first we didn't see him sitting at the table.

"Well, hello," he said in his old, genial voice. "Come in!" He had a glass of something in front of him. "Just enjoying an after-dinner drink," he said. "Join me." He went to the next room and came back with a bottle of Johnnie Walker. When we begged off, saying we had schoolwork to prepare, he refilled his own glass. "Cheers!" Some of the whisky spilled from his glass as he lifted it. "What's up with the two of you?"

"We just wanted to see how you're doing," Molly said. "We haven't talked for a couple of weeks."

"Oh, you've noticed, have you?"

"Well, yes," Molly said. "You don't stop by so often any more."

"Maybe I have better things to do."

"I'm sure you do," she said, sounding hurt.

"I didn't mean that," he said. "Forget it." He sat quietly for a few minutes, his head in his hands.

I began to think he'd fallen asleep. "Father O'Dea?" I asked. "Are you okay?"

"I don't feel so great," he said. "Look, you two go on home now. I'll talk to you later."

After Mass the next morning, he told us he had to go to Belize City and would be gone through the following weekend. "I'll stop by when I get back," he said.

That was the weekend Father Bosque offered to help me move my bed and belongings from my bedroom to another room in our house. I'd been sleeping in the bigger of the two bedrooms, one furnished with twin beds. Although the room had two windows, one facing south and the other west, the room heated up beyond bearing as the late-afternoon sun poured in. Almost as bad for sleeping, the west window opened onto Market Street, noisy even late at night.

That Saturday, he and Gilly moved the dining room furniture into a corner of the living room and carried a bed, chest and desk from my old bedroom into the new one, where the windows faced north and east and caught the sea breeze.

I don't know exactly how Father O'Dea heard about what Father Bosque had done – probably from Gilly – but when he came to look at the changes, I could see from his expression, as if he'd just sucked a lemon, that he was upset. I had to admire the way he controlled his emotions. All he said, with a sour look in my direction, was, "You know, if you and Molly were uncomfortable in this house, you could have said something to me about it."

Only then did we realize the extent of our treachery.

In the former breakfast room just off the former dining room, which was next to the former bedroom where I was teaching Jane Austen's *Pride and Prejudice* to the IB literature class, Ana Zacharias led her IIA Spanish class through the conjugation of irregular verbs. She was the only local teacher and the only layperson, besides Molly and me, in the school. The sisters taught all the other classes, except the senior theology class, which Father Bosque had taken over.

"*Haber*," Ana said in a high, piercing voice that travelled around corners and down hallways. "'To have', the auxiliary."

"*Haber*, 'to have', the auxiliary," the class recited.

"*He*," she said. "'I have'."

"*He*, 'I have'," they responded.

"*Has*, 'you have'."

"*Has*, 'you have'."

"*Ha*," the cheerful chant continued. "'He has'."

In her orderly fashion, Ana guided her students through present, past and future tenses. I envied the comparative simplicity of her task as I tried to explain entailed estates, aristocratic titles and social precedence to my baffled students, only half of whom had copies of Austen's novel.

"Why we read dis book, Miss?" one of the girls asked.

"It's a classic and by a woman," I said. "Isn't it interesting to read a book by a female for a change?"

"Why, Miss?"

"Well, it's about women's lives and their way of seeing things."

"But English people difrant dan us, Miss, 'specially de old-fashion womon. Hard a unnahstahn."

"Okay," I said. "Here's another reason. The novel is required reading for the exams you have to pass to get your diploma. And if you don't get your diploma, you can kiss a good job goodbye. So, read on, Cassie, if you would. Second full paragraph on the page."

The class heaved a mutual sigh and bent over their shared books. The Cambridge O- and A-level exams were the answer that explained and justified almost everything in the curriculum.

After class, I ran into Ana in the hallway.

"Can you and Molly come over this evening?" she asked. "We'll listen to some music if the power stays on, and you can meet the rest of my family."

We'd met several of her brothers a few days earlier. After school, she'd stopped by our house for tea, and as we were saying goodbye on our balcony, a Jeep full of boys drove up and stopped.

"*Hola*, Ana!" they called.

"My younger brothers," she said.

"You wan go foh ride, Teachahs?" they called.

"Talk good English!" Ana yelled. "Where are you going?"

The driver got out. He was older than the others. "To the valley, with a message for Javier."

"You want to drive along?" Ana asked us.

"Is there room?"

"The little boys can sit on our laps."

I ended up next to the driver, with a boy of about ten perched on the edge of my seat. Molly and Ana sat in the back, each holding one of the younger boys.

"You are Abigail. Yes?" the driver asked, looking over at me, pronouncing my name as in Spanish: "*Ah-vee-gah-eel.*" Like Ana, he had large, dark eyes, with lashes even thicker and longer than hers.

I asked him how he knew my name. He said he'd seen me one day on the street and asked Ana.

"I'm sorry," she said. "I should have introduced you properly. Molly and Abby, this is my brother Eduardo." She introduced the boy sharing my seat as Jaime, and the two youngest, she said, were Miguel and Tomas.

On our way out to the valley, Eduardo said that he had graduated the year before from the agricultural college in Pomona Valley and now worked for his father.

"What kind of work?" I asked.

"Whatever he gives me to do," he said. "He has some citrus walks that I help him with, and I work at the Caribbean Club in town in the evenings, and at some other clubs that my older brothers run when they need me to help. The Sportsman Club in the valley is one of them. When I'm ready, my father will give me my own farm and my own club to run. Until then, I'm learning about the businesses."

We pulled up before a small but neat concrete house, whitewashed and shaded by mango trees. Eduardo climbed out. As he walked away from us, he looked long-legged and too lean for his height, like a puppy that's had a sudden growth spurt.

"How old is Eduardo?" Molly asked.

"Almost twenty," Ana said.

"Isn't that young to be finished with college?" I asked.

"You forget that we use the word 'college' like the British do – it's like the American high school, only it takes five years. After that, it's 'university', but we have to go abroad for that, and almost no one does."

Eduardo stood talking to a middle-aged woman at the door of the house. She looked Mestizo, with straight, dark hair and dusky skin.

"Javier must not be home," Ana said.

When I asked who Javier was, she identified him as another of her brothers. He ran the Sportsman Club, Ana told us. He lived with "that woman", who was old enough to be his mother. She got him to settle down, and they had a baby together, but her father didn't want them to get married.

"What does your mother think?" I asked.

Ana's face flushed bright red. "She doesn't live with us right now. She's in El Salvador. I'll explain to you later."

"Our *mami* isn't his *mami*," Tomas, the littlest, said, pointing at Jaime next to me. "But our *papi* is all of ours."

Mr Zacharias was a big man and must have been handsome before he gained all the weight. He sat in a wooden armchair in the dining room of the big apartment above the Caribbean Club, a goblet of dark wine in his left hand. On his thick forefinger he wore a gold ring with a smooth black onyx embedded in it.

He looked Molly and me over as we were introduced, asked us a few questions about where we were from, where we had gone to school, what we had studied, and then said to Ana, "Take the American young ladies to meet Marita."

We followed Ana into the darkened parlour, where black-haired Marita, the mother of the two youngest boys, sat on a cushioned chair in a corner, smoking a pungent cigarette. She smiled at us, switched her cigarette into her left hand, and shook hands limply, first with me and then with Molly. She too wore gold, in her ears and wrapped around her wrist. She was a beautiful woman. We exchanged a few words, she in her vaguely Spanish accent, and we in ours, obviously American.

"Enjoy your visit with Ana," she said, turning back to the window that overlooked the Angel Creek River, now shimmering with light reflected from the club below.

There was no sign of the little boys as we went with Ana to her room at the back of the house, but it was almost nine and they were probably in bed. I looked around for Eduardo, but he wasn't there.

Ana put on a Paul Anka single, "Hello, Young Lovers", with the volume turned low, and we listened for a while in silence.

"Doesn't that music make you wish you were in love?" she asked.

"I am in love," Molly said.

"Who with?" Ana asked.

"Someone from back home," she said. "He's very smart and very handsome, and I miss him. We're planning to get married when I get back."

"Are you in love, Abby?" Ana asked me.

"Not now," I said. "For a long time I thought I was, but he – his name was Chris – was away at one school, me at another, and we hardly ever saw each other. That's probably why it lasted as long as it did. Then, I met someone else I really liked, but once again, just too much long distance, especially with me coming here."

"You didn't tell me any of that!" Molly said.

"It's all over and done with," I said. "What about you, Ana? Have you ever been in love?"

"No, never. I would like to be sometime in my life, but it will be an accident if it happens."

"What do you mean?"

"My father will pick my husband. Right now, he's looking for a husband for me. Until he finds the right person, he allows me to teach. I just turned twenty-one, so there is still time."

"Don't you have any say in the matter?" Molly asked her.

"If I really didn't like the man my father picked, he would look for someone else, I think. And if I saw someone I liked, I could suggest him, but unless my father approved, that would be the end of it. Everything must go forward with my father's knowledge and consent, especially marriage."

"Is it the same for your brothers?" I asked.

"They can pick their mistresses," Ana said, "but my father must say yes to their wives. We get that tradition from both sides of our family, Syrian and Spanish. As long as my father is alive, we must do what he tells us."

Ana switched off the record player because a band had started playing in the club downstairs. Most of the songs were American pop music from the 1940s and 1950s: "Stardust," "Mood Indigo," and every now and then a fast piece like "Blue Suede Shoes" or "Rock Around the Clock."

"I go to sleep to that music every night," Ana said. "It's the background music of my life."

That night, Ana told us more about her family. She said that Emmanuel Zacharias was a son of Syrian parents who had immigrated to Central America with their children after the First World War. They settled in British Honduras, but they had relatives scattered all over Central and South America. Her father met her mother in El Salvador when she was only seventeen and he was still a young man. She was the eldest daughter of a Salvadoran who had business dealings with the Zacharias family.

"She was beautiful, and he was handsome," Ana said, "but they didn't marry for love. It was to bring the families closer. My mother once told me there was someone she had liked and hoped to marry, one of her cousins. He was sweet and gentle and later became a priest. You've seen my father. Not sweet and never gentle. She had no choice."

Together the Zachariases had eight children, six sons and two daughters. An older brother and a sister, now a nurse, had moved to the States. The three youngest, Ana, Eduardo and Jaime, still lived at home. Of the others, all sons, only one was married; two lived with mistresses. Ana said that her mother, who'd grown up on the Pacific Salvadoran coast, thought of Angel Creek as the other side of the world. She never learned much English, and throughout her marriage had gone back to El Salvador for long visits with her family. As the children grew older, she began leaving them behind for months at a time. During one of those long absences, about three years earlier, Mr Zacharias's mistress, Marita, had moved into the family apartment with her two little boys and a baby girl. Mrs Zacharias refused to return as long as Marita stayed, and Marita refused to leave.

"I don't think my father wants my mother to come back," Ana said. "If he did, it would happen."

"Do you ever see your mother?" I asked.

Ana shook her head. "Eduardo does, because he goes to El Salvador on business for my father. He brings back messages to me and Jaime."

She rubbed tears from her long lashes with the heels of both hands. "It's hardest on Jaime. My father won't let him live with my mother, even though Jaime wants to and my mother would love to have him. Marita favours her sons, and that's only natural, I suppose, but she doesn't belong here, in my mother's house, sleeping in her bed. There have been other mistresses, but nothing like this. It's a scandal. There's nothing I can do about any of it, though. You see how beautiful she is. She wraps my father around whatever finger she wants."

The next day, Ana pulled me aside after class. "My father likes you and Molly," she said. "He says he would be happy if we become friends. He wants to know if the two of you want to come with me and Eduardo to the club this Saturday night, as our guests. Eduardo says a very good band from Jamaica will be playing. Is nine o'clock too late? Nothing starts before then."

"Thanks for the invitation," I said. "It sounds like fun. I'm sure Molly will want to come. I know I do!"

The Caribbean Club reminded me of the dingy tropical bars I'd seen in old black and white movies. Overhead, a ceiling fan rotated slowly, agitating the stale, smoke-filled air. Along one wall was a bamboo bar with a cloudy mirror behind it and tall stools lined up in front of it. Scattered around the room were round tables and mismatched chairs, most of them already occupied. Off to one side was a small open space for the band and for dancers. There was no paint on the walls, and no decorations except the mirror.

Eduardo stood behind the bar, serving drinks. When he saw us come in, he said something to an older man working with him and came over to us. He led us to a table near a window that had the chairs propped up against it to signal that it was reserved.

"It will be cooler here," he said. He brought us each the Coke we requested, with ice, a rare treat. He then went off to tell Ana we'd arrived. As we sat there waiting for her, David Lewis and Andrew Todd came in.

"What luck to find you here," David said. "In fact, we stopped by your house on our way here and were disappointed to find you gone. Mind if we join you?" He claimed a chair and sat down next to Molly. "The club is packed tonight. How did you manage to get the best table in the place?"

"Friends in high places," Molly said. "What have you been up to?" We hadn't seen him or the Todds for several weeks.

"Sorry to have been out of touch for a while," David said. "We've been repairing roads and rebuilding washed-out bridges. These rains do terrible damage all through the summer and into the fall."

"Where's Julie?" I asked when Andrew returned from the bar with a whisky for David and another for himself. "I hope she's feeling okay."

"She said she was tired, wanted to turn in early. Actually, she doesn't feel like drinking now and doesn't care for all the smoke and noise."

"When is the baby due?" Molly asked.

"Just after Christmas."

"Will she have the baby here?"

"Not if she can help it. She'll probably go up to Belize City. At any rate, that's the plan right now."

Eduardo led Ana over to the table and pulled up a chair for her between Molly and me. "These are your friends?" he asked, looking across the table at David and Andrew.

I nodded, and as Molly introduced them, they stood and shook hands with Eduardo. Ana kept her hands folded in her lap.

"Excuse me," Eduardo said. "We are very busy tonight, as you can see."

He returned briefly to deliver a cold lemonade to Ana, who then sat sipping her drink, saying little. I could tell from her face she was upset by the presence of the Englishmen, and I was relieved to see the band assemble and start to tune up. There were four musicians, a drummer, a bass player, a saxophonist and a guitarist.

Because the band was from Jamaica, I had thought it would play the sort of calypso music popularized by Harry Belafonte: "Banana Boat Song", "Brown-Skin Girl", "Jamaica Farewell". But their sound took me by surprise. It had a beat like nothing I'd ever heard before, not swing, not rock and roll, not jazz, not blues.

"It's called the 'Blue Beat' or 'ska'," David said, introducing us to what would be the precursor to reggae. "And I hear it has spread from Jamaica to England. The emphasis is on the upbeat, not the downbeat. Irresistible, isn't it, once you get used to it?"

The band interspersed Latin tunes, old Glenn Miller favourites and calypso songs with their own pieces, played in that odd and insistent rhythm. I found I liked it. When David asked Molly to dance, Ana took my hand and pulled me onto the floor.

"I don't want to dance with those Englishmen," she said. "My father would kill me."

She led expertly, and I followed. She was an excellent dancer, and I imitated her movements, trying to roll my hips like she did.

"I grew up dancing with girls," she said. "You'll see when we have a dance at school. The nuns don't allow mixed dancing. Relax, Abby, and listen to the music."

Molly and I took turns dancing with David, Andrew and Ana. She refused the men, saying simply, "I don't dance with men except my brothers."

"Not even married men?" Andrew asked.

"Especially not married men," she answered.

The club was packed, and through the windows we could see people dancing in the street. The whole town seemed to have gathered in or around the club. At about ten, Father Bosque came in with his sister Lydie and a short, blue-eyed man she introduced as her husband, Allan.

"So you de Americans evrybady be talkin about," Mr Quinlan said.

Coupled with his light skin and blond hair, his unabashed Creole patois took me by surprise. No matter what language people spoke at home, most tried their best to speak to us in standard English. As Molly and I discovered, what we saw was what we got with Al Quinlan, a straightforward, unassuming man.

"Why aren't you girls dancing?" Lydie asked, leaning over and hugging first Molly and then me. Her big breasts pressed softly against my shoulder as she squeezed tight.

"Get me a rum and Coke," she told her husband, "and see if you can find a couple of chairs!"

"Chairs? You know you gone be dancin' ahl night."

David offered Lydie his chair, and she sat long enough to smoke a cigarette and swallow half the drink her husband had brought her. Then she and he joined the dancers on the floor, and we didn't see them again all evening.

Father Bosque leaned against the windowsill near our table, talking to a young Garifuna man. Eduardo brought the priest and young man each a Corona and then stopped at our table.

"Would you like to dance?"

"Me?" I asked, surprised.

"Yes, you, Abigail." I loved the way he pronounced my name.

He took my hand and led me onto the dance floor. His palm was cool from carrying the beer. It was too noisy to talk, so I silently moved with him to the music. He, like Ana, was an excellent dancer.

"Do you like to dance?" he asked when the music stopped.

"Yes, I do," I said. "But it's a strange custom, isn't it? Bringing people so physically close, even if they're strangers."

"It's a beautiful custom."

Every half hour or so after that, he'd reappear to claim a dance with Ana,

Molly or me, dividing his breaks among us. But was it my imagination? Each time I glanced in his direction, he seemed to be looking in mine.

About midnight, Ana said it was time for her to go. After saying our goodbyes, Molly and I walked out with her.

"Ana," I said as we stood outside the door to the upstairs apartment. "I hope you weren't upset that our English friends sat with us all evening."

"We know them, and also Andrew's wife," Molly added. "They've been very kind to us, so we invited them to sit with us. The other tables were full when they came in."

"Never mind," Ana said. "It's all right."

"It was so kind of you to invite us," I said. "Please thank your father and Eduardo for us. Tell them how much we enjoyed ourselves."

"I will bring Eduardo to see you, and you can tell him yourself."

"Yes, do," I said. "And bring your other brothers, too. They're such nice boys. We'll have a little party of our own."

"So you think of Eduardo as a boy?" Ana's eyes watched my face as she asked the question.

"Well, not exactly a boy. But he's younger than we are. Two, maybe three years. That's a lot at our age."

"He's older than his age," she said. "More serious. You'll see, when you get to know him."

The next morning, Molly and I went back to Hawkens Creek with Father Bosque.

"You both were up late last night," he said as we drove past the Caribbean Club, shutters closed, on our way out of town.

"So were you," I said. "Did you enjoy the music?"

"Yes, I did. You both seemed to be having a good time. And that's good. You need to have friends and some fun." He hesitated. "I don't want to butt in or be a killjoy, but I have to warn you about some of your friends."

"Not another warning," Molly moaned. 'First the nuns saying we shouldn't see the local people, then Father O'Dea warning us against the British. Now who?"

"Father O'Dea is right about the British, Molly. If you spend too much time with them or the rich Zachariases, you'll be seen as no different than they are. The British exploit the workers, and the townspeople know it and hate them for it. Old Mr Zacharias has his hands in dozens of things without too much concern about how dirty they get. And his sons are just as bad. Ana is a nice girl, but you see how the father treats her and the younger children, bringing his mistress into the house to take their mother's place. It's not the kind of family you want to get too involved with."

"I think you should judge people on themselves," I said. "Not who they're related to."

"I agree," Molly said. "I like Ana a lot. How can she be blamed for what her father does?"

"It can be hard to separate individuals from their families here," Father Bosque said. "Be friendly, sure. Just be careful."

We bumped along the rest of the rough road in silence.

At Hawkens Creek, there was a baptism, and Mass took longer than usual. Afterward, the young Creole couple, whose first child it was, invited us to the christening party, a pig roast for the whole camp. Father Bosque said we'd be expected to stay, at least for a while, even though none of us had planned on it.

To make matters worse, at the party Señora Salazar cornered Molly and me and delivered a long speech in Spanish. We understood nothing. She then pulled us over to Father Bosque.

"She says this new mother is many years younger than you," he told us. "You must hurry to catch up!" He made the mistake of laughing, increasing my irritation.

The pig just wasn't getting done and we had to leave before it was ready. We'd driven maybe three miles when a sudden downpour stopped us for over an hour. The road was slow going even when it was dry, and we didn't arrive back in Angel Creek until close to dark. Evening benediction was going on in the church as we drove into town.

"Come over to the rectory," Father Bosque said. "We have a canned ham on the shelf and I'm sure we can scrape together a meal. Let's have some food and cheer each other up."

By the time the three of us had gathered together enough food to feed ourselves, we were friends again. The electricity was off, so we lit a kerosene lamp. We sliced the Danish ham, gelatine dripping from it in the heat, and in the cupboard also found some crackers, a glass jar of cream cheese with olives and pimentos in it, and a can of peanuts. We carried our food into the study, where we laid it out on the coffee table.

We were just sitting down to our improvised meal when Father O'Dea walked in.

"I thought you'd be back in time to do Benediction," he said to Father Bosque. Every Sunday evening, one or the other of the priests, usually whoever hadn't said the High Mass that day, led the evening service. Its climax was the elevation of the host in a glass and gold monstrance, bells ringing. People from town flocked to the service, which was more popular than Mass.

"I thought I'd be back earlier," Father Bosque said. "But you know better than anyone how unpredictable these mission trips can be. The road was terrible, as usual. And there was a baptism, of the Godwin baby, and a party afterward. Have you eaten? Join us."

Father O'Dea sat down in an armchair at one end of the low table, and Father Bosque, sitting across from him in a straight-backed chair, blessed the food. Molly and I sat on the sofa. After taking a slice of ham and a cracker, Father O'Dea rose and went to a cupboard in the corner and pulled out an unopened bottle of Johnnie Walker.

"You drink your beer if you want to," he said, referring to the glasses of Corona in front of us. "I'm having this." He poured himself half a tumbler of the whisky.

He listened sullenly, sipping steadily from his drink, as Father Bosque, Molly and I shared details of our trip. After the meal, as Molly and I started piling up the plates, he refilled his glass for the third time.

"Leave those f'Gilly," he said. "Si' down."

Molly and I sat back down on the edge of the low couch.

I'd never seen him so far gone. He splashed whisky into the three empty beer glasses and pushed them towards us in no particular order. Father Bosque reached out as though to stop him, and Father O'Dea swatted at his hand, missing him.

"So, another li'l black Cath'lic in the world," Father O'Dea said, and held up his glass. "Le's drink to that!"

"Father O"Dea, why don't we call it a night," Father Bosque said. "It's been a long day."

"Damn right!" Father O'Dea's voice was a snarl as he turned to Molly and me. "And a helluva long coupla weeks since that black bastard arrived." It took me a second to realize he was talking about Father Bosque. Relentless, he went on. "Can't count on that one for a damn thing! Chases around in that goddamn Jeep, hangs out in bars half the night. What kinda priest is that?"

"You know that's not true," Father Bosque said without raising his voice, but his face was flushed, his hands clenched. "We've been through all this before. I don't go to bars for pleasure. I go because we'll never reach half the town if all we do is stay in the church and the rectory."

"What a prick!"

"Father O'Dea," Molly said, her voice shaking, "please don't talk like that."

"Lis'n here, you two," he said, leaning forward. "Don' you ever trust that black bastard any farther 'n you can throw him. Don' let him fool you. He's as black as the rest of 'em, and they're all alike. I never knew a single one of 'em not after jus' one thing from a female. You stay away from him, you hear?"

Father O'Dea struggled up, spilling the rest of his whisky all over himself. He reached across me, grabbed Molly's arm, lost his balance, and fell sideways onto me. Father Bosque jumped up and came behind him, catching him by his shirt tail and flinging him back into his chair.

"You sonuvabitch," Father O'Dea yelled, trying but unable to pull himself up again.

"How can you talk to Father Bosque like that?" I cried out. "I know you're drunk, but that's no excuse!"

"You don' know a damn thing, Miss Smart-Ass!"

"Don't pay any attention," Father Bosque said. "He doesn't know what he's saying. You go, and I'll get him to bed."

"How can you stay here with him after this?" I asked him.

"It's the liquor talking. He won't remember any of this tomorrow. Just go home, and don't worry." Father Bosque no longer looked angry, just tired.

Father O'Dea lay sprawled in his chair, breathing heavily. I was shocked to see he'd fallen asleep.

"We'll let him sleep it off here," Father Bosque said. "Now go home, Abby and Molly, and try to forget this ever happened."

Chapter 8

DARK MOODS

EARLY THE NEXT MORNING, before sunrise, I dressed in the dark, wrapping my Mexican shawl around my shoulders, and went softly out the front door and down the steps. People rose early in Angel Creek, but now no one else was out yet. I made my way down Church Street to Front Street and struck out across the field that edged the sea. In the predawn light, the orange windsock at the north end of the field looked grey.

The long pier stretched towards the horizon. Careful not to trip on the uneven boards, I walked to its end and sat there with my feet dangling, my flip-flops hanging from my toes, waiting for the sun to rise. It was a relief to be alone, a new day just starting, the breeze tart on my skin and the choppy waves slapping at my heels. The sky was overcast and promised early rain. After the scene in the back room of the rectory, I longed to disappear into the general gloom.

Molly and I had stayed up late into the night, trying to help each other understand what had caused the scene we witnessed. How responsible were we for what had happened? I wished I could wipe my memory clean. Instead, I saw Father Bosque's face, which smiled so easily, pained and angry. With loathing, I heard the echo of Father O'Dea's voice, lifted not in prayer, as I most often heard it, but heavy with curses. How could I ever again go to Mass if he was the celebrant?

Gradually, the morning world came alive. Human and animal sounds blended with those of the wind and sea. From a distance, dissonance vanished and an intricate harmony remained. When the church bells rang just before six, I hesitated, and then headed for the church.

To my relief, it was Father Bosque who came out of the sacristy, clothed in black vestments. After Hattie, almost every daily Mass was a Mass for the Dead, requested with a donation by some grieving person in the congregation. For once, the mood matched mine. I had a feeling of loss, though I couldn't say exactly what was gone.

I opened my missal to the English translation of the Latin prayers that opened the liturgy: *"Introibo ad altare Dei*: I will go up to the altar of God." The significance of the altar as a place of sacrifice hit me. *Put your illusions there*, I told myself. *Offer them up!* The problem was sorting out illusions from ideals.

"*Ad Deum qui laetificat juventutem meam,*" I read. "To God, the giver of youth and happiness." I'd never before noticed that phrase. In a rush of emotion, it dawned on me that the altar of God is also a place of thanksgiving. This Mass wasn't just a memorial for the dead, an offering for the uneasy spirits in purgatory. It was to comfort the living, to hearten those of us still in the flesh by reminding us of God's abundant gifts to us, including life itself.

I left Mass determined not to allow disillusionment to overwhelm my sense of life's blessings. Nevertheless, it would be a week shadowed by dark moods.

The oldest man in Angel Creek died that Monday morning, just about the time that I was sitting on the edge of the old pier. He had so many children and grandchildren that he was related to most of the Garifuna families in town. Sister Veronica dismissed classes early so that our students could attend the funeral service and burial that afternoon. Left to nature, corpses decayed quickly in the heat of late July.

When Molly and I arrived, the church was packed. As they did on Sundays, men stood at the back of the nave or in the vestibule, but today they also lined the outside aisles and some sat in pews. Molly found a seat near the front, but I stood in the back, near one of the confessionals. Father O'Dea led the service, assisted by Father Bosque. Watching them perform their priestly roles in perfect tandem, I wondered if the night before had been an evil dream.

The profound human silence of the funeral procession was like nothing I'd ever experienced. A stream of mourners three blocks long walked double file along the sea from the church to the graveyard, almost half a mile to the north. The only sounds were the shuffling of hundreds of feet and the whipping in the wind of skirts and jackets. Halfway there, rain returned for the third or fourth time that day, and those who had umbrellas opened them. I tied the ends of my black lace mantilla under my chin and wore it as a rain bonnet. My skin was still hot from the crowded church, and the rain and wind felt cold against it.

In the cemetery, Father O'Dea stood in the midst of the crowd with Father Bosque behind him and rapidly read some prayers out of a little book he carried with him. The branches of a spidery tree scratched at the sky behind him, and while he prayed, pools of water deepened and spread at our feet. The homemade pine casket was lowered into the open grave and, as we watched, men with shovels set to work, filling the hole with pates of soil, from which long grasses grew like hair. Moans and a sound like chanting rose and fell from the inner circle of the crowd.

Like the coffin, its rough wood splintering the hands and backs of the pallbearers, the burial itself was raw and primitive. Hadn't some philosopher written that however fine the rest of the play, the end is always the same: a box with dirt thrown over it? This burial stripped away any illusion of sleep and waking and made clear how different these are from death and resurrection.

There was a supper of some sort somewhere, the first of many to be held over the coming days, I heard. Without speaking to either of the priests or waiting for Molly, I went back to our house, peeled off my wet clothes, and with a towel wrapped around me, filled the bathtub, squandering our precious water, which was piped into the house from an outdoor vat. Sliding down in the tub, I took a deep breath and went under to wet my hair so that I could wash it. For a full minute, I lay submerged and listened to my heartbeat, reassuringly strong and regular.

The next evening, Molly and I went to a wedding at the Anglican church, on the other side of the Angel Creek River. The bride was a lovely young Creole girl named Lillian Jones who lived catty-corner to us on Market Street. We knew that she already had one child, a little boy, by the groom and that she was seven months pregnant with a second child by him. She was just sixteen.

When we arrived a little after eight p.m., the tiny church was lit only by candlelight. Besides the minister, whom we hadn't met before, and the two of us, the only others present were the bride and groom, along with a couple introduced as the maid of honour and the best man. I expected more people to come, but the service started soon after we arrived and the only others who appeared were a dozen neighbourhood boys who peeked in the door and windows while the priest conducted the short ceremony.

Lillian stood at the altar in a strapless blue-net formal. In her arms, she carried white paper roses. Her honey-coloured hair, usually smooth and straight, hung down to her shoulders in long, loose curls. The groom, whom we met for the first time at the ceremony, wore a short-sleeved Guayabera shirt over his black trousers. He had greying black hair, slicked straight back, an eyebrow-thin moustache, and a sagging jawline. He looked to me at least twenty-five years older than his bride. I'd imagined someone altogether different, and felt disappointed for her.

Afterward, we all walked together back to a reception at the house near ours, where the bride and her young son lived with her parents, her siblings and several of her grandparents, all crowded into four not-very-large rooms. There, the rest of the family and their guests greeted us. The house was new and clean, lit with candles and lanterns, and decorated with crêpe paper. Lillian told us that her husband had built the house for her and her family after her son was born.

Someone who had a battery-operated radio – the house had no electricity – tuned in a station with dance music, and the party started. People of all colours, ages and sizes mamboed, chachaed, and twisted indoors and out, together and alone, with time out for station identification. Dodging the dancers with infallible timing, a pet parrot hopped around the middle of the room.

I danced the "Twist" with a Carib gentleman (yes, <u>black</u>) and the jitterbug too. It was really fun, I wrote my family afterward, wishing I could see their faces as they read my letter.

Elvis's "Love Me Tender" came on the radio, and the crowd cleared a space for the bride and groom to dance together. All eyes were on them as the groom put his arm around his bride and they moved to the music. It was an absurd scene – her growing belly between them, their little boy toddling towards them, and the parrot twirling at their feet – but tears stung my eyes. Sitting beside me, the bride's younger sister sighed. "One day, me wan' weddin' jes lak dis one."

It dawned on me that I was taking part in a distant version of the fairy-tale weddings of my friends back home. I don't know why that depressed me, but it did.

"Your uniforms are dirty, and you are dirty too! Everything you touch turns dirty!" Sister Veronica snapped as she marched up and down the second-storey balcony of the school building.

All our students stood in lines eight across and six long. It was the usual start of the school day, when attendance was taken and instructions were given, but today Sister Veronica's anger transformed the list of announcements into a docket.

"Stand up straight, Angelina Lopez! And Marcia Lambey, straighten your tie! Victoria Stanley, your uniform looks like you slept in it. And what have you spilled on yourself, Arcella Jones? You're a disgrace, every one of you. Pay attention to details, or you'll never get your lives in order! And you'll never amount to anything!"

Joining Molly and Ana in the hallway as we waited for the students to enter their classrooms I asked what had set her off.

"Just the usual," Ana said.

The "usual" referred to the students' starched white uniforms with light blue ties at the neck. They were a source of constant concern for Sister Veronica and of demerits for the students. To maintain the pristine condition she expected, they had to be laundered at least twice a week, a major undertaking in a town where few houses had running water and most laundry (including our own, done by Josie) was scrubbed at the mouth of the Angel Creek River, laid on stones to bleach and dry, and pressed with irons heated on coals. Halfway through the week, the cumulative effects of perspiration, spilled lunches and splashed ink became apparent. Sister Veronica ritualistically made her disgust known.

"I'd feel better if I thought it was just about the uniforms," I muttered. "Listen to her voice. It sounds like she despises the students!"

"I think she hates being Negro," Ana said.

"Well, don't most Negroes?" Molly responded. "Or at least they must hate the way they're treated because of it. I would."

Ana shushed us as the students marched in silently for class.

It must have seemed like a good idea to send Negro nuns here from the States, I wrote in my journal that evening, *but I don't think they like the students very much. They are awfully hard on them, downright insulting at times. It seems like they want to make them ashamed. The sad thing is, the worst one of all is the nun who was born here. It's like she's trying to outdo the others. Or maybe that's just how she sees her job as principal. Probably she's just treating the students like she was treated years ago, when she was a student here.*

I can't put my finger on exactly how, but it seems different to be Negro here than it is in the States. Not such a big deal. For some reason, that really seems to bother some people. They want to make it a big deal.

I didn't specifically mention the scene between Father O'Dea and Father Bosque in my diary, but it was on my mind as I wrote. *I'm determined to stick it out here, no matter what happens, and really, there are a lot of happy things about this place, like the teaching, which I really love. It's just that otherwise good people can be petty and even perverted about some things, like race, and that makes me sad, disillusioned and discouraged.*

That week marked the end of our first month as teachers. Every day, five days a week, both Molly and I taught seven fifty-minute classes that required five different preparations. Some of the teaching was drudgery, especially the basic composition courses: vocabulary, spelling, grammar, and punctuation drills in class and daily correction of homework, quizzes and essays. But we both loved aspects of our jobs.

Teaching is good, I wrote, *but I find it tedious sometimes. I always have loved to teach, but only what I myself just learned. When I must drill and drill to make a class understand, it almost kills me. Some days are soaring; others make me sick. If I'm doing anything, it's making the girls look at the world around them and love it, but how much they're learning from their erratic teacher is hard to say. I take delight in the offbeat nature of all my classes, but I'm pretty sure the principal doesn't approve. I think the kids benefit more from my telling them about Russian icons or a great concert hall in Vienna occasionally than from sticking to a dull, dry syllabus prepared by some wizened British educationalist.*

As part of her extra-curricular duties, Molly had been assigned the task of salvaging the remnants of the school library, badly damaged by Hattie. She'd spent two summers working in the Racine public library, where she'd had some training. She had set up an area at the back of the school, in what was once a pantry, and for an hour or so several times a week, she meticulously repaired, organized and catalogued the salvaged books. As much as teaching, maybe even more, she loved reclaiming those books with all their different bindings, shapes and sizes. Molly said she even loved the humid smell of their warped pages.

To celebrate the first-month anniversary, we asked Ana to join us for afternoon tea. As we drank lemonade and snacked on *empanadas* – the spicy

Figure 7. Molly and students in our temporary high school building. Photo courtesy of Malilee Zimmers.

dumplings sold door to door by some of the village kids – we talked about our classes, and that led us into a discussion of some of our students. Ana proved to be a storehouse of local gossip about them and their families.

When Molly mentioned the Pérez sisters, Sarita, Marta and Maria ("all so smart and interesting and one prettier than the next"), Ana told us that there were two older sisters too. One of them, Catharina, had been in school with her, she said. She married an Englishman from the Forestry Service. Many Englishmen in British Honduras had mistresses, but few ever married them. "That tells you how beautiful she is, and clever too." Ana added that she was sure they lived in British Honduras because his family in England wouldn't accept her.

She then moved on to something she said she'd just heard from one of her brothers. She made us promise to keep it a secret. "He says Susanna Mendez is no better than she has to be and is playing around with her stepfather. Her mother knows and looks the other way."

Susanna was the doe-eyed Mestizo girl with masses of soft black hair who sat in the back of my junior literature class. If anyone ever looked sweet and innocent, it was Susanna. She was a good student and a hard worker, although she was often absent.

"That's shocking," I said. "And hard to believe. But if it's true, shouldn't we try to help her?"

Ana asked why she would need help. "Some girls are bad that way," she said.

"But what if it's her stepfather's fault?" Molly asked.

"Girls have ways of stopping things like that if they don't want them to happen."

"I don't think that's always true," Molly said. "What about rape?"

"Nice girls don't get raped."

I had to admit that Ana was only saying what most people at the time accepted as true, certainly in British Honduras but also in the States. It explained why, at twenty-one, Ana put up with almost constant chaperoning.

"Maybe we should try to talk to her," I said, looking at Molly.

Ana shook her head. "I shouldn't have told you anything. You don't understand how big a mistake that would be. It's a family matter. Even if it was her stepfather's fault, the men rule. No one could do anything." She paused, then added, "Don't look so upset. I don't make the rules. I'm just telling you how it is."

The next morning, I stopped Susanna Mendez after class.

"You seem tired today, Susanna. Don't you feel well?"

"It's hard to finish all my homework, Miss. I stay up very late."

"Why is it so hard? You're a smart girl."

"My mother, she's not well. I have to help in the restaurant."

Her family ran La Cena, a small restaurant that served basic but well-prepared dishes like Creole rice and beans and Mexican tamales. Molly and I had eaten there a few weeks earlier with Father Bosque and the Quinlans, and Susanna had served our table. Father Bosque seemed to know her and her family well, and he teased her when she mixed up Mr Quinlan's order with his.

"What you dreamin' 'bout, Susanna? Wake up, gal!"

Susanna had blushed prettily and hurried back to the kitchen. That night, we had met her stepfather and her mother, but I hadn't paid much attention to them.

"If you come by my house this afternoon, I'll give you some extra help," I told her. "Why don't you come at four. Bring your books. And your notebook."

"If I can, Miss," she said.

Four o'clock came and went with no sign of Susanna.

The family lived above the restaurant, not far from the river. I convinced Molly to swing by there on our way to our afternoon swim. The restaurant was closed until six, but when we went around the back to look for the stairs to the second-floor apartment, I saw Susanna chopping onions and peppers at a table in the kitchen. I stuck my head in the open window and asked her why she hadn't come that afternoon. She said her mother wasn't feeling well and she had to work. At that point, her stepfather came into the kitchen from the restaurant. I remembered his face and his first name, Johnny, but not his last name, different from Susanna's.

"Come in, Teachahs," he said, opening the back door. He shook our hands and smiled, showing even, white teeth. "Susanna, she's not in trouble at school, is she?"

"No, not at all," I said. "She was absent last week, and I wanted to help her catch up."

"It's okay, *Padrasto*," she said. "I will go for help Monday, if I don't work."

"Sure, she will come then," he said. "She is a smart girl, a hard worker. Her mama and I want her to do well in school."

"She seems tired some days," I said. "If she could get a little more time for study and for sleep it would help her to do well."

"It is a busy time, and we all work hard," he said. "And her mother, she's not so well. But we will try."

As Molly and I walked towards the sea, I asked her, "What do you think?"

"He seems nice," she said. "And well educated. It's probably just gossip. She's pretty, and he's still a young man. People's imaginations can work overtime."

"You're probably right," I said. "You have to wonder how such things get started. The sad thing is, the gossip itself can do a lot of damage, even if it isn't true."

I hoped it wasn't Eduardo who had passed the gossip on to Ana. Eduardo had been on my mind. He'd stopped by our house to drive Ana home after our little celebration. For the first time, he came inside and sat down with us at the table, occupying our fourth chair. We offered him some beer along with the remaining *empanadas*, but he took only a glass of lemonade. I remembered then that Ana had told me he rarely drank liquor and never smoked, unlike his older brothers.

"He's the serious one and the hard worker," she'd said. "My father expects him to move ahead fast. He'll have his own club soon."

As I glanced at Eduardo, he looked up and returned my gaze, not at all hesitant or shy. His boldness surprised me.

"I like your house," he said. "I have a place picked out in the valley along the river where I will build my own house someday. Already, I've drawn up plans. It will be large and beautiful, with room for many children."

"So you like children?" I asked him.

"I love them," he said. "They are the best thing in the world."

While Ana gathered up her belongings, he moved his chair closer, so near that I could feel the hair on his arm just touching mine.

"May I come back to visit sometime?" I could see traces of a moustache on his upper lip. His cheeks, though, were as smooth as an olive skin.

"Of course," I said. "We'll be happy to see you anytime."

"I would like to come to see you," he said softly, stressing the *you*.

"Let me think that over."

"I hope you will say yes. If you are willing, I would like us to know each other better."

I felt as though warm liquid were being poured into me, swirling as it filled me. Eduardo gave me one last look and then stood and followed Ana down the stairs.

Do I want this? I asked myself. All the warmth drained away.

After they left, Molly said to me, "It's really sweet, the way he looks at you with those big, puppy-dog eyes! I'm sure he has a huge crush on you, Abby. If only he were a few years older! God, he's beautiful, though."

"Who says that men have to be older?" I asked. My own mother was several years older than my stepfather, though I didn't mention that to Molly.

"You're not seriously interested in him, are you?"

"For heaven's sakes, Molly," I said. "He's Ana's little brother! And I only just met him."

On Saturday, Molly and I were working in the sacristy of the church, making communion hosts for the following week. The nuns usually did it, but they were having some sort of retreat that weekend and had asked if we could take over for them. One of them showed us what to do and left us to our work. It was surprisingly hard and slow, made worse by the muggy weather. We were in a room without much ventilation, working with a hot press that reminded me of a big waffle iron. We poured a thin, starchy liquid into the mould, pressed it and, timing carefully, removed the crisp, white wafers, ready for consecration.

I'd always savoured the taste of the melting host on the flat of my tongue. It had the chaste flavour of holiness itself, its delicacy at once piquing and staying my fasting hunger. I don't know whether it was Molly or me who first began sampling the rejects and some of the trimmings, but we soon overcame our fear of sacrilege and snacked on one misshapen host after another. After a while, I felt like I was eating paper and stopped, sickened. The sense of mystery and yearning the taste once evoked in me had entirely vanished.

Sweaty and irritable, we were just finishing up when Father O'Dea came in. Father Bosque had been gone most of the week, first to Belize City and then to some of the more distant missions.

"Thanks for doing this," Father O'Dea said. "Come join me for supper. Gilly did the cooking tonight, so it will be better than usual."

I hesitated, remembering the dinner of the week before.

"I have something I have to tell you tonight," he added, not waiting for an answer.

We washed and changed our clothes. Maybe in memory of his former kindness to us and to make up for our growing distance from him, we both tried to look nice. Molly put on a flowered dress with a scoop neck, and I changed into my favourite pink and white striped dress with a full skirt. A land breeze swept in from the north, signalling a change in the weather, as we walked across to the rectory, where Father O'Dea had gin and tonics waiting for us.

"I'm going to miss you," he said.

"Where are you going?" Molly asked.

"I received word a few days ago that I'm being transferred back to the States. Soon."

I didn't know what to say. Molly, too, was silent.

He raised his glass. "To two great gals. I wish you all the best."

He clinked glasses with each of us in turn, but his eyes lingered on Molly. She looked lovely as she sat there, her face flushed from the work of the afternoon, her eyes bright with tears. Seeing his hands tremble slightly, I felt pity for Father O'Dea, and feeling pity, I found it possible to remind myself of the many people I knew who shared his bigotry. My stepfather, in many ways a kind man, firmly believed that no black man could be trusted around a white woman. In fact, I doubted most of my parents' generation – those like Father O'Dea who grew up in the era of Jim Crow – would have consented to live on equal terms in the same house or share a meal with any person of colour, no matter how white his skin. That didn't make what Father O'Dea had done and said any less reprehensible, but it helped me remember what years of Catholic education had taught me: never reduce people to their worst acts.

During that meal, our last together, Father O'Dea was on his best behaviour. He vigilantly watched what went into and came out of his mouth, and it was easier for me to recall some of our good days with him. We said our goodbyes that night, even though he stayed on in Angel Creek until mid-August.

Was he a flawed priest or a failed one? An evil man or a wounded one? In my darkest moods, I thought of him, even though he was a priest, as no better and no worse than most of us.

Chapter 9

SHERRY, SISSY AND JEAN

"MISS, MAY I COMB out your hair?"

Startled, I opened my eyes and saw one of my students standing over me as I lay on my towel on the sand. I recognized Sherry Cain, one of the light-skinned, Creole girls, the full-breasted one, tall for her age, who sat towards the back of the first-year composition class.

"Why? Is it a mess?" I sat up and ran my fingers through my damp hair. To bathe and cool off, I'd been swimming at the mouth of the river where it flowed into the sea. I usually came with Molly, but today I was there alone.

"Oh, no, Miss. I like to fix hair. If I fix it for you, it will dry nicer." She spoke slowly, carefully, using her best English.

"Haven't you been home yet?" The school day had ended more than an hour earlier, but the girl still wore her white school uniform and carried her book bag.

"I must wait for my father – or whoever he sends – to pick me up. He runs the citrus factory in the valley, where we live."

"Will he be able to find you here?"

"Soon, Miss, I'll go where he meets me. He won't be there yet."

"That must be boring for you, to have to wait so long every day."

"Sister Veronica lets me stay at school if I want, and I can go to the shops."

"Sit down, Sherry." I made room on my towel.

"If my uniform gets dirty, I get demerits." She sat gingerly on the edge of the towel. "I have a comb, Miss," she said, opening her bag.

"That's awfully nice of you, Sherry, but I can do it. I have my own comb here somewhere."

"Please, Miss, let me. I want to be hairdressah one day, in Belize City or maybe the States."

Without waiting for permission, she knelt behind me and smoothed my hair back from my face, then firmly pulled a comb through it, holding my head steady with one hand.

"Oh, Miss, your hair so soft! I wish mine be like yours."

"But your hair is lovely."

Sherry's hair and eyes were golden brown and her skin the colour of coffee with cream. I could not imagine a more beautiful fourteen-year-old girl.

"No, Miss. Mine stiff, like wire."

As I gathered up my things I turned and saw that the front of her starched skirt was damp where it had pressed against my bathing suit. The cotton would dry wrinkled.

"I used to comb my mum's hair," she said, rising too.

"And you don't any more?"

"She died three years ago."

"I'm so sorry, Sherry. Is it just you and your father, now?"

"No, Miss, now I have a stepmother and baby brother too. Everything different."

"A good change, I hope."

Sherry shrugged.

I pulled my loose dress over my bathing suit. "I'd like to hear more about you and your family, but it's getting late and I have to go home now. I enjoyed talking with you, Sherry. I'll see you in class tomorrow."

"Your class is my favourite, Miss. I'm glad you came here from the States to teach us."

The next afternoon, Sherry ran up behind me as I left the school.

"May I walk you home, Miss?" she asked, falling into step beside me.

When we reached the house, I stopped at the foot of the stairs to our front door. She looked up at the closed door. "Your house is pretty," she said.

"Would you like to come in?"

"Oh, yes, Miss!"

I led her inside. On the table, Josie had laid the mail, which came twice a week by boat.

As I sorted through it, Sherry said, "Miss Portah, do you think I can write someone in the States? A pen pal?"

"Sure, if you want to." I picked up a letter from a friend who was in grad school at Notre Dame. "This letter is from my friend Vince. He's very nice, and if you write a note telling him about yourself, I'll put it in the next letter I send him, and then he can answer you directly, if he has time."

"Shall I write it now?" she asked.

"Why don't you write it at home and give it to me tomorrow?"

"No, bettah now," she said, drawing a chair to the table.

She took a piece of notebook paper out of her schoolbag and spent the next twenty minutes hunched over it. When she'd finished, she carefully folded her letter in thirds. "Sometimes I think I want to be a writah one day."

"I thought you wanted to be a hairdresser."

"Yes, Miss, that too. I dream many things."

Sherry loved American pop music and movies. Her favourite singer was Paul Anka, she said, and one day she brought a glossy, autographed photo of him to show me. She had written away for it and called it her "best thing". His singing was fine, but the real reason for her devotion, she confessed, was that he reminded her of her father. "My dad, he don' sing, but he only handsome, Miss, jes like Paul Anka."

Sherry was right about that. After her second visit, she had her father pick her up at our house. He introduced himself as Jerry Cain. He was a trim, dark-eyed man who did look a little like Paul Anka. He wore a white shirt, open at the throat and showing lots of black chest hair.

"Thank you for being so very kind to my daughter," he said. He spoke with the hint of a British accent.

"I'm glad to spend time with Sherry, Mr Cain," I answered.

"Maybe you and the other teacher will come with Father Bosque for supper on Sunday? The two of us go way back. We were in school together in Belize City, so it will be a reunion after many years. We will be pleased if you join us."

That Sunday afternoon, Sherry greeted us at the door of the Cains' bungalow with her unbound hair radiating corona-like around her face. I'd seen her only in her school uniform, with her tawny hair reduced to a puffy ponytail held tight by a rubber band. The uniform made her look like she'd been stuffed into a child's outfit, and when she stood or walked, she bowed her head slightly and rounded her shoulders as if to make herself smaller and shorter.

Not today. A sleeveless blouse and a bright, swinging skirt had liberated her body, and she looked almost as tall as her father, who came up beside her.

"You look lovely, Sherry," I said to her. "All grown up!"

"See how long my hair grow, Miss?" She pulled a coiled strand so that it touched her collarbone. "Someday I straighten it – I know, Daddy, talk good English," she said, in response to a nudge from her father. "I mean, someday I will straighten it – so it will be long, long, long. I want it to reach down to my waist. Nothing so beautiful as gals with long hair."

"You look fine as you are," I said.

"Only a little fine," she said.

Sherry's stepmother, Iris, was a plump little woman with a darker complexion than her husband or stepdaughter. She guided us to the most comfortable chairs on the veranda, and while we talked with the men, she busied herself refilling our glasses of lemonade before they were empty. Like many women in British Honduras, she looked older than her husband, almost too old to have the toddler she referred to as "Jerry Jr". Usually little children in British Honduras stayed close to their mothers, especially around strangers, but Jerry Jr arched his back and turned rage red when his mother tried to confine him to her lap.

"Let the boy go, Iris," Mr Cain said.

Iris turned him loose to do what he wanted. The little boy pulled off his shirt and screamed until she took off his shoes and socks. He then ran back and forth across the porch, his little bare feet slapping the floorboards.

The Cains lived on the edge of an orange walk, not far from the Beaumont factory Molly and I had toured the day we begged paint for our classrooms. Driving in with Father Bosque this time, we'd passed the tiny houses where the workers lived. Families sat outside on their steps or in the shade, enjoying their day off. Some of the men, recognizing the priest, raised their straw hats in greeting as we went by. Women and children waved. Cars, scarce after Hattie, commanded interest and respect.

About a quarter of a mile farther down the road, we came to a cluster of pretty white bungalows we hadn't seen on our previous visit. The bosses lived here with their families, Father Bosque told us. Mr De Santos, who had shown us around the factory, lived in one of the houses and the Cains in another. The Beaumonts, we learned later, lived in a big house up the valley, in the mountains.

Sherry had a room to herself, where she showed Molly and me her collection of pop albums and movie magazines, along with a few novels – *Treasure Island*, *Little Women*, *The Wind in the Willows* – arranged neatly on shelves. She had a record player and a short-wave radio, and a closet full of pretty clothes made by the best dressmaker in town. She said she'd give us the name of this woman, who just looked at you, took a few measurements, and made the dress or blouse or whatever you wanted. Lee Wong's store had the nicest fabric for party clothes. There was also a man in town who could copy photographs of shoes and make them to fit your foot. She promised to tell us how to get in touch with him too.

On her bureau I noticed a framed photograph of a young woman who looked a lot like Sherry, only older. "Is this your mother?" I picked up the photo to look at it more closely. The woman's hair was straighter than Sherry's, and longer, but the facial features were the same.

"Yes, Miss," she said. "Everyone say I look just like my mum, but my name is just like my dad: 'Sherry' and 'Jerry', you see. So we're the same, too, just like she and me."

"May I ask how your mother died so young?"

"She always sick, Miss. Always, I remember, she be very sick with fever."

"How hard for you," Molly said. "And for your dad. You must be very close."

"Like this," Sherry said, crossing her middle finger over her forefinger.

Over Iris's excellent roast chicken, conversation flowed pleasantly at first. Molly and I answered the usual questions about where we were from and why we'd come to a place as remote as British Honduras. Then Mr Cain turned to Father Bosque.

"You know, Charlie," he said, "I have never been so surprised as when you joined the priesthood. There we were, flirting with all the girls – " He turned to Molly and me. "They were all in love with Charlie or me," he said, winking slyly. "Then we graduated, and within a month, I married Sherry's mum, and Charlie joined the Jesuits."

"Part of me was always attracted to the priesthood," Father Bosque said. "My mother is very religious, and she encouraged me to think about it seriously. My father was against it. He said the Americans, even the priests, were just as prejudiced against the colonials as the British. They called us 'coloureds' back then, you recall. My dad died my last year in school, and the principal at St John's said he'd recommend me if I decided to apply to the

American Jesuits. There weren't any native Jesuit priests at the time – just one in the seminary. But changes were coming in the Church, it was clear, and I decided to try it."

"And it's been good for you?"

"Well, I stuck it out and now I'm here, for a while, anyway."

"How long will you be in Angel Creek?"

"It's a temporary assignment, so only six months or so. I still have my tertianship ahead," he explained. "That's the last part of training before permanent assignment to a parish. I'll probably be sent to one of the Jesuit houses in South America to finish up. My superiors want me to work on my Spanish."

"So we'll have two new priests in Angel Creek?" I asked.

"By the time I leave, Father Peck won't be new any more," he said. He turned towards the Cains. "Have you heard that Father O'Dea is returning to the States in a few weeks? They're sending Father Peck down from Belize. You remember him, Jerry."

"He taught us math at St John's," Mr Cain explained to Molly and me. "A bit of a character. He's an avid ham radio operator. In fact, I heard he was the one who got the word out about Hattie last year when all the phone lines were out." He shook his head. "He spent most of his free time on that radio. I wonder what sort of parish priest he'll be."

"He's a good man," Father Bosque said. "Strict, but reasonable. Before he settles in here, I believe he's going to Jamaica for some of the ceremonies." Jamaican independence from Great Britain would be celebrated in a matter of weeks.

One after another, former colonies around the globe were exercising their right to self-determination, a right proclaimed in 1960 by the United Nations General Assembly Declaration on Granting Independence to Colonial Countries and Peoples. Newspapers and magazines in the United States had been full of stories celebrating the explosion of freedom in former African colonies – seventeen in 1960 alone. In 1961, in an address before the UN General Assembly, President Kennedy had inaugurated a "UN Decade of Development" to enable developing countries to help themselves.

"Will British Honduras have its independence soon?" I asked.

"Maybe not full independence, but at least home rule," Father Bosque answered. The PUP – that's the People's United Party – has been working for it ever since the party was founded after the Second World War. Of course, the independence movement goes back much earlier than that."

"In my opinion, complete independence for British Honduras any time soon would be a mistake," Mr Cain said, slicing more chicken and serving it as he spoke. "I think it's all right for Jamaica, but it would be – I do not mean to exaggerate – a disaster for us."

"How can you say that, Jerry?" Father Bosque demanded, putting down his knife and fork.

"How can you say anything different, with things so unsettled in this part of the world?" Mr Cain addressed his next remarks to Molly and me. "You see, young ladies, Jamaica is an island, but unfortunately we are not. There are revolutions and civil wars all around us. Guatemala claims British Honduras as rightfully hers, and we have no way to defend ourselves." He turned back to Father Bosque. "The day British troops move out, Guatemala moves in, and we'll have total collapse."

Almost from the day we arrived, we'd heard about Guatemala's claims on British Honduras. Some Guatemalan maps, according to Ana, who was our main source of information, identified British Honduras as one of its provinces. Guatemala wanted British Honduras's coastline and its resources, she said, and there had been frequent skirmishes along the border and even a couple of attempted invasions.

"I know that's the old argument," Father Bosque replied. "We give up our right to rule ourselves in return for British protection – even though we need protection mostly because of Britain's self-serving treaties with Spain over a century ago, with British Honduras and Guatemala as bargaining chips. It's clear the British government wants to wash its hands of the mess it's made. And I admit we need their military support for the time being. But they could and should give us a lot more control over internal matters. And give our representatives a voice in negotiations with Guatemala. We're second-class citizens in our own country and have been for over a century. They've stolen our resources and exploited our workers for so long we take it for granted."

"I work for an Englishman, and he compensates me very well, I can assure you. I wouldn't call that exploitation."

"Yes, he pays you well. I can see that. But what about the men who work under you? Your family is well cared for, but what about theirs? You and the other bosses keep the colonial system running. And you do it by breaking the unions and making slaves of the workers, who owe their souls to the company store. Good for you, but not so good for them!"

"Before we can rule ourselves, this country must be developed, and unions prevent that!"

"How can we develop when the British take our raw materials and return them to us from Liverpool and Leeds in packages at ten times the price? Can't you see they don't give a damn about developing us? It's a rotten system, and the United Nations has rightly called for an end to it!"

"Why? So US corporations can move in?" Mr Cain's voice rose. "You and your American Jesuits would love that. Englishmen like Mr Beaumont have lived here all their lives. They have as much of a stake in this country as we do."

"Yes, but they send their children 'home' to England for their educations. Their British wives spend half their time there. Meanwhile, and I'm not talking about Mr Beaumont, he's a decent man as these men go, but can you deny that most of the masters have their mistresses and their brown-skin babies scattered all over the districts? That's a kind of exploitation we haven't touched on yet! You and I are living proof of it."

"Charlie!" Mr Cain slammed his hand down on the table. "Just shut up and eat your chicken, will you?"

I jumped and my fork clattered across the floor. Iris, Sherry and Molly mirrored my dismay. We all looked at Father Bosque.

"I'm afraid I can't possibly do both of those things at once."

Even Mr Cain had to laugh.

Iris hurried to bring me another fork, while the two men went back to eating and polished off the chicken.

After class towards the end of the following week, Sherry waved a red-white-and-blue–edged airmail envelope in my face.

"Vince ansah me! I have a pen pal!"

But a few days later, Sherry came by our house before school, a tragic look on her face. "Iris say I can't ansah Vince." She dropped her book bag and slumped into a chair.

"But why not?"

"She say young gals have no business to write a strange man."

"Oh, Sherry, I should have thought of that. It was a stupid mistake on my part."

"No," she said. "Iris just mean. She always say no, no matter what."

"I'll find you a female pen pal. One closer to your age."

"No, Miss! I want to write Vince. Maybe he can send my letters in your letters?"

"That would be very sneaky."

"Please, Miss."

"I can't do it, Sherry." I said. "Iris is just trying to protect you."

"No, Miss! She hate, hate, hate me."

"What does your father say?"

She didn't answer.

"So he doesn't approve, either?"

She shrugged. "If I ask him, he will let me."

"That settles it, Sherry," I said. "Listen, I'll send one more letter for you. In it you have to tell Vince it's the last one, and why."

"It's not fair!" she said, crying.

"Maybe not, but you have to live by your parents' rules."

"I thought you will help me, Miss."

"I'm trying the best I can to do what's right, Sherry."

She wiped her eyes and sat down to write what I thought was a last letter to Vince.

In Vince's next letter to me, I found one addressed to Sherry. *Thanks for delivering this to Sherry*, he wrote.

"Okay, Sherry," I said when I showed her the letter from Vince. "What's going on here?"

"Can I have it, Miss?"

"No."

"Please, Miss. It's mine!"

"I told you I wasn't going to cover for you, Sherry. I'm sending this right back to him."

"My dad, he knows now. He says it's okay. Just don't tell Iris."

"Why do I find that hard to believe?"

"Ask him, Miss."

I did, that afternoon, when he came to pick Sherry up. She stood at a distance, watching as we talked beside his Land Rover.

"My wife can be too strict with Sherry," Mr Cain said. "What harm can there be in a pen pal, especially if you know this person? I've never seen Sherry so excited."

"I'm not really comfortable doing this," I said.

"It will be our secret," he said.

I silently handed Sherry the letter.

She threw her arms around me and hugged me. "I love you so much, Miss," she said.

Then she climbed in the Land Rover beside her father. Even before they drove off together, she tore open the envelope and started reading Vince's letter.

Sherry didn't give me any more of her letters to enclose in mine, and Vince didn't send anything else for me to deliver. When I asked whether they were still writing, he replied that he hadn't heard from her in weeks and was just about to write me to be sure she was okay.

My impression is she's a complicated young lady, he wrote. *I'm a bit concerned about her. Get the impression the family situation isn't the best. Glad she has you to look out for her.*

Sissy Quinlan, Father Bosque's niece, was the opposite of complicated. With Sissy as with her father, what you saw was what you got.

"I didn't do my homework last night, Miss. Instead I listened to American baseball," she confessed one day when I called on her in class. "Go ahead, Miss, and give me the consequences."

Sissy loved sports. In our after-school baseball games against the Camelot Boys, she was our star player, even though she was more than a year younger than the other ninth-grade girls. She played barefoot and, feet planted wide, swung the bat left-handed with all the force in her lean, lithe body. Half the time she struck out, but the other half she hit home runs with bat-cracking power. She ran like a gazelle, long yellow-brown hair streaming out behind her.

When we played water polo with Father Bosque and the other Quinlans, she was the one who always managed to steal the ball from "Uncle Charlie". He accused her of being part water sprite because, he swore, she could stay under water longer than most fish. He nicknamed her "Ondine" after a mermaid in a legend. "She hair be seaweed, she bones be pearl," he chanted, making things up as he pursued her. "On her skin, me see a fin! Web do grow between her toe. Under water I hab caught her! Dis e no de Quinlan dahtah! Who she be, dis strange young gal? She Ondine, wid fishy tail!"

At twelve, Sissy looked if not like a mermaid, like a changeling. Her androgynous body still lacked breasts and hips. Clothes looked wonderful on her, even the school uniform, although she didn't seem to care or even notice.

After school, she wore what must have been hand-me-downs from her older sisters: oversized striped jerseys with holes in the sleeves and plaid cotton skirts with ripped hems that on her looked marvellous.

Her voice was high-pitched, befitting the child she still was, but her eyes, big and brown, were much older and always aware. "I used to want to go to the States," she told me. "But now I hear about Paris and Vienna and think maybe I rather go there."

Once when we were talking, Lydie, her mother, said that she was in despair over Sissy's hair. "I just don't understand hair like hers, and I don't know what to do with it. It's so straight and limp. She doesn't care, at least not yet, but I do."

Lydie's dark brown hair was thick and naturally curly. She pulled it back from her face with a headband, exposing her broad forehead and distinctive widow's peak. Her hairstyle had the added advantage of showing off her handsome profile.

"The other girls have such lovely hair, full of body with such rich colour." Sissy's two older sisters, Betty and Alma, were brunettes like their mother. "Sissy takes after her father's family. They're all blondes. I know a lot of people admire blond hair and envy the Quinlans theirs, but I never cared for it. It's often thin and fine and looks dingy – at least to me. Unless you bleach it, of course, and then it looks fake. I never could see what's the big deal about being blond. The same with blue eyes. Blue eyes look faded to me. I'm surprised people can see out of them. Thank God Sissy's eyes are brown."

I enjoyed listening to Lydie's stream-of-consciousness monologues, delivered in a deep, throaty voice, probably the result of too many cigarettes. It was like listening to jazz. Molly thought Lydie's conversation was disjointed and hard to follow, but I found her delightfully offbeat and unpredictable. When I had nothing else to do, I sometimes stopped by the Quinlans' house on Front Street, happy to spend half an hour with Lydie, who never failed to cheer me up.

One afternoon, I ran into Lydie in Lee Wong's store. As we waited to pay for our purchases, she picked up a pink cylinder from a bin on the counter.

"Do you know how to use these things?" she asked.

"You mean hair rollers? Sure."

"You Americans amaze me," she said.

I paid my bill and went on my way.

The next afternoon, Sissy appeared on my doorstep with a bag in her hand.

"My mum sent me," she said. "With these."

She emptied out a dozen pink jumbo hair rollers, a card of bobby pins and a comb. "Mum says you'll fix my hair if I ask you."

"Do you want me to?"

"If it makes my mum happy, why not?"

She followed me into the bathroom, where I helped her wash her hair. But her mane was so thick and slippery that the rollers popped out and spun across the linoleum the instant I let go of them. I called Molly, and it took both of us working together to tame her hair. Then we sat her in the sun till her hair dried and the curl had set.

When we were finished, I handed her a mirror. "What do you think?"

"I'd rather have a real present, if it was me."

"What do you mean?" I asked her.

"Today is my mum's birthday, and this is what she asked for," Sissy said, gathering up her rollers. "Oh. She said for you to stop by later for some cake."

That night, Lydie pulled me aside. "Thank you," she said. "You helped me see it."

"What?" I asked.

"That Sissy is as beautiful as her sisters."

In one of her essays, Jean Martinez wrote about a little boy from her village:

> From the moment we met, there was no one dearer to my heart than this little boy; he was not handsome nor was he rich. He was only a plain little chap, without any fine hair or blue eyes. There was nothing attractive about him, and yet I loved him well. What made me love this boy so much? Think as I might, I never understood. Sometimes I fancied that I loved just for the sake of loving, so I decided that it was something natural.

Who was this student who, so young, pondered the source and meaning of love? Like the boy of whom she wrote, something in frightened, tongue-tied Jean, who wrote so much more fluently and freely than she spoke, moved my heart. She almost never spoke in class, never sought me out or mumbled anything but "Hello, Miss" when I ran into her on the street. She called attention to herself only by her extreme shyness.

But from the beginning, I noticed her eyes. Hungry eyes. I often thought of her as I prepared my lessons, adding morsels of whatever learning I had that I thought might satisfy her, and I gauged her responses as I taught.

Her first essay was so good compared to those of the other ninth graders that I was afraid she'd copied it from somewhere. I asked her to stay after class. At first, hunched over her desk, she hid behind her hands, crossing and recrossing her legs, so nervous that she could barely manage to complete a sentence.

"I'd like you to write something for me about yourself, Jean," I said. "Right now, please."

In her copybook, she wrote an essay that began, "The family to which I belong has little to go with our name. Depending on the season and the sea, our hands and our stomachs are full or empty."

As I read her paragraph, I imagined Jean and her family in their tiny Garifuna village, much like the ones we visited with the priests. I'd seen how such families lived, crowded into a hut roofed with palm or coconut leaves. Plagued by mosquitoes and flies, they slept in the rainy season in a single bed or on the floor, and when the weather was warm and dry, rolled up three and four to a hammock like peas in a pod. They all went to the village school, where one teacher taught everything. The difference for Jean, I eventually learned, was that when she'd gone as far as she could – standard six, the same as eighth grade in the United States – the teacher took her on as his assistant and paid her wages, a few dollars a month. During the next three years, she managed to scrape together enough for her dream: to attend high school in Angel Creek.

"Five dollars BH a month is all it costs to come," I said to Molly, "and it took her three years to earn enough for a year's tuition. And she still has to work for room and board."

"I agree with Father Bosque," Molly said. "This system stinks. How can people work so hard and be so poor?"

"I don't know," I said. "But I do know this girl is remarkable and deserves everything we can do for her. English isn't even her first language – she speaks it only in school, and you know how that goes – and she writes like Jane Austen! Or, on second thought, more like a Victorian, like Dickens, maybe."

I found out that Jean was living just around the corner from us with an aunt and uncle, who traded room and board for help with their seven children. In my journal, I described their house as *zinc and boards leaning against each other and at least ten people crowded in there. Newspapers and magazine illustrations for wallpaper. No running water, electricity or heat in the house. Meals cooked in a lean-to in the yard. I don't even know if they have enough to eat.*

One evening, passing by the house, I heard someone playing a concertina in the backyard, and the music – wistful and playful at the same time – drew me around the corner. It was Jean playing, with all her little cousins dancing around her in the moonlight.

During the second month of school, at my suggestion, she began coming by our house two or three afternoons a week to write in the quiet of the living room while I prepared the next day's classes. She would sit across the table from me, writing until I told her to stop. I offered her cookies and whatever else I could save from our big noon dinner to take home for the little children – otherwise, she wouldn't eat anything I served her during our visits but would save it for them. Several times, she brought the three smallest of her cousins along with her, and to keep them quiet while she wrote, I had them sit for a group portrait. I wasn't a good artist and certainly not a trained one, but the kids were delighted with the drawing and promised to "keep it fohaybah".

The next afternoon, Jean turned up with an old piece of slate and a stump of chalk. She hesitated before she thrust them into my hands.

"Can you draw someone with hair like mine?" she asked.

"I'll try," I replied. "But wouldn't you like me to use paper?"

"No, Miss, just this, if you please. So I can see how you see me."

Sherry often came to study with me, too, while she waited for her father. It could take her a long time to settle down. She would start to read or write, and then out of the blue say something like, "Excuse me, Miss, but there a good movie at the Silver Dream this weekend. I forget the name, but Frankie Avalon's in it. If you and Miss Molly go, I'll see you there."

In response to my impatient look, she would pick up her book again.

"Miss, you know that girl, the one who sits next to me in first period, Jean? She *sixteen*, Miss!"

"Another interruption, Sherry, and you go."

"You only strict," she said. "Okay, I be quiet now."

One afternoon of a particularly tiring day, Sherry followed Molly and me home from school, tagged along with us when we went for our afternoon swim and trailed us back to our house.

"My dad say to tell you he be late today," she said. "I tell him to come by here."

"If you wait with us," I said, "you have to be very quiet. Miss Molly and I have a lot of work to finish this afternoon."

While Molly and I changed clothes, Sherry settled down and began reading. When I came out of my room and sat down with my own book, she didn't say a word. For once, she had a peaceful look on her face. We sat that way until her father honked for her.

"It's nice to see you so calm, Sherry," I said. "And happy."

"Only now, when I'm here with you, Miss. It's like the feeling I used to have with my mum."

Then, of course, I felt awful for wishing her gone.

Chapter 10

THE JESUS TREE

LIKE EVERYONE IN ANGEL CREEK who could afford the admission price, Molly and I went to the Silver Dream Theatre at least once a week to see movies that had shown in the States, often years before. The films usually changed nightly, and we saw dozens of them. Whether they were set in the Far East, like *The Inn of the Sixth Happiness* or *Love Is a Many-Splendored Thing*, or the American West, like *Springfield Rifle*, each was a quick trip home through familiar accents and faces. We discovered classics like *The Bridge on the River Kwai* and enjoyed things I would have mocked at home – tearjerkers like *All that Heaven Allows*. I even came to relish Elvis Presley movies, especially *King Creole*. That was a good thing, because the Presley movies were so popular that they were screened repeatedly, always packing the house.

The only films I dreaded were the old Second World War movies set in the South Pacific, because the crowd cat-called and stomped their feet whenever the Asian villains came on the screen. No matter that they were Japanese, not Chinese; any actor who even vaguely resembled the merchant Lee Wong, to whom almost everyone in Angel Creek owed money, was hissed and booed.

Ana sometimes joined us there, and now and then Eduardo, when he had a night off from the Club, turned up. As I sat silently in the dark next to him, our elbows or knees occasionally touched and I'd shift away, my entire body tingling. Within minutes, he had repositioned himself so that one of his arms or legs once more touched mine. It was eighth grade all over again.

One evening, Eduardo asked if he could walk Molly and me home after we dropped Ana off. Molly soon went up to bed, and he and I sat for a while on the bottom porch step. It was the first conversation we'd had with no one else present.

We started by talking about Elvis Presley, whom we'd just seen in *Jailhouse Rock*. I told Eduardo how much I'd disliked Elvis's singing the first time I heard it at age fourteen. His voice had sounded burpy to me. "Like he needed an Alka-Seltzer," I said. Eduardo looked puzzled. "You know, for indigestion." He didn't know.

I told him I liked Elvis in his movies and even liked his singing now. That Elvis in his movies was sweet and clueless – like a kid – until he sang, and then he was exciting. Dangerous even. You felt his power.

Eduardo asked me if I thought Elvis was handsome. "Sort of," I answered. "But he looks to me like he needs a good bath and a change of underwear." Again Eduardo looked puzzled.

Burping? Dirty underwear? It crossed my mind that I was babbling. Why did he make me feel like I was the teenager?

"Do *you* think Elvis is handsome?" I asked to cover my confusion.

"Yes, I do, but it doesn't matter what I think. It's the girls who have to think so." He hesitated, and then asked, "Which movie stars do you think are handsome?"

I told him I thought most of them were: Cary Grant, Clark Gable, Rock Hudson. That's what movie stars were – handsome.

"Do you have a favourite?"

My real favourites were the heroes in books: Mr Rochester, Heathcliff, Fitzwilliam Darcy, Captain Wentworth, but I didn't tell Eduardo that. Instead, I told him I used to have a crush on James Dean. I was fifteen and looking for someone like Lord Byron, whose poetry I liked at the time, someone "mad, bad, and dangerous to know". James Dean was all that and more. I fantasized that if we ever met, it would be love at first sight for both of us. And then he died in that car wreck.

"I saw *Rebel Without a Cause* right after his funeral and cried all through it," I said. "Not because he was dead, but because it was the last movie he'd ever make."

I had expected Eduardo to laugh or at least smile at my foolishness, but he listened with a seriousness that threw me off guard.

"What about you, Eduardo? Which movie stars do you think are handsome? Or 'beautiful', I should say. Funny how we save 'beautiful' for women."

He answered right away that his favourite female star was Natalie Wood. *Splendor in the Grass* had played at the Silver Dream a few weeks earlier, and he said I reminded him of her in that film. "Especially the part before she cut her hair."

I felt flattered, but said, "Except maybe for the hair, I don't look anything like her, Eduardo."

"To me you do."

"But it's just a fantasy if it isn't true."

"It is true," he insisted. "I see her and I think of you, and I see you and I think of her."

In a movie, at this point James Dean would have kissed Natalie Wood, but sitting on the steps, in full view of the convent and the rectory and anybody walking by, we turned away from each other and went on talking. I don't remember much of anything else we said, but I do remember clearly the feeling of sitting next to him on the steps and not wanting it to end.

"What did you two talk about for so long last night?" Molly asked the next morning.

When I admitted it was mostly about our favourite movie stars, she said, "That sounds deep."

"What do you and Paul-at-Harvard talk about? Truth, beauty and goodness?"

"Of course."

"Actually, we did talk about beauty."

"What did you say?"

"Not much. Just who we think are the most handsome or beautiful movie stars. It was a way of talking about ourselves, I guess, without getting too personal. As one of my teachers used to say, 'Tell me who or what you admire, and I'll tell you who you are.'"

"We'll talk more tonight," Molly said, picking up her schoolbooks. "We haven't had an 'orgy' for a long time."

Molly and I called our late-night conversations "orgies" because they frequently involved cigarettes and alcohol. We usually had a half-empty bottle of something alcoholic on hand, left behind by David Lewis or the priests, and a supply of candles and Benson & Hedges, purchased with our orgies in mind at the Blue Beat, a shop across the street from us. Whenever the mood struck us, usually once every couple of weeks, we poured a glass of something and lit up. Sometimes we included others, but usually we orgied alone.

That night, after class preps were done, I lit one of our candles, a black one. The town generator had gone out again and the Blue Beat had sold out of the white ones we usually bought because they were cheaper. I liked the way the black candle vanished in the darkness and the flame appeared to float in a void.

Molly shook a Benson & Hedges from the pack we shared and lit it in the flame. I poured us both a taste of gin and added lots of tonic, along with big squeezes of lime juice. No ice, alas.

"Since this morning, I've been thinking about beauty," Molly said. "And its effect on others." She puffed on her cigarette. Neither of us was a smoker, really – we inhaled only by accident. We were good girls misbehaving.

"Most people assume that being born beautiful is a great blessing, especially if you're female. They think that the more beautiful you are, the more attractive you are to other people, especially men, and the nicer they treat you. But I'm not so sure. Let me tell you about my friend Celeste."

We sat cross-legged on the floor, the flame between us.

Molly said that Celeste was her closest friend in college, and people were in awe of her, almost like she was some sort of goddess. They'd stop on the street to gawk at her. Men pursued her like a prize. Women envied her. They'd also imitate her. If she wore something, it didn't matter what, others would run out to buy it. Molly said she'd done so herself.

She went on to describe what we would now call "stalking", although then we had no name for it. "Some people became obsessed with her," she said, "and just wouldn't leave her alone. One guy – she didn't even know his name – followed her around for months! She'd leave the dorm, walk down the street, and there he'd be, right behind her. Wherever she went – to class, to the movies, to the library – he'd turn up. He never said or did anything, just watched her from a distance, but after a while, she was afraid to leave her room."

"That's a sad story," I said.

"All I can say is that before I met Celeste, I used to envy really beautiful people. Now I feel a little bit sorry for them. You know, in a strange kind of way, they're scapegoats."

"What do you mean?" I asked.

"I think we humans project our dreams and desires as well as our guilt and sins onto others and then make them suffer for it."

I thought of Celeste and the curse of great beauty a few days later when we heard the news. It was Sunday morning, and as Molly and I usually did on Sundays, we had a long, leisurely breakfast after eight o'clock Mass. The convent always sent over something special: pancakes or scrambled eggs. It was raining outside, so we lingered over coffee, happy in the thought of a free day.

After a while, Molly turned on the battery-operated radio, and I went into my room to write letters home. Within minutes, over the sound of the radio and the rain on the tin roof, I heard Molly cry out, "Abby!"

I ran in to see her sitting with her elbows on the table amongst the dirty dishes, eyes fixed on the radio.

"What's wrong?" I asked her.

"Marilyn Monroe was found dead!"

"Dead! Where? How?"

"In her house. It happened sometime during the night. They said the cause of death is still being determined, that it could've been an accident, but it sounds more like suicide to me. I don't know which would be worse."

Music began playing. Molly reached out and spun the dial, searching for more news. She couldn't find any. News coverage on Radio Belize was brief, as on most stations at the time. The only other news we could find was in Spanish. We'd have to wait for the next day's *Belize Times*.

"I only heard the last part of the announcement," Molly said. "We'll catch the next broadcast."

I sat down at the table. "Was she one of your favourites?"

"Not like Audrey Hepburn or Grace Kelly, but she was a real star. It's always a shock to hear someone famous has died, especially someone still young and beautiful."

"My grandmother says bad news always takes a while to sink in. Then it seems inevitable."

"If it was suicide, I wonder why she'd take her own life."

"I don't know," I said. "Maybe she wanted to escape. Or be rescued."

I could see her image, icon-like, before me, Marilyn on the subway grate, her head tilted back, silver-blond curls tousled, open mouth laughing, long, pale legs bare under the lifted white skirt. And in my mind's eye, I saw another girl, not yet Marilyn – Norma Jean, in a halter top and short shorts, playing pin-up girl.

"She wasn't a very good actress," Molly said. "You could tell she was acting."

"She seemed that way even off-screen," I said. "Like Marilyn itself was a role she was playing."

"I think a lot of people must feel like that, like they're playing a role and it really isn't them. Especially a lot of women."

"Especially Marilyn. How do you play the ideal woman, the twentieth-century Venus? An impossible part for anyone. You couldn't get old!"

"She didn't," Molly said.

The first time – that I know of – that my mother tried suicide was when I was eight years old. She swallowed an entire bottle of aspirin and then told me what she'd done. I told my father. "Call the ambulance, Daddy. Call one now!"

He said, "Let her die if she wants to," and then he picked up the phone.

The second time was a couple of years later. She slit her wrists with a razor blade. For that one I only remember the ambulance coming, although I found myself imagining the scene for years afterward, her climbing in the bathtub at my grandparents' house and lying in the bloody bath water until my grandfather broke down the door.

Right around that first time, I found a wonderful stone. I collected stones and kept them in a Yardley's English Lavender soapbox. This particular one was black with a silvery white substance swirling through it, and I called it my magic touching stone. It reminded me of stars in the night sky – the Milky Way, in fact. When I felt nervous or sad I touched it, and everything felt better. Much later, I heard behaviour like that called "magical thinking". It had worked for me.

I also built a shrine to the Virgin Mary in my bedroom closet. I was scared of the dark, and the little night-light that illuminated her statue comforted me. Still, I often couldn't sleep soundly until dawn. During that year, I, who loved school, was often late or absent.

Then, one night while praying as I *had* to do before the statue, I felt myself drop into a hidden place. With great certainty, I knew that I had fallen into God's room. From then on, I didn't really need the stone or the shrine any more, except to remind me that God was down there, living inside me.

"Weh you gat dese candles?" Josie asked. She had come across our box of black candles while she was cleaning.

"At the Blue Beat," I said. "Why?"

"Wat you wan' wid dese?"

"Light, of course," I said.

"Why dese?"

"It's all the store had left. The electricity has been out for a week," I reminded her.

She looked uneasy. "Dese foh *obeah*."

What's that?" Molly and I both asked.

"Foh mek de charm an' de spell," she said. "Foh mek de magic. Wen you rite de name of sonebahdy on de candle and it burn down, dey ded!"

"How awful!" said Molly.

"Only witch womon gat black candle," Josie said.

"And local merchants stock such things?" Molly asked.

She nodded. "If you gat enemy, de witch womon make hex foh you. If you need be heal, she hep you. If you wahn mon go crazy foh you, you go see witch womon. But don' let fahdah or de sistahs know!"

"Josie," I said, "surely people wouldn't think we're witches just because we bought black candles!"

"Yes, Miss. Dey do."

"So what do we do now?" I asked.

Josie bit her lower lip and shook her head. "Me no know."

"But we go to Mass every morning," Molly objected. "How could people think we practise witchcraft?"

"Only mek de *obeah* strongah."

"Take these candles and get rid of them." Molly tried to hand them to Josie, who squealed and hid her hands behind her back.

"Well then, we'll give them to Father Bosque and he'll get rid of them for us," I said.

"Yes, Miss. Dat gud way foh do it. Arrite, Miss Abby and Miss Molly. Ah go now!" Josie, who rarely hurried, hurried away, leaving us to finish our own dusting and mopping.

We told Father Bosque the candle story, and he said, "If it will make you feel better, I'll talk to Leon over at the Blue Beat. And I'll say something to my sister. Lydie can get the word out that you're not witch women, so you won't have people lining up at your door to have spells cast."

He was joking, but we were still concerned. "Will people suspect us of doing harm to them?" I asked, images of machetes slashing through my mind.

"I wouldn't worry about it," he said. "Just don't buy any more of these black candles." Once again, we were sitting in a circle around a lighted candle, and again it was one of the black ones because the electricity was still out and they were all we had. "And don't sacrifice any chickens."

"I know you think it's funny," I said, "but Josie was really upset."

"I'm not saying people here aren't superstitious," he said, helping himself to a Benson & Hedges from the pack Molly and I brought out for our orgies. "I see it all the time. I believe in good luck charms myself. I even believe in ghosts."

"Have you ever seen one?" Molly asked him.

"No, but that doesn't mean they don't exist."

"Does *obeah* exist?" I asked him.

"I'm not sure how widespread it is, but yes, I'm sure that some people try to work their will on others, and on nature, and use ways against both reason and Christian belief to do it. Many such practices came with the slaves from Africa and have been passed down generation to generation. You'll find forms of *voodoo* and *obeah* all over the Caribbean and the West Indies."

"What's the difference?" Molly asked.

"Basically it's the same thing with a different name," he said. "In some places, it's called *santería*. By now it's blended with Christianity, as you'll see on some of the high holy days, like Easter. The chanting and ecstatic dancing goes on for days. The priests and nuns have tried to stop it, but without much success."

Father Bosque added that many of the local folk tales and legends had African roots too. "Surely the boys have told you stories of Anansi the spider and his tricks. Those go back to legends that are widespread in Africa."

"Yes, we've heard some of those," I said, remembering one in particular that had reminded me of Br'er Rabbit and the tar baby, only it was Johnny Anansi, not Br'er Rabbit, who was the tricky hero. In the story the boys told us, Johnny made a baby out of the sticky sap of a tree to catch a spirit haunting the bush.

Father Bosque spent the rest of the evening telling us folk tales and ghost stories. Most of them involved men and dangerous, seductive women, like the story of the beautiful woman with flowing hair who lures a man into the bush. They start making passionate love, and it goes very well until, suddenly, she starts choking him. He pulls out his knife and plunges it deep into her heart, saving his life by killing her, and then runs home as fast as he can go. The next day he returns to the bush to find her body, and there where he left her lies a huge snake with his knife in its heart.

Not long after this conversation, Ana lost her purse. We'd gone to a movie and on the way home, stopped by the Caribbean Club for something to drink. Suddenly she looked around, panic on her face, and asked if I'd seen it.

"No," I said. "You had it when we paid for the tickets."

We headed back to the Silver Dream, searching the street with a flashlight, and talked to the manager, who said nothing had been turned in as lost. He switched on all the lights, powered by his own generator – the city lights were still out – and we went row by row through the empty theatre. No sign of Ana's purse. We walked her back the way we came, still searching for it.

"Did you have much money in it?" Molly asked her.

"No, that's not why I'm worried." She lowered her voice. "It's my period, and I took some pads and an extra pair of panties along, just in case. Now, anyone finding them will have complete control over me."

"What in the world do you mean?"

"If the wrong person gets their hands on those panties, they can use them to cast a spell – the *obeah*, you know. That's how it works."

An entire lifetime without hearing it, and now that word again, for the second time in one week.

"Oh, Ana, can you really believe that?" Molly asked.

"Yes, of course! Everyone knows it works like that." She burst into tears. "I was so foolish to take something like that with me."

When I saw Ana at Mass the next morning, I asked her if she'd found her purse. "No," she said, "but Marita gave me this." She pulled a gold cross on a chain from inside her blouse. Attached to it by a thread was an unpeeled garlic clove.

"Why the garlic?"

"Marita says it has special power to protect against evil," she said.

So that explained the strings of garlic I saw hanging on the doors of some of our neighbours.

During one of our visits, our neighbour Therese told us about a certain kind of tree that bled on Good Friday. She called it "de Jesus Tree".

"Go een de bush dat day, an' you see it!" she assured us. "No uddah day, jes dat day, and it bleed ahl day. Or maybe it only bleed aftah noon. Ah fohget. But it bleed!"

When we next had supper at the Forestry Station with the Todds and David Lewis, we asked them about the legendary tree.

"Never heard of any such tree," Andrew said.

"It's probably just a fairy tale," David said. "There are some trees with reddish-coloured sap, like the sapodilla tree. If you cut it, the sap vaguely resembles blood. But it doesn't just bleed on its own, and it bleeds whenever you cut it, not just on Good Friday."

Do we all, I wondered, need a Jesus tree on occasion – some object or image that gives us a glimpse of supernatural influence and sometimes terrible beauty, which we appropriate for ourselves and use as the spirit moves us, to comfort, console, create or destroy?

Chapter 11

DYING FOR ICE CREAM

THE SCRAWL WAS HARD to read, one line invading the next, the margins uneven. Word by word, phrase by phrase, I deciphered the note Molly had handed me.

"My dear Molly," it began. "It is probably a good thing I am being transferred back to the US." What followed could only be described as a love letter. It ended with the request that Molly either tear up the letter or burn it.

"He must have mailed this just before he left," Molly said. "It's postmarked 'Belize City'."

We'd last seen Father O'Dea almost a week earlier in the convent parlour, where the nuns held a farewell tea for him. By now, he must be back in the States.

"Molly, he'd die if he knew you showed me this," I said, handing back the letter.

"Well, I can't handle something like this all on my own. What should I do?"

"What he says. Get rid of it."

"Why in the world would he write something like this?"

"The madness of the moment. Probably he'd been drinking when he wrote it."

"Of course. I should have thought of that. But he must have been sober when he mailed it."

"I don't know, Molly. He probably couldn't help himself. I never understood him very well."

"Do you think I should write him back?"

"What would you say to him?"

Molly reread the letter, refolded it and slid it back in its envelope. "There's no return address, so I guess he really doesn't expect me to answer. He probably just wanted to get this off his chest."

Father Matthew Peck, Father O'Dea's replacement, was at least six and a half feet tall, looked to be in his early forties, and reminded me physically of his namesake, the actor Gregory Peck.

Mother Eugenie brought him over to meet us. "Father Peck is famous," she said after she introduced him. "He's the one who radioed for help during the hurricane last fall." She tilted her head back to look up at the priest. Her veil hung down like a medieval maiden's hair, almost to her ankles. "Father Peck is an expert radio operator."

Even when she was most serious, Mother Eugenie's Louisiana accent had a coy lilt to it. Now the lilt was pronounced. Interacting with our new pastor, she laughed, talked and gestured with more animation than usual. She seemed almost girlish. "Did you bring all your equipment with you, Father Peck?"

"All my equipment? Oh, the radio stuff. Sure. It's already set up." Father Peck was surveying our living room. "Father O'Dea did a nice job on this house. I heard he built most of it himself. Do you mind if I look around?"

He stuck his head into each of the bedrooms, and then headed for the kitchen and bathroom. "I'm going to have to do something about the rectory. It's a wreck."

Molly and I nodded, trying not to laugh. We'd been calling it the "wrecktory" for months.

Mother Eugenie, right behind him, said, "Let us know if we can help, Father Peck. The sisters and I will be happy to do whatever we can. Just say the word."

We heard the faucet running in the kitchen, and a moment later the toilet flushed.

"The water pressure at the rectory is terrible," he said, coming back into the living room. He turned abruptly to Molly and me. "You girls like it here?"

"Very much!" we said.

"Glad to hear it!" He shook our hands vigorously and, without another word, headed for the door.

"Wait just a minute, Father Peck," Mother Eugenie cried out. "I'll show you the school!" She said a quick goodbye to us and hurried down the stairs after him.

"A whole new Mother Eugenie!" Molly said. "She certainly is showing him her softer side."

"I don't think he noticed. He was much more interested in the plumbing than in her or us, although he seems nice enough. I'd say he's one hundred per cent woman-proof. He's not going to be writing anybody love letters when he leaves!"

"Don't tease," Molly pleaded.

It was the end of August, and even though the daily downpours that drenched Angel Creek through July and August had tapered off, it was still hot and muggy. No air moved. In the distance the sea lay flat and still, as if exhausted. I sat at the desk in my bedroom grading exams. My hands were so slippery with sweat that I couldn't keep a firm grip on my pencil. When I tried to write in the margins of the exam books, the students' ink transferred itself onto the heel of my hand. I rubbed it off on my dark blue skirt and tried to concentrate.

As part of their history final, I'd asked each of the first-formers to pretend she was a crusader and write a letter home describing her experiences, thoughts and emotions, developed with relevant historical details. I read:

> Dear Wife, How are you? I am fine. Here it is already the beginning of the ~~11th~~ 12th? century. The First Crusade is going fine. We made it all the way to Jerusaland. I think we shall have the Jerusalanders beat soon. I will soon come home to you and the children, back to Eureop where we live. I will bring presents maybe some silk for everyone and a few spices. Darling, I long to kiss your ruby lips and hug you a hundred times. Your slave, Marcella Hernandez. PS Please write back.

I turned to the short-answer section of Marcella's exam. When I read that the Portuguese prince responsible for the European exploration of Africa was Prince Henry the Alligator (someone else thought it was Prince Henry the Aviator), I didn't know whether to laugh or cry.

No less than the other students, Marcella had done her best to make sense of the odd assortment of names, dates and disconnected stories I'd fed the class, but the exams convinced me that I'd failed to communicate any real sense of history or why they should spend time learning about it. I recalled the day one of the students had asked me what the Africans thought about the Europeans who came to explore them. I didn't have an answer. I could only repeat what the text said about why the Europeans had wanted to explore Africa. I couldn't even ask the students to imagine the response of the Africans because I suddenly realized how little I knew about Africa.

"Too bad sonebody don' write ahl dat down," the student said.

"It's only history if somebody keeps a record of it" was all I could think to say.

In 1962, the books we read and history we studied were entirely European. During the first term, we'd studied the Middle Ages and the Age of Exploration and Discovery from the point of view of European Christians. My own education hadn't prepared me to challenge that perspective, but I often found the language and allusions in our few surviving textbooks, all of them British, almost as hard to understand and apply as my students did. When the textbook pointed out by way of clarification that medieval monasteries were a part of the status quo as accepted as the House of Lords or Oxford and Cambridge universities, I wondered exactly what that meant. Was it good, bad or indifferent to be like "Warwick shaking his bells"? Who was Warwick, anyway, what sort of bells was he shaking, and why was he shaking them? What did it mean "to come a cropper"?

Unless I remembered to ask David Lewis or the Todds, I usually offered my best guess from the context and moved on. Unfortunately, such details were exactly the ones the students often fixed on, parroting them back without any understanding.

I vowed that next term I'd do a better job of finding and substituting language and examples that were relevant to me and to my students. And I'd ask them the question I was asking myself more and more often: not *what?* but *so what?*

A recent episode had crystallized my impressions of the education at St Monica's and, by extension, in the colony as a whole. My literature students were taking a test, and as I walked around the room monitoring them, I clearly overheard the geometry lesson going on in the next room.

"Who can explain this proof?" Sister Veronica asked.

I looked through the open arch between the rooms. Sister Veronica tapped impatiently on the board with her pointer.

"Surely, one of you can explain this proof! We spent all last class on it."

I saw one little girl slowly raise her arm. It was Jessie, one of the students in my first-year comp class.

"All right, Jessie."

Jessie stood and recited the proof perfectly, then sat back down.

"Excellent! Now, who doesn't understand it?"

Again, slowly, one arm went up. Jessie's.

"How will you go to Belize City?" Eduardo asked me. He had pulled up beside me in his Jeep as I walked along the edge of the soccer field on my way back from turning in my marks to Sister Veronica.

"We're taking the truck," I said.

Open-backed trucks fitted with wooden planks for seating and a canvas covering were the most common form of public transportation in British Honduras. There were fleets of them, like buses at home, all looking the same but each with a distinctive name, such as *Maya Princess* and *Jumping Jaguar*. For about a dollar each way, Molly and I could travel the ninety miles by road to Belize City.

"That's a rough and dusty way to go," he said. "If I didn't have to work, I would drive you there."

"Thanks for thinking of it, Eduardo, but it'll be a new experience to take the truck."

"At least let me drive you home."

"But it's just a couple of blocks," I said.

"I was hoping I would see you before you left. I want to ask you something."

I climbed in beside him, curious and a bit apprehensive.

"Let's drive the long way round," he said, passing by Church Street, where I lived. "Maybe Ana told you I've been in El Salvador for the past two weeks. Otherwise, I would have come to see you before now."

"She told me you were away."

"I know you think I'm too young for you, but I'll soon be twenty."

"You're still a teenager, Eduardo, and I'm more than two years older than you. At our age, that's a big difference."

"My brother Javier is with someone who is almost fifteen years older, and they're happy. I like that you're different from girls my age. You're more serious. They only think about catching themselves a husband."

We'd reached the end of Front Street. He turned onto the street that bordered the cemetery, turned again on Market Street, and drove slowly in the direction of our house.

"The weekend after next, Ana and I are going to Half Moon Creek for the baptism of our brother Emilio's first son. Would you like to come along? My father has given us permission to ask you. Will you say yes?"

"If Ana is going, then yes, I'd like to come."

"Then we'll make plans."

"I'll be back here in four or five days, and we can talk more about it then."

I decided to wait to tell Molly until I was sure the trip would happen. Especially as I'd forgotten to ask if the invitation included her.

Father Bosque stopped by soon after Eduardo dropped me off at home, bringing Molly and me some oranges to take on our trip.

"I'm sorry I can't go with you," he said, "but Father Peck needs me here until he's settled in. Here's my mother's address in Belize City. Stop by if you have time."

"Will she know who we are?"

"I sent word you might come. I told her you were Sissy and Alma's teachers and friends of mine."

That night, as I pulled on my nightgown, I heard a harmonica playing across the way. Looking out, I could see a shadowy figure sitting on the flat roof of the rectory. In the moonlight, I recognized Father Bosque, who must have climbed out his attic window. He was playing an old folk tune, "The Water Is Wide". Until that moment, I had no idea he played, and quite well. The music made me vaguely sad, aware of distance and of time passing.

"It feels like the end of something," Molly said as we lifted our suitcases into the back of the *Lightning Bolt*, already crowded with passengers, bags and baskets loaded with fruits and vegetables. There was also a well-behaved dog with a rope leash looped around its neck and a chicken in a cage.

"Ends are usually the beginning of something else, aren't they?" I said, repeating another of my grandmother's sayings.

"David Lewis came by yesterday afternoon while you were out. To say goodbye. And before I knew what he was doing, he kissed me. And I kissed him back."

"Shall we head for the hills while we can? Eduardo said goodbye to me too. No kiss, though. Actually, I think it was just an accident I ran into him."

"It was good before," said Molly. "I'm not sure I'm ready for things to be different."

"But I like things to happen. Don't you?"

"Good things."

"Let's hope *only* good things happen."

We sat in the back of the truck, near the opening, hoping to enjoy the landscape that everyone said was the most beautiful in the entire country, but the truck kicked up so much dust that we couldn't see much of anything. Nor could we talk over the roar of the engine. Bumping along the Hummingbird Highway, I thought of all that had happened in the past two months and wondered what the future would hold.

When we stopped briefly in the valley to pick up two more passengers, I caught a glimpse of the flowering citrus walks on both sides of the road and, in spite of the smell of diesel, inhaled a hint of their pungent fragrance, a promise of things to come.

As Molly had hoped, we learned on our arrival in Belize City that Kate Mannion, one of four new volunteers, would be returning to Angel Creek with us. Father Weaver told us that she would arrive from the United States the next afternoon, and we arranged to go with him to the airport to meet her. Molly said that she didn't know Kate well – she was actually a friend of Molly's boyfriend, Paul – but she liked her. "She'll fit right in," she assured me. "I know we'll have a great time together."

When I first saw the young woman walking towards Molly and me across the airport lobby, I saw a foreigner. Blond hair, forget-me-not blue eyes, a trace of freckles across a turned-up nose. She had a bounce in her step.

I wondered what made Molly think Kate would "fit right in". She couldn't help but stand out, everything about her so light and bright. People were turning to look at her.

I could see her scanning the crowd with anxious eyes, clutching her purse to her breast with one hand and holding onto an overnight case with the other. When she at last saw Molly and me coming towards her, she tried to wave and dropped her purse. People hurried past her as she bent to pick it up, and for a moment, we lost sight of her.

"I'm so glad to see you!" she said when we reached her.

Molly embraced her. "I forgot how blond you are."

CHAPTER ELEVEN

"And look at you!" Kate said. "You look like a gypsy. I almost didn't recognize you! Here, would you hold my purse and this bag for a minute?"

Kate peeled off her woollen sweater. "It's so hot here! And humid! When I left Minnesota, it was in the low sixties. I guess I have some adjusting to do."

Once we were in the privacy of our room at PAVLA House, resting before supper, Kate shared her first impressions. She said the airport was so new and modern that she had expected the rest of the city to be too. She didn't want to say anything in front of Father Weaver, but quite honestly, conditions in Belize City were a bit of a shock.

"Everything looks so rough and raw," she said. "Kind of like a gold rush town. It all seems – I don't know – haphazard. The houses, the stores, the roads, the bridges, they all look improvised. To think that people actually live like this in the twentieth century!"

"Before long, you'll get used to it," Molly said, "and then you'll see it differently."

"I can't imagine ever getting used to it," Kate said. "It seems somehow wrong to get used to it."

"At least PAVLA House is nice, don't you think?"

"But it makes all the other places look worse!" Kate said. "Aren't the townspeople jealous?"

"No one seems resentful," Molly said. "I guess they just expect the Americans and the British to have more money and to live better. Not that it's fair. That's just how things are."

"My God!" Kate said. "The spread of communism makes much more sense when you see a place like this."

"You're right, of course," Molly said.

"The question is, what can be done about it?"

"It may be hard to believe," I said, "but I think we're supposed to be part of the answer to that question."

That evening, all sixteen of the volunteers gathered for an informal meeting in the living room of the renovated PAVLA House, sitting on new chairs and sofas. Father Weaver introduced the four arrivals, a married couple who would live at PAVLA House in a third-floor apartment, a young man from Kansas (but not from St Ben's) who would join the Ritters in Punta Gorda, and Kate.

We each talked briefly about our experiences during our first few months in the colony and gave advice to the new volunteers. As the meeting neared its end, Father Weaver said, almost as if it were an afterthought, "As many of you are no doubt finding out the hard way, probably one of the biggest challenges of this year is the challenge of community living."

The group fell silent. Rumours of trouble in various households had already spread among us. Nick and Dave, who had driven from the States in Carlos the Car, were no longer best friends. We could all see they weren't speaking to each other, although nobody knew exactly what the problem was. At the meeting that night, they'd chosen chairs on opposite sides of the room. There were also hints of divisions within PAVLA House itself. The English volunteers went their own way, and I noticed that Peg and Sue Ella were polite to each other but distant.

Father Weaver said he knew from experience that community living wasn't easy. "It's based far more on shared values and goals than on liking someone," he said, "and it depends more on commitment than on compatibility. What it takes is charity – another word for Christian love." His final words of advice: "Try not to sweat the small stuff."

After comparing notes with the other volunteers, I realized that the "small stuff" made a lot of difference. Class loads varied widely, as did extra-curricular responsibilities. The Belize City nuns, a white European order whose convent and school were next door to PAVLA House, kept Peg and Sue Ella and the English volunteers under constant scrutiny, as Diana had predicted they would. They were demanding taskmasters who left little time for the volunteers to do anything but work. Consequently, Peg and Sue Ella had seen nothing of British Honduras beyond the city. Nor did they have much to do with their students or their families outside school activities. Apparently the limits our nuns had tried to set on Molly and me were actually enforced in Belize City. By comparison, our nuns seemed considerate and easy-going, and I gained a new appreciation for their many acts of kindness.

Few of the other volunteers saw much if anything of their parish priests. They were surprised and envious when Molly and I told them that Father O'Dea and Father Bosque regularly took us with them on trips into the bush. The one other exception was the priest in the southern district, Father McCall, who had involved Judy Ritter, a nurse, and her husband, Ken, in health care in some of the Maya villages and encouraged the couple to offer marriage counselling for those who wanted it.

To my surprise, the most enterprising volunteer was quiet Maureen Bone, who'd been sent alone to a town on the Guatemala border. Isolated in a Spanish-speaking village, she had taken matters into her own hands. Father Weaver congratulated her on initiating a beginning science course at the high school where she taught, one of the poorest in British Honduras. Working through her bishop in the States, Maureen had acquired not only textbooks but also laboratory equipment for the students. The orange and bright blue paint for our classrooms that Molly and I had begged from Mr Beaumont paled by comparison.

Maureen was the one who told me that Father Weaver had agreed to house some of the Peace Corps workers in various PAVLA houses around the colony. One of them was being sent to live with her. "Frankly, the Peace Corps sounds awfully disorganized," she said. "Father Weaver told me that the staff is still scrambling to find housing and jobs for some of the volunteers, and they're due here any day."

Peg added that she had heard the prime minister – called at that time the first minister of British Honduras – went to Washington looking for aid money and ended up instead with twenty Peace Corps volunteers. "He didn't really want them, but he couldn't come back empty-handed. Now he's stuck with them, and he doesn't know what to do with them. The government here would much rather have the million US dollars it's costing to send them. It makes you wonder who's helping whom!"

I repeated the Peace Corps story to Molly and Kate, who found it as ironic as I did. New as it was, the Peace Corps already had a reputation for looking down its nose at PAVLA and other church-related volunteer organizations. At the same time, the story brought to the surface a new concern, which was beginning to dawn on each of us. Had President Kennedy and Pope John XXIII launched an invasion of young Americans on the developing countries of the world, causing more trouble than we were worth? As I wrote in my journal:

> *Maybe all of us American and British volunteers are more of a burden than a help in the eyes of the people who live here. Or at best, superfluous. To be honest, I'm sometimes afraid we're not doing much good for anybody but ourselves. And I sometimes feel a little bit like a fake because I know that I'm learning so much more than I'm teaching and getting tons more out of being here than I can ever hope to give.*

"I can't believe all the problems people are having living together," Molly said when she, Kate and I were back in our room on the second floor of PAVLA House. We were already identified as a threesome: "the Angel Creek Girls", "Angels" for short, as though we were a sports team.

"Well, at first I was surprised," I said. "Especially by Dave and Nick, who were best friends. But the more I think about it, it's maybe more surprising that we haven't had more problems, Molly. In fact, we really haven't had any."

"I hope the three of us will get along as well as the two of you have," Kate said.

"Well, I know people say, 'Two's company, three's a crowd'," Molly replied, "but I think the more the merrier!"

"Three has always been my lucky number," I said.

"In a drama class I took last year," Kate said, "the teacher told us that threes are more dynamic and interesting than twos, at least on the stage."

"Like Chekhov's three sisters?" I asked.

"Exactly. And the three witches in *Macbeth*."

We thought of other famous "threes": fates, furies, graces. "And don't forget the musketeers," Molly laughed, "and the three Wise Men. And, of course, the biggest trio of all, the Trinity."

"Father Weaver had some good things to say about community being based on shared values," Kate said. She added that she thought about friendship in the same way.

"But I'm not sure about Christian love being different from liking someone," Molly said. "I agree that you can like someone without loving them, but I just can't see how you could love someone and not like them."

"But he might have a point," I said. "If loving and liking go together, how can we ever love our enemies, as Christians are supposed to do."

"Besides," Kate said, "feelings change, and if love is going to last, wouldn't it have to be based on something more than feelings? On reason and choice?"

"But is that how you want to be loved by your boyfriend?" Molly asked.

"Well, I would certainly hope the relationship would be based on more than just feeling all soft and gooey around him," Kate said.

Just then the lights flickered and went out. Molly found and lit a kerosene lamp.

"In my opinion," she said, "love or friendship that comes from the mind or that's based on some rule or other pales in comparison to love that comes from the heart. It's kind of like this kerosene lamp. It's for when there's no electricity!"

For some reason this set us all to laughing. One of the British girls in the next room called out, "Quiet down in there, please!"

"I'm so glad we don't have to live with them!" Molly whispered.

Molly and I had promised each other that while we were in Belize City, we'd find ice cream. We'd been more than two months without it, and it's what we longed for most, more than M&Ms or peanut butter.

"If you want the best ice cream," Peg told us, "you have to go to the Regency Club. That's the social club where all the British and Americans hang out. And the Royal Creoles. But it's expensive, and anyway, you have to be a member or else be invited by a member. You can always go to the ice cream parlour over on Albert Street, but the stuff there is made with condensed milk."

When we asked who the Royal Creoles were, she replied, "They're the European British Hondurans, the ones who've been here for generations. The mostly white ones, even though some have intermarried. The rich ones."

"How can we meet some of them?" Molly asked. "I want to get in the Regency."

"Well, there's Julian Martin. Sue Ella and I know him. He's an announcer for the BHBC – the British Honduras Broadcasting Corporation. He and all his friends are members. We've been there with them a couple of times. I'll see if he can arrange something."

"In the meantime, let's go see Father Bosque's mother," I suggested.

"I forgot all about that," Molly said.

"I can always go alone if you'd rather do something else," I said.

"We only have one more day here, and I need to go to a bank and do a couple of other errands," Kate said. "And I need to find a pair of sandals. Flip-flops, like both of you have."

"I could use a new pair myself," Molly said. "You don't mind going alone, Abby? We'll meet her the next time we come."

I found my way to the address Father Bosque had given me. It turned out to be a large, weather-beaten house not far from PAVLA House. The woman who answered the door was obviously Father Bosque's mother; she had the same high cheekbones, green eyes and husky voice. Her thick hair, still dark but threaded with grey, was pulled back from her face like Lydie Quinlan wore hers, and when she smiled, I could see that a few side teeth were missing. She apologized for not being able to shake hands with me; her fingers were knotted with arthritis.

"You must let me kiss you, instead," she said, beckoning to me to lean down so she could brush my cheek with her lips.

"Bitsy!" she called out. "One of Charlie's girls is here!" She sounded just like Lydie as she said it.

An even smaller woman, completely white-haired, hurried into the hallway. Mrs Bosque introduced her as her sister, Elizabeth Usher.

"Everybody calls me 'Aunt Bitsy'," she said. "I hope you will too."

Sitting with them in the front parlour with its scuffed hardwood floors, half-open shutters and high ceilings, I drank the limeade and munched the ginger cookies they offered me.

"How long will you stay?" Mrs Bosque asked.

"Maybe half an hour," I said. "I hope that won't be too long."

Mrs Bosque and Aunt Bitsy laughed. "I don't mean your visit to us, my dear. I hope that will be as long as it may be, but your stay in the British Honduras." Mrs Bosque's phrase was something I would expect to find on one of David Lewis's old maps at the Forestry Station: "The British Honduras" as distinct from "the Spanish Honduras".

"We'll be here through the end of the school year, next April," I answered.

"My goodness!" Aunt Bitsy kept exclaiming. "Oh my goodness! To have come all this way from your home! You amaze me. Such an adventurous young lady!"

"And is our Charlie watching out for you?" Mrs Bosque asked.

"Oh, yes! He takes me with him into the bush when he goes to the villages to bring the sacraments. Well, not just me but also Molly, the other American teacher. And now another teacher has come, named Kate."

"He mentioned Molly," Mrs Bosque said, "but you are the one he talks about. He thinks you might have a vocation."

"A vocation?" I felt my heart shift gears.

"Yes, as a nun," she said. "Looking in your eyes, I see why."

Vocation: the call from God, issued only to the chosen ones. The ultimate distinction, as the nuns who had taught me made clear to me and my classmates.

"You embarrass her," Aunt Bitsy said.

"No, I'm not embarrassed," I said. "Just – surprised."

"Is it so surprising that God would choose you to serve him?"

"There are many ways to do that, I hope," I said. "Like you've done, being a mother and raising such wonderful children. Not just Father Bosque but also Mrs Quinlan, who has invited us so often to her home. Do you have other children?"

"Yes, I do," she said. "Four daughters and two sons. And another son who died, my very first child. It was a miserable way to start, losing him before he was even a year old. That's one of the questions I'm planning to ask God: 'Why? Why did you give him to me only to take him back so soon?' The others came one after the other, all good and healthy children, so I had to stop crying, even though I didn't think I ever would. Charlie is the youngest. He came with wheels, so to speak, all boy, and I was always running to keep up with him. It's true I was getting old by that time."

Mrs Bosque paused to pick up her glass for a sip of limeade, using both hands as a child would, because of the arthritis, and carefully put it back down again before going on.

"Even though Charlie grew up in the city, he loved the outdoors. He was so quick, he could catch a hummingbird with his hands. His father taught him to hunt, but he also taught him to kill only what he could eat. When he was twelve, Charlie killed a crow with his new pellet gun. I'll never forget how his father made him pluck it, cook it and eat it. He never killed for killing's sake again, that I know of."

Aunt Bitsy added in her fluttery voice, "He was a great tease. When he was seven or so, he put his pet mice under his mother's and my best hats. Do you remember that, Mamie? It was quite a sight to see those hats with their bows and feathers scooting around the living room floor. And the other thing he did, he was always making up funny poems about us. I can't recite them for you; they were just silliness, and besides, they were often quite naughty. I would never have expected him to become a priest."

"Oh, I always knew," Mrs Bosque said.

The atmosphere in the room where we sat reminded me of a church after High Mass, when the candles have been blown out but a sweet smell of wax, fresh flowers and incense hangs in the air. Listening to the soft voices of the old ladies, I felt like a spell was being cast over me. Around me, the wood glowed with a dark lustre in the late-afternoon light slanting through the shutters, and the paintings and objects on the walls took on a jewel-like radiance. An ornate silver and gilt crucifix hung alone on one wall, and on another was a small icon illuminated with red and gold. It was an image of Jesus, his exposed heart pierced by thorns, drops of blood falling.

I'd seen pictures of the Sacred Heart countless times before and found them either cloying or disgusting, sappy or morbid. This icon was different, and my eyes fixed on it. There seemed to be a light radiating from the eyes, and I couldn't tell whether it was part of the painting or some sort of reflection off its glossy surface. Whatever its source, the light transformed the entire image, one I'd always connected with suffering and death. Now, it unmistakably depicted love – passionate, divine love – made visible.

"That's a wonderful icon," I said. "I went to a Sacred Heart school, and there were pictures of the Sacred Heart all over the place, but I've never seen one quite like yours."

"It's a treasure, isn't it?" Mrs Bosque said, turning to look at it. "It came down through the family. Charlie has always loved it. We'll tell him you noticed it."

"You know the promise, don't you?" Aunt Bitsy asked. "That a house where the Sacred Heart is displayed and honoured will be a refuge, filled with love and blessings."

"Timid hearts will fill with fire and tepid hearts with zeal," Mrs Bosque added, probably from some prayer or other.

"I can tell that this is a special place," I said, knowing already that it would be almost impossible to convey the spirit of the place to Molly and Kate.

Later, when they asked me about it, I said, "I understand Father Bosque a lot better now. But it's something you have to experience for yourself."

"So you are the Americans dying for ice cream," Julian Martin said when the three of us met him the next afternoon at PAVLA House.

I immediately recognized his resonant voice with its cultivated British accent from listening to Radio Belize, but he looked totally different from the James Mason type I'd imagined. He was short and stocky and no older than we were, with dark, wavy hair. He had on a plaid sport shirt and khaki pants, much like the ones the male volunteers wore.

"Well, come along, dahlings, and I'll take you to the infamous Regency. You'll have your choice of vanilla and vanilla. That's all they serve, I'm afraid."

Outside he hailed a taxi, and we drove north from the centre of town for maybe fifteen minutes, along the sea. The club sat back from the road, enclosed by a stucco wall. The taxi dropped us off in front of the main building, also stucco, long, low and modern.

"The Regency isn't much to look at on the outside, or on the inside for that matter, but it's the best club in Belize. Would you like a look around the grounds before we go in?"

He walked us across a green lawn and past a tennis court, where a game of mixed doubles was going on. The players were dressed in regulation white. Nearby, Julian pointed out a medium-sized swimming pool, one of the few in the colony. Everyone in it, mostly women and children, was white, as were all those who sat under wide umbrellas on a concrete patio, having drinks after tennis or a swim.

As we entered the building, the doorman recognized Julian and greeted him by name. "Good afternoon, Mr Martin," he said. "Mr Kerr and Miss Gregg have already arrived. They're waiting for you in the dining room."

"I asked two of my friends to meet us here," Julian said to us. "I thought you'd enjoy meeting some of the locals."

Inside the club it was dark, with curtains drawn against the sun. I expected luxury – carpets, cushioned chairs – but all I saw were some simple wooden tables and chairs, a big dance floor, and a bar off to one side.

"These are the three young women I told you about," Julian said, introducing us to his friends. "Miles and Mimi, meet Kate, Molly and Abby, who are dying for ice cream."

"Well, you've come to the right place," Miles said. "The only place, as a matter of fact."

I wondered why Julian had called Miles a "local". He was actually a Londoner sent out by Lloyds Bank. Only twenty-five, he was already an assistant manager of the local branch after a mere two years in the colony. He told us he had his own apartment above the bank offices and invited us to stop by.

"There's a lovely little garden atop the roof of the building," he said.

"There's a quite funny story about that," Mimi said. "We all went up on Miles's roof to watch the changeover of traffic. The government decided it would be better for trade, you see, to switch from the British way of driving on the left to driving on the right, as the rest of the Americas do. It was the biggest event of the year a few years back – except for the hurricane, of course. It happened at midnight, and we took some champagne to celebrate. Then someone – I'm sure it was you, Julian! – started dropping pebbles from the roof, and then we all did. The police came and hauled us all off to jail. It was hilarious, though it didn't seem so at the time. All the bigwigs were down at the station bailing their kids out, including the chief of police!"

Molly, Kate and I joined in their laughter. Mimi, we learned, was one of *the* Greggs, the family that owned the biggest department store in British Honduras. Without any doubt, her father was a bigwig in town. She mentioned that she was just about to leave for her first year at Cambridge.

Julian said he hadn't gone away to university because he'd landed a job with the BHBC after finishing at St John's College.

"I didn't always talk this way," he said, referring to his accent. "It's an occupational necessity."

"He's our Eliza Doolittle," Mimi said, although her accent didn't sound much different from his.

"That makes me his Professor Higgins," Miles said. "His accent is good enough to fool even a member of the royal family. When Prince Philip visited the colony last year, he was totally taken in. Thought Julian, like me, was born and bred in Britain."

At last our ice cream came, cold and white as mounded snow. It was served in plated silver bowls surrounded by shaved ice in larger silver bowls. I took my first taste. Velvet in my mouth. It clung to my tongue, coated my teeth. Molly and I took a long time to finish ours. Each drop was precious.

As little as I like to admit it, it was a relief to linger in such a clean, comfortable place, surrounded by so much white! Ice cream, tablecloths, tennis outfits, all the men and women who wore them. They had found a way not to be the minority.

Chapter 12

THE GAME

MOLLY, KATE AND I had been back in Angel Creek only a day or two when Father Peck told us that we would temporarily have another housemate. Dorothy Jefferson was a Peace Corps volunteer who needed a place to stay until permanent housing could be found. We asked where we would put her.

"You'll figure something out," Father Peck answered. He said he'd have Gilly bring over an extra cot from the rectory and whatever else was needed.

Kate's bedroom (once mine) was the largest but also the hottest and noisiest. Molly's and my rooms, whose windows faced the sea, we judged too small to hold a second bed, desk and dresser.

"I guess she'll have to go in with me," Kate said.

That was the plan, until we met Mrs Jefferson. She was an African American more than twice our age, soft-voiced and apologetic about all the inconvenience she was causing us.

Gilly brought her bags up when I was alone in the house. "Wey dese go?" he asked.

"My room," I said, making a quick decision.

I gathered up my things and moved them into the room that was now Kate's, an easy matter since I still had everything except essentials in my luggage. I kept meaning to unpack everything and store my luggage at the convent as Molly had, to put up some pictures and arrange the few photos and other things I'd brought with me, but I just hadn't taken the time. It shocked me that I'd already been in Angel Creek three months, but in fact, the more time that passed, the more I resisted unpacking. Somewhere in the back of my mind, I kept thinking, *You'll only be here eight more months, and then you'll just have to pack everything back up. Why bother?* I often felt the same way about making my bed in the morning, but I usually did that, not wanting to leave it for Josie.

When Kate and Molly came in later that day, I explained what I'd done. "She's older than my mother," I said. "I just couldn't put her in that oven."

Kate sighed. "I'd rather room with you than a stranger, anyway."

None of us said anything about Mrs Jefferson's race, far more of a surprise than her age. Right or wrong, I think we all felt we owed her special consideration because of both.

At supper that night, Mrs Jefferson told us she was born in Mississippi but had moved to California after the Second World War and lived there ever since. She was a war widow, she said, with two daughters, now grown.

Mrs Jefferson was nothing like my stereotypes of African-American women, set for the most part by movies and books. They included the mammy, the torch singer and the athlete, personified respectively by the movie stars Hattie McDaniel and Lena Horne, and the tennis sensation Althea Gibson. In her quiet way, apart from age, Mrs Jefferson was our counterpart, just as educated and eager for adventure as we were. She'd joined the Peace Corps for many of the same reasons we had joined PAVLA.

She told us that she had worked for many years at the Better Business Bureau in San Jose. Most recently, she'd been employed in the audio-visual department of a local college there. When she heard about the Peace Corps, she decided to apply because it seemed like a wonderful way to see how people lived and worked in a different part of the world. She'd been assigned to teach secretarial skills and bookkeeping at St Monica's and also at St Michael's, the tiny Anglican high school in town. "I hope my business background will help these young people advance themselves," she said.

After supper, we offered to take her to meet the nuns and the priests. She said she'd be happy to meet them, but added, "I must tell you, I'm not a Catholic. Between us, I've always found nuns and priests a little intimidating."

"So do most Catholics," I told her.

I don't know who looked more surprised, Mrs Jefferson to find a convent full of black women, or the nuns to meet an African-American Peace Corps volunteer. Mrs Jefferson's jaw went slack, and Mother Eugenie looked from Mrs Jefferson to us and back again as though we were playing a trick on her.

"So you're Dorothy Jefferson," she finally said. "I had a letter from

Washington, DC, about you and also about a Mrs Moss. When will she arrive?"

"As soon as the Peace Corps finds permanent housing for us. I came ahead because I'm teaching, to be here for the start of the new term. I'm so grateful to these young ladies for welcoming me into their home."

"Of course, that house belongs to the Church," Mother Eugenie said. "It was originally meant to hold at least four, two in each bedroom. Father Bosque had the good idea of turning the dining room into another bedroom. I suppose we could house five or even six there, if need be."

Molly, Kate and I exchanged silent glances. I think we all felt a snarl of emotion at the thought of a permanent fourth or fifth housemate, of turning our home into a dorm. I know I did.

"Do you know the other Peace Corps volunteer very well – did you say her name is Mrs Moss?" I asked Mrs Jefferson on the way to the rectory.

Mrs Jefferson said she'd met her during training, that she was also a widow lady, a bit past sixty, who would be doing continuing education for adults in Angel Creek. She'd probably be moving from Belize City to Angel Creek in a couple of weeks.

Father Peck answered the door at the rectory. "All moved in, Mrs Jefferson?" he asked, shaking her hand. "Gilly told me you'd arrived. I hear you're someone who knows something about bookkeeping."

Mrs Jefferson nodded, looking up at him. She was tall, but he towered over her.

"Our parish records are a mess, thanks to Hurricane Hattie," he said. "I was just in there, in the study, trying to make sense of them. We could use a whole new system of record keeping. And so could the convent. Would you be interested in helping out with that sort of thing?"

Again, Mrs Jefferson nodded.

"Wonderful! Why don't you come over tomorrow afternoon around three so I can show you what needs to be done?"

Mrs Jefferson looked stunned. She still hadn't said a word.

"Well, I better get back to business," Father Peck said, ushering us to the door. "Father Bosque is out at the moment, but I'll send him over to meet you as soon as he gets back."

Back at the house as she unpacked her things, Mrs Jefferson asked us if we happened to have a phonograph player. "Mine is being shipped but hasn't arrived yet."

We told her there was one at the rectory.

"I ask, because I brought several of my albums with me, and I would love to share them with you. If you like opera, of course."

"We often listen to music with Father Bosque, the assistant pastor," I said. "He loves opera, and I like what he's played for us."

"If he loves opera, I'm especially eager to meet him," Mrs Jefferson said. "And Mrs Moss will be too. Opera is our passion."

"Do you sing?" Kate asked.

"A bit," Mrs Jefferson said. "Only in choirs. But I love singing." She hummed a few bars from an aria she identified as "Vissi d'arte" from Puccini's *Tosca*.

"Can you sing it?" I asked.

"I really can't do it justice. But I have a beautiful recording by Renata Tebaldi. I'll play it for you if the priests' machine is in good condition and if they'll let us use it. If they're careful people, I'd also consider lending them some of my albums."

"Maybe we can all listen together," Molly said.

"Yes! We could have opera nights," Kate suggested.

"What a splendid idea!" Mrs Jefferson said.

Molly, Kate and I were rearranging the furniture in Kate's bedroom when Father Bosque knocked on the door.

"Where's the new arrival?" he asked.

Even though it was only nine-thirty, Mrs Jefferson was already in bed.

"She's asleep," I said. "But she really wants to meet you. She's an opera lover, just like you. In fact, she's going to ask if she can use your record player."

"She has some albums, then. Sounds like we're going to make beautiful music together."

When he came into Kate's bedroom to help us move some of the furniture, the first thing he said was, "It's like an oven in here."

"Can you think of any way to make it cooler?" Kate asked.

He said the house was poorly designed. Bedrooms needed to face east, to catch the sea breeze. The only solution he could think of was to open up the interior wall between Molly's bedroom and Kate's. His question was whether we were willing to sacrifice privacy for cross-ventilation. We agreed it wasn't ideal but had to be done.

The next day, Father Bosque and Gilly removed a large section of the wallboard between the rooms. The breeze swept through the opening, blowing all the loose paper off Kate's desktop. She whooped for joy.

"Such a mess," Mrs Jefferson said, looking on as the men cleaned up the debris. "I'm so sorry if my staying here has caused all this upheaval."

"Not at all, Mrs Jefferson," Father Bosque assured her.

The opening in effect transformed the two bedrooms into one. An advantage was that, when we wanted to, the three of us could talk late into the night while Mrs Jefferson slept undisturbed across the hall.

"I'm just glad that Father O'Dea isn't around to see what's happening to his house," Molly said. She paused. "I probably shouldn't say anything because it will make me sound petty, but it would really make me angry if Mother Eugenie and Father Peck put Mrs Jefferson in here permanently without consulting us. And I wouldn't be surprised if they crammed this other person, Mrs Moss, in here too."

"I agree," I said. "It would be different if they were part of PAVLA. Or closer to our age. On the other hand, they obviously need someplace to go."

"Mrs Jefferson seems like a lovely person," Kate said.

"It's not about Mrs Jefferson, don't get me wrong," Molly said. "And I know we have room to spare, especially when you consider how everyone else here lives. What I object to is the way the nuns and priests do things. Everything is decided for us."

"But nothing is decided yet, is it?" Kate asked.

"That's the trouble," Molly said. "We wouldn't know if it was."

After a few days of living together, I decided that in Mrs Jefferson's case, age and temperament were far bigger differences between us than race. She was much more ladylike than Molly or me, or even Kate, who was something of a lady herself. Mrs Jefferson never slumped when she stood nor crossed her legs when she sat. She wore nylon stockings, even with sandals, and looked elegant even in her school uniform. She always had a fresh handkerchief handy and never left the house without her black leather handbag hanging from her arm. She smiled often, seldom raised her voice, avoided religion and politics as topics of conversation, and rarely asked a personal question.

Although she never complained, she must have found Molly and me, in particular, unpredictable and undisciplined housemates. We both loved variety, happily dropped whatever we were doing if something more interesting turned up, and stayed up far too late at night.

Unlike Molly, Kate or me, Mrs Jefferson held Josie to a high standard. "You missed some dust under my bed," she said the first day Josie cleaned her room. "Come, bring your broom, and I'll show you how to do it properly."

Another day, with her comb in her hand, she accosted Josie. "I found some hairs in this that aren't mine," she said in her usual quiet way. "You must never, ever use any of my personal things, Josie. I must insist on that, my dear."

Josie stood mutely staring first at the comb and then at the floor.

"Some of these townspeople seem content with sloppy work and uncivilized ways," Mrs Jefferson said one night at dinner. "We'll have to work hard to lift them above their upbringing, especially the young ones, like Josie."

"Dat new teachah lady, she no lak you an' Miss Molly an' Miss Kate," Josie grumbled not long after Mrs Jefferson's arrival. "She picky. And stahnoffish." Josie kissed her teeth in disdain. "She tink she bettah dan us. She worse dan de nons!"

Without walls between us, Kate, Molly and I usually talked ourselves to sleep. On one of our first nights together in the combined bedrooms, Kate told us about her family and the small town near the Canadian border where she grew up. Her father owned Mannion Motors, the General Motors dealership, she said, and her mother had been principal of the local high school until she became pregnant with her first child, Kate's older brother, Mark. By that time, she was in her late thirties.

"She stopped working to raise my brother and me," Kate said, "but she continued to run the town – or try to, anyway – from the kitchen, using the telephone. She's a strong woman, a force to be reckoned with. Everyone does what she says, including my father. He's just the opposite, low-key and laid-back."

"Who are you more like?" I asked.

"I'm probably a blend of the two of them," Kate said. "I usually go with the flow, like my dad, but I also have a lot of my mom's idealism, and I share her desire to make a positive difference. I guess that's one reason I came here."

Kate went on after a pause. "My mother is a great mother, but she's made me wonder if marriage and children are enough in themselves to satisfy an intellectual, high-powered woman. I wouldn't say that she regrets her decision to marry and have kids – she loves her children and her husband without question, and would do anything for us – but I'm sure that she wishes she could have continued her career. I guess she thought that she couldn't do justice to both and that she'd be missing out if she didn't marry and have kids."

"Interesting," Molly said. "I've always assumed that a woman would pick marriage over a career any day, if she had a choice, and that no one except nuns and priests would actually choose to be single."

"I wish it didn't have to be either–or," Kate said. "I know it's hard for a woman to do both, but I don't think I'll be able to choose one over the other. It's a dilemma!"

"Do you have a serious boyfriend?" I asked.

"No. For a while I was serious about a graduate student from Spain. Armando. I met him my junior year at Marquette."

"I remember him," Molly said. "From Barcelona, right? Nice looking, with a sexy accent. You introduced him to Paul and me. I think we went out for pizza together once."

"He's a great guy," Kate said, "funny and intelligent and a real gentleman. We even talked about getting married someday." She said he'd returned to Spain the previous January. They wrote, and things seemed fine between them, but when she saw him there in July, he was like a stranger. All the differences between them hit her like a slap in the face. She realized then that even with the most intelligent and understanding husband in the world, it would be hard to bridge such a big cultural gap. And the personal isolation, living in a foreign country, would be terrible.

"I'm sure it would be a huge adjustment," Molly agreed. "That's one reason – besides Paul, of course – that I don't want to get too involved with David Lewis." Molly was silent for a long minute. "Kate, I have to tell you about David." She paused again. "I know you were Paul's friend before you were mine, and you know him a lot better than you know me. I certainly won't do anything to hurt Paul, but I do like David – actually, it's more a case of his liking me. He's English, and he works at the Forestry Station. We're just friends, but he'd like it to be more."

"Does Paul know?" Kate asked.

"I did mention David in a letter to Paul, but that's all. Really, it's nothing serious. David and I have hardly ever been alone together. Why upset Paul for nothing?" I could hear the springs of her bed creak as she turned over. "You know, we ought to get to sleep. It's late. I'll tell you more tomorrow.

And Abby can tell you about her admirer, Eduardo. He's still a teenager and positively gorgeous."

"Great way to change the subject, Molly," I said.

"Sleep tight," she said sweetly in the darkness.

Eduardo sent word through Ana that the trip to Half Moon Creek for their nephew's baptism was scheduled for the following weekend, the last before the beginning of the new school term. Ana delivered the message when she stopped by to meet Kate and Mrs Jefferson, and at the same time invited both Kate and Molly to come along. I don't think it occurred to Ana to invite Mrs Jefferson, or to Mrs Jefferson – or any of the rest of us – to wonder why Kate was included and she wasn't. I think the age difference explains it, but I'm not sure.

Molly said that she and Kate had other plans; they would spend the weekend in Chetumal, just across the Mexican border.

How we were spending that weekend was a sore spot between Molly and me. The day before Ana stopped by, Molly had come home all smiles.

"I have a ride for us to Mexico next weekend!" she announced. She explained that she had run into Lydie Quinlan downtown with a man she introduced as her brother-in-law, married to one of their sisters – hers and Father Bosque's. As they talked, he mentioned he was driving up to Chetumal with one of his sons and offered to take the three of us along if we could get a ride out to meet him at his place, about an hour's drive from Angel Creek. "He said he'd bring us back too," Molly added.

That was when I told Molly and Kate about Eduardo's invitation.

"Why didn't you say something sooner?"

"I'm still not certain that it's going to happen," I said. "But if it does, it will probably be the same weekend as the Mexico trip. I'll talk to Eduardo or Ana about it, to be absolutely sure."

"I'd rather go to Mexico," Molly said. "You've been there, but I haven't. We can always go to Half Moon Creek some other time. There's not much there anyway except a lumber camp."

"I'm eager to see Mexico," Kate said. "I can practise my Spanish, which I need to do before I start teaching it next week." Kate, who'd studied Spanish through most of high school and college, had been assigned an introductory Spanish grammar and conversation class.

"Come with us," Molly said to me. "It will be more fun."

"But I promised Eduardo and Ana I'd go with them."

"You didn't promise for us, too, did you?" Molly asked.

"No, of course not. To be honest, I wasn't sure who was included in the invitation. I should have asked, but it all happened so fast, and then we left for Belize City. I haven't seen Eduardo or Ana since we got back."

"There's no reason we should do everything together," Molly said, but I could tell that she was upset.

"I'll happily go with you and Kate if I can," I said. "I'll find out the dates of the baptism for sure."

"It's up to you. Do whatever you want."

"I want to do both," I said.

"Then do whatever you want to do most."

Father Bosque offered to drive Molly and Kate out to his brother-in-law's on Friday afternoon to catch their ride. I wouldn't be leaving for Half Moon Creek until the next morning, so he invited me to come along. His two nephews were coming, too, he said, and he knew a great place where we could swim on the way back.

Molly climbed into the front next to Father Bosque, and Kate and I sat in the back with the boys, James and Ian, squeezed between us. Molly and I hadn't talked much in the past few days. It was our first falling-out, and I wasn't sure exactly what had caused it.

"You're going to miss a great time," she said with a sad smile as she hugged me goodbye when we dropped them off. "Take care of yourself, Abby."

Watching her and Kate drive away, I felt abandoned, even though I realized that they no doubt felt deserted, especially Molly. It was the first time we'd be apart for any length of time since our arrival in mid-June. Being on my own felt strange – but liberating too. Not that I was alone. There were Father Bosque and the boys, of course, and tomorrow, there would be Ana and Eduardo and their family. And Mrs Jefferson was waiting for me back at the house. But I felt joined to Molly, and now Kate, in a special way. A way I was afraid I'd jeopardized.

"Go ahead, take the wheel," Father Bosque said to me, climbing in the passenger seat.

As I drove, he gave me directions to the swimming place. After the rainy season, everything was lush, moist and green. Every couple of miles, the road crossed another stream rushing from the mountains towards the sea. All the bridges were one lane, but there was so little traffic it really didn't matter.

When we came to an unpaved side road, Father Bosque took over. He drove to the end of the road, and then for another quarter of a mile we bumped along a broad creek bed where the water spread out over flat rocks. When the creek deepened, we parked, changed into our bathing suits and walked another fifteen minutes upstream to a pool that looked blue-green under the overhanging trees. When we plunged in, the water was so clear that we could see to the bottom.

After a while, Father Bosque and I sat on one of the flat rocks while the boys continued to play around in the water.

"How are all of you getting along?" he asked me. "You, Molly, Kate and Mrs Jefferson."

I told him it was a big change, four in a house instead of just two, but added, "You know how close Molly and I are, and Kate's a wonderful person. Couldn't be easier to live with. Mrs Jefferson keeps pretty much to herself, but she's also very nice."

"Why didn't you go to Chetumal with Molly and Kate?"

"I'd already promised Ana I would go to Half Moon Creek with her. Her brother's baby is being baptized."

"I know. I'm doing the baptizing. How are you getting down there?"

"Eduardo is driving us."

"The three of you could drive with me."

"I think Eduardo's driving the truck down, loaded with supplies for the club. We're keeping him company."

"So you'll be staying with the Zachariases, then."

I nodded.

"So will I," he said. "There aren't many places to stay in Half Moon Creek."

"Do they have a big house?" I asked.

"It's an apartment over the club, like the Zacharias apartment here. Lots of room, but noisy. I recommend earplugs."

Father Bosque went back into the water while I stretched out on one of the flat rocks and almost immediately fell asleep. When I woke up, I saw that he had taken some bread, butter, jam, chocolate and oranges out of his bag and spread them out nearby.

"Oh good!" Ian, the eight-year-old, cried out as I opened my eyes. "She's awake! We can eat now."

"Uncle Charlie made us be quiet so we wouldn't wake you up," James added. He was a couple of years older. "It was hard because we were starving."

"Well, thank you for waiting!" I said. "I'm starving too."

"That must be why you waked up," Ian said. "You probably heard your stomach growling."

We didn't start for home until close to sunset. "Uncle Charlie said we can look for eyes in the bush on the way home," Ian announced.

"What does that mean?" I asked.

"That means we can help him hunt," James said. "Eyes mean a wild animal, and if we spot the eyes, he can shoot whatever it is."

"Only if she doesn't mind," Father Bosque said.

"What sort of wild animals?" I asked, looking at the bush all around us.

"Peccaries," Ian said.

"That's wild pigs," James said. "If we shoot one, we can roast it or stew it. My mum knows how. Very good."

"Okay," I said. "I've never hunted before, but I'll give it a try."

"Just look very hard for anything that glints," Ian instructed me.

Father Bosque always had his rifle in the back of the Jeep when he drove into the bush. That night, he drove with it across his knees.

We travelled a few miles in the gathering darkness. "Eyes!" Ian said, grabbing Father Bosque's shoulder in his excitement. "Right side, two o'clock."

Father Bosque put on the brakes and raised his rifle. I saw only darkness. "Gone," he said.

A few more miles. "Eyes!" This time it was James. "Left side, nine o'clock." I saw eyes, and then I didn't.

We lurched our way back to Angel Creek. It was after nine when we pulled up in front of the house.

"No luck tonight," James said.

"Just as well, James," I said. "I'm just getting used to this hunting business."

"Uncle Charlie says that's how life is," James said, "and we better face it. Life feeds on life. That's where hunting comes in."

"I'm just quoting your grandfather," Father Bosque said. "Remember: not killing for its own sake, but death for life. And remember, that works two ways: to a jaguar, you're fair game, young man. You're a delicious dinner!"

Early the next morning, I sat in the front seat of the Zacharias truck between Ana and Eduardo. He was a silent driver, focused entirely on the road. The pavement ended ten miles out of Angel Creek, and from there on it was ruts and dust the rest of the way to Half Moon Creek.

Mid-morning, Father Bosque came roaring by in the blue Jeep. He passed us with a grin and a taunting wave of his hand. An hour later, we came to a wide, shallow river and saw him sitting cross-legged on a rock by the water, reading his breviary. As we drove by him, Eduardo pressed his foot down on the accelerator and spun up a cloud of red dust.

Within fifteen minutes, Father Bosque was passing us again at top speed. I thought I heard him yell, "Eat dust, Eduardo!"

When Eduardo dropped Ana and me off in front of the Zacharias club, I saw a figure at an upstairs window, and a few minutes later a round-faced woman with glossy black hair and two small girls with exactly the same face and hair came down the outside steps. Eduardo said he had to park the truck and drove off.

"This is Emilio's wife, Elena," Ana said. "My sister-in-law. She's from El Salvador and understands more English than she speaks."

Elena nodded vigorously, greeting me in English: "You are most welcome to be here," she said. The little girls looked at me from a safe distance.

"These are my nieces, Blanca and Clara," Ana said.

"How old are you?" I asked.

"Four," Blanca said in a surprisingly loud voice. "Clara is two."

"Two!" Clara repeated, holding up her tiny hand and slowly uncurling first her middle finger and then her forefinger.

"This is our friend, Abigail," Ana said, taking me by the hand. "Say hello."

Blanca, the older girl, took the hand I offered. "You wan' watch Clara go pee-pee in the toilet bowl?" she asked me.

Ana and Elena both laughed. "Elena is potty training Clara," Ana said.

"Is struggle," Elena added.

She led us upstairs to the big apartment, where Father Bosque sat at the kitchen table with a man who looked like Eduardo probably would in another ten or twelve years, fleshy but still handsome, with large, luminous eyes and the beginning of a double chin. He stood when we came in the room, and Ana introduced him as her second oldest brother Emilio. He shook my hand with a few words of greeting and offered me his chair.

Eduardo soon joined us, and the two little girls ran to him. Blanca climbed up on one of his long legs, and he lifted Clara onto the other.

"They love their Uncle Eduardo," Ana said. "More than me."

Blanca wrapped both arms around Eduardo's neck and kissed him repeatedly on his cheek. Clara caught hold of his ear and his nose and pulled his head towards hers.

"Kiss Clara," she said.

Blanca pulled him towards her. "Me first!"

"Quite the ladies' man, Eduardo," Father Bosque said. "How does it feel to have girls fighting over you?"

"I don't mind," he said, kissing first one and then the other.

A baby cried in another room, and Elena said something in Spanish to Ana and hurried off.

"She says dinner is almost ready," Ana said, "but she has to feed the baby first."

Ana and I set the table, reaching around the men to place the plates and glasses. Elena brought out her infant son, named Emmanuel after his grandfather, and handed him to Ana on her way to the stove. The baby drew me like a magnet, and I happily took him when Ana went to help Elena arrange *chiles rellenos* on a platter and put the meal on the table. Emmanuelito fit perfectly in the crook of my left arm. I looked up and, embarrassed, saw that all three men were watching me.

It felt good to be in a family again, to have children to care for and household tasks to do. After the midday meal, Emilio and Eduardo went off to take care of the things we'd brought in the truck. Father Bosque stayed on in the kitchen with Elena, the children, Ana and me, switching between Spanish and English. He fascinated the girls by making a coin disappear, only to find it behind one of their ears. He couldn't do it often enough for Blanca, who would shriek with delight at each discovery, commanding, "Do it again!" Clara would repeat, "T'gain!" not quite understanding what was going on but excited nonetheless. They played until Elena took them in for a nap.

On the way to the cupboard with a stack of clean plates, I walked by Father Bosque. He grabbed the edge of the apron Elena had lent me and asked in a teasing voice, "Having fun playing housewife, Abby?"

I put the plates down and fluffed up the apron. "Do you like my outfit?"

"Are you sure it fits?"

"You think it doesn't?"

"It might be too small for you. But only you can tell."

"Maybe I'm just trying it on for size."

"Well, then, how about bringing me another cup of coffee?"

"I'm not playing waitress."

He laughed. "Okay, I'll get it myself."

"No, I'll get it. As a favour. Because you never make fun of me."

"Can't help it," he said. "You know I love to tease."

He drank his coffee, and then left to make arrangements for the Sunday services. No church had been built yet, he said, and he had to be sure the mess hall at the mill, the only large space in town except for the club, was free. Otherwise, we would have Mass outside, in one of the empty lots.

Ana and I spent the rest of the afternoon helping Elena prepare food for the Christening celebration the next day. The kitchen was big and bright but lacking most of the conveniences and appliances of a kitchen in the States. Besides a couple of free-standing cupboards and some shelves, it contained only a sink, a stove and a tiny refrigerator fuelled by gas. The one luxury, if you could call it that, was a beautiful table made of local mahogany. I sat there chopping onions, peppers and tomatoes on a cutting board, while Elena expertly plucked, cleaned and cut up chickens – a smelly, bloody job – and Ana did the baking.

About three o'clock, Eduardo came in and sat down across from me with a glass of water. I glanced at him, then looked down and continued chopping.

"Do you like to cook?" he asked me.

"Yes," I said. "The problem is, my grandmother and mother are both terrific cooks, so I usually only do desserts."

"What kind do you make?"

"Cakes, mostly, but out of boxes, and cookies. Snickerdoodles are my specialty. I've made a pie or two. My mother says I make good pie crust."

"Pie crust is very hard," Ana said from across the room.

"It's easy to do one thing at a time," I said, "but I can't imagine having a whole meal ready at the same time."

"You could serve courses," Eduardo said, lowering his voice, talking only to me.

"Dinner could take two or three hours that way," I said, also lowering mine. "That would require long dinner conversations. If you came to my dinner party, what would you like to talk about?"

"Your life in the States," he said.

"Pretty boring most of the time."

"I don't believe it. You have so much there to do."

"But there never seems to be enough time to do it."

"What do you like to do?"

"Same things I do here. Enjoy friends, go to new places, meet new people, learn new things. Read books. And I like nature."

"What do you like about nature?"

"Being outdoors. I like natural beauty, I guess. The sea, the mountains, birds, flowers – even insects can be beautiful." I finished chopping the last of the vegetables. "What do you like to do?"

"Be with my family. Work hard and accomplish things. Make other people happy."

"How do you make other people happy?"

"Find out what they like or want and give it to them, if I can." He paused. "I would like to give you something."

"Me? Why me?"

"I would like to make you happy."

"I am happy."

"But you often look sad. Lonely."

"Come to think of it, you often look kind of sad yourself," I said. "Or if not exactly sad, very serious."

"I know how to tell who is more serious."

"How?"

"It's a game we used to play when we were younger. That's what we called it: 'The Game'. You have to look each other in the eyes, and the first one who laughs or looks away loses."

"I remember that game," Ana said, coming over to the table. "It's harder than you think. Eduardo always won, at least when I played with him."

"It really doesn't sound all that hard," I said.

"Let's try," Eduardo said.

"Are there any other rules besides not laughing or looking away?"

"No talking or making faces."

"What are the stakes?"

"Anything you want."

"All right," I said. "The loser has to find something to make the winner smile."

"Excellent," he said.

"I'll act as judge," Ana said, sitting down between us.

Eduardo and I settled ourselves on opposite sides of the table. He took a last gulp of water.

Elena came over to stand behind Ana's chair and watch. She asked Ana something in Spanish, and Ana replied in English, "They're playing a game."

"Tell us when to start, Ana," Eduardo said.

"Now!" she said.

He was ready before I was, and the intensity of his gaze caught me off guard. My eyes widened in surprise, and I almost looked away to get my bearings. At the same time, I felt a nervous giggle bubble up in my throat. I swallowed, clenched my teeth, and steadied myself. I willed myself to return his stare, strong and penetrating. The temptation to say something, anything, irritated me like an itch. How else to distract the mind behind those eyes and divert it from its sharp scrutiny? I felt exposed, vulnerable and, without knowing why, cowed by feelings of shame. I sat up straighter and, resisting the feeling of panic that swept over me, held firm.

Paradoxically, the look of mastery in Eduardo's eyes strengthened my resolve. He thought he had bested me, and my sense of how close he'd actually come strengthened my resistance. I scrutinized him in turn, searching his eyes for some sign of weakness. His gaze wavered slightly as mine grew more determined.

The excruciating absurdity of the game suddenly hit me. I bit my lip and scrambled mentally for sad memories. Lady, my beloved fox terrier, who disappeared when I was eight. Didn't work. I squeezed my hands together under the table until the flesh stung and the bones crackled.

"What's going on?" It was Father Bosque's voice.

"They're playing a game," Ana said. "Eduardo challenged Abby, and they're both really good at it."

I felt my concentration slipping. My willpower went with it. I blinked and realized I had unconsciously been holding my breath. I gasped for air and let it out in what could have been mistaken for a laugh. At exactly that moment, Eduardo glanced over at Father Bosque.

"Too close to call," Ana said. "You'll have to do it again."

"I'm ready," Eduardo said. "What about you, Abigail?"

I felt dizzy and disoriented. My hands, still in my lap, tingled as though they'd been burned. "No," I said. "I need a break."

"How about taking me on, Eduardo?" Father Bosque asked. "I'll sit in for Abby."

Eduardo swallowed another drink of water. "Have a seat."

I gave Father Bosque my place and went to stand next to Ana. My hands were still slightly trembling and my legs felt wobbly.

Ana explained the rules to Father Bosque. The two men put their elbows on the table and leaned towards each other. "Get ready. Go!" Ana said.

Eduardo and Father Bosque faced off. The priest's entire body looked alert, just as it had the night he and his nephews had looked for eyes in the bush. It was as if Father Bosque had Eduardo in his sights and was staring down the barrel of his rifle at him. Eduardo frowned and realigned his shoulders. Five minutes went by and stretched to ten. After a quarter of an hour, Eduardo's face and neck were slick with sweat, and his shirt was damp with it. Without moving his eyes, he slowly wiped his jaw with the back of his hand. As he did, his elbow bumped his water glass, tipping it over. Water spilled all over the beautiful table and the glass rolled towards the edge. As Eduardo grabbed for it, he momentarily looked away.

"Father Bosque wins!" Ana shouted.

Eduardo nodded, wiping his face with the tail of his shirt.

"I didn't win," Father Bosque said. "Abby did. Don't forget, I was playing for her."

"Thanks, but I play for myself," I said.

"Then you'll have to take me on as well as Eduardo," Father Bosque said. "But not right now. Right now, I need some help. I'm hoping you and Ana will go around town letting people know where and when the Mass and baptism will be tomorrow. I'll put up some signs while you're going door to door."

"Of course, Father," Ana said. "That way, I can show Abby the town."

Half Moon Creek had existed for more than a decade, Ana said; nevertheless, the town looked recent. In many ways, it reminded me of a larger version of Hawkens Creek, where Molly and I had often gone with Father Bosque. None of the houses were painted, all the streets were unpaved, and the air smelled of resin from the sawmill. The mill was the main source of employment in the area, with logs brought in daily by boat from the rain forests to the south.

The population of Half Moon Creek was not only larger than that of Hawkens Creek, it was also more diverse, with many more Garifuna. Ana said most Garifuna didn't live in town but came by dory to Half Moon Creek from fishing villages along the Placencia Peninsula to the east, across the lagoon. Most came to sell their fish, but a few worked in the mill, as did a large contingent of Mexican immigrants.

Knocking on doors with Ana at my side, I no longer felt like a foreigner. Everyone I met assumed I somehow belonged to Ana's family. With my tanned skin and my embroidered Mexican blouse, I looked anything but North American.

"Weh you from?" a Creole woman asked me. "El Salvador?"

I said I was from the States.

"You lang time up dere?"

"Yes," I answered. "Almost my whole life."

"Wouldn't it be nice to be sisters?" Ana asked as we made our way back to the Zacharias apartment. "My only sister left when I was still small. I've always wanted a sister close to my own age."

"Is that why you're trying to match-make?"

Ana giggled. "Eduardo does like you, you know. All on his own."

"And I like him, but I hardly know him. We've spent very little time together. Even when we do, like driving down, he hardly speaks. I've seen him for maybe an hour since we arrived, and most of that was playing a game where we couldn't talk. The rest of the time, he's working!"

"Yes, he does work most of the time. It's his way of getting ahead as fast as he can. But I know he wants to spend more time with you."

"Well, then, why doesn't he?"

"He isn't sure you want him to. And my father asked him to go slow. You have to understand it's different here."

"I do understand that. But when it comes right down to it, I guess I'm not sure exactly what the differences are."

About eight o'clock that night, Eduardo came up from the club to shower and change. He came over to the table, where Ana, Father Bosque and I had just finished a supper of rice and beans and leftover stuffed peppers. Elena was putting the children to bed.

"Do you want some food?" Ana asked.

"I ate something downstairs," he said. "There's going to be a big dance tonight, and we're getting ready for a crowd. The band will start playing in about an hour. I hope you will come down."

"I don't dance," Father Bosque said.

"You can have a drink, though, and enjoy the music," Eduardo said.

"I'll escort the ladies, if they want to go."

"Oh, we do!" Ana said. "Abby and I can dance together."

"Be sure you save a dance or two for me," Eduardo said.

When we entered a little after nine, the Half Moon Club was already crowded. Men outnumbered women at least three to one. I'd barely walked through the door when a man who might have been Mexican came up to ask me to dance. Before I could accept, Eduardo appeared and stepped between the stranger and me. He said something in Spanish, and the man backed off without a word.

"You shouldn't dance with strangers," he said, taking my hand and leading me to the dance floor. "Ana will introduce you to some friends of ours."

"But what's the harm in dancing with a stranger? I'd like to meet some of the people who live here."

"There are some bad characters around. It's best to avoid them. Ana will introduce you to people we know."

When the music stopped, Eduardo guided me towards Ana and Father Bosque, sitting near the bar with two men and a woman. One was a young man named Alfredo, who said that he taught standard six at the local grade school. Every now and then, he asked Ana or me to dance, but most of the time he sat talking with the other man, Pablo, and the woman, Mercita, who were also teachers. Pablo and Mercita seemed to be a couple; in any case, they danced only with each other.

"You said before you don't dance," I said to Father Bosque while Alfredo and Ana and Pablo and Mercita were on the dance floor. "Is it because you don't know how or because you don't like to?"

"Neither," he said. "I would dance every dance if I could. But I can't. Not as a priest."

"Is it against the rules?"

"There's no rule that says, 'Thou shalt not dance.' But don't you think it would be inappropriate for someone everyone knows is a priest to be seen dancing with a young, unmarried woman?"

"But married people dance with other people's wives or husbands all the time, at least at home they do, and no one thinks anything of it. And people dance with total strangers. There's nothing wrong in dancing, is there?"

"Many people would say that as a priest I shouldn't even be in this bar, not to mention sitting here alone with you. And drinking this beer on top of it. It may seem arbitrary, but I draw the line at dancing. At least, couple dancing.

Even I wouldn't be comfortable doing that. But here comes Eduardo. He'll dance with you, I'm sure."

During the evening, Eduardo danced with me several times, but his breaks from bartending were too few to satisfy me. The band was very good, and I decided that no matter what Eduardo said, I'd dance with whoever asked me. But after that, no one asked, even though the room was full of unattached men looking for partners. Once they saw that I was with the Zachariases, they kept their distance.

At ten the next morning, Emmanuelito was baptized at an outdoor Mass. Ana, his godmother, held him, and his godfather, Eduardo, stood beside her. There were about fifty of us at the Mass, half of whom were Mexicans. We stood in a semi-circle around a table that had been carried outdoors from the dining hall at the mill. All around us were stacks of freshly cut lumber, waiting to be carted off.

As Father Bosque poured water over the baby's head, I saw Eduardo brush aside a drop that slid towards Emmanuelito's right eye. How carefully he protected those he loved!

Everybody but the Mexicans, who weren't invited, followed us back to the club for the Christening party. It went on into the afternoon. That night there would be another big dance with the same band, and Eduardo would stay on because his brother needed his help. Father Bosque offered to drive Ana and me back to Angel Creek, but he said we had to leave right away because he didn't want to drive those roads in the dark.

As I was packing my things in the room I shared with Ana, I heard someone tap lightly on the door behind me. Expecting her, I didn't turn around. "Come on in, Ana," I called out.

"No. It's me, Eduardo." He stood in the doorway. "May I come in?"

I nodded, too surprised to speak.

"I brought you something. A gift."

"A gift?"

"Because you won the game."

"But I didn't really win."

"It's not to keep. Just to remember."

I noticed that his hands were cupped, as if in prayer.

"What is it?"

"Open the shutters, and I'll show you," he said, nodding at the window. I did what he asked.

"Now, let's lean out together."

We did, our shoulders touching. He held out his hands and opened them. A butterfly, iridescent blue, emerged as from a cocoon. It hovered in the air in front of us as though reluctant to leave. We watched its erratic motion until zig by zag it disappeared into the distance.

I turned to Eduardo. "That's the best gift I can imagine!"

"Now I know how to make you smile," he said. "Next time, I'll bring you a bag of butterflies. We'll let them go one by one."

Chapter 13

A BUSY WEEK

THE FIRST DAY OF the new term had not gone well for any of us.

"How do you do it, day after day?" Kate asked as we waited for Josie to bring our supper. She was late, and we were hungry.

Kate was taking over some of the courses Molly and I had taught the previous term, along with one of Ana's beginning Spanish classes. Instead of seven classes, Molly and I now had only five each, as did Kate, but unlike her, we were at loose ends, wondering how best to use our free time.

Her biggest worry, Kate said, was her Spanish class. "I was so excited to be teaching Spanish, because I thought it would force me to become fluent. Only to find out I have two native speakers in the class! What am I going to do? They already know so much more than I ever will."

Mrs Jefferson, too, voiced concern over her teaching load. She was in the classroom from eight in the morning until four in the afternoon, she said, with time off only for the midday meal. Because she was teaching at two schools, she had to walk back and forth between St Monica's and St Michael's three times each day, carrying all her books. "At least I'll be in fine shape by the end of the term," she said with an uncharacteristic hint of sarcasm.

"And the classroom building!" Kate said. "First of all, it looks haunted. Everything falling down, the yard full of debris. And then, to have Sister Veronica teaching math at one end of the classroom while I'm teaching history at the other end. I know we're in a temporary building and don't have enough classrooms, but it's dreadful. And worst of all, in the middle of literature class this afternoon, a chunk of the ceiling fell down. It missed me by inches! It's only luck it didn't fall on a student."

"This morning, the first thing Sister Veronica asked me was why Kate and I had missed Mass this morning," Molly said, with a pointed glance in my direction.

When they had arrived home from Chetumal the night before, sometime after midnight, I'd woken just long enough for them to ask me to get them up at five a.m. so they wouldn't miss the opening Mass of the school term. The next morning when I was unable to rouse them, I decided to let them sleep on until breakfast.

"What were you thinking?" Molly wailed. "You should have thrown water on us."

"When you didn't wake up, I decided it was crazy for you to try to teach all day on four hours sleep, so I didn't keep trying."

"Well, it's a crummy way for us to start the new term. You know we're all expected to be there. Kate and I counted on you!"

At that point, Mrs Jefferson remembered to tell us that she'd heard from Mrs Moss over the weekend. "She's hoping to come down from Belize City next week. They really don't have anything for her to do up there."

"Does that mean the Peace Corps found a house for you?" Molly asked.

"No, not yet, I'm afraid."

"Is Mrs Moss planning to move in here too?" I asked, trying to sound nonchalant.

"I had a talk with Mother Eugenie yesterday morning, and she said she'll work something out."

Just then, Josie came in with our supper tray. "Ahl de students talkin' 'bout de new teachah wid de blue eyes an' de blond hair," she said. "Dey tink you only sweet, Miss Kate! You jes like de angels, dey say."

"I wish they'd judge me on something more substantial," Kate said. "I had nothing to do with the colour of my eyes or hair. They're just accidents of birth."

"As are many of the things that matter most, my dear," Mrs Jefferson said, managing a smile. "Please don't underestimate their power."

As soon as we finished eating, Molly stomped out of the house. She returned an hour later in a visibly better mood.

"Where did you disappear to?" I asked her.

"I'm sorry I've been so bitchy lately," she said. "I haven't been feeling well. The bites are still infected, and I noticed in Mexico that I have a swelling in my armpits. I decided to go see the doctor."

"The one Father O'Dea said was a quack?"

"Dr Bauer is definitely not a quack. He's great. It wasn't his office hours, but he invited me in. He has a wonderful house. It's his office too. So old-world, and filled with nice things. An oriental carpet on the floor and a Tiffany-style lamp with an amber shade. He examined me and said I should let the hair grow on my legs and under my arms. Says he doesn't know why American women shave themselves like we do. The hair is protective, he says, and keeps off the bugs. And he said the lumps are because I've been shaving my armpits too close, and it irritates the glands, or something like that. I feel so much better just having talked to him."

"What a relief," I said. "I'm glad it's nothing serious."

"He wouldn't take any payment. Not a penny. And he said he'd teach me German! He'll teach all of us, if we want. He invited us to stop by for schnapps this evening, sometime after eight, when his evening office hours are over. He said he'd love to get to know us."

"I don't think I can come," Kate said. "I have too much class prep. I still need a couple of hours before I'll be ready for tomorrow."

"I'll come," I said. "I've always wanted to taste schnapps."

"Maybe I can go just to meet him," Kate said, "and leave after half an hour."

Molly hesitated a moment before she asked Mrs Jefferson if she would like to come too.

"It's kind of you to ask, Molly, but no," she said. "You know how early I go to bed. You can tell me all about it tomorrow."

Dr Bauer's combined house and office was on the corner of Front Street and Doctor's Alley. I'd passed it many times on my way to the river and had occasionally seen the doctor around town, although always from a distance. He was Angel Creek's only MD, a general practitioner who was also the town's dentist. Father O'Dea had fumed because the "quack" didn't fill teeth, only pulled them – at five dollars BH a tooth, half a week's salary for most people in Angel Creek. "He's not only incompetent, he's mercenary," he told us.

"Ah, *lieblich* Molly!" Dr Bauer said when he opened the door. "And these are her charming friends." His voice was deep, and he spoke English with quirky syntax and a thick German accent that we found quaint. Instead of shaking our outstretched hands, he bowed briefly over them and brushed them with his lips.

He was a well-fed man of about fifty, with bushy eyebrows, lively brown eyes, thick grey hair and a full beard, rosy cheeks and moist, red lips whose touch I could still feel on my hand. He wore a short-sleeved white shirt, walking shorts with multiple pockets and expensive-looking brown leather sandals with socks.

"Come in! It is too long we have not met. We must become friends!"

The room was full of books, most of them in German, and smelled of pipe tobacco, a spicy scent that was strong but not unpleasant. He sat the three of us down and poured the promised schnapps into fragile, gold-rimmed glasses.

"To your good health!" he said, raising his glass.

I cautiously wet my lips with the clear liquid. It stung, and when I licked my lips, I tasted peppermint.

"So you are the young ladies from the States." He regarded each of us in turn. To my surprise, he then set down his glass, leaned forward, grabbed hold of my ankle and lifted my leg for closer inspection. "You too have the bites very bad, young lady," he said to me. "I will tell you what I have told Miss Molly here – please do not shave the legs! You must realize hair on the legs and underarms gives natural protection and also is very much attractive!" He returned my leg to its former position. "You, Miss Kate (he pronounced it *Kaht-eh*), do not have this problem."

"I just arrived," Kate said, "and so far the bugs seem not to notice me."

"Still, promise that you will let grow the hair on the legs."

"Thank you for the advice, Dr Bauer," Kate said.

"And so, for the German lesson!"

Before Kate could excuse herself, he pulled out a few books and for the next hour, impressed on us that the German language was the tongue of poets, philosophers, scientists and scholars. In his resonant voice, he read aloud a passage he said was from Goethe's *Wilhelm Meisters Lehrjahre*. He said he had selected it with us especially in mind:

> "*Kennst du das land, wo die Zitronen bluhn?*
> *Im dunkein Laub die Gold-Orangen gluhn,*
> *Ein sanfter Wind vom blauen Himmel weht,*
> *Die Myrte still und hoch der Lorbeer steht –*
> *Kennst du es whol?*
> *Dahin! Dahin!*
> *Mocht ich mit dir, o mein Geliebter, ziehhn!*"

"What does it mean?" Molly asked.

He translated for us:

> "Do you know the land where the lemon trees bloom?
> In the dark leaves, golden oranges glow,
> a slight wind blows from the blue sky,
> but the myrtle is still and the laurel stands tall –
> Do you know it well?
> There! There!
> I want to go there, oh my beloved, with you!"

He paused, holding the book open in his hands. "Can you say why I have chosen this passage?"

"The description reminds me of Angel Creek," Molly said. "Especially the part about the lemons and the oranges. Is that why?"

"Very good!" He beamed. "Can you think of perhaps something else?"

"We can relate to the poet's desire to leave his ordinary world for a different, more exotic one," Kate said. "I guess that's a universal longing."

"*Brava!* You are very smart young ladies."

"It sounds to me like the poet wants an erotic adventure," I said. "But I'm not quite sure how that relates to us."

"The erotic impulse – is not that what underlies all longing?" the doctor asked, looking at me over the top of his reading glasses. "Does not the sexual impulse fuel all desire? Define all beauty? Drive all knowledge? Propel all discovery?"

He closed his book, set it on the table next to the amber-shaded lamp, took off his glasses and put them on top of the book.

"Until you can understand this wonderful author in his own language, you should not have satisfaction! It is like hearing of the orange blossoms without smelling them, to have only translation. I will help you know their fragrance!"

"Could we really learn that much, Dr Bauer?" Molly asked, her voice breathy. "We don't have much time."

"You can begin. But you, young ladies, must give yourself entirely to my instruction. You must prepare the lessons I give you and come faithfully at least twice in each week. If so, you will make great progress."

"May I think about it?" Kate asked. "I don't want to take on something I can't finish."

"Of course," he said, lighting and sucking on his pipe.

"You make it sound very tempting," I said. "But I'm trying to learn some Spanish, and I'm afraid I'm going to mix them up."

"These languages are very different."

"I would love to come whenever you have time," Molly said.

During study hall on Tuesday morning, Ana came into my homeroom and whispered in my ear, "Eduardo came back from Half Moon Creek yesterday. He asked me to give you this." She handed me a white envelope and hurried back to her own classroom.

It was an invitation to the movies, written in a strong, flowing hand. If I accepted, he wrote, Ana would join us so that everything would be "proper".

When I saw her in the hall between classes, Ana looked at me expectantly. Obviously she already knew what was in the message. I nodded my consent.

At our midday meal, I told the others that Eduardo had invited me to the movies and would be picking me up at seven-thirty.

"Good, I'll get to meet him," Kate said.

The film was *All the Fine Young Cannibals*, and it starred Robert Wagner and Natalie Wood. I sat between Eduardo and Ana, and midway through the film, he leaned close and whispered, "Now do you see the resemblance?"

I shook my head. As before, the comparison made me uncomfortable, as though I were a stand-in for the real Natalie.

After the film, Ana and Eduardo both walked me home. She waited at the bottom of the steps while Eduardo took me up to the door. As we said good night, Father Bosque drove up in the Jeep. He stopped, said a few words to Ana and then called out over the sound of the engine, "Come on, Eduardo, and I'll drive you and Ana home!"

"I'll see you again when I can," Eduardo said. "If you agree."

"I'm always happy to see you, Eduardo," I said.

As the Jeep drove off, I wondered just what I'd agreed to.

"Things seem to be very friendly between you and Eduardo Zacharias these days," Father Bosque said as he balanced his plate on one knee. He'd brought his food over to where I sat on a folding chair in the Quinlans' front parlour and pulled up a chair next to mine.

I took a bite of the spicy chicken with black bean sauce. "Mmm! This is very good! Happy birthday, by the way! Were you surprised?"

"That you and Eduardo are so friendly? Oh, you mean the party."

"Stop teasing me, Father Bosque! You know I meant the party."

"Yes, I was surprised. I haven't had a party like this since I was a kid. Why don't you want to talk about it?"

"The party?"

"Okay. I know it's none of my business."

"There's not much to talk about."

"That would be a sad day, if we had nothing to talk about."

"You know I don't mean that."

"Where do you think Lydie got the crazy idea to throw a surprise birthday party for me?"

"She said the older we get, the more surprises we need."

"I'm not all that old," he said.

"She said you're thirty-two."

"I don't think that's very old. Do you?"

"Not very," I said. "Anyway, you seem a lot younger."

"How young?"

"Sometimes, like tonight, about twelve!"

He let out a loud laugh. "Well, you like younger men. No true?"

Without responding, I took another bite of my chicken. He'd touched a sore spot, and I could tell from the sly look in his eye that he'd intended to.

Lydie had issued invitations to the party only the day before. "If I did it any earlier, he'd be sure to find out," she said. "Don't breathe a word. He thinks it's just a family dinner. He's coming at six, so everyone else should come at five-thirty."

"I'll bake a cake," I offered.

"If you bake it, we'll eat it."

After class on Wednesday, the day of the party, Kate and I went over to the convent to bake the cake for Father Bosque while Molly shopped for a present. The cake turned out lopsided, but we iced it and decided to take it to the party anyway. Molly found a crucifix made of straw at Lee Wong's store, and we wrapped it in red tissue paper. She also bought two boxes of tiny red candles. We counted out thirty-two and stuck them on the trapezoidal cake.

Lydie had asked me to invite Ana, who at first accepted, but at school on the morning of the party said she'd changed her mind. "There are bad feelings between Betty and me. I'm sure she'll be there, and I'd rather not see her."

Betty was the oldest Quinlan daughter, Ana's age, already married and the mother of a six-month-old son.

As Molly, Kate, Mrs Jefferson and I were leaving for the party, Eduardo drove up in his Jeep. He looked me over with a smile. "You look nice," he said.

I'd pulled up my hair in a French twist and put on my sleeveless, raspberry-coloured dress. He handed me two bottles of wine, wrapped in cellophane, and asked me to take them to Father Bosque from his family.

When we arrived, the Quinlan house, one of the largest in Angel Creek, was full of people. All the Quinlans and their neighbours and friends, along with Father Peck, Mother Eugenie, Sister Veronica and Gilly, were there. Mrs Jefferson sat spellbound with Father Peck and the two nuns, listening to their eye-witness account of Hattie. Lydie had her arm around Kate and was introducing her person by person to everyone at the party.

"Ana sends her regrets," I told Father Bosque as we finished our supper. "Apparently there's some misunderstanding between her and Betty."

"Did Ana tell you they were once best friends?"

"No, she didn't tell me anything."

"Ana was determined that Betty should marry Javier, one of her older brothers."

"You mean the one who lives with the older woman?"

"That's the one. Apparently, at one time they were interested in each other, but then Betty met Phil. When they started seeing each other seriously, Ana took it as a personal betrayal. At least, that's what Betty says. I'm sure Ana has her side of the story. In any case, they haven't spoken since Betty and Phil's marriage a year and a half ago."

Father Bosque's comments made me uneasy. How many of Eduardo's feelings came from him and how many from Ana? That question, which almost unnoticed had been nibbling at the back of my mind, suddenly bit hard.

"I really would like to talk to you about Eduardo," I said. "Later, when you have time."

"Let's get some more wine and go out on the veranda. There's a full moon rising."

The Quinlan house was on Front Street and faced the sea. I headed for the front door, but Father Bosque took my elbow and guided me to the stairs.

"Let's go to the upper balcony," he said, and led me up and out onto the deserted second-storey porch.

"Shouldn't you visit with some of your other guests?" I asked him.

"I have, and I will," he said. "But it's my birthday, after all. Isn't that moon spectacular? Who could ask for a better birthday present? And as a reward for putting up with my teasing, I'm sharing it with you."

We leaned together on the railing, our eyes on the moon.

"Why do you tease me about Eduardo?" I asked.

After what seemed like a long time, he answered, "Honestly, I don't know. I tease my nieces too. I guess it's a sign of affection. And curiosity, to see how they'll react. And maybe a little bit of a warning, to let them know I'm noticing something that I think they ought to be aware of. Would you rather I didn't?"

"I really don't mind. I tease you too." I paused and then forced myself to ask, "Do you think I'm making a mistake to be friends with him – with Eduardo?"

"It's not what I think that matters," he said. "What do you think?"

"What you said about Ana and Betty worries me. I'm afraid maybe Ana's pushing him – and me too – into a relationship. And I feel like you're warning me off for some reason."

"It's more like trying to bring things into the open."

"But why, if they're my private feelings?"

"So, you do have feelings for him?"

"I'm not sure what I feel. That's part of the problem."

Just then, we heard Lydie call out, "Charlie? Has anybody seen Charlie? We're going to cut the cake! He has to blow out the candles!"

"We'll continue this later," he said.

"Just one request," I said as we went down the stairs.

"What's that?"

"When you hear who made the lopsided cake, try not to tease."

As Molly, Kate and I were leaving the party, Ruthie Archer, a friend of Lydie Quinlan, called out to us.

"You three have to help Lydie and me out," Ruthie said. "Please say yes!"

"If we can," Molly said.

"The Jamaican football team – I guess you call it soccer – is playing here tomorrow afternoon, a demonstration game, and the Beaumonts are throwing a party for them afterward, at the Sportsman Club in the valley. Lydie and I are helping organize it. It's a last-minute thing, and we need girls to come, lots of young, pretty girls. Won't you help us out?"

"Of course!" Molly said. "At least, I will."

"It sounds like fun," I said.

"If you're both going, I'll come too," Kate said.

"I'll pick you up a bit after eight. The game is at four, on the field, if you'd like to watch some of it. Wear your prettiest clothes. To the dance, I mean. What you have on would be fine."

Walking home in the moonlight, Kate asked in a worried voice, "How do you ever find time to prepare for class? There's always something going on."

"There's lots of time," Molly said. "After Mass, during your free period, right after classes. On weekends."

"It isn't always this busy," I said. "It's one of those weeks when there's a lot happening."

"I'm worried not just about Spanish," Kate said. "The 'Gracious Living' part of the composition class is giving me trouble too."

"Gracious Living? What in the world is that?" Molly asked.

"Well, I think that the students need to work on their manners," she said. "So I decided to include etiquette in our composition class. After all, we're educating tomorrow's leaders. Some will have careers, and many will be the wives of important men. And of course have children to raise."

"What are you teaching them?" Molly asked.

"We're working on introductions at the moment," Kate said, "but we're almost through with those. I want to talk about table manners. But I have to think of ways to have the students practise things like how to set a proper table and use the right fork. I don't have any equipment to work with."

"Have you seen how our students live?" Molly asked. "Some don't even have tables in their houses. Certainly not dining tables."

"But it's an important part of an education," Kate said. "What good will it do them if they can talk about Jane Austen and the Magna Carta, but don't know a butter knife from a steak knife?"

"When you put it that way, I guess it makes a certain amount of sense," I said. "Maybe Josie can borrow some silverware and plates from the convent for you. Or you can make some out of cardboard."

"What a great idea!" Kate said. "But all that takes time."

"I can help," I said, "if you really think it's important."

"Yes, I think it is," Kate said. "It's knowledge every civilized person ought to have."

Overnight, the weather changed. On Thursday, the sky was overcast and the wind had an edge to it. By late afternoon, a drizzle had started. After class, I put on a sweater and walked down to the field along the sea to watch part of the football game. It was hard to see the field because people were lined up two and three deep along the sidelines. Not far off, I saw David Lewis standing alone and went over to say hello. I hadn't seen him since our return from Belize City, and so far as I knew, neither had Molly. He hadn't yet met Kate.

"I've stopped by your place a couple of times," he said, "once over the weekend and again last night, but I haven't found anyone at home. You're not avoiding me, are you?"

"Why would you think that? We're just busy."

"Molly was supposed to send me a note when you got back from Belize City, but I haven't heard a word."

"Maybe she forgot. Honestly, there's a lot going on." I explained about our new housemates.

"Have you heard that there's a party for the Jamaican team tonight? If you're not too busy to make time for another event, I'd be happy to give all of you a lift out to the Sportsman Club."

I told him we already had a ride but thanked him and said we would see him there.

As we waited for Ruthie to pick us up, I said to Molly, "I ran into David today, and he thinks you're avoiding him."

"Well, I am, in a way," she said. "I don't want things to get any more complicated than they already are."

When we walked into the Sportsman Club, the entire Jamaican team, substitutes included, were already there, some thirty or forty of them mixing with a crowd as diverse as Angel Creek itself. As host of the event, Mr Beaumont greeted us and introduced his wife, recently returned from a visit to England. We also met the Olivers, who owned everything in Paloma Valley that the Beaumonts didn't. Together, the two families employed most of the town in one or another of their enterprises.

Many of our friends and acquaintances were there: the Todds, our neighbour Therese and her sister-in-law, Mr DeSantos, who'd given Molly and me paint for the classrooms, and an elegant woman he introduced as his wife.

We made our way around the room, greeting those we knew and introducing Kate.

The Cains were there, too, without Sherry. "She's at home, supposed to be doing her homework," her father told us. "In any case, as you probably know, the sisters frown on their students attending mixed parties like these."

No wonder Rosie had been so eager to have us attend. Some of the unmarried female teachers from the grade school, also recruited by Rosie, arrived in a group. Otherwise, I saw no single women there without a brother or other family member to chaperone them.

I knew that Javier, one of Eduardo's older brothers, ran the Sportsman Club, but when I first saw him behind the bar, I thought he was Eduardo. I kept looking in his direction, wondering why he didn't show some sign of recognition. Only when I moved closer did I realize my mistake. So this was Javier, four or five years older than Eduardo but looking enough like him to be his twin. And the man working with him must be Alberto, another Zacharias brother. Alberto resembled his Syrian father more than his brothers, who must take after their Salvadoran mother.

Ana had described Alberto as the black sheep of the family, interested only in pleasure. She said he worked as little as possible. Still, his father favoured him, making excuses for him and keeping him on the family payroll. He lived with a young Creole woman named Posey. According to Ana, they were a "lethal" pair. They both drank too much, she said, fuelling their hot tempers. When it came to verbal and physical abuse, though, Posey could give as good as she got.

I'd seen Posey around town; she was the sort of woman you couldn't ignore. Not only was she striking, with her honey gold skin and masses of auburn hair, but also she flaunted her good looks. In a town where most of us wore flip-flops, she wore spike heels. Her skirts, a couple of inches shorter than anyone else's and twice as tight, revealed long, smooth legs; her low-cut blouses barely constrained what I can only describe as buoyant breasts. There she was, perched at the end of the bar, alternately smoking a cigarette and sipping a Corona straight from the bottle.

With his oiled, Elvis-style haircut, tight trousers and black shirt with the collar turned up in back, Alberto's good looks were just as flamboyant as Posey's.

"You must be Alberto," I said after Kate and I had ordered our drinks. "I'm

Abby, and this is Kate. We're friends of Ana and Eduardo. Do you know if they're coming tonight?"

"No, I don't." For several seconds, he silently sized us up. Then he called out above the noise of the crowd, still looking at us, "Javier, are Eduardo and Ana coming tonight?"

"Not that I know of." Javier came over, and Kate and I introduced ourselves. "So you are the American teachers," he said, adding that he'd heard about us from Ana. "I think Eduardo went to Belize City on business this morning and won't be back till the weekend. Ana wouldn't come alone."

Alberto handed us our Heinekens, his eyes on Kate. "Later, maybe I'll come ask you American teachers to dance." I could see Posey watching from her end of the bar.

"It looks like you're very busy tonight, with this crowd," Kate said.

"Too busy to dance," I added.

"I doubt you'll be needing partners," he said.

There must be some soccer players in the world who are not good dancers, but none of them were at the Sportsman Club that night. *They certainly are a rhythmic group*, I wrote later in my journal. *What footwork! And stamina!* If any woman young or old at the party wanted a rest, she had to go to the ladies' room to get it, because as soon as one of the Jamaicans released us, another was there to claim the next dance. Many cut in on their teammates, joking as they made off with their partners.

Kate never once sat down. She was a good dancer, light on her feet and able to improvise a plausible response to any music. On the dance floor, reserved, controlled Kate became, as Lydie put it, "who she was born to be."

David Lewis walked in alone not long after the music started. Molly saw him and waved, but he finally had to cut in to dance with her. Not long after, I saw Molly heading for the door with David. As she passed Lydie on the dance floor, I saw her stop to say a few words.

"Molly said to tell you that David will take her home," Lydie said to me later, while the band was taking a short break.

"But it's not even nine o'clock," I said. "I hope she's all right."

"She twisted her ankle. She can walk, but she said it's starting to swell."

It was after midnight when Ruthie dropped Kate and me off at our house. When we turned on the light in the hallway, we saw that Mrs Jefferson's door was closed but Molly's was open. Her room was empty. Just then we heard a car drive up. From the front window, I could see that it was David's Simca.

David got out and helped Molly up the outside staircase, and after a few minutes, the door opened and Molly limped in, holding onto his arm.

"Have you been home long?" she asked.

"Just got here," I said. "We were surprised and a little worried when you weren't here."

"David and I went to his place so I could soak my foot." Her face was flushed.

"David, meet Kate," I said. "Kate, David." They shook hands. "Just say hello right now, because it's late, and we don't want to wake Mrs Jefferson."

"We'll all get together soon," David promised.

When he'd gone, I turned to Molly. "How are things between the two of you?"

"Good," she said. "We talked for a long time, and I think we understand each other better now. I made it clear that I'm still committed to Paul."

"How did he take that?" I asked.

"He said we'll just be friends, if that's what I want."

"Is that what you want?"

"What I want is to go to bed."

"How's your foot?" Kate asked.

"Swollen," she said. "But it doesn't hurt if I don't put much weight on it. I'll see the doctor tomorrow."

The next day, Molly's left ankle was discoloured and twice its usual size. Leaning on the two of us, she managed the short walk to school.

"You should have stayed home," Sister Veronica said. "If you want to go home now, we can cover your classes for you."

"It's easier to stay now that I'm here," Molly said. "At least until I can see the doctor."

We all knew that an illness or injury that seemed insignificant in the States could have dire consequences in Angel Creek. Almost weekly, we heard stories of townspeople, many of them children, dying suddenly of dysentery, fevers, infections, and common childhood diseases like measles and chicken pox.

Over the noon hour, Kate and I took Molly to see Dr Bauer, who was just finishing his midday meal. He asked us to join him, saying the roast beef was excellent. When we told him we couldn't, he said, "Oh, yes, I forget Friday is fish day for Catholics." He asked his houseboy to bring us some cheese and bread. Molly happily accepted, and Dr Bauer said he would drive her home after he examined her ankle.

I was eager to get back to school, because this was the afternoon that the IIIB composition class would select articles for the first issue of our school newspaper. I'd decided to delay publication until after break, knowing I'd have more time to work on it once Kate arrived. I had also hoped for more submissions. Any student could contribute, but as my most advanced group, the IIIB class would edit the paper and have final say on what to include. The class took its editorial responsibility seriously, knowing that we had only about a hundred sheets of legal-sized paper to work with. We had to get all the news onto the front and back of a single sheet.

When I arrived at class, one of the juniors, Phyllis Lopez, was arguing with her classmates about whether it was too late to submit an article for consideration. The deadline had been the first day of the new term.

"I couldn' write it befoe now," she protested. "It jes happen! Dis be *new* news."

"What's it about?" I asked.

"Miss Molly accident."

"We ahlready have too much news," one of the students said. "Save it for de next issue."

"But she be ahl bettah by den."

"Den you have a happy ending," said another student.

"But what if she get worse?"

"Den you have a bettah story," a third replied.

The class decided to sit on the story and wait for further developments.

By consensus, they chose as their lead an account of an event hosted by their class the week before break. The headline read: POWER FAILURE AND MERENGE LEND EXCITEMENT TO JUNIOR TEA PARTY. One of the juniors had written:

> The tables were set and the eats were ready at the junior class party on Thursday evening, 23 August 1962, when the lights went out. The love songs that the students had been dancing to stopped and so did the dancing. The American teachers began to sing, and everyone joined in until someone brought a gasoline lamp from the convent. By its dim light the delicious food, not cold yet, was served and eaten. The meal ended with cake and pudding, some of it spilling on the floor when the students started dancing again in the gloom and bumped into a table. Everyone sang while they danced the Twist and then the Merengue.
>
> Miss Zacharias began to dance the Merengue along with the students. Believe

it or not, neither Miss Eliot nor Miss Porter knew how to Merengue, so Miss Zacharias and the students showed them. Miss Eliot went this way and that while Miss Porter went that way and this. Everyone sang and danced until the party was dismissed at approximately 9 p.m.

There was some debate on how much junior class news was allowable. The students reluctantly agreed that the Tea Party article was enough and settled on reports of a sophomore class party and various club activities as their other news stories. All of them focused on the St Monica social scene.

ORIGINAL SKIT OPENS FIRST MEETING OF ENGLISH CLUB, submitted by another junior, reported on an event that all of us who had been present recalled as one of the highlights of the first term. The skit had been set in an English classroom where students of various ethnic backgrounds struggled to speak and make sense of standard English. The teacher, played by one of the students, became increasingly irate over the mispronunciations and grammatical errors committed by her students. The more mangled the sentences of the students became and the more contorted with rage the teacher's face, the harder the audience laughed.

"Why we haf to learn dis English?" one of the students in the skit had asked in a stage whisper when the teacher's back was turned. "It only hard!"

"Le's ahl speak our own language!" another student had suggested.

"Arrite den!" they all agreed, and each one began speaking fluently in a different language.

I'd recognized Garifuna, Creole, Spanish and Chinese, and there may have been some Hindi and Arabic in there too. At least one student in the school, and often many more, spoke one of those languages at home.

"Wha' you say?" each questioned the others in English, only to have the babble repeated.

Rapping her ruler on her desk, the teacher faced the class and delivered the moral of the play: "You silly gals! You cannot understand each other without English! Now you know why you must study and use proper English!"

"Dis de troot, Teachah!" the students responded in unison. "We shall complain no mo. We ahl shall study an' speak propah English now!"

Most of us, students and teachers alike, realized that what passed for "English" was actually closer to Creole, the dialect (many would say language) that almost everyone – including the speakers of Garifuna – could speak more fluently than English. English, however, was the official language of the schools, whereas Creole was the language of the streets. In Angel Creek, neither was the language of the majority. That was Garifuna (called "Carib" at the time). In essence, the education of most of our students took place in a foreign language.

The "English Only" policy in the schools – there was a fine for speaking anything other than standard English on school property – was the subject of our lead editorial, written by one of the Creole students: WHY SPEAK ENGLISH, MON?

> The English language can be difficult in its pronunciation and proper word arrangement, especially for those who use another language at home, but English must be studied and learned. Who knows? Sometime we may be called upon to speak or deliver our opinion as educated people. How embarrassed we would be if we could not keep from stumbling over our words! We must encourage each other to speak English properly. This is the reason for the school rule banning Creole and Carib from the classroom. Only with constant practice can we know the right thing to say at the right time in perfect English.

I was surprised that the students chose this particular editorial, because in spite of its provocative title, which we all liked, it unquestioningly supported the school policy.

"What would you say most students think of this school rule?" I asked the class.

"Dey complain," several students said.

"Then I think you should be prepared to defend your reasons for choosing an editorial that argues in favour of it."

"We choose it because it explain de reasons foh de rule," one student said.

"Yes," another added. "It hep us unnahstahn why we have dis rule."

"You don't want to question the rule, or argue against it?"

"Oh, no, Miss. We complain, but we know it foh de best."

Like the students, I understood the reasons for the school policy and could live with it, but that didn't mean that I liked it. Especially the mindless way it was enforced. Just that week, Sister Veronica had chided me – not unkindly, but pointedly – for inviting some of the Garifuna students in my religion class to teach the rest of us the Lord's Prayer in their language: "I know you mean well, but if you give the girls an inch in this matter, they'll take a mile," she had warned.

Class was almost over, but there were still a few questions I wanted to raise. In a section called FLASHES AROUND TOWN, one of the first-form girls had written: "Warning! Beware on Saturday nights, for the 'killers' are in town: recklessly driven Jeeps, buses and bikes that endanger the lives of St Monica High girls."

"Is this a real problem?" I asked. Not counting the vehicles at the Forestry Station, I could think of perhaps five Jeeps in the entire town and only a couple of Land Rovers. There were no more than ten trucks that served as buses to different parts of the colony and maybe twice as many bikes.

"Oh, yes, Miss," the students assured me. "So many vehicle on de weekend dey come from bote direction at once!"

"One final decision," I said. "And it's an important one. What are we going to call our newspaper?"

Silence.

"How about the *Three B Newspaper*?" Phyllis Lopez finally suggested.

"But it a newspapah for de whole school," the class objected.

"Den how about the *Busy Bee*? We de B class, and we be like busy bees gettun ahl de news, like de name say – and evrybady in de school be busy, too, doin' ahl de tings we report."

"Dat right!" everyone agreed.

It was a wrap. We were ready to go to press.

When Kate and I arrived home from school that afternoon, we found Mrs Jefferson and a tiny, wrinkled woman with masses of wild, grey hair drinking tea together in the living room. There was a pile of luggage in the corner. Alice Moss, the other Peace Corps volunteer, had arrived on the afternoon truck from Belize City.

"I couldn't stand it there one day longer," she said to us after the introductions were over. "Belize is the most unpleasant city in the world, with those hideous canals crawling with rats, and the streets so crowded and noisy. It seems much nicer here. Up there I just sat in the filth and the heat waiting for something to do. I'm eager to get started on real work."

"You know we don't have a house yet, Mrs Moss," Mrs Jefferson said in her gentlest tone.

Mrs Moss looked around doubtfully. "Is there room for me here?"

"You'd have to double up with someone," Mrs Jefferson said. "And there's only one bathroom. It hardly seems fair to these young women to crowd them like this."

"There has to be someplace I can stay until we have a house."

Figure 8. Assembled students, with teachers. (To the left, the temporary girls' high school and background right, the Papal Volunteer House.)

"Let's finish our tea. Then we'll go see Mother Eugenie. She's the superior of the convent, and she promised to help find a place for you."

After they left, Molly called out from behind her closed door, "Come in. I'm awake." She was lying on her bed with her swollen foot propped up. Dr Bauer had put an elastic bandage on it and given her some pain pills.

"He doesn't think it's broken, just a bad sprain," she said. "What's going on out there? When I woke up, I heard Mrs Jefferson talking to somebody, but I couldn't tell who it was."

"Mrs Moss has arrived from Belize City with all her luggage," I said.

"So she's moving in here?"

"Probably," I said. "Where else can she go?"

"We don't know for sure," Kate said. "They've gone over to talk to Mother Eugenie."

Just before supper, Mrs Jefferson and Mrs Moss returned, followed by Gilly. "I'm joining the convent," Mrs Moss announced. "Gilly is moving me in."

"She's not really joining," Mrs Jefferson assured us. "But the sisters are kindly putting her up in one of their spare rooms. They have a very nice one on the first floor. Mother Eugenie said the two volunteers lived there last year, before this house was built. Mrs Moss can stay there until we get our own place. In the meantime, I'll continue sleeping here, if you don't mind. But I'll be eating over there with her from now on."

"Wouldn't you both rather eat here with us?" Kate asked, always the gracious one.

"It's kind of you to offer, but it would be difficult for Josie to carry so much over and back. This way will be easier for everyone. In fact, maybe you can join us there for some meals."

"Yes, we'd like that," I agreed, and the others nodded.

"Mother Eugenie really surprised me," Molly said later. "I'm embarrassed that I jumped so quickly to conclusions. I guess I underestimated her."

"I have to confess I didn't feel particularly welcoming when Mrs Moss showed up," I said.

"You know, I just arrived myself," Kate said. "And from my perspective, you've both been extremely hospitable, not just to me but also Mrs Jefferson. But Molly's right. At times you can be pretty hard on the nuns."

"Well, they should have talked things over with us – " Molly began.

" – before the guests started arriving!" I finished.

After such a busy week, Molly, Kate and I decided to spend the weekend catching up on schoolwork. Molly was still nursing her ankle, staying off it as much as possible, and Kate had a pile of unmarked quizzes and essays. They spent most of Saturday in their rooms. Without a desk after Mrs Jefferson's arrival, I usually worked at the dining room table, now in the living room.

Mid-afternoon, I thought I heard a faint knock on the front door. I waited a minute and heard it again. Couldn't be Father Bosque. He usually called out as he came right in.

When I opened the door, there stood Jaime, the Zacharias son who looked like Eduardo must have at eleven. He held out a sealed envelope with my name written on it. "Eduardo sent you this, Miss Abigail," he said, as shy as ever.

"Come in, Jaime," I said. "Sit down. How about something to drink? Orange juice?"

"No, thank you," he said. "Eduardo said you should read it right away."

"I will," I promised, "but sit down at least for a few minutes. I haven't seen you in ages. What have you been up to?"

"School, Miss. Eduardo came home from Belize City late last evening, so today I helped unload the truck. And then he said please to bring you the letter while he finished."

"Thank you," I said. "Do you need to wait for an answer?"

"Yes, Miss. He said to wait."

"Then have some juice."

I took the envelope into the kitchen with me, opened it with a knife and read it there.

> Dear Abigail, I am back from another trip away. May I come to see you tonight around seven? May I come alone? Eduardo.

I brought the juice to Jaime. "Drink this while I write back," I said. I took a piece of notebook paper from my binder, but I couldn't think of what to say. Where could we meet? Privacy was the rarest privilege in Angel Creek. I decided I'd figure that out later.

> Eduardo, Yes, I'll see you here at seven tonight. Abby.

Only after I'd stuck the folded note in an airmail envelope, the only kind I had, and sealed it did I remember that he always called me Abigail.

"Did you say yes?" Jaime asked.

"It's private, Jaime," I said. "Why do you want to know?"

"He said he would take me to the movies tomorrow if you said yes."

When I told Molly and Kate about Eduardo's imminent visit, they both assured me they wouldn't mind spending the evening in their rooms.

"I have enough work to keep me busy for a week," Kate said.

"I'd go visit Therese or Dr Bauer," Molly said, "but I'd have to walk there. I'll catch up on some letters."

Mrs Jefferson, who'd begun having her meals with Mrs Moss, had already told us she planned to spend the evening with her, maybe take her to the movies.

When he arrived at seven, Eduardo and I had the living room to ourselves.

"I hoped to see you before now," he said, sitting on the edge of the armchair, the cup of tea I'd poured for him untouched beside him. "Things keep coming up, like the trip to Belize City. Someone else was supposed to go, but at the last minute, I had to."

"Even when you're here in town, you're usually working when we see each other," I said.

"I know. I don't like working in the clubs or driving the trucks, but I have to start at the bottom before I can do what I want."

"And what is that?"

"To cultivate citrus. To own and work in the groves. I love every part of that. It's my dream. Mile after mile of orange and lemon and grapefruit trees, blooming and bearing fruit. And my house on a hilltop – it will have a red tile roof and white stucco walls – looking over it all."

I smiled, imagining the sweetness of such a life.

"Do you realize this is almost the first time we've seen each other alone?" I asked him. "With time to talk? Even in Half Moon Creek, you were usually working."

"That's how things are here," he said. "Young people aren't supposed to be left alone. Of course, they find ways."

"But people live openly with each other, like some of your brothers do." His face reddened, so I didn't mention his father and Marita. "I guess I just don't understand."

Eduardo took a minute to drink some of his tea and carefully put the cup back on its saucer. "Those relationships have nowhere to go. Even when there are children. Men only marry girls with good reputations. At least, in my family."

"But how can people get to know each other if they don't spend time alone together?"

"I know it's different in America. And my father knows that too. I have a brother and a sister who live there, and they try to explain things to us. That's what I want to tell you. Yesterday, I asked my father for permission to get to know you better. And he said yes."

Eduardo reached out as if to take my hand. I leaned towards him, but by then he'd drawn back. "But my father also said it won't be easy because this is a very busy time. In a few days I have to go to El Salvador for a week or two, and in a few months, I may have to live with Emilio and Elena in Half Moon Creek, to help out at the club there."

"What does it mean, Eduardo – that your father gave permission? For what?"

"I said already. For us to see each other."

"But what does that mean if you'll be gone most of the time?"

"That nothing stands in the way. That he approves if we want to go forward."

"Do you mean . . . fall in love?"

Eduardo blushed deeply, his face shining like polished brass. "I mean come to an agreement."

"An agreement? That sounds like a business deal, not a friendship."

"Friendship? That's for you and Ana."

"You mean males and females aren't friends here?"

"Maybe small children. Usually, though, boys and girls stay apart, except for brothers and sisters."

"It's just so different in the States. I wish I understood how things work here; what the codes are."

"Codes?"

"Of behaviour. The things you know just by living in a place that outsiders like me need explained. What you can or can't talk about, for example. Things that tell you where you are in a relationship, like a pin or a ring does back home. Or whether you even are in a relationship, like flowers or a phone call after a date."

Eduardo looked lost. "If you have questions, Abigail, ask, and I'll try to answer. Or maybe Ana can explain for you."

"Well, there is one thing I'd like to know." It was the question that had been bothering me ever since Father Bosque's birthday party. "Is seeing me your idea? Is it something *you* want?"

"It is, of course," he said, looking me in the eyes. Then, briefly, his gaze wavered. "But I wouldn't want it if my family didn't want it too."

It was my turn to look lost. I understood his words, but nothing in my experience of family could help me imagine that sort of connection and control.

The minute the front door closed behind Eduardo, Molly's door opened a crack. "Can we come out now?" she asked, peeking round it.

"He's gone. You can come out too, Kate."

Kate's door immediately swung open. She looked sheepish.

"You have to tell us everything," Molly said.

"Weren't you listening at the door?"

"Of course not!" Molly said.

"With all the noise in the street on a Saturday night, we couldn't hear a thing," Kate said. "I mean, even if we'd tried."

We all sat down, and I did my best to sum up the conversation. When I finished, which took a while because they both kept interrupting with questions, I said, "As you can probably tell, the gist of all this is I'm really not sure what's going on."

"I think he was telling you that his intentions are honourable," Molly said. "That he plans to court you, with his father's blessing."

"I don't think we're anywhere near that yet."

"Where do you think you are?" Molly asked.

"I don't know exactly. But it feels to me a little like passing the entrance exam for college. You're in the door but still a long way from graduation. In this case, though, I honestly don't remember applying for admission."

"That's my question," Kate said. "Did Eduardo ask you whether you want to – what did you say his words were? – 'go forward'?" Kate asked.

"No, come to think of it, he didn't. That's another reason I think he wasn't proposing anything more serious than, say, going on a first date would be back home."

"Would you ever consider living here permanently?" Molly asked.

"Whoa! That's jumping way ahead!"

"It's something you should consider," Molly said. "To be honest, I don't think I'd want to. Not permanently. No matter how much I like it here. It's a hard life."

"I would if I loved somebody, and he loved me," I said.

"It seems to me," Kate said, "that instead of wanting you to move here, whoever it was would probably want to move to the States."

When Molly and I laughed, she said, "I'm only half joking."

Glad to have something to take my mind off my conversation with Eduardo, I spent most of Sunday afternoon in the study at the rectory typing the stencils for the *Busy Bee*. Father Peck had gone for the weekend to one of the missions, and Father Bosque suggested I use the priests' Underwood typewriter. It was bigger and would do a better job than my little portable.

When I finished, I took the stencils to the mimeograph machine and lined up the paper, feeling extremely proud of myself.

Father Bosque stuck his head in the door. "How goes it?" he asked.

"Good," I said. I started the mimeograph machine, expecting to see columns of type. Instead, plain paper flew out.

"What's wrong?" Father Bosque came over to look. "You forgot to remove the protective paper before you started typing," he said. "It has to be done all over again."

"More than two hours of work for nothing! Do I really have to do it all again?"

"No," he said.

"No? Do you mean it's okay after all?"

"I mean that I'll retype it for you."

"Oh, no, Father! Why should you do that?"

"Because I want to. Show me what you want done."

He was a far better typist than I was, but it still took him over an hour to redo the stencils. I sat next to him, interpreting the handwriting of the students and showing him the layout I'd worked out on my first try.

"Some of these articles are really imaginative," he said as he finished retyping the newspaper. "Did Victoria Flores come up with the idea of interviewing you and Molly about your impressions of Angel Creek and St Monica's all on her own?"

"She certainly did."

"So you think the students at St Monica's are willing to learn and have a great deal of wonder? That wonder is the beginning of knowledge?"

"Yes, that's what I think."

"Tell me a little more about the connection you see between wonder and knowledge."

"To me, wonder is a mixture of doubt and curiosity and amazement. All of those emotions, if that's what you want to call them, get the mind going. And when the mind gets going, it learns."

"So learning starts with the emotions?"

"I never thought of it that way before, but yes, I guess it does. As a teacher, I do spend an awful lot of time trying to get the students to care about what they're learning."

"I guess that explains your statement here about Angel Creek being a wonderful place to 'love and learn'."

"I didn't say that! I'm sure I said 'live and learn'. See, here it is in Victoria's original."

"My mistake." He grinned at me. "It's going to be hard to change it now. You may just have to 'love and learn'."

Chapter 14

THREE FIRES AND A DISAPPEARANCE

THE HOUSE THAT THE Peace Corps found for Mrs Jefferson and Mrs Moss was a couple of blocks from ours. The day they received the key, Gilly piled their luggage into the blue Jeep, and Josie, Molly, Kate and I followed on foot, carrying buckets, a mop, a broom, dust cloths and sponges. The house had been empty for weeks while the Peace Corps negotiated a lease. We were on our way to help the women at last move in.

"Mrs Jefferson was certainly an interesting and considerate housemate," Kate said. "I'm going to miss her."

"I don't disagree," Molly said, "but I have to wonder how comfortable she was with us. I don't know much more about her now than I did when she arrived. She made herself invisible most of the time."

Kate opened her mouth to reply, but Josie interrupted. "Hah! She invisible to you, but Ah see plenty a dat lady, and I cahn tell you, she don' miss noting! 'Don' do it lak dat, Josie. Do it lak dis!' Dat all I heah fro she! She be sweet lak coconut meat to you, but Ah gat de shell!"

"Maybe she was only trying to help you by setting high standards," I said.

"It no hep you be high if sonbahdy mek you feel low ahl de time."

We stopped before an unpainted wooden box of a house that sat smack on the sandy ground. Inside, there were four small rooms, and each room had one window. The living room had scarcely enough space for a bench-like wooden sofa, a matching armchair, and a four-person dining table and chairs. When we entered, a big bookcase that wouldn't fit anywhere else in the room occupied the middle of the floor.

"We must find a place for it," Mrs Jefferson said.

"De only place it gone fit be de kichin," Gilly said. "In front ah de window."

"That will have to do," Mrs Jefferson said. "A bookcase is a necessity."

While Gilly carried in the luggage and moved the bookcase, Josie washed windows. The two women showed us around the house.

"Quite snug," Kate said.

"What a good way to put it," Mrs Jefferson said. "We hear that since the hurricane, housing is almost impossible to find. We're lucky to have this."

"Only an optimist could think so," Mrs Moss said. "I'm glad we have a place to ourselves, but it's far from satisfactory. With our things, few as they are, we hardly fit!"

She complained that the nearby houses were much too close and blocked the breeze. Even with all the doors and windows open, it was going to be hot and stuffy. "If the Catholic Church can afford a house like the one you girls have for its volunteers, the US government ought to be able to do at least as well by us. I intend to tell them so."

"I'm sure the government did the best it could," Mrs Jefferson said. "The furniture they provided is quite nice."

"Dorothy, you'd be pleased in a mud hut!" Mrs Moss said. "You have to learn to stand up for yourself. Be more demanding." I saw Josie do a double take. "How will those in authority know what needs improving if we don't let them know?"

"I suppose you're right, Mrs Moss." Mrs Jefferson turned to Molly, Kate and me. "I have to say that I never thought I'd be staying a month with the three of you. I appreciate how considerate you've tried to be, and I do thank you. You young people certainly lead very busy lives. I'm sure I must have been in your way."

"No, of course not, not at all," we protested.

As we were leaving, Mrs Jefferson shook hands with each of us. "I hope that we'll continue to see each other often, and not only at school. As soon as my record player arrives, we'll start our opera nights." Father Bosque's machine had failed to pass inspection, and we had yet to hear Mrs Jefferson's music.

"That's another thing we should complain about," Mrs Moss said. "Our trunks should have arrived long ago! How many weeks can it take a cargo ship to sail from the United States to Belize City?"

As we all drove back in the Jeep, Gilly shook his head. "Bettah dose ladies stay whey dey cohn from."

"Do you feel the same way about us, Gilly?" Molly asked.

Gilly looked surprised. "No, Miss Molly! You difrant. You happy yah, and dat mek us happy you be yah."

That afternoon, I moved back into my old room. With Josie's grudging assistance, Mrs Jefferson had left it in spotless condition. I unpacked all my suitcases and hung my clothes in the wardrobe and my pictures on the walls. The blue-trimmed curtains swelled in the breeze, and the bed, swathed in gauzy mosquito netting, looked big and comfortable compared to the cot I'd been sleeping on in Kate's room. It was as if I'd just arrived and was seeing the room for the first time.

As I carried all except the smallest piece of my empty luggage over to the convent storeroom, I realized I no longer thought of unpacking as wasted effort but as a commitment to life in the here and now.

From now on, I vowed, wherever I am, I'll always unpack my suitcase. Even if I'm spending just one night in a hotel room.

"Let's have an orgy," I said that night after we finished our class preps.

"An *orgy*?" Kate asked.

Molly explained while I found a candle, the remnants of a bottle of gin and a tin of grapefruit juice.

"So we just talk about anything?" Kate asked.

"That's the idea," Molly said. "By the way, our cigarettes have gone stale. It's been over a month since our last orgy."

"Doesn't matter," I said, lighting one. "They taste terrible even when they're fresh."

We sat cross-legged on the floor and clinked our glasses.

"To friendship!" Kate said. She cautiously sipped her drink. "Not bad!"

"How is 'Gracious Living' going, Kate?" I asked. The quixotic course continued to intrigue – and amuse – me.

She said that in the beginning, things went just fine. The students understood very well about introductions – why you introduce the younger person to the older one as a sign of respect. That came naturally to them. And table settings were clear enough, especially using the plates and silverware she borrowed from the convent. But she'd had trouble with the table manners themselves.

"What sort of trouble?" Molly asked.

"I didn't quite understand how different the local diets are from ours. And the same is true of their eating habits. We talked about what food you can eat with your fingers. It turns out they eat almost everything with their fingers. I explained that according to the rules of etiquette, you should only eat things like appetizers that way. Never heard of appetizers! I told them they were like snacks before the main course, and they asked why you would eat snacks before supper." Kate paused. "Actually, their questions make me wonder about some of our customs. They sound downright silly when you try to explain them.

"Anyhow, I decided to move on to letter writing. That's been much easier to teach. They'd learned about return addresses and salutations in the lower grades, so all I had to clarify were the different types of letters – you know, business letters, personal letters. But when we got to thank you notes, one of the students asked if you had to write a thank you note when the person you were thanking couldn't read."

"What did you tell her?" I asked.

"That she should go ahead and write, of course, because surely the person she wanted to thank could find someone to read the note aloud."

"You've got to be kidding," Molly said.

"Why?" Kate said.

"Because, to start with, thank you notes are ridiculous. I almost never write them and certainly don't expect them."

"Why ever not?" Kate asked.

"They're so artificial."

"But all manners are artificial," I said. "They're just a set of conventions. But don't you agree that they improve the quality of life?"

"I think they're made by snobs for snobs," Molly said.

"But you have very nice manners," I objected. "I think you're just playing devil's advocate."

"Oh, I admit I usually go along," Molly said. "My mother raised me to be polite and would be horrified to hear me say this, but I think conventional politeness can devalue real feelings. When you turn a feeling like gratitude into a formula, that spoils it. Diminishes it. Makes you feel like you've paid off some sort of debt, when all you've done is send someone a worthless piece of paper. When I receive a thank you note, I feel like someone has tried to pay me back with counterfeit money."

"Do you mean you wouldn't thank someone for a gift?" Kate asked.

"Gifts ought to be freely given. No thanks expected. If a gift puts me in somebody's debt, then the debt ought to be paid with something of equal value, not a thank you note or a mouthful of words!"

"I'm shocked to hear you say that," Kate said.

"Of course you're shocked," Molly said. "You obviously believe in all this etiquette crap if you're teaching 'Gracious Living'!"

Kate took a big swallow of her gin. "I think life would be crude and very unpleasant without manners."

Molly shrugged, pouring more gin.

"I'm having a problem a bit like Kate's," I said. "Not teaching etiquette or anything like that, but making what I teach relevant to the students. That was the idea behind starting the newspaper, so the students could put their writing skills into practice. But I'm having a devil of a time trying to bring history and religion to life. I'll admit it's probably because I don't know enough to be teaching either subject, but sometimes I think there's a deeper problem, and it's just what Molly said about etiquette. I'm afraid what I'm supposed to be teaching is a lot of irrelevant crap."

"Good heavens!" Kate said. "First Molly throws out manners and now you're junking Christianity and western civ!"

"I know history is about remembering, and I value that," I said, "but why remember mostly battles and kings – mostly European ones, at that – and not other things? The only relevance for these students that I can see is that they have to know them to pass their Cambridge exams. There must be a deeper reason, but I can't for the life of me figure out what it is. Then there's religion, which is reduced to a long list of dos and don'ts."

"Sounds like holy etiquette," Molly said, with a side glance at Kate.

Kate ignored her. "I don't know about religion," she said. "But could you have the history students write their own family stories? Their own pasts? And it would give them a sense of doing history. I think I'm going to try that in my class."

"Maybe they could act out scenes," Molly suggested, getting excited. "And see parallels to their own lives. I'm trying that with my lit class. They've been reading Thornton Wilder's *Our Town*, and they're going to perform a couple of scenes from act 3. Do you think people would come if we scheduled the performance after classes?"

"I'm sure they would," Kate said, and I agreed. "They could invite their families and friends."

"I know nothing could seem farther away from Angel Creek than New Hampshire, but once the students thought about it, they saw a lot of similarities between life in Grover's Corners in the early twentieth century and life in Angel Creek today. Especially the way Emily dies. They all seem to know of women who've died in childbirth." Molly shook her head. "It's tragic, how many must die that way here. And just as sad, the students also say a lot of babies die before they're a year old."

"I never thought of it before, but life here is probably a lot like life in the States when our grandmothers were young," Kate said.

"Makes you realize how quickly life in the States has changed," I said. "In only a few generations, we've gone from slow and rural to fast and suburban."

"I wonder what this country will be like when we're grandmothers," Kate said. "Life here could change very fast, because now the technology exists, even if this country doesn't have it yet."

"That's true of the whole world," Molly said. "Soon there won't be any remote places left. That's why it's important for you to visit the bush, Kate. Some of the villages, like the one Abby and I visited with Father O'Dea, are just the same as they were hundreds of years ago. But they probably won't be that way much longer. In a few years, they'll probably all have television sets!"

It was the most preposterous thing we could think of.

"Going to Sand Bight is like revisiting the past," Molly said. "Like Emily does in *Our Town* when she relives her twelfth birthday. It's a much simpler world."

Meanwhile, at that moment, in the simple world of Angel Creek, a house was burning down. No fire alarms. No fire trucks. No fire hydrants. Too far to haul water from the river or the sea. Nothing for the hapless family to do but stand, surrounded by neighbours, and watch fat flames consume everything they owned.

We stubbed out our cigarettes, blew out our candle, and went to bed without looking out the window or paying attention to the shouts in the street as those out late saw flames in the distance and headed towards them.

At Mass the next morning, Father Peck prayed for the family that had lost its home and gave thanks that no lives had been lost. He announced that a special collection was being taken up for the family. Contributions could be made through the church. We didn't know the family, but we went through our closets and took some of our clothing over to the rectory. If the family couldn't use the dresses and other things we brought, Father Peck assured us, they would sell them or trade them for something they could use.

A few nights later, after midnight, another building caught fire. This time we knew the place and the owners. It was La Cena, the restaurant owned by the family of our student Susanna Mendez, who lived above the restaurant.

When we arrived at school the next morning, we learned that Susanna and her mother had managed to escape from the building unharmed, but Susanna's stepfather, whose name was Johnny Young, had been burned, some said badly. The women said they hadn't been able to wake him or move him, so they had to leave him in the room where he was sleeping, directly above the restaurant kitchen, where the fire started. One of the neighbours risked his life to save him. Johnny Young was in the Angel Creek Hospital, we heard, but only until he could be transferred by plane to the hospital in Belize City.

"He was drunk," Ana told me. "That's why Susanna and her mother couldn't wake him."

"How do you know?" I asked her.

"The neighbour who rescued him told us. You know, their place is close to ours. Our whole block could have gone up in flames."

Ana shared more gossip between classes. "People think the fire was set. The police found what looked like a kerosene tin near where it started. My father says that Johnny Young has a lot of gambling debts, so maybe someone was trying to scare him into paying. But I don't think so. They wouldn't destroy the source of his income."

"Who else would have done such a thing?"

"We'll probably never know for sure. No one is going to ask too many questions. Everyone knows that Johnny Young deserves to be punished, so it doesn't matter how that fire started, whether God did it, or some person."

Once again, Molly, Kate and I went through our things and filled a bag with clothing. After supper, we took the bag to the house where Susanna and her mother were staying with relatives. A cousin went to find Susanna, and she and her mother joined us on the veranda. The cousin reappeared to serve us lemonade.

"Thank you so much," Susanna said, looking through the bag of clothes. "These will fit very well."

"We can certainly use these nice things," Susanna's mother said, "but we are better off than the other family whose house burned. They lost everything. With our neighbours' help, we managed to save many of our things from the fire."

"How is your husband?" I asked her.

"He is badly burned," she said, "and he suffers. God will decide if he lives."

Kate and I decided to stop by Lee Wong's store after the visit with Susanna and her mother, but Molly said she was tired and wanted to head home.

Everyone we met was eager to talk about the fires. The clerk at Lee Wong's, who sold us toothpaste and airmail envelopes, said she believed that there was an arsonist at large in Angel Creek. Several of the other customers agreed.

"We best be watchful," one of them cautioned.

Another, however, disagreed with that advice. "Nothing we cahn do. Bad tings allays cohn in threes. Dere be one mo fire soon."

After that ominous exchange, we ran into a group of our students, clustered with the crowd in front of the roped-off ruins of La Cena. They told us that the two fires had made the national news.

"De BHBC announsah describe dem as 'mysterious in origin'," one of the girls said, "an' 'suspicious in nature'."

We also stopped to chat with Ana, who was on her way to the movies with her stepmother, Marita. When Marita heard that the Youngs had salvaged many of their household items from the fire, she replied cryptically, "I'm not surprised."

It was almost eight by the time Kate and I arrived home. The house was empty.

"I thought Molly was coming straight home," Kate said, switching on the light. "Did she leave a note?"

"Don't see one. She probably stopped by Therese's or one of the other neighbours' houses. Or maybe she ran into David. She'll be back soon."

I went into my room to write letters and get ahead on some of my classes. Around eleven, Kate knocked on my door.

"I'm starting to get really worried," she said. "All the stores are closed by now, and the movie is over. Most people are in bed. Where could she be?"

"You know Molly," I said. "She forgets all about time when she's with someone and having a good time."

"Would you mind walking around with me, to see if we can find her?"

Kate left a note in case Molly came back while we were gone.

First, we stopped by Therese's house. She answered the door in her nightgown. "Me no see Molly lang time," she said.

As we expected, the lights were out at the Peace Corps house, and we walked from there to the Caribbean Club. Only a few people were in the club, none of whom we knew.

"Should we try upstairs, at Ana's?" I asked.

"Since we're here, I guess we should."

I knocked on the downstairs door, and we waited a long time. Finally, the shutters on one of the upstairs windows opened, and Marita leaned out.

"We are all in bed!" she called down. "Oh, it's you, Abby and Kate! Is something wrong?"

We apologized for disturbing her and asked if she or Ana had seen Molly. They hadn't.

"Let's try the doctor's," I said.

"Why would she go there?"

"I don't know, but it's the last place I can think to look."

We headed towards Front Street and, turning a corner, ran into Father Peck, out for a late-night walk.

"Where are you two going?" he asked.

"We're looking for Molly," Kate said. "She's disappeared."

"What do you mean, 'disappeared'?"

"We last saw her around seven this evening, when she said she was going straight home," Kate said. "But she wasn't there when we arrived a little later. When it got to be so late, we decided to go looking for her."

"She shouldn't be out this late alone," he said. "And neither should you. I was just on my way back to the rectory, but I'd better go with you. Where are you going?"

"Dr Bauer's," I said.

"Was she feeling sick?" he asked.

"I don't think so," I said. "But he's been teaching her German."

"At this time of night?"

"Well, no, not usually."

Sure enough, Molly was at the doctor's, having a late supper of toast and cheese, her foot in a basin of purple water. The sweet smell of lineament was in the air.

"So you search together for the lost Molly!" Dr Bauer chuckled. "Come join us." He insisted on pouring us glasses of iced tea; then he offered to toast bread for us, but we declined. Molly and the doctor were both in a jolly mood.

Father Peck drank his tea in silence, and then stood up, dwarfing the rest of us. "It's time to go," he said.

Molly dried her foot and slipped on her sandals. "I sprained my ankle a few weeks ago, and it was hurting tonight," she explained as we walked home in the moonlight. "Dr Bauer said to come anytime I needed a treatment, so I did, and then we got talking, and then we got hungry."

"This is no time for medical treatment, unless it's an emergency," Father Peck said. "I shouldn't need to tell you that it's a bad idea to disappear like you did, without a word to anyone."

"But Father Peck – "

"Your behaviour was what I'd call thoughtless and inconsiderate, and it shows very poor judgement," he said in his no-nonsense, schoolmaster's voice. "If something like this happens again, I'll send you home."

"All right, then," said Molly, in a tone my grandmother would have called "huffy". In spite of her hurt ankle, she strode ahead of us, not saying another word.

Kate and I said a hasty good night to Father Peck at the rectory gate and ran to catch up with her.

"Molly, we were worried about you!" Kate said.

"So you had to bring Father Peck into it?"

"We ran into him by accident," I said.

"All I know is, you got me in trouble for nothing!"

"Wait a minute," I said. "You got yourself in trouble."

"What do you mean? Did I ask you to come looking for me?"

"That's what friends do," Kate said. "They look out for each other."

"That's what busybodies do! I can look out for myself, thank you."

"We're not here on our own," Kate said. "We have to remember we're part of a team."

The next morning, a Saturday, dawned cool and dazzling.

"How would you like to go to Sand Bight next weekend?" Father Bosque asked us after Mass.

Kate and I showed our delight, and Molly, who had gone to bed indignant and risen depressed, brightened.

"We were talking just a couple of days ago about how much we want Kate to see Sand Bight," I said. "You read our minds."

Father Bosque said that Father Peck had been scheduled to make the trip but now didn't have the time. Instead, he needed to go to Belize City to meet with the bishop before he left for Rome and the opening of the Second Vatican Council. I was surprised to hear that the first session of the Council would last several months.

Since his arrival, Father Peck had done most of the travelling into the bush, in order to visit each mission personally. Sand Bight was the farthest of all. On our first trip, we'd taken the sea route, but this time Father Bosque said he intended to go by road. We'd leave the Jeep in Half Moon Creek and take a dory through the mangrove swamps, coming into the village, situated on the narrow Placencia Peninsula, from the west instead of the east.

"It could be a rough trip," he warned us. "The southern roads are in pretty bad shape because of all the rain." Although the daily rains had stopped, the hurricane season wasn't over yet, and storms, when they came, were often violent. "Are you sure you want to go?"

"Can't wait," Kate assured him. "I hear it's just this side of heaven."

Not long after breakfast, the church bells began clanging. Why would they summon us more than two hours after the call to six o'clock Mass? I went out on the porch, and in the clear air of a perfect day, saw smoke rising.

"My God, it looks like another fire!" I called out to Molly and Kate. "Somewhere to the north along Front Street."

Molly grabbed her camera, and we walked to the corner of Church and Front streets. The nuns were on their upper porch, and Mother Eugenie shouted down to us, "It's the Quinlan house!"

"Oh no!" I yelled and started running. "Sissy and Alma! Lydie! The boys!"

Kate struggled to catch up with me. Molly walked behind, nursing her ankle.

The bells were still clanging, and as I sprinted up Front Street, the blue Jeep filled with ten-gallon cans sped by, river water splashing out and wetting the road. Gilly was behind the wheel. A few other cars, similarly laden, honked past us, followed at a distance by donkey carts. This was the best Angel Creek could do in the way of a fire brigade.

As we came closer to the Quinlan house, we could see that it was already too late for help. Black smoke rolled out of the second-storey windows, chased by orange flames that leaped towards the roof. Father Bosque, the Quinlans and some of their neighbours were throwing things out the downstairs windows and dragging furniture and other objects out of the house. Chairs, tables, beds, desks and dresser drawers, their contents spilling out as they sailed through the air, piled up around the burning house. Shirts and dresses had blown into the trees and bushes as though flung there by a drunken laundress. All the objects of everyday living – kettles, skillets, cups, plates, pitchers – were scattered across the yard.

People formed a chain to pass the containers of water, but by then, smoke was swelling out of the downstairs windows too. I heard a cracking like bones breaking.

"The roof is going soon," someone yelled.

"Get out! Get away!" Father Bosque yelled. "We've saved all we can." His face was streaked with soot and sweat.

"Count the kids!" Lydie screamed. "Where's Ian? Alma, find Sissy!"

"We're all here, Mum!" James yelled.

The girls were still in their pyjamas. Standing with the family, watching their house burn down, Lydie told us that she'd come back from Mass that morning and cooked breakfast as usual for the family. Everyone had just finished their pancakes when Mr Quinlan smelled smoke. He went upstairs, and the front bedroom was already on fire. He'd sent his eldest son, Joseph, to find Father Bosque and call for help. He'd done what he could to put the fire out, but already it was too strong to fight. Fanned by the sea breeze, it had engulfed the entire second storey no more than twenty minutes after he discovered it. The family rushed to save whatever they safely could, most of it from the ground floor.

"Hattie, she barely touch us!" Mr Quinlan said as the fire like an X-ray revealed the scaffolding of the house. "But dis house, she doom ahl de same."

"Thank God this is only a personal tragedy," Lydie said, hugging her daughters, both of them weeping. "The whole country doesn't have to suffer, like Hattie. Really, this shouldn't even be called a tragedy, not like the Youngs' fire, because no one was hurt."

"But I'll miss our home," Alma said, tears streaking down her face. "It was a wonderful house, wasn't it, Uncle Charlie?"

"Yes, that it was," Father Bosque said. He turned to the crowd, the burning house behind him. "Let us pray together," he said, moving away from the roar of the fire into the field.

Figure 9. The Quinlan house, engulfed in flames. Photo courtesy of Malilee Zimmers.

He reminded us how quickly the things of this earth pass away and urged us to remember that, unless the Lord builds the house, we labour in vain who build it. Wind, water, fire might destroy all we had, but they could not destroy the firm foundation of a life built on faith.

Once again, Molly, Kate and I went through our things. I threw in my pink striped dress and a pair of white leather sandals that were almost new and donated a paperback collection of Emily Dickinson's poems and a hardback copy of Anne Morrow Lindbergh's *Gift from the Sea*, two favourite books I'd brought with me. I had a big bar of hard-milled, scented soap in a pretty box, too good to use for every day, that my mother had given me, and I added it at the last minute, hoping Lydie would use it.

The whole family had temporarily moved into Ruthie Archer's house, next door to the school. When Molly, Kate and I took the bag of things to them, the visit turned into a party. Father Bosque and some of the neighbours were there, having a beer with Mr Quinlan. They'd spent all afternoon moving most of what they had salvaged from the fire into the same convent storeroom where I'd recently put my luggage. James and Ian were playing Chinese checkers with Ruthie's sons, and Alma and Sissy were helping Ruthie and Lydie cook supper.

"Stay for supper!" Ruthie encouraged us. We'd already eaten, but Ruthie and the Quinlans, unfailingly hospitable, insisted we keep them company.

"How can you all be so cheerful?" Molly asked as we sat around the table.

"'Don' cry ovah spill milk!' as we say in Creole," Mr Quinlan said.

"We say that in the States too!" Kate said.

"Gud advice de world ovah," he said.

"What we lost today can be replaced," Lydie said. "It's only right to thank God for what we still have, all the most important things. Our lives. Our health. Our neighbours and friends."

Father Bosque put his arm around his sister. "As our mother always says, 'What little we have is as much as we need. Let's thank God and make the most of it!'"

Mrs Jefferson and Mrs Moss settled in, and, once their trunks arrived, had their entire neighbourhood enjoying – and often imitating – the high art of Puccini, Verdi and Bizet. Molly, with tears, apologized to Father Peck and Kate and me not for going off on her own but for being thoughtless about when and how she did it. After a brief investigation, the local police concluded that all three fires were accidental. The town took up a collection for the family we didn't know who'd lost their home, and they rebuilt with improvements. The Quinlans slowly began rebuilding, too, in the style of the home the flames had consumed. Johnny Young spent months in the hospital recovering from his burns. The town agreed they had spoiled his good looks but made him a better man. With the restaurant closed, Susanna's attendance at school improved markedly. She soon took her place as one of the best students in her class. Her mother, miraculously according to some, regained her health, reopened La Cena, and cared without complaint for her invalid husband.

Chapter 15

GOING BACK

WE TRAVELLED MOST OF the way from Half Moon Creek to Sand Bight in twilight. Even before sunset, it was dark in the mangrove swamp. The dory was built to hold six – big enough for our Garifuna guide, Father Bosque, Molly, Kate and me and our overnight gear. While the rest of us paddled, the guide steered, telling us when to shift our paddles from one side to the other. Somehow, he found passages through the clumps of massive mangrove trees whose tangled roots spread wide in the brackish water. The trees grew far out into the lagoon that separated the mainland from the Placencia Peninsula to the east.

After about forty-five minutes, we emerged from the swamp into the open waters of the lagoon, and at the end of another hour of steady paddling in a northeast direction, we drew near enough to the far shore to see the light of cooking fires. As we came closer still, we saw the flames of kerosene lamps glowing like fireflies among the shadowy palm and coconut trees.

Our approach to the village was like coming in a back door at night – there was something both familiar and furtive about it. No one saw us arrive and carry our paddles and our gear through the grasses that grew along the sandy shore. Only when we came to a cluster of houses did dogs begin to bark and a general cry go out that "Creole Fahdah and de American teachahs" had come.

We were just in time for a simple supper with the schoolteacher and his family, followed by a big event at the thatched-roofed schoolhouse. The village troop of Boy Scouts was performing in their annual talent show. When they saw us file in and sit in places of honour among the village elders, the boys, about a dozen of them, stood visibly taller. Most were between twelve and sixteen and looked a lot like our Camelot Boys in Angel Creek.

Dressed in their khaki uniforms with big kerchiefs around their necks and dark berets on their heads, they recited poetry, sang and danced for an hour and a half. Most of the acts were group performances of Garifuna dances and songs accompanied by drums and rattles – now known as *punta* – but some of the music was obviously imported, like a group number, "The Road to Mandalay", and a show-stopping rendition of Elvis's "Blue Suede Shoes" by a shoeless Boy Scout with a guitar. None of the Scouts wore shoes with their uniforms.

The presence of a Boy Scout troop in the village amazed me. On our first visit, Sand Bight's remoteness from the modern world had seemed to be its defining characteristic. Now, probably because of four months in Angel Creek, I saw the village with keener eyes. When we went round to greet people and inform them of the time of church services, I now recognized the signs of family members working abroad and sending money home – a bicycle at the door, a battery-operated, short-wave radio on a table – whereas before I'd seen only roofs thatched with kahuna palms and dirt floors. On some of the walls, I noticed calendars from Half Moon Creek, Angel Creek and Belize City businesses. Several of those who lived in the bigger, more prosperous houses, the ones with tin roofs and wooden floors, had children in high schools in Angel Creek and Belize City.

Kate, Molly and I made a point of meeting the parents of the St Monica students from Sand Bight. Kate and I both taught Elspeth Williams, one of the first-year students, and in the morning we went together to visit her mother. Elspeth's father, we discovered, was working in a factory in New Jersey, living with relatives in the States.

"How Elspeth do?" Mrs Williams asked, offering us cellophane-wrapped pieces of butterscotch candy, only slightly gummy from the humidity.

"She's very well behaved and always does her homework," I assured her. "And she wrote a very good article for our school newspaper."

"Yes," Mrs Williams said, "she send me dat newspapah. Oh, my! So much hapm dere!" She giggled, covering her mouth with her hands and rocking back and forth.

"And she's a good speaker," Kate added. "I'm helping Elspeth prepare for the St Monica speech contest. If she's one of the finalists, she'll go to Belize City for the national competition in a few weeks."

"You such gud teachahs!" Mrs Williams said. "Eat mo cahndy. It frahn de Stay-uhts!"

That morning, two young women with babies approached us. The first of them we knew: Annie Boyd. Molly and I had witnessed her wedding to Joseph Losey on our first visit to Sand Bight. She and her husband were bringing their newborn son to church to be baptized.

"Dis de secon' bway," Annie said, showing us the baby. "Evrybady say he look jes lak Joseph."

"He only handsome!" Joseph said, his smile wide.

"What a lovely family," Kate said afterward. "But so young to have a child."

"There are two more babies at home," I told her.

Not long after, a second young woman with a baby came up to us. This one we didn't know. She held out the infant, who was about the same age as Annie Boyd's, to Kate.

Kate took the baby in her arms. "A beautiful baby!" she said. "Is it a girl or a boy?"

"She a girl chile," the mother said.

"You must be very proud of her," Kate said as she tried to give the baby back.

"No," the woman said. "She foh you."

"For me?"

"Yes, Teachah, she foh you. Tek she bahk to de Stay-uhts. Me no wan girl baby. Bwayz bettah. She be fine wid you. She have gud life in de Stay-uhts. You tek she wid you."

"Thank you, but I can't!" Kate said firmly, forcing the child into her mother's arms. "Babies belong with their mothers!"

"Please, Miss!"

Kate lowered her head and walked off. After a long look at Molly and me, the woman turned away towards the village.

In the dory on the way back to Half Moon Creek, Kate described the incident to Father Bosque. "I didn't know what to do," she said in conclusion. "I couldn't believe it was happening!"

In response, he said that many young mothers were unmarried, not just in Sand Bight but in the country as a whole. Fair or not, a son might convince the father to marry the mother or make her family more willing to support her and the child. Boys fished. They were a necessity in the sea villages. Girls were considered something of a burden, especially when they were the eldest. It was likely that this particular mother, with her own limited view of things, was trying to make a better life for herself and also the child.

"Better?" Kate echoed in disbelief. "Could anything be worse than for a mother to offer her own child to a stranger – and her only child, at that! It doesn't seem natural. It seems heartless."

"Maybe if you thought of it in terms of adoption, Kate, it might not seem so heartless. Look at yourself through her eyes. You're a stranger, yes, but she knows a lot about you. You're obviously white and American, so you must be rich and able to take good care of her child. You probably seemed the answer to that poor girl's prayer."

"The first time we visited, I thought Sand Bight was paradise on earth," Molly said. "It's still beautiful, but I guess it's not as perfect as I thought."

Beautiful or not, perfect or not, I was impatient to get back to Half Moon Creek. Eduardo was there, and I wanted to see him.

"If you're going through Half Moon, would you mind stopping at the club?" Ana had asked the day before we left for Sand Bight. "I have some things Elena needs for the babies, and I'm not sure when I'll get down there again."

"Of course," I said. "I'm sorry we don't have room to take you with us."

"I couldn't go anyway. I'm helping Sister Veronica plan the school fair and we're having a big meeting on Saturday."

I stopped by the Zacharias apartment after class to pick up the packages. She gave me a box containing cloth diapers and tiny undershirts for the baby and a bag of things for the two girls.

"I love little kids' clothes," I said when she showed me matching red dresses for Blanca and Clara. "They'll look so cute in these."

"Eduardo picked them out the last time he was in Belize City," she said. "But he probably won't go down to Half Moon for another month or so. I know Elena will be happy to have them sooner."

"I haven't seen Eduardo for a long time. How is he?"

"He's been on the road a lot – to and from Belize City, mostly, with a long trip to Salvador – and the rest of the time, he's been staying with Javier in the Valley, helping him out. He hasn't been home here for over a week, but we expect him for supper tonight."

"Tell him hello," I said.

"Tell him yourself. Here he is, coming in the door. *Hola,* Eduardo!"

"*Hola!*" he said. "Hello, Abigail. I was going to stop by your house tonight. I have something for you from Belize."

"Stop by any time."

"Don't you want it now?"

"I can wait."

"All right, then. About seven-thirty. But I have to be at the club by eight."

After supper, I bathed and washed my hair and put on a clean blouse and skirt. I sat on the steps drying my hair in the breeze, waiting for Eduardo to come. Father Bosque saw me from his balcony, waved and came over. He took the stairs two at a time and sat down next to me at the top.

"You look fresh," he said. "But washing your hair was a waste of water. Once we get on the road tomorrow, it'll be full of dust after a mile or two."

"I know. But for now it feels nice and clean."

He leaned close. "Mmm. Smells good too. Like coconut."

"That's the shampoo."

Eduardo drove up.

"Look who's here." Father Bosque sounded amused.

Eduardo joined us but didn't sit down. He stood with his feet on different steps, facing us at eye level. He carried a big tin of fancy imported cookies, which he rested on his raised knee.

"Ready for another game of Stare, Eduardo?" Father Bosque teased.

"Not unless Abigail wants to play," he said. "You beat me, no question."

"I was playing for Abby. She gets the win."

"Then I've met my match."

No one said anything for a minute. Eduardo glanced down at the cookie tin and then held it out to me. "This is for you," he said.

"I don't know what the occasion is, but thank you, Eduardo." I set the tin on my knees. "This is heavy! And much too expensive, I'm sure."

"It's nothing," he said. "I have to go now, but I'll see you soon."

"We're leaving for Sand Bight tomorrow," I said. "Father and the three of us."

"I know. Ana told me. Goodbye for now."

When Eduardo had gone, Father Bosque asked me to join him in the rectory for "that talk we've been promising each other." The evening was so fine he'd love to go for a walk, he said, but "better not." Like most nuns and priests at the time, Father Bosque was cautious about being seen in public alone with someone of the opposite sex. Groups were fine, but one-on-one could start gossip.

"Tell me if I'm butting in," he said, once we'd settled in the rectory parlour. "But I was thinking now might be a good time to talk about Eduardo – before those cookies sweeten you up."

"I've been meaning to bring up the subject again," I said, "but I'm not sure where to begin."

He suggested that I start talking and see where it led. I shivered involuntarily, as though about to plunge into icy water.

"Here's my predicament," I began. "I have no idea how to interpret the mixed signals Eduardo sends me. He does really nice things, like bringing me the cookies. He seems interested in me and says he wants to get to know me better. Even gets his father's permission to see me alone. I gather that's a big deal down here, at least in his family. But then he disappears for days and weeks without a word. It's like he takes a step or two towards me and then two or three back."

"What sort of signals are you sending him?"

It took me a minute to answer. Talking about my feelings for Eduardo was just as hard as I had feared it would be. It was possible only if I looked straight ahead or down at my hands, folded in my lap like a schoolgirl's. If I closed my eyes I could almost imagine myself in the confessional, talking to God through a priest as I'd been trained in childhood to do – even though I did it as seldom as possible. I forced myself to go on.

"At first, I hardly noticed him. He was Ana's nice younger brother." I paused. "But soon I began to admire certain things about him, especially his love for his family and his way with children. That's what I love about him, the way he looks out for Ana and his little brothers, and how sweet he is with little Blanca and Clara. You've seen how they adore him. I like his seriousness. And his kindness to me, of course. I'm sure he knows I want to get to know him better. In fact, I've told him so." I paused.

I heard Father Bosque take a deep breath before he asked me in his throaty voice, huskier than usual: "Would you say you're in love with him?"

"No!" I answered, quickly this time. I knew my face was flushed, and I wished he couldn't see it. "To be honest, I don't know Eduardo very well. And my feelings for him are all mixed up with my friendship for Ana and my love for this place. But if he's like I think he is, then maybe I *could* fall in love with him."

"Then he's very lucky."

"I don't know. Falling in love – that seems to me the easy part. But I don't know what I think about what would come next, the being together part. I haven't seen many good marriages. My parents' was bad."

Before I could think better of it, the story I'd never told anyone in its entirety came spewing out. Irresponsible, alcoholic father; unstable, pill-popping mother. Seven children abandoned, left to grandparents and friends of the family to raise.

"Are you in touch with your parents?" he asked me.

"My father, not often, but a few years ago, my mother reappeared with a new husband. And then last year, she had another baby, a little boy. She's trying to include me and my two oldest brothers in her life, but I don't think it's going very well. She tries to act like nothing ever happened."

"Have you tried to discuss it with her?"

I fought back the tears that always came when I tried to talk about my family. "Not really," I said, explaining that I didn't think it would do any good, just make her depressed and me angry, not caring what I said, not caring if I hurt her, wanting to hurt her.

Now that I'd started talking, I found it hard to stop. I admitted to Father Bosque that my grandmother, after the adoption, had asked me not to be so hard on my mother. My grandmother blamed the war. She had lived through two world wars, she said, and seen how they damaged people. She reminded me that both my parents were still in their early twenties at the start of the Second World War. My father enlisted in the Navy after Pearl Harbor, and when he shipped out to the South Pacific, my mother was left with two babies under three and another on the way. Once he came home, four more were born, one right after the other, and there was a miscarriage in there too. "Eight pregnancies in twelve years," my grandmother said, "and your mother not yet thirty-two." She told me to keep that in mind.

"I can see they both felt overwhelmed, Father Bosque," I said, "and I feel sad for both of them. But as I told my grandmother, even though I love my parents, I blame them. I blame them for leaving us, first him and then her. And I blame them for not finding a way to keep us all together."

I stopped, sorry now that I'd said so much. "I hate talking about it. Just like my mom, I guess. You know, I haven't told Eduardo or Ana or even Molly and Kate about any of this."

"We all have things we don't want to talk about, Abby," Father Bosque said. "When you're ready, you'll tell people. Or you won't. It's up to you." He surprised me by what he said next. "Others aren't entitled to know everything about you."

"But I sometimes feel so dishonest. I try not to tell actual lies, but leaving things out and keeping secrets is also lying, isn't it?"

"Not exactly. Not always."

I sat silently, remembering the response of the nun I'd tried to talk to about my family early in my first year of college. She said that if my mother was divorced and remarried, then she was ex-communicated from the Catholic Church, and I shouldn't have anything more to do with her. That *nun* was the one I decided not to have anything more to do with. But from then on, all through college, I kept quiet about everything: the divorce, the adoption, my mother's remarriage and the baby, born the summer of my junior year. When I came to British Honduras, I radically changed the story for reasons I couldn't entirely explain, even to myself, admitting the divorce but leaving out a different part, the four adopted children.

"I'm sorry, Father Bosque," I said at last. "I meant to talk to you about Eduardo. I'm not sure how I got from him to my family."

"I'm glad you did," he said. "Won't you look at me, Abby? I want to be sure you know you're not responsible for your parents' actions. Of course, they affect you and may affect other people's opinions of you, however unfairly, but you aren't to blame for what happened."

I returned his steady gaze. "I know that. But the problem is that I was like a mom to the littlest kids. It feels like I deserted them too."

"Ah! That's hard." He sighed. "You know, we all have to live with circumstances beyond our control, including the bad choices of people we love. Keep in mind, though, that you can choose for yourself now. Try not to judge and, if you can, choose forgiveness, for yourself as well as them. Remember that God wants only the best for you – and expects the best from you."

"But what if I pick something at twenty that I don't want at all when I'm forty? Like my parents did. What good is freedom, if you can end up trapping yourself with it or hurting people you love?"

"There are lots of risks in life, Abby, especially in loving. The question is whether you're ready to take some of those risks for Eduardo."

"To be honest, I'm not sure. As far as I can tell, Eduardo's a good person, but we both come from such different cultures. And such mixed-up families."

I have to admit part of me thinks a relationship with him would be a big mistake. At the same time, I'd regret not giving it a chance."

"Then I'll help you if I can. You're like a dear little sister to me. That's what I told my mother – that she should think of you as her youngest daughter. I wasn't thinking of marriage for you, but if that's what you decide – well, I just want you to know you can count on me, Little Sister. Whatever happens."

Was that the moment I first realized that I didn't feel like a little sister to him? That I cherished every moment I spent with him. Couldn't wait for our next conversation. That he was the one I looked for when I entered a room where I thought he might be; missed when I wasn't with him. If so, I pushed that glimmer of consciousness back down into the dark and secret place where it belonged.

Thanks to a spell of dry weather, the road to Half Moon Creek had been in better shape than we expected. We stopped along the way for a leisurely picnic lunch overlooking one of the many rivers on their way to the sea. When we were packing up, we saw a red cloud of dust in the distance. As it came closer, I recognized one of the Zacharias trucks. Behind the wheel, I was astonished to see Eduardo.

He pulled up beside the Jeep. "I thought you would already be in Half Moon Creek by now," he said. "What held you up?"

"The beauty of the day," Father Bosque said. "What brings you this way?"

"My father decided he needed me to bring a few things down to Emilio. You'll be stopping at the club, won't you?"

"Yes," Father Bosque said. "But not for long. We'll be leaving for Sand Bight as soon as I can make arrangements for a dory and guide."

Father Bosque knew I planned to drop off packages that I could just as well have handed over to Eduardo right then and there, but neither of us said a word.

Although they welcomed all of us warmly, Emilio and Elena were just as surprised to see Eduardo as I'd been. Once we'd settled down at the big mahogany table with coffee and cake, I handed Elena the packages from Ana. She was mystified.

"Why you bring, not Eduardo?"

Before I could answer, Eduardo explained that his trip was a last-minute thing. "In fact, I only had time to load a few things on the truck."

Emilio looked amazed. "What a waste of petrol, especially when we have everything we need till next month. What's *Papi* thinking?"

Eduardo shrugged.

When it was time for us to meet Father Bosque, who'd gone off to arrange for the dory, Eduardo insisted on driving us to the pier in Emilio's Buick sedan. Emilio told us his eldest brother, who lived in the States, had driven it down for him a few years earlier. We knew that such automobiles, no matter how old and ill suited to the roads in British Honduras, were the ultimate status symbol.

The sun was already low in the sky by the time we reached the water. Except for a few workers preparing to leave by dory for their villages, the area was deserted at this time of day.

As we drove up, Father Bosque waved to us. Molly and Kate hurried to help him transfer gear from the Jeep to the dory. As I slid across the front seat towards the door, Eduardo put his hand on my arm.

"Don't go yet."

I turned towards him.

"I wanted to see you," he said. "That's why I came."

He leaned close and for the first time kissed me.

I was more surprised than anything. I drew away gently, then leaned back into him and kissed him first on his cheek and then on his lips. After a moment, without speaking, we got out of the car and walked to the pier, where he helped me into the dory. He said he hoped to see us at Father Bosque's Mass in Half Moon Creek when we returned the next day, and he wished us a safe journey.

Looking up at his tall figure, backlit by the setting sun, I saw a young Apollo in jeans and a blue cotton shirt. Why in the world, I wondered, would someone like him be interested in someone like me? And why in the world, I asked myself, would I be interested in him?

On our return, I half expected to see Eduardo standing exactly where we'd left him, but of course, there was no way he could know when we'd be back. I looked for him all through Mass, but he never appeared. When I asked Elena, who was there, if she knew where he was, she said he'd taken the truck back to Angel Creek that morning.

"But I thought he said he'd be here through the weekend."

"Eduardo say tell you he has go back. Rain later maybe and road bad for truck."

The skies looked clear to me.

On the long trip back to Angel Creek, Molly, Kate and I took turns spelling Father Bosque by driving on the better stretches of road. The closer we came to Angel Creek, the less he drove, but he refused to nap, introducing one song after another: all the Belafonte hits – "Banana Boat Song," "Brown Skin Girl" – followed by a mix of folk songs and popular music from the radio and movies. Father Bosque always led, singing melody in his raspy baritone. I usually joined him, while Molly and Kate supplied harmony. It was our customary road music, a way to stay awake and scare off any menacing eyes in the bush. On that particular evening, I didn't much feel like singing, but the energy of the others lifted my spirits.

On Monday morning, Ana told me that Eduardo had already left on another trip to El Salvador and would be gone at least a week.

"He wanted to see you before he went," she said. "That's why he decided to drive to Half Moon, even though he didn't really need to go. I was surprised that my father said yes, but he is in favour of you."

"In favour of me?"

Ana looked flustered. "I only mean that he prefers you."

"Prefers me?"

"To anyone else."

"Ana, who else is there?"

"No one you need to worry about," she said.

Worse than the mosquito and sandfly bites that I'd picked up on the trip through the mangrove swamps, Ana's remarks stung. Whether from jealousy or vanity I wasn't sure. Maybe they were the same vile thing.

Chapter 16

WELCOMING THE DAWN

ON THE MORNING OF Thursday, 11 October 1962, the Feast of the Motherhood of Our Lady, Father Bosque emerged from the sacristy clothed in white vestments trimmed with gold. Because Father Peck was away, Father Bosque offered the High Mass to celebrate the opening of the Second Vatican Council in Rome. Along with the daily congregation of school children, more townspeople than usual filled the pews. As on Sundays, thick wax candles illuminated the sanctuary, and incense hung like clouds in the early morning air. Facing the altar, Father Bosque chanted the prayers of the liturgy, and we, the congregation, sang our responses, all in Latin.

During the Mass, Father Bosque preached a homily that gave voice to the anticipation we all felt. This was, he stressed, a time of hope in spite of great darkness in the world. We all knew, he said, that the shadow of communism, with its dismal denial of God and the Spirit, obscured the light of faith in many places around the globe. But today, we welcomed the dawn of a new era.

Truth, as we know, does not change, he reminded us; the message of the Church is for all people and for all times, to unite us on our journey to God. But truth must be reinterpreted for a changing world. That's why our bishop and hundreds of other bishops were at that very moment gathered in Rome, called there by Pope John XXIII for the first Council in almost a century.

The eyes of our bishops were on the morning star, he said, a sign of a new day to come. Father Bosque exhorted us to follow their lead and to remember that ours is a Church not only of antiquity but also a Church for today and for the future. He prayed that each and every one of us might embrace the changes and challenges to come.

As the students filed up to the communion rail, I was happy to see Jean Martinez among them. My conversations with humble, earnest Jean had helped me see more clearly why we needed a Church for our time. Jean and I often took walks together, usually after her late-afternoon writing sessions at our house. We talked about her opinions on the books she read as fast as I could get them to her. I lent her whatever we had in the house and also managed to pass on some books and magazines borrowed from the rectory along with a few from the Todds, but it was hard to keep up with her.

"You're going so fast you're approaching the 'read' limit, Jean," I teased her. "You're running out of books. I think you're going to have to move to a town that has a public library. Or rebuild one here."

"That would be a good thing to do, Miss, but it's not my dream."

Her comment surprised me. Jean rarely spoke about personal things. "What's your dream, Jean?"

"You will think I'm reaching too high if I tell you, Miss. Besides, it is only a dream. I could never do this thing. I am not good enough."

"I can't imagine anything you wouldn't be good enough – or smart enough – to do."

She spoke so softly, I had to strain to hear her. "Not even become a nun?"

"Not even a nun, if that's what you wanted."

"Ever since I was eight years old, before I ever saw one but only heard about them, that's what I wanted, Miss – to be a nun."

"Why do you think you're not good enough?"

"God only chooses the best. That's what Sister Veronica says."

"Maybe so, but only God knows who the 'best' are."

Jean looked as though she were debating with herself. I waited as she took several rapid breaths and then blurted out, "Miss, I don't feel like the best. Even though I would like to, I don't go to communion every day. I don't feel worthy. How could I ever be a nun?"

"In this case, I think you should listen to your desires and not your fears, Jean, and go to communion. Let me tell you something. Before communion, the priest says three times, 'Lord, I am not worthy that you should enter beneath my roof, but only say the word and my soul will be healed.' He's saying those words for all of us, himself included, because we're all sinners who need forgiveness."

"But how do you know what the priest is saying, Miss?"

"I have a little book that translates the Mass from Latin into English, so that anyone who reads English can understand it. Do you want to take it to Mass with you tomorrow and follow along? I'll lend it to you."

"Can there be such a thing, Miss? I thought it was a secret language, and only God and the priest could understand what the words he says at Mass mean."

"That's the problem with Latin – usually the priest and God *are* the only ones who know what the words mean. But Vatican II will probably change that, and before long, our priests here will be saying Mass in English, so that even little children will be able to understand."

When we returned to the house, Jean took the black leather book with its gold-edged leaves into her trembling hands. I explained that it contained all the prayers in all the masses through the liturgical year in both Latin and English, and showed her how to use it.

Returning the book a few days later, Jean admitted that even though she still didn't understand many things, even in English, she saw now that she should think more about God's love and forgiveness than her own unworthiness.

Jean revealed to me what is perhaps obvious – that the institutional changes we all expected from Vatican II had the power to change people's attitudes and affect their personal lives and relationship with God, often profoundly. Pope John XXIII was opening not only a window in an ancient structure, but also the eyes and minds that viewed the world through its apertures.

"What excites you most about Vatican II?" I asked Father Bosque during one of our now-daily conversations. We were drinking mugs of tea together in the rectory kitchen after I'd helped him mark a set of quizzes from his senior theology students. He'd become my coach for the first-form religion class I taught – basic catechism – and in turn I occasionally helped him read and respond to student work, not his favourite part of teaching.

"So much!" he said, holding his cup in both hands with elbows on the table. But what excited him most was something Pope John had said in his remarks at the opening of the council: that human differences can lead to the greater good of the Church. The idea that Catholics should value difference instead of regarding it as divisive signalled, he said, an inspired change in thinking and feeling. In that statement alone, he saw the possibility of true transformation. Respecting difference – religious, cultural, individual – and using our different gifts and perspectives to work together for a better world: what could be more hopeful?

I'd grown up in a Church encrusted in ancient traditions that elevated the papacy and priestly hierarchy above laypeople. A Church shrouded in mysterious rituals like the Latin Mass and defined by arcane practices like abstaining from meat on Fridays. A Church that stressed its authority through doctrines like papal infallibility and its universality through the rejection of local customs. In contrast, the Council implicitly acknowledged the Church's human dimension, subject to change and in need of revision and reform. It affirmed that Church leaders as well as those of us in the pews could – and should – open ourselves to the best that other religions and the secular world had to offer.

My experience in British Honduras confirmed the need for and value of such change.

"We feel we must disagree with those prophets of doom, who are always forecasting disaster, as though the end of the world were at hand," Pope John XXIII told the assembled Council, as reported on Radio Belize.

Within days, seeming to vindicate those who saw disaster ahead, news reached us of an ominous situation developing in the waters off the Florida coast. President Kennedy addressed the nation on American TV and radio the night of Monday, 22 October, although we didn't hear about what became known as the Cuban Missile Crisis until the next morning. At the time Kennedy was speaking, Molly, Kate, Father Bosque and I were at the Peace Corps house with Mrs Jefferson and Mrs Moss, listening to *Madama Butterfly* on Mrs Jefferson's record player.

Crowded in the tiny living room, we passed around the libretto as the music washed over us like a tsunami. Unaware of what was happening a few hundred miles northeast of us, we followed Puccini's tragic tale of doom, ironically set in Nagasaki. Cio-Cio-San's farewell to her son suggested that some chasms are too great to bridge.

"It sounds like the end of the world," I said as the last notes of the opera died away.

At Mass the next morning, Father Peck asked us to pray for a peaceful resolution to the crisis brewing near our shores. He'd picked up the news over his ham radio and told us the essentials, which the local stations and newspapers reported later that day: that Kennedy claimed the Soviets had built up sufficient military weapons in Cuba to hit targets within a radius of a thousand miles, and as a consequence, the United States was setting up a blockade – called a "quarantine" by the president – to keep additional weapons carried by Russian ships from reaching the island.

"A radius of a thousand miles!" Kate said. "That means that missiles already in Cuba could reach Cape Canaveral – and maybe even Washington, DC!"

"As well as the entire Caribbean area," I added. "And Mexico and Central America."

"My God!" Molly said. "We could be annihilated at the push of a button. Or watch the entire Eastern Seaboard go up in a mushroom cloud. The fallout could kill us all."

"I don't know that I trust Kennedy to deal with this," Kate said. "Remember the Bay of Pigs. What a fiasco!" The attempted invasion of Cuba by CIA-trained exiles from Castro's Cuba had occurred a year and a half earlier. At first, the Kennedy administration disavowed all knowledge of the mission, which was quelled by Castro's military within three days.

"I think there would a bigger chance of war if Nixon were in the White House," I said. "He hates the Russians."

"But what if Kennedy gives in? We'll be sitting ducks," Kate said.

"And if he doesn't give in, our goose could be cooked."

"I don't care who gives in," Molly said. "I just want this to be over and my family to be all right. It's horrible to be this far away. Even if it makes me late for classes, I'm calling home."

We headed for the post office, which had the only public telephone in the area. The phone wasn't working. Molly conjured up visions of cities already destroyed and telephone lines down across the United States, until the clerk assured us that it was only a local problem.

Our generation had lived with the threat of nuclear war almost our entire lives, watched films of the destruction of Hiroshima and Nagasaki, seen short subjects at movie theatres on atom and hydrogen bomb tests, and read magazine articles on how to build a fallout shelter in our backyards. It was easy to imagine that the end game had begun.

We decided to go over to the rectory to see what Father Peck was picking up on his ham radio.

"There's lots of chatter, but it's not always reliable," he told us. "From what I can gather, President Kennedy is exploring diplomatic channels and using the UN and the Organization of American States to put pressure on the Russians to pull back. The British are backing us up."

"Are people panicking at home?" Kate asked.

"There might be some hoarding going on, but most people have a wait-and-see attitude. You girls go on to class and try not to worry."

"Go to class and don't worry, he tells us!" Molly groused as we headed to school. "Doesn't he realize that going to class might be the last thing we ever do? I'm not sure I want to spend my last day on earth that way. Of course, I'm not sure I want to sit around thinking about the end of the world all day, either."

We went ahead with life as usual, but with the sense of dread people have when an airplane they're riding in unexpectedly experiences turbulence.

That afternoon, as planned, Molly's literature class staged the last act of *Our Town*. She turned the two big classrooms (formerly a living room and dining room) into a stage by lining up all the desks and chairs horizontally along one wall. Ordinarily, the lack of any door or divider between the rooms was a problem, but today it was an advantage. Students, teachers and the families and friends of the actors crowded into the rooms until they were filled and soon overflowing. Latecomers leaned on the sills and looked in through the veranda windows. The entire Quinlan family was there, because Sissy had the lead.

Father Bosque came in just before the performance began and stood in the doorway.

Dressed in a pink striped dress that I suddenly recognized as having been mine, Sissy delivered her lines in the same intense way she played baseball, throwing herself completely into the moment. The mature Emily of the play disappeared in the twelve-year-old Emily/Sissy, who personified all that is most fleeting: youth, innocence and childlike wonder.

"Wait! One more look," Sissy as Emily pleaded. "Goodbye, Goodbye, world. Goodbye, Grover's Corners – Mama and Papa. Goodbye to clocks ticking, and Mama's sunflowers. And food and coffee. And new-ironed dresses and hot baths – and sleeping and waking. Oh, earth, you're too wonderful for anybody to realize you. Do any human beings ever realize life while they live it? Every, every minute?"

In the case of *Madama Butterfly* the night before, art had been eerily attuned to the moment without our realizing it. Today, we were conscious of the connection. The poignant sense of the fragility and beauty of small, everyday things stayed with me long after the play ended.

On Wednesday, Sister Veronica brought a short-wave radio to school and kept it on all day. It was hard to keep my mind on classes, and the sound of the announcer's voice in the background lured me away from my lesson plan. Often I'd pause, sometimes in mid-sentence, straining to hear the latest news bulletin.

Throughout that day, periodic updates charted the mounting tension. According to reports on Radio Belize, the government of British Honduras had officially expressed its deep concern over the build-up of offensive weapons in Cuba. We heard a bit later that President Kennedy characterized the build-up as the result of deception and warned that if it were to continue, Cuba would rival the United States in military power within five years. He demanded an immediate end to the build-up and called for the dismantling and removal of the missiles already in place. In the afternoon, we learned that the Soviet government had cancelled all military leaves in apparent preparation for war.

The most worrying news was that a fleet of Russian ships was on its way to Cuba in spite of the blockade. The fleet was scheduled to arrive at eight the following morning, and there was no sign of their stopping. Pope John XXIII appealed for peace, urging negotiations at all levels and asking for a rule of wisdom and prudence.

With our supper tray, Josie brought over a copy of that day's *Belize Times*. The headline read, STOP THEM OR SINK THEM! The newspaper reported that if the Russian ships didn't stop or allow a search of their cargo, US ships had orders to sink them. And that would mean all-out war.

"De Russians no fools," Josie said. "Dey no wan fight de USA." Like many of the townspeople, including our students, she didn't seem terribly upset by the crisis.

"I don't think most of the people here understand about nuclear war," Molly said. "We've grown up with images of Hiroshima and Nagasaki. They haven't, and so they can't imagine it."

"I think it's their *que sera, sera* attitude," Kate said. "A kind of fatalism that I've noticed in their thinking."

"Maybe it was living through Hattie," I suggested. "After something like that, you learn the things you can't control, so you don't waste your time worrying about them."

Whatever its cause, I found their stoic reception of unfolding events reassuring, even though I couldn't imitate it.

After class, Molly went by the post office to see if the phone was working

– it wasn't – and Kate and I stopped by the rectory to see if Father Peck had any more news. He repeated what we already knew.

"Let me give you a few things," he said. He disappeared for a minute or two and came back with a box of thick candles, matches, a flashlight, some bottled water and a bottle of Scotch whisky.

"Just in case you need any or all of these," he said. "Not that I expect doomsday, but there's a storm brewing, and I'm pretty sure there won't be any electricity tonight."

"What's the Scotch for?" Kate asked.

"Any emergency that might arise," he said, with the hint of a smile.

"That was so nice of him," Kate said as we carried everything home.

"Maybe he is human after all," I agreed.

The last thing I wanted to do was go back to school after supper, but I'd promised Ana I would help her with the school fair, to be held the coming weekend. She'd scheduled a dress rehearsal for the fashion show, the main event of the afternoon of the fair. Seamstresses from town had contributed a dozen outfits to be modelled by our students and auctioned off to the highest bidder. We had to select the models from a pool of volunteers, and this evening was to be the trying-on session. Like teenagers anywhere, the students loved this sort of thing.

Ana was at her best organizing such an event. Like the impresario she was, she shrewdly assessed each student in terms of size and appearance and was rarely wrong in assigning the dresses to be auctioned off to the girls who could wear them to best advantage. I'd expected an array of ethnic costumes, but every one of the dresses imitated US fashion at the time: shirtwaists, sheaths, and circular skirts worn with frilly blouses. Ana announced in advance that those who weren't lucky enough to fit into one of the dresses to be auctioned off could also model, wearing their own best outfits.

Ana swiftly interspersed the chosen models among the fifteen or so who had agreed to wear their own clothes, lined them up, gave them a few tips on carriage and demeanour, had them walk through the programme a couple of times, making minor adjustments in the lineup, and we were finished.

"You really didn't need me," I said as we locked up the building. The sky was dark and the wind was picking up.

"I wanted to see you," she said. "We haven't had a chance to talk. Come home with me for something to drink."

"Just for a few minutes," I said. "I don't want to leave Molly and Kate alone tonight."

We settled into Ana's room in the Zacharias apartment with iced Cokes that Ana had sent up from the club.

"I want to explain about Eduardo," she said.

"What about him?" I asked, feeling uneasy.

"He's confused right now," she said. "He really likes you, but there's this cousin in El Salvador. When he saw her on his last trip, I guess he noticed her. She's crazy about him, and now he's wondering what to do. He went down to Half Moon when you were there to test his feelings, and then he went back to Salvador."

My fingers were numb from holding the icy Coke. I switched my glass from one hand to the other, warming my fingers on my flushed cheek. Ana leaned forward, speaking rapidly but softly.

"My father doesn't think she is good for Eduardo. She's only sixteen and very spoiled. But she's also very beautiful. I know he will see through her, so I'm glad he went back. Whatever feelings he has for her will wear out quickly. But in the meantime, be cool to Eduardo. Don't let him touch you. That's my advice. My father thinks you are the right one for him, and that means a lot. You have the most to offer him. But you must be careful how you handle Eduardo. I know him, and he likes what he has to work for. What's hard to get."

"The most to offer him? What in the world do I have to offer him?"

Ana looked at me as though I were daft. "You're an American!"

I needed air. "I have to go, Ana," I said, putting down the untasted Coke. Without saying goodbye, I headed for the door.

"Abby, you're upset, but don't be. I'm sure everything will work out fine. Just think about what I said."

I left her sitting on the edge of her bed, steered clear of Marita, who sat smoking at her usual place by the window, and hurried down the stairs. Outside, the wind was gusting and the rain came in spurts. I ran most of the way home, splashing through puddles I couldn't see in the dark.

I burst into the house, letting in a rush of wind that extinguished the flame on the candle in the middle of the floor, but not before I caught sight of Father Bosque sitting in a circle with Molly and Kate. Molly relit the candle, and I noticed they'd already opened the bottle of emergency Scotch.

"Oh, I'm so glad you're all here!" I gasped.

"You're drenched," Molly said. "Hurry up and change clothes. We were wishing you'd come."

I put on whatever clothes came to hand in the darkness, grabbed my Mexican shawl from the hook on the door and joined the circle.

"A terrible night," Father Bosque said. "In every sense of the word."

"I keep imagining those Russian ships out there, headed for Cuba, and our US ships ready to torpedo them!" Molly said. "It makes me crazy!"

"Father Peck says he thinks the Russians would never have tried anything like this against Nixon; that they're testing Kennedy, and if he holds firm, they'll back down," Father Bosque said. "Of course it's a dangerous game. But I can't believe the Russian people want war any more than Americans do."

"I hope you're right," Kate said. "But then why are they building up weapons in Cuba?"

"For the same reason the US has nuclear weapons in Turkey," he said. "As a deterrent. A defensive strategy."

"I didn't know we had nuclear weapons in Turkey," Molly said. "But even so, I can't believe we'd ever be the first to use them."

"Of course, you did, in the Second World War," Father Bosque reminded us.

I was taken aback by his implicit distinction between us as Americans and himself as British Honduran.

"But we only did it to end the war," Molly said, "because the Japanese wouldn't surrender otherwise."

"Perhaps so," Father Bosque said, "but if you were Russian, wouldn't you want as much security as possible with such a formidable enemy?"

"Then disarmament is the only answer," I said.

"Nations won't voluntarily give up their weapons," Kate said. "And the UN is too weak to make them."

"I agree," Molly said. "And you can't unsplit the atom or forget how to make atomic weapons once you have them."

"Then what hope is there?"

"The hope that Kennedy and Khrushchev find in themselves some of that wisdom and prudence that John XXIII prayed for," Father Bosque said. "And that they're doing some serious negotiating even as we speak."

That's how we spent the worst night of the Cuban Missile Crisis – not praying the rosary, as I suspect the nuns were doing, but having one of our orgies while the wind screeched and the rain beat on our zinc roof. Even after the last of the emergency Scotch was gone, the four of us stayed in the circle, keeping vigil through the darkest time of night.

Chapter 17

LOCAL CRISES

AS THE CUBAN MISSILE Crisis lifted, thanks in large part, it seemed, to the negotiations, wisdom and prudence John XIII had prayed for, local crises set in.

It wouldn't stop raining. Day after day, it rained, a cold, drenching rain. On the Friday morning before the school fair, rain was still coming down. Ana went to Sister Veronica, asking to have the fair postponed. Sister Veronica sent her to Mother Elaine, who told her to go see Father Peck. She begged me to go to his office with her over the noon hour.

"Rain or not, we're going ahead," he said. "The pig for the hog roast is being butchered today, the band for the dance has been hired, and everything else is set. If it rains tomorrow, we move indoors."

"Indoors!" Ana said. "There is no indoors big enough."

"Then people will just have to get wet."

"And when will we put up decorations?"

"We'll do without decorations."

"No one will come!"

"They'll come," he said.

"Oh, that priest makes me so angry!" Ana said as we hunched under a shared umbrella on our way back to school. "We start with a parade. Of course, that has to be outdoors. All the contests and games have to be outdoors. The hog roast is outdoors. The dance is outdoors. Only the fashion show is indoors! If it doesn't stop raining by the end of school today, we'll never get the lights and decorations up. And I don't care what Father Peck says. People might come, but they won't stay long. And if they don't stay, they won't spend their money."

We had been planning for the fair ever since the fall school term began. Molly, Kate and I had all written letters home, asking for donations, especially costume jewellery. New or used, it was always in demand, Ana told us. She was in charge of the St Monica events, with me as assistant; the boys' high school and the grade school each had their own coordinators. The name chosen for this year's fair – "Hurricane Halloween" – surprised me. Hattie had occurred only a year earlier, almost to the day.

"Life goes on," Ana assured me. "The contrast between last year's disaster and this year's prosperity will only make everyone more grateful and more generous."

"How much money does the fair usually raise?"

"About four thousand dollars BH. Last year, luckily we had the fair the weekend before the hurricane, but all the money went into the relief effort after Hattie, and that makes this year twice as important. The schools split the money and use it for books and scholarships. It's one of the biggest events in Angel Creek. Probably the biggest except for Settlement Day. That goes on for a whole week," she said, referring to the November celebration of the arrival of the Garifuna people in British Honduras more than a hundred years earlier.

In mid-afternoon, during composition class, one of the Three B students called out, "Look, Miss! De rain stop!" The class began to buzz, and I heard a similar sound from nearby classrooms.

Not long after, Sister Veronica stuck her head in the door to announce that classes were dismissed for the rest of the day so that we could work on preparations for the fair. We had part of an afternoon and an evening to complete work that usually took three or four days.

Until late that night, nuns, priests, teachers, students and quite a few parents worked together to string up coloured lights, set up games (one involved blowing up hundreds of balloons to be pierced by darts) and decorate booths and tables to carry out the Halloween theme. The concept required twisting together dozens of yards of orange and black crêpe paper and cutting out scores of pumpkins, cats and witches' hats labelled, maybe a bit too obviously, "Hattie".

Most of the evening, Ana and I worked side by side decorating the double classroom where the fashion show would be held. After we finished and the students who'd been helping us left, I decided that now was as good a time as any to talk to Ana about Eduardo. For days, he'd been on my mind.

"Let's go out on the balcony for a few minutes," I said.

As we sat looking out over the sea, savouring the cool breeze, I took a deep breath and began talking a bit too fast, stumbling over my words. "Ana, I've thought a lot about what you said not so long ago – about Eduardo, I mean, and his cousin – and I think now – well, what I thought at the very beginning. He's too young for me."

"We've been through this before," she said.

"He needs more time before he's ready to settle down."

"Won't you give him a little more time? You're young, too, you know. Twenty-two isn't exactly old age. Don't rush things. In fact, it's best to hold back. Men like that."

"I won't play hard to get, if that's what you mean. Once Eduardo gets me, then what?"

"Then everything will be fine."

"But that sort of game isn't something to build a relationship on. In my opinion, that's not love. It's infatuation. And manipulation."

"I don't think feelings, whatever kind, are all that good to build a relationship on," said Ana. "Of course, you know I want love for myself, but only if other things are there too. Eduardo is attracted to you, Abby, if that's what you're worried about. But even more important, he respects you. And you would be so good for him! It would be sad if you turned away now, when the road ahead is clear."

"But it's not clear, Ana. What about your beautiful cousin?"

"I shouldn't have told you about her!" she said. "But I thought it would make you want to fight harder, not give up!"

"It's not the cousin. It's the feeling I have that your family is pushing Eduardo – and me too – into something we're not ready for. Really, Eduardo is the one I need to talk to about this."

"No! It's not something you should ever mention to him. It will spoil everything."

"Not being able to talk to him about it will spoil everything for me!"

"Please don't even think about talking to him," she said. "I'll talk to him soon and find out what he's thinking. Promise you won't say anything to him before that."

"I doubt I'll have the chance. He's still in Salvador, isn't he?"

"We expect him back tonight or tomorrow."

The morning of the fair reminded me of a fall day back home. The sky was overcast, and the wind raised goose bumps on my arms. Ana said it was sure to rain before the day was over. As I lined up my homeroom for the opening parade, I crossed my arms to stop my shivering. The students shivered, too, waiting for the band – a group of local musicians hired to play for the dance that evening – to start us off with marching music.

"Can you believe it? Floats!" Molly pointed to a side street where a dozen floats perched precariously on the backs of trucks or the tops of cars were waiting to join the parade. In the back of one truck, real oranges and grapefruit swung like pendulums from cardboard trees. Boys from the agricultural college in the valley propped up the top-heavy trees.

When things got going, wheels and feet soon churned up the muddy streets, spattering the skirts of the students' white uniforms. The mud sucked the flip-flops that most of us wore right off our feet, and that slowed our progress as we stopped to retrieve them. Making things worse, some of the floats that pulled into line ahead of us got stuck in the mud, and we had to march around the truck that carried the quivering citrus grove and a Ford convertible filled with models from the fashion show, who continued to smile and wave to spectators.

Each school in town had its own float, and the procession culminated with ours. One of the Pérez sisters perched on a chair in the back of the blue Jeep, dressed in flowing robes and holding a baby doll. I would have mistaken her for the Blessed Mother holding the infant Jesus except for a sign arched over her that identified her as the patroness of our school, St Monica, holding baby Augustine. By the time the mud-speckled parade entered the big schoolyard next to the church, where most of the games and food were set up, it included half the town.

Sitting at a table outside the schoolyard gate, Mrs Jefferson sold tickets for the events and food. Mrs Moss went around collecting used tickets from the various booths and concessions and returned them to Mrs Jefferson to sell again. Throughout the day, between drizzles, townspeople competed in foot races run barefoot in the sandy field across from the church and lined up for a variety of balloon-popping, ball-tossing and weight-lifting contests. To the winners went a dollar's worth of tickets each and a blue ribbon, pinned to shirts and blouses as a badge of victory.

The nuns and some of the mothers took charge of selling the food they'd prepared, roast pork dinners with rice and beans and cassava pudding; orange sections sprinkled with hot pepper flakes; sugar cookies iced with orange frosting; newspaper cones of salted cashews and others of fried plantain chips; and bottles of imported soda pop.

Molly staffed a booth that sold the mounds of dime-store, pop-on plastic pearl necklaces, coloured glass bracelets and enamelled brooches that she, Kate and I had collected from family in the States. Kate, wearing a turban and my Mexican shawl, read palms at ten cents a hand in a little tent set up in the schoolyard. Ana and I ran the fashion show, which was delayed until the convertible was dug out, pushed and pulled from the mud, and the mostly unsullied models were delivered to the high school. Just as the fashion show began, the rain started falling hard, but that worked to our advantage; we had a standing-room-only crowd at twenty-five cents a head. As the last student strutted down the runway, the rain stopped, as if on cue.

"Now, if only the rain holds off until after the dance tonight!" Ana said. "We need that ticket money!"

With the exception of Eduardo, the entire Zacharias family was at the fair. They had shut down the clubs in town and in the valley so as not to compete. As I walked across the schoolyard after the fashion show, I saw Alberto Zacharias and Posey lined up to have their fortunes told. When Alberto stayed in the tent a little too long, Posey pushed aside the tent flap and pulled him out by the sleeve of his shirt. Alberto was laughing, and Posey looked like it was all in fun, but later, they began a shouting match in the middle of the schoolyard. She shoved him, he shoved back, and she ended up sprawled on the muddy ground. He turned to walk away, but she was on his back in an instant, pummelling and clawing. Shaking her off, he grabbed her by the waist and half dragged, half carried her off with him.

I watched them later that evening, wrapped in each other's arms on the dance floor. I despised their violence even as I envied their passion. And I realized I myself would probably choose it over the self-controlled love Ana proposed.

Mr Zacharias, his big belly filling his lap, sat on a wooden bench with his three youngest sons, watching Marita dance with Ana. Molly, Kate and I sat on the next bench, where Ana and Marita eventually joined us. When the music started again, Marita beckoned to the boys, and they came over to us in a group, looking very serious.

"May I have this dance?" Jaime, the eldest, asked me, holding out his hand.

Even though I wanted to laugh, I managed to mirror his seriousness. He led me onto the dance floor and carefully put his arm around my waist, the top of his head just even with my chin. Miguel chose Molly, and Tomas, the youngest, followed with Kate. They were all good dancers, and the people around us backed off to watch them lead us through a calypso number. As it ended, the onlookers applauded, and the boys bowed, first to us and then to the crowd.

"Did Ana put you up to this?" I asked Jaime as we walked back to our bench.

"We wanted to do it," he said.

I stopped. Eduardo was there, standing next to Ana. Even though the dance was over, I felt as if I'd been whirled around. I heard him say, "Are you boys flirting with girls already?" It was kind, gentle Eduardo, at ease with his little brothers. The memory of our twilight embrace in Emilio's Buick – awkward, sweet – swept over me.

"Papa said we should dance with them!" Miguel answered. "Didn't he, Ana?"

"I'm just teasing," Eduardo said.

I saw that he was smiling at me over their heads.

I returned his gaze but not his smile. Suddenly, I felt like crying and wished I'd been able to slip away before he saw me. At the same time I wanted to talk to him, but alone. We stood there, not saying anything to each other. The strings of coloured lights that lit the dance floor swung in loops and arcs, tossed by the wind. I turned away as Molly and Kate joined us and began a conversation. The only thing I said to him was a hasty good night.

"Well done!" Ana said the next day, stopping me after Sunday Mass. "Eduardo thinks he's done something to offend you, and he's going to stop by this afternoon to see you and invite you to the movies. My father even gave him the night off."

"It won't do any good, Ana," I said. "Molly, Kate and I are leaving for the Pine Ridge in a couple of hours. We're spending our break there." The Pine Ridge was a forest preserve in the Maya Mountains, half a day's journey over rugged roads.

"Well, that's good and bad," Ana decided. "You're missing an opportunity to get closer to Eduardo, but maybe it's good he should worry for a while. And miss you."

"I don't want him to worry or to miss me, Ana! I'm not doing any of this to make Eduardo more interested in me."

"Don't you like him any more?" She looked upset.

"It's not working out, Ana!" A wave of anger swept over me. What concern was it of hers, my relationship with Eduardo? "I have to get ready to leave right now. I'll talk to you when I get back."

"Well, what is there to talk about if your mind is made up?"

"Ana, what I feel or don't feel for Eduardo shouldn't change our friendship."

She looked at me wordlessly, turned and walked away.

Chapter 18

BETRAYALS

"YOU'RE CERTAINLY SPENDING A lot of time with the British these days," Father Bosque observed.

It was true. Over our break, David Lewis had taken us to the Pine Ridge, where we stayed in cabins maintained by the Forestry Service. The Todds came, too, and with them we explored for the first time the western region: the ancient Maya Mountains, with their rapid streams and vast pine forests; the Macal River Valley, teaming with wildlife and exotic vegetation; and the Spanish-speaking town of El Cayo, also known as San Ignacio, not far from the Guatemalan border.

Bit by bit, David had become a constant presence in our lives. Everyone, even Molly, realized that he was in love with her. He must have decided that since he couldn't develop a one-on-one relationship with her, he'd include Kate and me too. He and I were good friends, but after Kate's arrival, he formed an even closer bond with her. The two of them would sometimes sit talking long after Molly and I excused ourselves to run an errand or prepare for class. Under other circumstances, they might have made a good couple, I sometimes thought, both of them genial, polite, logical, disciplined and reserved.

On most weekends that autumn, David turned up at our house on either Friday or Saturday evening. Often Father Bosque or some of our other friends would drop by, and suddenly we'd find ourselves in the midst of a party. Some of the local bachelors were regulars – Simon, the twenty-year-old son of the Morrises, who ran the pharmacy and drugstore, and a few of the teachers from the agricultural college in the valley. Mrs Jefferson and Mrs Moss had introduced us to one of the Peace Corps workers, Larry Jessup, who taught math there. He usually brought with him the Spanish teacher, Maestro Rodriguez, with whom Kate had long conversations in Spanish – just practice, she assured us, nothing personal. One October night, a dozen of us piled in Father's Jeep and David's Simca and drove down to the new pier, built a bonfire and watched the moon rise.

When David suggested the trip to the west, Molly, Kate and I immediately took him up on his offer. He managed to get time off when we were free and picked us up the Sunday after the fair. On the drive, which under the best conditions took three hours, we took our time. We stopped along the road at Roaring Creek, where there was a gas station and general store, for *empanadas*, the spicy dumplings we all loved, and took time to splash in one of the dozens of mountain streams that rushed to the sea over wide, flat rocks.

We reached Augustine, a tiny village on the side of a mountain, a little before nightfall. Andrew and Julie were already settled into one of the stone guesthouses, perched on a cliff above the village, and as we arrived, we smelled a wood fire burning. We ate our supper looking out the window at faint pinpoints of light in a distant valley under a sky emblazoned with stars.

Molly, Kate and I had our own small cabin next to the one the Todds and Richard shared, and we slept on army cots under woollen blankets. Even though the windows were open only a crack, the scent of pine spiced the cold air.

After an early breakfast, we drove in the Todds' Land Rover to the Rio Macal, a wide, fast-moving river at the foot of a winding road. We parked along the road near the bridge, and David led us on a long walk into the bush that was busy with scarlet macaws, spider monkeys, giant iguana and scores of bright blue butterflies, some at least six inches across, which David identified as blue morphos. I felt as if I'd entered a natural metropolis whose exotic inhabitants, absorbed by daily affairs, scurried on their way, hardly noticing us as we passed.

Most of our walk was not the difficult trek through tangled undergrowth that I had expected. As David explained, the thick canopy of trees blocked the sunlight so that the forest floor was, for the most part, clear. Only in the river valley itself and in occasional clearings did the term *bush* actually apply. There, vegetation grew dense and impassable without a machete to clear the way.

After a picnic lunch, we took off for Baldy Beacon, driving over narrow mountain roads until, it seemed, we had reached the top of the world. We stood on the windswept peak, looking towards the Coxcomb Ridge that rose like a dragon's back in the distance. No one spoke, the wind too strong and the view, down long river corridors to the sea in one direction and Guatemala in the other, too breathtaking.

We then drove back down to the Macal River Valley along a road called Angels' Drive and hiked to another section of the river, where huge trees trailed tendrils into darkly deep pools of water. David said that some of the mounds we saw along the trail were most likely the ruins of ancient Maya villages, covered now by the vegetation of the rain forests indigenous to the region. He pointed out the towering ceiba trees, also called kapok, held sacred by the Maya as their link to the spirit world. It was as if the spirit of that ancient people, who had lived and worshipped for centuries along these waters, hovered over and around us as we moved.

The landscape we explored that day and in the days that followed was ravishing, and David was at his best in it, knowing which mountain trails offered the most spectacular views, which pools and streams were best for swimming, and which part of the forest at which time of day afforded the most interesting insects, birds and wildlife. I wasn't surprised to see Molly's regard for David grow as the days went by. Kate's and mine did too.

Molly and David became a twosome on that trip as never before. They often wandered off together while the rest of us read or napped. In the evenings, wrapped in sweaters and scarves, the two of them sat outside in the chill night air.

"I think we have something happening here," Julie said to Kate and me, her voice uncharacteristically excited, as we hiked along a mountain trail one afternoon. David and Molly were well ahead of us and Andrew was bringing up the rear. Even though she was seven months pregnant, Julie kept pace with the rest of us, easily it seemed. It's true that she was in excellent shape and had gained little weight during her pregnancy. "It's no worse than carrying a rugby ball around," she assured us. Still, we worried about her and tried to slow her down a bit.

"Are you feeling all right?" Kate asked, alarmed. "You're not having contractions, are you?"

"Gor blimey, no!" she laughed. "I mean that things are happening between David and Molly. Haven't you noticed all the sparks flying these past few days? I'm so happy for David. He really cares for her, you know."

Neither Kate nor I responded, but later, when we were alone, Kate said to me, "I feel sorry for David. I don't think Molly really loves him."

"Maybe she's starting to."

"I think she's in love with love."

When I told Kate that I'd never understood exactly what that phrase meant, she replied, "I think it means the feeling is more important to you than the person."

I had to admit that as my feelings for Eduardo diminished, so did my interest in him. "But the problem," I said, "seems to be telling the feeling of love from love itself."

"I'm not too clear on that myself," Kate admitted. "I think it might be easier for others to see than you yourself can."

Early Thursday morning, we said goodbye to the Todds, who were staying on through the weekend. It was All Saints' Day and David had agreed to take us to El Cayo for Mass before we started for home.

"We're sorry to leave so early," Molly explained to the Todds. "But we have to go to church."

"Whatever for?" Julie asked.

"It's All Saints' Day, a holy day of obligation."

"What does that mean?"

"It means we have to go to Mass."

"Why?"

"It would be a sin not to."

"Do you mean you'd be damned to hell if you didn't go?" Andrew asked with the ironic look that always accompanied any reference he made to religion.

"Well, yes, if we should die before we could confess our sin."

"Do you actually believe that?" he asked.

"Yes, of course," Molly said.

"And you too?" Andrew said, looking at Kate and me.

We both nodded, although I'm pretty sure all three of us had our doubts.

Andrew persisted. "Presuming for the moment there's a hell, I can see damnation for mass murder, maybe. But for missing a Mass?"

"It's one of those things, if you're a Catholic, you don't question. Like not eating meat on Friday," Kate said. "It's an obligation, as Molly said before. We do it because we believe, as a sign of faith."

"And if we take time now to argue about it, we'll miss Mass for sure," Molly said, her tone playful.

"Well, I wouldn't like for you to be damned," Andrew said, "But it's a damned shame to waste this beautiful morning. It's perfect for a parting swim."

David shook his head. "We really must go."

"And are you going to this Mass?" Andrew asked.

"I might try it," he said.

"I guess Paris is worth a Mass."

I couldn't quite recall the allusion, but I knew Andrew was mocking the Church, and I resented it. As with a family, however mixed up, only members could criticize it.

As it turned out, David waited in the square while we knelt in the Spanish-style church filled with women, children and old men. Afterward, we found strong coffee and sweet bread for breakfast and wandered through the hilly, dusty roads, admiring the bright textiles for sale on the street corners, brought over from Guatemala, only a few miles to the west.

"It's a pity we can't stay till tomorrow," David said. "I'm told they celebrate the Day of the Dead instead of Halloween in this area. Very colourful – processions, decorations, all sorts of interesting rituals."

We wanted to stay, but we'd already accepted invitations back in Angel Creek for the weekend. We did, however, decide to stop by the Papal Volunteer House on our way out of town. Several times, volunteers had dropped in on us, and we all expected that if we were near a PAVLA house anywhere in the country, we'd find a warm welcome and, if necessary, a place to stay.

Maureen Bone kept us talking on the doorstep for what seemed like a long time and then, reluctantly, I thought, invited us in. As she was introducing us to her roommate, one of the Peace Corps volunteers who'd arrived in September, a sleepy-eyed young man came out of one of the bedrooms, barefoot, buttoning his shirt. Maureen and her roommate exchanged embarrassed glances, and then the Peace Corps worker cleared her throat and explained that the man was her husband.

"Please don't mention this," she pleaded. "We got married last weekend, against the rules. If the Peace Corps finds out, we'll both be sent home."

We promised to keep their secret. As we had tea together, the couple explained that they'd met during training, fallen in love and with a free week ahead, found a minister to marry them. The husband was posted in Orange Walk, more than a hundred miles away. They knew they wouldn't be able to be together very often, only over holidays and breaks, but they didn't think they could postpone marriage any longer.

"Now, we just have to find a way to keep it a secret for the next two years!" the young man said.

"We hated to do this to Maureen," the bride said, "but we couldn't afford a honeymoon. She's been wonderful about it all!"

"It's fine for you to be here together, no matter what the Peace Corps says," Maureen replied. "You're married, after all."

That's how it was in 1962, and most of those I knew accepted that marriage and sex should go together, and in that order, for decent people, anyway.

One of the invitations that kept us from staying in El Cayo for the Day of the Dead was from the Pérez family, the one with all the beautiful daughters. The other was for Sunday supper with the Olivers, one of the most prominent British families in our district. The Pérezes had invited us as well as David for a family baptism on Saturday and the Olivers for dinner on Sunday evening.

Around four on Saturday afternoon, Molly, Kate and I drove with Father Bosque to All Saints, the tiny church in the valley. It was used only on occasional Sundays, when one of the priests from Angel Creek was available to say Mass, or for a special occasion like this baptism. He unlocked the door, and we opened the windows. The air smelled of stale incense and candle wax, not quite covering an unpleasant, mouldy odour. As family members and friends began to arrive and settle in the pews, we helped him set up the altar and the baptismal font. The baby was the first child of one of the Pérez daughters, Catharina, and her English husband, Jack Hitchens.

Catharina and Jack were both famous, she for her beauty and he for the combined toughness and ingenuity that had made it possible for him and his crew to construct and maintain roads in some of the most remote parts of the colony. Like many of the British in our area, he worked for the Forestry Service. We knew from David that the men on the crews adored Jack and had turned him into something of a local hero. He was known for his exploits: killing a rattler with his bare hands, saving a workman who slipped into a swollen river. He turned out to be a big, handsome guy, broad-shouldered, blond, with brown eyes and a deep tan. Catharina was a smooth-skinned, dark-haired beauty, with full breasts and a tiny waist, even so soon after the birth of her baby. All the Pérez sisters were beautiful, but Catharina was the sun that obliterates other stars. The baby was dressed in a long, lacy christening gown sent from England by Jack's mother. According to David, she'd vociferously opposed the marriage, perhaps because of his conversion to Catholicism or maybe, he said, because he'd chosen to settle in British Honduras.

Just as the ceremony was about to start, half an hour late, a hairy black tarantula emerged from a corner and scuttled towards the altar. Catharina clutched her baby and let out a shriek. "Jack, do something!" Her husband scooped up the spider with a palm-leaf fan from one of the pews and flipped it out an open window into the hibiscus bushes.

Once again, Father Bosque launched into the opening prayer, but a few seconds into it, a Land Rover full of British foresters who had driven all the way from Half Moon Creek roared up, and Father Bosque stopped again and waited until they all came in, laughing and greeting people as though the party had already started.

With the baby safely baptized, we drove in a caravan farther up the valley to the Pérez house. It was bigger inside than it looked from the outside – we found out later that the family had taken down an interior wall just for the party – and had a back veranda that overlooked a creek that was still cloudy after the recent rains. When we arrived, some of the younger kids, who hadn't attended the baptism, were swimming in a pool formed by an improvised dam upstream. In addition to Catharina and the three Pérez daughters who were our students at St Monica's, there were also three boys of school age, a couple of younger children, one still too young for school, and the oldest sister, Celia, also married, and the mother of three small children.

Late in the evening, "Mama Pérez," as we were instructed to call her, served a spicy chicken *relleno* with black sauce that was quite possibly the best food I'd ever eaten. Then the toasts started, round after round of raised Heineken bottles and glasses filled with whisky or wine.

"Miss Abby!"

I'd been daydreaming, and the sound of my name startled me. Papi Pérez's voice boomed in the crowded room, repeating my name. "Miss Abby, may we ask you to offer a toast on behalf of the American teachers?"

"Me?"

"Yes, please, Miss Abby, if you will be so kind."

When I blurted out that it would be the first toast I'd ever given, probably because I'd only recently reached the drinking age in the States, everyone laughed.

"A toast to love, then, which knows no boundaries, and to the marriage of nations this new child represents." Everyone waited for more, but I couldn't think of anything else to say. I raised my glass and in my nervousness shouted out, "To the Pérez family, past, present and future! Oh, and the Hitchens family too!" Far and away, mine was the shortest toast of the evening and, I'm sure, a disappointment in a culture that valued length and admired eloquence and expected no less from a teacher.

Later, when the music started, as it inevitably did at any celebration, Jack Hitchens asked me to dance. I could tell from his flushed face that he'd already had too much to drink. He held me so close I could hardly breathe. Over his shoulder, I saw Father Bosque taking his leave. I hadn't had a chance to talk to him all evening. Since our return from the western region, I'd exchanged no more than a sentence or two with him. I wanted to tell him about our trip, but he was out the door without a goodbye before the dance finished.

"Let me tell you a thing or two about love and marriage," Jack said, drawing me off to one side. He held onto my waist, even though the music had stopped. "They're damnably overrated!"

"I beg your pardon?"

"Overrated. Most definitely overrated."

"Why do you say that?"

"Because you seem like an intelligent girl. Educated. You wouldn't want to make a big mistake."

"What sort of mistake do you mean?"

"A lifelong one. I hear you're seeing one of the locals, one of the Zacharias boys. Don't get sucked in."

Angel Creek was a small town, and I knew the townspeople watched our every move. I hadn't expected the British to do the same.

"I'd think you'd be the last person to give me such advice," I replied.

"It's good advice," he said. "I know what I'm talking about. It's another world, this country. Like going back in time." I felt his hand slide from my waist down to my buttocks. "So god-damned much they don't know."

I backed away and retreated to one of the benches along the wall, squeezing in next to Molly, who was sitting beside David.

"Did you get a chance to talk to Father Bosque?" I asked her.

"Not for long. He said he has the early Mass tomorrow and needed to get some sleep."

Kate was dancing with Maestro Rodriguez, the Spanish teacher from the boys' high school in the valley. Jack Hitchens tried to cut in, but the Spanish teacher didn't want to let her go. "Wait your turn, mon," I heard him say.

Jack then asked Molly to dance, but David said, "Sorry, Jack; this one's mine." He rose and led Molly onto the dance floor.

Jack looked at me with a lopsided grin. "Guess I'm going to have to ask my wife to dance."

The Olivers lived on a hilltop above Paloma Valley in a hacienda-style house surrounded by gardens. The two priests had also been invited, but Father Peck turned down the invitation. The Olivers weren't Catholics, but the family generously supported the schools. They monopolized the sugar cane industry in the south and employed many workers from Angel Creek and the surrounding villages. One did not turn down an invitation from them lightly, but Father Peck refused most invitations, saying the parish kept him too busy for a night out. Father Bosque agreed to go as a favour to us. He let us know he didn't like the idea of hobnobbing with the "colonials" but would take us if we wanted to go. We decided we wanted to see how the upper crust lived.

As we drove into the courtyard, we saw an in-ground swimming pool off to one side and down a level on the terraced hillside. The entire valley fanned out around us, and in the distance, we could see the Caribbean, docile now that the season of storms was past.

"This is the life!" Molly exclaimed.

Father Bosque commented, "You're certainly spending a lot of time with the British these days."

His remark made me uneasy, as if we were somehow betraying our PAVLA mission and, worse so far as I was concerned, disappointing him.

But unaccustomed luxury is seductive, and the Olivers offered the closest thing to luxury in our part of the colony. A white-coated servant greeted us in the tiled entryway and led us into a long, airy living room with paintings on the walls, fabric on the chairs and couches, and shaded lamps and vases of cultivated flowers on the tables. The floors were solid mahogany, polished to dark brightness, covered here and there by rugs. Through the archway, I could see crystal, silver and china glinting on the dining table. Mr and Mrs Oliver, he in a print shirt that looked like silk, open at the throat, and she in a flowery skirt and dark green blouse, came to welcome us. He was in his mid-fifties and his wife about the same age, although with their hair gone grey they looked older.

They introduced us to two of their children, both adults, and several visitors, among them Mr Oliver's brother, visiting from Jamaica. "Call me Richard," he said, shaking our hands.

Richard seemed delighted to meet three young, unmarried women and soon had us cornered. Father Bosque eyed us from across the room, poised, I knew, to come to our rescue.

"I had no idea there was a trio of young American girls living in Angel Creek," Richard said. Five minutes into the conversation, he mentioned that he was on the board of a private girls' school in Kingston, where there might be an opening for the "right" girl.

"Let's go sit in those chairs over there and talk it over," he said. "But first, you need some more wine and I could use another whisky." He gestured to the white-coated servant, who brought us the drinks.

Richard guided all three of us to a corner of the room and launched into a description of the school. It was the best in the Caribbean, he assured us. He asked us about ourselves and our educations, and whether we might be interested in applying.

What about you?" he asked, looking at Molly.

"Well, to be honest, I'm engaged," said Molly, "and I'll probably be married by this time next year."

Kate and I exchanged glances. Too bad for David.

He turned to Kate. "You?"

"Possibly," Kate said. "But I'm thinking of grad school for the fall."

"I might be interested," I said.

Molly and Kate excused themselves, leaving me alone with Richard.

"You know, you remind me very much of my son's fiancée. Charming girl. French. Looks just like Leslie Caron." He said he was sure he could find something for me if I was interested. Shortly after that, he excused himself and went over to say something to Mrs Oliver.

Father Bosque came up behind me. "Is he bothering you?" he asked in a low voice.

"No, not at all," I said. "He's very kind. He's offered to recommend me for a teaching job in Jamaica next year."

"What sort of job offer is made over a Scotch and soda? Just be careful what you get yourself into, Abby, especially with a notorious womanizer like that one."

"You're the second man in two days warning me about other men!" I snapped.

"I sometimes think Kate is the only one of the three of you with any sense!"

"Thanks a lot," I said, and walked off.

I was relieved when Mrs Oliver seated me at the opposite end of the table from Father Bosque and wasn't at all displeased when she put Richard Oliver next to me. We talked through the entire meal, at first about Jamaica and the school system, the sort of classes I might be teaching, and the incredible salary I'd receive. But soon he was leaning close, telling me about his unhappy marriage to an unsuitable woman. For the most part, they lived separate lives.

"I'm sure we can work out a suitable arrangement," Richard said at the end of the evening. He handed me a card with his name and address engraved on it. "Contact me if you'd like to pursue this."

By then, I'd begun to think better of the offer. "You know, I really don't think I'm the kind of person you're looking for," I said.

All the way home, Father Bosque was silent. Not a word except a curt good night.

"To tell the truth, I thought the evening was a disappointment," Molly said as we prepared for bed. "For one thing, the dinner itself was pretty poor. In fact, I thought it was an insult to the guests."

"What was the main dish?" Kate asked. "I've never had it before."

"Cottage pie, that's what it was," Molly answered. "Basically, mashed potatoes and hamburger. I didn't expect steak – well, maybe I did. In any case, I certainly expected something better than that! All that silver and crystal and china for hamburger!"

"It's a lovely house and a wonderful location, though," Kate said, "and they were good to invite us."

"I think they invited us because we're young and not bad looking and it livens things up for them. Old Richard was certainly enjoying himself. What in the world were you two talking about for so long, Abby?"

"I thought I was being interviewed for a job. In fact, I think he may have been propositioning me."

"How disgusting!" Kate said.

"I feel like I need a bath," I said. "And I've had enough of the British for a while."

"I think from now on we should be more careful accepting invitations," Kate said. "Maybe that's what Father Bosque was trying to tell us when he said we were spending an awful lot of time with the British. Do you think that was why he was so quiet most of the evening?"

"I think he was upset with Abby," Molly said.

"Why do you think so?" I asked, fearing she was right.

"He probably thought you were flirting, sucking up to the British."

By this time, I knew Father Bosque well enough to know that he would regard any such thing as a personal betrayal. And I knew that to a certain degree, I was guilty.

Chapter 19

TIGER

NOT FOR THE FIRST time that year, I wished I were older – safely past youth. If I were beyond it, and the emotions and desires that went with it, I told myself, I could concentrate entirely on teaching my students, enjoying my friendships and doing good deeds. I wouldn't inadvertently attract lecherous old men like Richard Oliver, wouldn't be vulnerable to the attention of handsome young men like Eduardo, and above all wouldn't do anything to jeopardize the good opinion of someone like Father Bosque.

My only comfort was perverse: Molly shared my condition, fretting over both David and her fiancé Paul. She was by turns hot and cold to both, sometimes ignoring Paul's correspondence for weeks and then writing him ten-page, single-spaced letters; sometimes avoiding David, to whom she denied any real attraction, and other times welcoming his attention. Only Kate seemed impervious to the sexual waves Molly and I rode, even though I suspected she felt a ripple of attraction to David.

"How do you control your emotions so well?" I asked Kate at breakfast the morning after dinner with the Olivers. "No matter what, you're always cucumber cool."

"Oh, I have my emotional moments," Kate said. "But I guess I'm still getting over Mandy – Armando, my Spanish friend. And I haven't met anyone here who attracts me strongly in that way."

"I'd say you attract Maestro Rodriguez and also Alberto Zacharias in that way," Molly said.

"I can just imagine taking Alberto Zacharias home to my little Minnesota town to meet the folks," Kate said, not looking up from her grapefruit.

I tried to imagine Eduardo in Missouri. But of course, we'd live in Angel Creek. In the house he would build in the valley, with orange groves just outside the back door and our beautiful children, all of them looking like him, playing in the garden.

"By the way, Kate," Molly asked, "why did Alberto stay so long in your palm-reading tent?"

"That was very strange and kind of humorous," she said. "I told him his fortune, but he kept asking me to tell him more, and then he grabbed my hands and tried to tell *my* fortune! Suddenly, in came his girlfriend and pulled him out by the ear. You know what happened next." She sighed. "Posey has nothing to worry about. I'm not looking for romance. I'm just trying to teach my classes, follow the rules and stay out of trouble."

"What rules?" I asked.

"Well, as I understand it, we aren't supposed to date or get involved with anyone while we're here."

"Rules like that are meant to be broken," Molly said. "You can tell that priests and nuns made them. If you meet someone you're attracted to, you naturally want to be with that person."

"What would Paul say to that?" Kate asked.

"That's really nobody else's business," Molly said, heating up. "Just so you know, I'm not dating David, and I'm really not all that attracted to him. We're just good friends. I was thinking of Abby. It's Abby who's dating."

"Leave me out of this!" I said. "Eduardo and I aren't dating. Actually, we're not even friends! A couple of kisses and he's off to greener pastures!"

"You kissed him?" Molly cried. "When? And what greener pastures? Tell us!"

"Another case of nobody's business," I said.

"You brought it up, Abby Porter! You're a tease!"

Now my temper rose. "I am not a tease! And I'm not saying another word!"

"That's right, bottle it all up," said Molly.

"Wait. Isn't that my thing?" Kate asked with an edge to her voice.

We managed a laugh, but we spent the rest of the day avoiding each other.

Now that our fall break was over, Molly, Kate and I threw ourselves into our teaching. We went in early to school and stayed late. Other teachers did the same thing. It seemed to have dawned on all of us, teachers and students alike, that we'd fallen way behind the syllabus sent out from Britain. It was easy to blame our late start and lack of books, but the three of us felt particularly guilty. We'd spent precious time on innovations not part of the regular curriculum: my newspaper and, along with Molly, the English club, Molly's production of *Our Town* and Kate's "Gracious Living" sessions. In addition, preparation for the school fair had taken time away from classes, as had the oratory contest.

The contest was a national event, and not long before the fair, Molly and Kate had taken two St Monica's students to Belize City to compete against finalists from all the high schools in the country. One of our students won a top prize for "Original Oratory" with her speech entitled "Needed Virtues in British Honduras" – respect for oneself and others topped the list – and the other came home with "Honourable Mention." The honours were a first for our school, and Sister Veronica called an assembly to recognize the award winners.

"We are proud of your outstanding performances," she said to the prize winners, one of whom was Elspeth Williams, the girl from Sand Bight, "and we commend Miss Mannion and Miss Eliot, who coached the winning students.

"I'm also happy to announce that the fair cleared forty-four hundred dollars, the most in its history. Miss Zacharias deserves credit for organizing the event so well and also Miss Porter for helping her. Everyone deserves thanks for working so hard to make both events a grand success."

This was rare praise from our usually dour principal, and we sunned ourselves in it while it lasted.

"But as we all know," she went on, and a familiar frown eclipsed the unaccustomed smile, "the future of every student here depends on doing well on the exams. All the extra things are good in themselves, but steady progress towards the leaving exams is the crucial thing."

At the end of their high school programme, most students took the Cambridge O-level exams in a range of subjects. A few students then stayed on for an extra year or two to prepare for and take the A-level exams. This year, five fifth-year students comprised a special class taught by Sisters Veronica and Marietta; they were slated to take their A-levels in December. Every morning, this select group climbed the stairs to the attic room at the top of the house reserved for their use. The students in the lower forms regarded them with hushed deference.

In many ways, I had to admit that the students were getting an excellent education, one that would enable them to compete for government jobs and qualify for scholarships at foreign universities. But I found its heavy reliance on memorization one-dimensional and its detachment from our students' lived experience short-sighted and closed-minded. As I would later describe it, the curriculum was designed by males for males and by Europeans for Europeans, not girls from Caribbean villages. Like Kate and Molly, I searched for ways to energize my teaching and bring the students' learning to life.

Occasionally, it happened with the material I was given to teach. John Masefield's "Sea Fever" worked like magic, calling forth my students' intimate knowledge of the sea and transforming it through art into a new way of imagining the world around them. Their own sea poems were acts of observation heightened by imagination. Jessie Nunez, one of the best poets in the first-year class, wrote a sequence of inspired poems about the sea.

"Like a dog following its master, the sea follows the seasons," began one of her poems. Another concluded: "When the seaweeds come to call the waves, / The waves just smile and show their white teeth around." I hoped for many more such revelations.

Struggling most of all with my history class, I started a current events discussion once a week – another activity not on the syllabus but the only way I found to give the subject a bit of vitality. Even though we were living it, history was the discipline most detached from the daily life of my students and also from my own. In those days, history was almost entirely a male province, concerned mostly with warfare and politics, areas where females traditionally played only an occasional or incidental – at any rate, unrecorded – part. I didn't question that orientation; I assumed it went with the territory. But in high school, I'd taken a social studies class that included current events, and that precedent gave me the idea of widening our discussions for fifteen or twenty minutes a week to include whatever was in the news.

Even though momentous events were going on in the world – the Cuban Missile Crisis, Vatican II – I doubt I would have taken such liberties with the curriculum if the hurricane hadn't washed away most of our textbooks.

In History 1A early in November, I mentioned the notorious Francisco Sagastume, whose name had been all over the *Belize Times* for the past couple of weeks. I knew the main features of his story: he was a twenty-five-year-old Guatemalan who, with only nine or ten followers, had invaded southern British Honduras a year earlier in the name of independence. Not long before

Molly and I arrived in Angel Creek, he was tried in our district, the judicial centre for the southern region, and the townspeople's memory of him was fresh and strong.

"Tell me about him," I asked my students.

Every hand in the class shot up.

"He *young*, Miss. And he only handsome!"

"He *danjrus*, Miss!"

"Why 'dangerous'?"

"He try an' tek our land foh Guatemala! Guatemala tink she own us."

"He say he cohn hep us mek our own country. He say he ready to die foh our independence! But we no ask he cohn heah an' hep us!"

"Cho! He no wan hep us. He burn de Union Jack and put up de Guatemala flag in San Antonio!"

"He and he men, dey hab guns and dey say dey gone kill ahl de English people!"

"Dey wan de Ketchi people join dem, Miss! An' de Carib people too. But we no do dat!"

In their excitement, the students were all trying to speak at once.

"Wait! Talk standard English! First, exactly what did he do?"

"He came into BH in the south, where many Indians live," Alice Wong volunteered, "and he tried to start a revolution, like they always do in Guatemala."

"Then they were captured," Sissy Quinlan said, "him and his followers, but most of them were just sent back to Guatemala. But not him or his friend Rosado. Those two were put in jail in Belize City. After the trial – I'm not sure which one because there were lots of trials and they went on a long time – he got ten years in prison, and so did Rosado."

"But now they soon will go free," said Alice, "after only six months! Why, Miss? I don't understand."

"According to yesterday's newspaper, there was 'a review of cases by visiting justices appointed by the British governor of British Honduras, and they recommended their release'," I said, reading directly from the *Belize Times*. "It seems as though he'll be freed by the British in exchange for some *chicleros* from British Honduras who were detained in Guatemala when they wandered across the border by mistake. Who can tell us what a *chiclero* is?" I hoped somebody knew, because I didn't.

"They gather chicle from the trees, Miss," said Juanita Lopez, who had cousins in Guatemala. "That's like gum, Miss." She paused a moment. "I think this exchange could be a way for British Honduras to keep the peace with Guatemala. We think he is an invader, but the Guatemalans think he is a hero."

"You make some good points, Juanita," I said. "Things look different, depending on where you are – which side of the border you're on, in this case. That's what it takes to get a perspective on something – looking at it from different viewpoints and considering different sides of the question." Trying to draw a lesson from our discussion, I said that things can look different in hindsight, reviewing them after some time has passed. That was important for all of us, not just historians, to remember.

"Well," Sissy said, "using my hindsight, all those trials seem like a big waste of time."

My students were absorbed by Sagastume's story, as was the rest of the colony. Some argued that he was an opportunist, seeking political power in his home country, but others regarded him as a romantic idealist who, however misguided, risked disgrace and death in the name of freedom.

Ana, who'd sat in on some of the trial the previous March, said that Sagastume knew something about the law and had cross-examined witnesses himself. He insisted in his own defence that he was in fact acting within British law in an attempt to show Her Majesty that she and her government were wrong to claim the country he called Belicé as her possession. Ana said that even though she herself wasn't in favour of a revolution, she admired the young man's courage. Even two months in the hellhole of a Belize City prison hadn't dimmed his spirit.

Events culminated in Sagastume's release in mid-December, when the government finally completed the proposed exchange of prisoners. SAGASTUME IS FREE! read the headline in the *Belize Times*. "They Let Him Go!" "They" presumably were the lieutenant governor appointed by the Queen and the officials elected by the people of British Honduras.

"He'll eat Christmas dinner in Guatemala," commented the leader of the opposition party. He and his followers claimed that the leaders of the PUP – the People's United Party, in power at the time – had caved in to British pressure. A few went so far as to suggest that the release of such a dangerous criminal confirmed rumours of a conspiracy to overthrow British rule. They hinted that fifth columnists in the Belize government had secretly backed Sagastume's invasion. According to some reports, he had tons of money on him when he was caught. Had the Guatemalan government secretly backed him? Had ambitious Belize politicians, hoping to lead the country if the British were ousted, bankrolled him? Or had he been enlisted by the United States to start a revolution?

Rumour had it that the United States was secretly supporting Guatemala's claim to British Honduras in return for Guatemala's support against Fidel Castro. If the British were driven out, Guatemala could move in and the United States could set up military bases along the coast. I dismissed such explanations as absurd. Even though I knew about the Bay of Pigs invasion, I couldn't accept that the United States would act in such an underhanded way, especially against our ally, Great Britain. Certainly not Kennedy's administration!

"Why do you think Sagastume was released?" I asked Ana.

"Our government is a joke." She shrugged. "It might be our Christmas present to him. That's how our system works. Grand gestures. That's our way."

During the entire week after break, Ana remained distant, nodding hello when our paths crossed but not stopping to talk. One Friday evening, Kate and Molly suggested a movie, and we decided to see if Ana wanted to join us.

When we rang the doorbell, Marita opened the upstairs window, saw us and called down, "The downstairs door is unlocked. Come up."

She stood at the top of the stairs, holding open the door into the living room. "I'm very happy it's you," she said. "Ana hurt her foot on the way home from school. It bled and hurt so much, we called the doctor. She must stay off her foot tonight, and she will be happy that friends have come!"

Marita led us into Ana's bedroom, where she lay with her right foot propped up on a ruffled pillow, her big toe thick with gauze, the instep swollen and discoloured.

"It feels like a toothache in my toe!" she moaned. "I can't get on any shoes, not even flip-flops, because my foot is twice its size, and besides it's so black and blue I don't want anyone to see it. It's too ugly. Everyone will laugh when they see me limping barefoot, but if they do, I'll strangle them with my bare hands!"

Ana dramatized the situation, and she made us all laugh as she explained ("step by misstep," as she put) how she stumbled and fell going into Lee

Wong's store. She'd fallen in such a way that she twisted her ankle under her and snagged her big toenail on a floorboard, tearing the nail almost off. It was still attached at the base by a shred of skin, and bleeding badly. Marita had sent Jaime for Dr Bauer, Ana said, who at four in the afternoon had already been into the schnapps.

"When he came in the room, his breath was so strong it practically anaesthetized me. That was good, because he terrified me. His hands were so shaky and his eyes so glazed over, I was sure he would amputate my foot, or at least some of my piggies!"

We put off going to the movies till the next night and let her entertain us. By the end of the evening, we were back to being friends.

Not long after our arrival, Eduardo stuck his head in the door. As though I were the anesthetized one, I glanced at him, feeling nothing, and turned away. He might have been any of her brothers. *I'm over him*, I thought. In the middle of her story, Ana didn't seem to notice my response, or if she did, she accepted it, probably even approved of it. Eduardo hung around in the doorway for a few minutes and then mumbled that he had to get back to work and left.

By the next morning, my composure had vanished. I stopped by the Zacharias house on the pretext of checking up on Ana. She was already up from her sickbed, hobbling around the house, less merry now that the pain pill had worn off. I spent an hour with her without seeing Eduardo, and went home, disappointed and depressed.

That mood passed, too, and the next time I saw him, almost a week later at a dance at the Sportsman Club, I chose to ignore him. He was busy at the bar, as usual, and had no reason to stop by our table because Ana, still nursing her foot, wasn't there. Molly spent the evening dancing with David, Kate looking on wistfully, even though she rarely lacked a partner. I was a bit wistful myself, watching Eduardo – who was sometimes watching me – from a distance. I felt like a passenger on a boat pulling away from shore. He seemed smaller every time I looked.

About ten o'clock, Father Bosque turned up and, eventually, came over to our table. It was the first time I'd seen him outside of church since the evening at the Olivers'. Just as he sat down and started to say something to me, Jack Hitchens approached from behind, put his hands on my shoulders and leaned over, his face near mine. I could smell the whisky on his breath as he asked me to dance.

"I'm sorry," I said, turning to look up at him, "but I'm not feeling too well."

"That time of the month, is it, love?" he asked, tugging my ponytail.

When I turned back to Father Bosque, he'd already gone – moved across the room to his sister's table. I started towards the bathroom, but seeing an open side door, slipped out into the cool, moonless night. For a few minutes I sat on the steps, my forehead on my knees. I realized as I sat there that my estrangement from Father Bosque made me far more miserable than my vanishing attraction to Eduardo. I felt something like despair, certain there was nothing I could do to regain Father Bosque's friendship.

I stood up and started walking, faster and faster, down the drive, turning up the highway towards town. The road was deserted at this time of night. Without a moon it was pitch black, and I liked that. It was easy enough to follow the edge of the pavement, but if I wandered into the ditch or even off into the bush, who would care? I certainly wouldn't.

About half a mile down the road, I came to my senses. Kate and Molly would be sick with worry about me, and even if nothing happened, Father Peck would be furious if he found out I'd wandered off alone. I turned around to go back and saw car lights coming towards me on the narrow road. I moved to one side, but the vehicle screeched to a stop.

"My God! It's you! Get in!" It was Father Bosque.

I went around to the passenger side of the Jeep and climbed in.

"What in God's name are you doing out here all alone?"

"Just getting some air."

"That's ridiculous. Plain stupid! You must never, ever go off alone like that in the dark. It's incredibly dangerous."

"But no one's around now."

"The bush is full of life – and death! I've seen rattlesnakes along this road. There could be jaguar."

"I'm sorry!" I said, my voice breaking.

He let me sob for a while, saying nothing, then abruptly turned the Jeep around and drove at top speed down the deserted highway. In front of the driveway into the club, he slammed on the brakes.

"Get out here, and get back in there before they miss you," he said. "I'll talk to you tomorrow. I'm too upset right now to make any sense."

I climbed out. He gunned the motor and was gone.

The following afternoon, a Sunday, Father Peck left for Belize City for the week. About an hour later, Father Bosque sent Gilly to ask me to come to the rectory.

"He no happy," Gilly said. "You cheer him up, Miss."

"I'm afraid I'm the reason he's unhappy," I said. "I did some stupid stuff."

"But you he fayvrit, Miss. You no need to worry."

As I followed Gilly to the rectory, I felt the tears coming back. He opened the door for me but didn't come in. Father Bosque was waiting for me in the back room, he said, and then he left.

I hated that room. It reminded me of Father O'Dea and the night he humiliated himself and insulted Father Bosque.

"Can we talk someplace else?" I asked.

"This is more private, but we can go in the kitchen if you want."

I nodded.

In the kitchen, he pulled out two chairs on opposite sides of the table and sat down across from me.

"I'm not sure what to say," he said. "I'm sorry I was so angry with you last night, but what you did was so foolish that I couldn't help myself. What's gotten into you lately?"

"I don't know why I did that," I said. "I know it was stupid to try to walk home. I was upset, and I wanted to get as far away from the club as fast as I could."

"Why were you so upset?"

"Things haven't been going well. Not with Ana or Eduardo. Molly's depressed. Her health hasn't been good, and she's mixed up over David. Kate's kind of remote these days. And if you want the truth, what upsets me most is I'm afraid you hate me now."

"Hate you? Impossible!" His voice became breathy, as it always did when his emotions took over. "But I have been disappointed in some of the things you've done recently."

"What things?" I asked. "I know you've been upset, but I don't know exactly what I've done to upset you so much."

"Choosing to spend so much time with your British friends." He drew in his breath and held it for a few seconds. "Playing up to Richard Oliver and Jack Hitchens. I hate to see you anywhere near such men. The way you looked at Oliver, like he was the whole world, eating up his lies and flattery. It made me sick. I've seen too many innocent young girls ruined by men like that. One of my own sisters – "

"Oh, I'm so sorry," I said.

His eyes searched mine. I returned his gaze even though I couldn't see him clearly through the tears.

"I admit I probably overreacted," he said. "Maybe I'm too protective. But you have to be careful not to give others a false impression, especially men."

"But how can I control what other people think?"

"Just be what you are, sweet and pure."

"I'm not the Virgin Mary, Father Bosque. Conceived without sin, and all that."

That made him smile, but he was soon serious again. "Don't deny your purity, your goodness," he said. "I saw it in your eyes the first day I met you. I know I'm not wrong about you."

My purity? My goodness? His praise left me with the uneasy feeling that his good opinion of me resulted not from anything I had done, but from things I hadn't done.

Ana, back on her feet, with shoes on, joined Molly, Kate and me for an evening meal towards the end of the following week. We were in the midst of a fried chicken dinner when the door burst open and Father Bosque rushed in. He was covered in blood.

"Come see!" he yelled. "I shot a tiger!"

We ran down the steps after him to the Jeep. A crowd of neighbours, mostly boys and young men, surrounded it. They parted to reveal a jaguar (everyone called it a "tiger") slung over the hood, its tongue hanging out and its tawny, spotted fur matted with blood.

"Fahdah only gud hontah!" we heard.

"I shot her with my .22," Father Bosque said. "I can't believe it, mon."

Molly ran back upstairs to get her camera. "Wait till my brothers see this!" she said.

"I'll tell you all about it later," he said. "But first I have to get out of these clothes."

Ana stayed to hear the story. Even though tigers were plentiful in British Honduras at the time, she let us know that killing one was an event. Usually, the animal did the killing. Since Hattie, she said, they had been sighted close to town, preying on domestic animals and livestock. "That priest is a hero from now on," she told us.

After a shower, Father Bosque came back, carrying his supper on a tray.

Figure 10. The jaguar Father Bosque shot with his .22 rifle, surrounded by townspeople. Photo courtesy of Malilee Zimmers.

Setting it to one side – he said he was still too excited to eat but knew he'd be hungry later – he began his story.

"I ran into my brother-in-law, Al Quinlan, this afternoon," he said, "and Al told me that he'd seen some wild peccaries feeding in a cassava patch on their farm along the Melena Road, not far from the place where we go to swim. So I got my rifle, a .22 Browning semi-automatic, and picked up my nephew, James, one of the Quinlan boys."

He looked at me. "Abby, you know those boys and how they love hunting. And most of all, they love roast pig. Well, James and I had the taste of it in our mouths the three miles out to the farm. We parked far enough away from the cassava patch that we wouldn't scare off the peccaries. We didn't see them, but found their tracks soon enough among the plants and decided to wait till they showed up.

"Just so you know, the edible part of cassava is the root. The plant itself is about four feet tall, with leaves that spread out sort of like an umbrella. James and I crouched under one and could see about twenty-five yards ahead, so I knew I'd have a clear shot if one turned up.

"About half an hour goes by, and then we hear the piam-piam, a bird like a blue jay, making a racket, like it does when it's alarmed. That was the signal that something was coming. I thought it was a peccary. Looking towards the sound, I saw a tail. And then I saw the jaguar. It was making short, slow leaps, coming towards us, head to the ground, following the scent of the peccary. By that time it was maybe fifteen feet away from us. We froze, watching it open-mouthed. I've never seen a live tiger so close before. When it was opposite us, it suddenly stopped. I guess it must have smelled us.

"As it started to raise its head, I took aim and fired and hit the tiger. I fired again, and that's when it fell. I went up closer and fired two more shots to make sure it was dead. Then I picked up a big tree branch to poke it to make absolutely sure it was dead.

"I gave James the rifle and slung the tiger over my shoulder. As I did, there was a deep growl from the head, which was hanging down by my buttocks. I admit it; I was terrified. I flung off that tiger and leaped away. But the tiger didn't move, so I guess the growl was air escaping from its stomach. James helped me carry it to the Jeep, and we threw it onto the hood and drove back to town. People who saw us followed after the Jeep, and by the time we got to the rectory, we had the crowd you saw when you came downstairs. Nobody can believe I shot her dead with a .22, but that's God's truth!

"After I left you, I measured her – six feet two inches from nose to tail – and took her over to a friend of Al's who knows how to skin her. He'll do it in return for the meat."

"What will he do with the meat?" Molly asked.

"Sell it," Father Bosque answered.

"People eat it here, you know," Ana said. "Not us, but some people."

"So it was self-defence?" Kate asked. "That's why you killed it?"

"I think it would have attacked us, but I wasn't going to wait and see," Father Bosque said. "I didn't think. I just fired. I think it was an old tiger – the teeth are pretty worn. If it wasn't, I doubt it would have been so near the town, where getting food is easier. And I doubt James and I would have survived the encounter."

"What will you do with the skin?" Molly asked.

"I'm going to tan it myself," he said. "It will make a good rug. People pay big money for such things."

"But you wouldn't sell it?" Ana asked. "If you do, my father would like to buy it, I'm sure!"

"No, no, of course I wouldn't sell it. But I might make a gift of it to someone."

"What a splendid gift!" Ana said. "It would have to be someone very special."

"Yes, indeed," he said. "Very special. Now for this chicken!" He tore into it with his hands, eating it as he did everything, with unabashed gusto.

Chapter 20

CELEBRATION

LIVING IN ANGEL CREEK taught me that one of the vital signs of any community is celebration. Every week provided some reason to celebrate, and groups of neighbours and friends – sometimes the whole town – gathered to process, pray, bless, drum, sing, dance, eat and enjoy.

In our region, the biggest celebration of all was Carib Settlement Day, 19 November (now Garifuna Settlement Day and a national holiday). Each year on that day, the Garifuna people remembered and gave thanks for their arrival on the shores of Central America. Everything else in town stopped as they re-enacted the events of more than a century before, when the dories of the first Garifuna settlers in Angel Creek landed.

We were told that this year's celebration would be extra-special because Hattie had disrupted events in Angel Creek the previous year. Preparations began weeks in advance and included dancing and drumming in tents set up on the edge of town. These dances, described as "practices", began after dark and continued far into the night.

The festivities began almost a week before Settlement Day itself, kicked off by a torchlit procession through the streets of Angel Creek. Molly, Kate and I joined in along with many of our students. Afterward, Molly and Kate went off in different directions, and I went home alone to grade papers. About an hour later, the lights flickered and went out.

I'd just lit the gas lantern when Father Bosque appeared. After our conversation in the rectory kitchen, he'd once again resumed his daily visits.

He said he was on his way to see the dances and asked me if I'd like to go. I was surprised that outsiders would be allowed to watch, but he assured me that the tents were just big canopies, and if we stood on the sidelines, no one would object.

We walked to the western edge of town where the tents had been pitched in a vacant lot. A few others, children and young people for the most part, had gathered to watch. By the light of the long-handled torches they'd carried through the streets, Garifuna men and women danced to the beat of the drums played with bare hands.

The basic dance was a shuffle, with lines of dancers moving in circles and sometimes circles within circles. Every now and then one of the dancers, usually male, broke free and moved quickly towards the drummers with intricate footwork while the others continued to dance in place. Sometimes a man and a woman paired up to dance suggestively in the middle of the circle, "back to back and belly to belly" as one calypso song of the time put it. Other times, two women danced together, and in a few cases one woman or man would dance with a group of the opposite sex. In addition to the drumming, a singer sometimes called out words in the Garifuna language and the dancers chanted a response, repetitive, hypnotic. These songs went on for half an hour or more at a time.

"Powerful, no?" Father Bosque asked, gauging my response.

"Incredible," I said, and asked if he knew what sort of dances they were.

He supposed they must once have had some sort of religious significance. Maybe they still did.

"It's like a spell being cast," I agreed.

He said that most of the Garifuna were good Catholics, Mass every Sunday, some daily communicants. A few priests still preached against what the Garifuna called "the ways of the ancestors" and condemned the dances as heathen and the rituals that went with them as devil-worship. With some success, they did their best to shame the Garifuna into giving them up. Many of the educated Garifuna were the harshest critics of those who followed the old ways. But now the attitude of many of the clergy and the sisters was changing.

It was still the case, he said, that some of the older priests and nuns gave the Garifuna a hard time for their "pagan" practices, but many now realized that all such attitudes accomplished was to cause resentment and push the rituals underground. The younger priests turned a blind eye.

"We call them 'Carib customs' or 'folk traditions' and leave it at that. There's so much we don't know about their culture."

"Even you?" I asked in amazement. "You've lived here all your life! Can't you ask for an explanation of their customs?"

He said that first of all, the words themselves would have to be translated from their language into English. And then the practices would have to be explained in English, a second language to most of them. Even that wouldn't necessarily help an outsider understand their meaning. He asked me if I'd ever tried to explain Catholic practices to someone who wasn't a believer. "It all sounds like mumbo-jumbo."

Even for those living next door to each other, it seemed, there were things too deep, too secret, to share. A revelation I found comforting.

"But at the very least," he added, "even if we don't understand them, we can try to tolerate differences, not deny or demean them."

"The music is so alive, so powerful. But there's something kind of frightening about it too," I said.

"It's natural to fear what is unfamiliar," he answered.

I thanked him for bringing me, adding that I probably wouldn't have come on my own. "To think I might have missed them!"

"I thought you would like them," he said.

I went home bewitched. Molly came in not long after in a similar state. The students had told her about dancing in the cemetery, she said, and she'd gone on her own to watch.

"I ended up dancing with them!" she said. "It was an incredible experience."

"Were there tents in the cemetery?" I asked.

"No, people were just drumming and dancing by torchlight. Someone pulled me into the circle."

"It sounds different from what Father Bosque and I were watching, Molly," I told her.

The next night, after a series of athletic competitions in the late afternoon, followed in the evening by a concert by the Angel Creek Police Brass Band, Molly, Kate and I headed together to the tents, where once again the dancers had assembled.

"These dances aren't the same as the dancing I did last night," Molly said, after watching for a while. "They're wonderful, but they're more choreographed, a lot less spontaneous. Do you want to go up to the cemetery and see what's happening there?"

I refused and so did Kate – prudently, as it turned out. The next morning Molly was called on the carpet by Mother Eugenie, who had heard about

Molly "dancing on graves", as she put it, and taking part in "ungodly rituals". For many, she said, Settlement Day was an excuse to relapse into "primitive practices". By condoning them with her presence and participation, Molly had disgraced herself, the Church and the civilized world.

Molly said she thought this time, for sure, she'd be sent home. Instead, she got off with a serious warning. "But it's definitely strike two," she said.

When Molly asked Father Bosque about what she'd stumbled into, he said he had no idea. He asked if she'd been hurt or disturbed by it in any way.

"Not at all," she answered. "All I can say is that it was a joyful time. It might have been worth being sent home for."

On Saturday night, the entire town followed the "official" dancers as they left the tents and went house to house in a public performance, dancing in the streets to the rhythm of the drums. On Sunday, most of the churches in town had thanksgiving services. Father Peck led ours. God had safely delivered the Caribs to their new home on the Caribbean coast after they had been cast out of their homeland on St Vincent Island. In British Honduras, they had thrived as a free people, under British rule, for almost a century and a half. Father Peck delivered his homily without a trace of irony, and the congregation, mostly Garifuna, received it impassively.

All the businesses and schools in our area were closed that Monday, Settlement Day itself. After breakfast, Molly, Kate and I walked over to the airfield to watch the arrival of the small plane carrying the lieutenant governor of British Honduras and the prime minister (called the first minister – "FM", for short). He was one of the so-called Royal Creoles who had attended St John's College in Belize. A large crowd had already gathered to greet the dignitaries. At the town end of the field, close to the post office, a platform had been erected for the speeches they would deliver later in the day.

It was the first time I'd seen either man. Both were middle-aged and rather handsome, dressed simply in white shirts and dark trousers (the FM wore what everyone called his "uniform", a long-sleeved Mexican Guayabera shirt). The lieutenant governor was taller, paler than the FM, and balding. The FM's tortoiseshell glasses made him look like a scholar, I thought. I wondered why he'd never married. Maybe, as some people said, he'd sacrificed his personal life to serve his country.

Soon after the two men left the aircraft, a cry went up from the crowd. Once it was pointed out to me, I could see a boat on the eastern horizon, pro-

Figure 11. Re-enactment of the arrival by dory of the first Garifuna settlers, Carib Settlement Day, 1962. Photo courtesy of Malilee Zimmers.

pelled like a gull by wing-like oars. Along with everyone else, I rushed to the beach to watch its approach. It came swiftly, reaching shore in a surprisingly short time. Townspeople dressed as the first Garifuna settlers jumped ashore carrying the flags of British Honduras and Great Britain. Some balanced basins of banana leaves and cassava roots on their heads, symbolic of the plants the settlers had brought with them. Caught up by the crowd, they processed to the square in front of the police station, where a young Garifuna woman, looking like a bride in her frilly white dress, was crowned queen of Angel Creek. After that ceremony, the Police Band led a parade of children in their school uniforms through the streets of the town.

At last, the long-awaited dancers, now in bright costumes of red and gold, lined up in the field along the sea. A truck pulled up, and men unloaded three big drums, each about half the size of a grown man. Someone told me that the pageant that unfolded on the field acted out events related to the settlement, but I had no inkling what those events were. Our Garifuna students rarely talked about their culture except in the most mundane and specific ways – how cassava bread was made, what a particular Garifuna word or

Figure 12. Garifuna drummers prepare for the dances. Photo courtesy of Malilee Zimmers.

phrase meant. If Molly, Kate or I asked about the Garifuna customs, especially anything verging on the spiritual, they looked away or responded, "We Catolic, Miss," or "Only de ole folk know dat, Miss."

The most flamboyant dance was performed by women carrying swords and clothed in red fabric from their elaborate headdresses to the hems of their tiered skirts. I saw some of the Camelot Boys in the crowd and asked them to explain what was going on. They shrugged. "We no know, Miss." In any case, in the bright light of day, elaborately costumed, the dancers lost their mystery and became a spectacle. I stopped trying to understand and just enjoyed the pulsing rhythms of the drums and the dancers' loose-limbed movements.

I didn't pay much attention to the speeches that followed. The boys and I found the swings in the park empty and, tired of standing, claimed them. We were too far from the platform to hear well, even with the loudspeakers. I kicked off my flip-flops and traced patterns in the sandy dust with my toes while the boys pumped their legs with their heads back. In the distance, I caught sight of Molly snapping pictures with her box camera. I'd lost track of Kate.

And then one more procession: Garifuna women clothed in white, with long white feathers in their hats, carrying a white banner before them, the schoolchildren assembled by class, Father Peck and Father Bosque in their flowing robes.

During the Catholic ceremony that ended the day, I sat near the back of the church. Marita and the little Zacharias boys were two pews in front of me. No sign of any of the Zacharias men, who according to Ana usually went to church only for sacramental occasions. Not so different from my own family, I had to admit.

Rounding the corner on my way home, I saw David sitting at the top of our steps. He waved when he saw me.

"Come on in," I said, opening the door. We rarely locked it except after dark.

"Molly on her way?"

"So far as I know. Supper's in half an hour if you'd like to stay, and there's sure to be something good. The nuns outdo themselves on Sundays and holidays."

Kate came in then. "David! Were you at the events today? I didn't see you."

"Lost in the crowd, I guess – one of the few days that can happen here." He settled in the big chair in the corner of the living room. "You know, I would like to stay for supper, if that isn't too much trouble, and spend the evening with all of you."

"Delighted to have you," Kate said. "I'll tell the convent we're having a guest."

Just then Father Bosque appeared on the doorstep. "Would you like to have supper here with us?" she asked.

"Love to," he answered.

"I'm on my way to tell the nuns," she said.

Molly arrived moments later. "Wasn't the day thrilling? I've never seen anything even remotely like it!"

Dinner was indeed delicious – a huge red snapper, far and away the best dish the convent served. Afterward, out came the cigarettes, gin and orange juice. We even had some ice that Kate had begged from the nuns. We lit a candle, a thick white one, and sat on the floor in our usual circle.

Father Bosque lifted his glass. "To the memory of those first settlers and to their children's children, our friends and neighbours."

"To the winds of fortune that brought us here strangers and made us friends," David said.

Kate, Molly and I offered our toasts in turn: to PAVLA and the nuns and priests who made it possible for us to be here; to the people of Angel Creek and all our students; to British Honduras, our second home. We clinked glasses.

Every time I thought of it, I was amazed that last year at this time, I hadn't known this place or these people existed. Now I couldn't imagine life without them and apart from Angel Creek. The lump in my throat made it hard to talk.

"I'd hate to think this is the high point of our lives, especially when chances are we still have so much life ahead of us, but sometimes I wonder if we'll ever be this happy again."

"It's before BH and after BH," said Kate. "In the future, everything will have to measure up against this year."

"In the meantime," David said. "Let's have another drink. Do you have any more ice, Kate?"

"Sorry. The little we had is gone."

"So it's an imperfect world after all!" He passed around the gin and orange juice. "It's one of the things I definitely won't miss," he said. "Not having ice for my gin and orange juice!"

"Can you not miss not having something?" Kate asked, laughing. She raised her glass: "One more toast, then. To all we're not missing by being here!"

Two days after Settlement Day, the nuns celebrated the founding of their congregation. After we heard Father Peck's congratulations at morning Mass, Molly, Kate and I made a card for them out of construction paper and dropped it off with a bag of sweets on our way to school. To our surprise, Mother Eugenie came out of her office just off the main parlour when she heard our voices greeting the young nun who answered the door.

"How thoughtful of you!" she said, taking our gift. She seemed sincerely pleased to see us and insisted we sit down for a few minutes.

Molly looked apprehensive, but Mother Eugenie couldn't have been more cordial.

"You won't be late," she said. "Or if you are, tell Sister Veronica you have my permission."

When we asked her about the history of the Holy Family sisters, she told us that a free woman of colour, Sister Henriette de Lille, had founded the order in 1842. It was one of the very first communities for Negro women in the United States. "Actually, Sister Henriette was a Creole, quite light-skinned and very well off," she added. From the very first, the sisters ministered to slaves and Negroes of all kinds and ages, starting a school for children as well as a home for the aged. They also cared for the sick and homeless.

She said her order had been in the southern district of British Honduras for over sixty years, since the turn of the century. The bishop of Belize City had invited them to come from Louisiana to found a school. "Just a few years ago, we managed to build this beautiful new convent. Thank God it survived Hattie! We have so much to be thankful for," she said.

"To think, tomorrow is Thanksgiving in the States," Molly said. "It will seem strange not to celebrate it."

"This will be my first Thanksgiving ever away from my family," Kate said, her voice teary.

"Poor darlings, I'm sure you miss your families very much! We'll have to see what we can do to cheer you up."

At supper that evening, Josie arrived, bearing a surprise: roast turkey, stuffing, sweet potatoes, green beans and pumpkin pie.

"It's what we always have for our anniversary," Mother Eugenie explained when we thanked her. "We have the turkey flown in from the States. We're Americans, too, you know."

Towards the end of the following week, Molly announced that Mother Eugenie was taking her to Belize City by plane.

Planes were for VIPS or emergencies. "She hasn't changed her mind about sending you home, has she?" we asked, only half joking.

"No, not that. She's worried about my health. She says I have to see a doctor there." Not only had Molly's bug bites not cleared up in the cooler weather but she'd also developed a condition that mottled the skin on her neck and shoulders and was spreading along her jawline. Worried, Mother Eugenie had made an appointment for her with someone Father Peck recommended.

"She insisted, so I gave in," Molly said. "Especially as she's paying for it."

Kate and I saw them off early the next morning in the single-engine plane that shuttled among Belize City and the six districts of the colony.

"I've always wanted to fly in one of these things," Molly said as she boarded.

Kate shuddered. "They don't look too safe to me."

"Think of the view," Molly said.

That weekend we had some of the finest weather that Angel Creek – or anywhere on the planet – could offer. The days dawned crisp and cool and as the sun rose towards noon, the air approached balmy perfection. While Molly was gone, Kate and I took long walks out the Melena Road towards the valley.

"You know, my handwriting is changing," Kate said, apropos of nothing, on our Sunday afternoon walk. "It's getting smaller. More studied."

When I asked her what she thought that signified, she answered, "I think it means I'm starting to focus." She took it as a sign she was learning to live on a smaller scale, thanks to life in Angel Creek, not trying to grasp everything like she used to. In her opinion, people often ended up with nothing of value when they tried to do too much. The problem, though, was that focusing also meant limiting yourself: limiting your aspirations as well as your actions. Limiting your freedom.

She paused, as though unsure whether to go on, and then continued. "I feel closer to God here, and I love that." Another pause. "I love our little church so much. You can hear the sea when the doors are open. Have you noticed? I've always connected the sea to God, and it's a daily blessing to live within the sight and sound of it."

We walked on in silence, breathing in the green smell of the grass that grew along the roadside. It was the first time Kate and I had talked seriously, just the two of us.

"You know, though," she said after a few minutes, "even here, even with so much interesting and different, I often feel extremely bored and maybe a little depressed. Life seems interesting, then dull, dull then interesting. I want challenges, change, growth. I'd be miserable doing the same thing day after day, year after year. I wonder how people here stand it."

"Maybe they expect less from life than we do," I said. "Or want different things."

"Of course I'm grateful to God for all I've been given and for the freedom I have." At the same time, she said, living in Angel Creek had made her realize that few people enjoyed similar opportunities. "It's so unjust, and I'm finding it harder and harder to deny that happiness depends on a person's situation in life. Some people seem to have everything, and others have nothing. When the people who have nothing realize it, they can't help but be miserable."

"I don't know," I said. "Most people here seem pretty happy to me. Even when they live in one room and have only rice and beans to eat day after day, the rituals and traditions seem to give their life meaning. And their families mean everything to them."

"Well, that's something I wonder about too," Kate said. "Family life. Marriage. I think about marriage a lot. Do you?"

"More lately," I admitted. "I've always assumed it's my ultimate goal, to have a husband and children, but now I'm not so sure."

Kate said that she was going through something similar. In fact, she was beginning to fear a permanent bond. "Up till now, my life has been a series of short periods, almost like a school day. If things got too bad or boring, I could always look forward to a change ahead. I guess I connect change with growth, and my question is whether people can continue to grow in a long-term relationship." She added that in most marriages she'd seen, both people seemed to suffer, not only physically but spiritually, living on top of each other all the time.

"Just imagining it makes me feel claustrophobic," she said. "And that makes me wonder if I'm too restless to remain consistent in a permanent relationship like marriage for the rest of my life. Won't I get fed up? Even come to hate someone for robbing me of my freedom? Won't children stunt my growth and hinder me? Won't I – or my husband – fall in love with someone else as time goes by?"

"It seems like there are a lot of ways for things to go wrong in life."

"I'm terrified of making the wrong choices. And even if I make the right ones, whatever those might be, I have the feeling an awful lot of luck is involved in a happy life."

"I feel exactly the same way."

After a few minutes, Kate sighed. "I'm sorry, Abby," she said. "I don't mean to ruin a beautiful day with such heavy thoughts. Sometimes I'm afraid I think too much and make problems for myself. Do you ever feel like that?"

"Father O'Dea once told me I'd be happier if I didn't think so much. He probably would have given you the same advice if you'd met him."

"I don't need to have met him; I keep giving myself that advice. I'm so afraid of thinking life instead of living it. I wish I could just do things, like Molly does, and not worry too much about them afterward. I've always tried to be objective and think things through before I act, but now I wonder if that doesn't just make me less human, cut me off from life and other people. I have so many fears, so many questions."

As I listened to Kate, I realized it could have been me speaking.

Late that afternoon, Molly returned alone by truck; Mother Elaine had gone on to New Orleans to a meeting of her congregation. Molly's news was that the ointment Dr Bauer had given her for the sandfly bites was about as good a treatment as any. The Belize City doctor diagnosed the blotches as a type of fungus picked up from sea bathing. He'd given her a different ointment for that.

"So much for modern science," she said. "But here's the real medicine. Close your eyes."

After several noisy minutes that kept us guessing what she was up to, she allowed us to look. From a Thermos container filled with ice, she had unpacked lobster meat, arranged it on a bed of leaf lettuce and dressed it with mayonnaise and lemon juice. She also had a bottle of white wine ready to pour.

"This is for my two dear friends," she said. "And also for me, of course! Mother Eugenie gave me some money to buy us a treat, and Julian Martin – remember him? The radio announcer? He sends greetings, by the way – he helped me find and pack everything. I swear he could get the devil into heaven. He knows everyone, and all he has to do is ask, and whatever he wants appears like magic."

"But only you, Molly, could have come up with the idea for something like this and found a way to make it happen," I said.

Our mouths full of the taste of the sea and the sun-soaked wine, we celebrated together the here and now.

Chapter 21

GIFTS

WHERE WOULD WE SPEND Christmas? Molly and I debated the question daily from Thanksgiving through mid-December. Kate was meeting her parents and her brother and his new wife in Acapulco. Several PAVLA volunteers had decided on Guatemala City and invited Molly and me to travel with them, but we liked the idea of going off on our own. Neither of us considered travelling home for the holidays. Flying back to the States would take far more money than we had, and any land or sea route, far more time. Besides, we wanted to see more of Central America. Molly had heard about Mérida, near the Gulf coast of the Yucatán peninsula, a city not far from the excavated Maya ruins at Chichén Itzá. That appealed to us, but we hesitated, even though the fall term was ending and we had to decide soon.

Part of the problem was that Christmas seemed a world away. The weather in Angel Creek was sunny and clear most days, often warm enough to swim in the afternoons. How could there be Christmas without Jack Frost nipping at our noses? In mid-November, we packed up inexpensive but beautiful souvenirs to send off to our families and friends: birds hand-carved from horn; embroidered raffia hats, boxes and mats; colourful napkins and tablecloths bought in El Cayo. My mother had written to ask what I'd like for Christmas, and I requested things that were luxuries in British Honduras: deodorant, shampoo, insect repellent and machine-made underwear.

In early December, I received a notice that her parcel was waiting to be claimed at the customs office in Belize City. When I finally received it, I saw that it was filled with expensive, impractical gifts: a silk nightgown and robe, lacy underwear – things she herself would have liked. I felt at once touched and exasperated. Why hadn't she settled for cotton? She also sent separately, direct to Angel Creek, a generous cheque, worth almost twice the amount in BH currency. After days of rigmarole at the local Barclays Bank, I found myself rich.

Molly, Kate and I did most of our last-minute shopping along Market Street, looking for small gifts that we could present to the nuns and priests and some of our Angel Creek friends. There wasn't much to choose from in Angel Creek. For the nuns and priests, we decided on boxes of English tea and biscuits, and for Ana, earrings for her pierced ears that Lee Wong swore were gold even though they only cost a couple of BH dollars. Molly and I had bought similar earrings for ourselves that Ana had admired.

Only a few weeks earlier, the two of us had had our ears pierced by one of the local women. In BH, even baby girls had pierced ears; back home, only old women and immigrants did. Kate refused to have anything to do with such a practice. Like many of our generation, she thought pierced ears outmoded. She also regarded it as a risky procedure, as in fact it turned out to be.

Josie had recommended the woman to us. Following her directions, Molly and I found our way to a one-room hut on the edge of town. We went after dark, but the moon was almost full and we found our way easily. She was probably in her sixties, her head wrapped in a bright kerchief of the sort many older Garifuna women wore.

"Josie seh unu gals wahn de pierce arze," she greeted us. "Arite, den, co'een, pets."

She understood us when we spoke English but replied in rapid Creole, not the pidgin English most people used when they spoke to us. We found it almost impossible to follow. Her native language, of course, was Garifuna, entirely beyond our comprehension.

In a tiny room lit only by a kerosene lantern, the woman heated a needle over a flame, rubbed our earlobes with alcohol and, holding a cork behind the lobe with one hand, she pierced it with the charred tip of the needle she held in the other. A drop of blood swelled where she pierced, and she wiped it off with a ball of cotton wool. She then inserted stiff bits of straw to keep the piercings open. That was all there was to it. It can't have taken more than fifteen minutes for both of us. We each gave her twenty-five cents BH for her trouble. She refused the money at first, but when we insisted, she accepted with smiles and thanks. As well as we could make out, following her gestures and asking her several times to repeat her words, she advised us to remove the straw often, clean it and our earlobes well with soap or alcohol, and reinsert the straw until the earlobes healed and the holes stayed open. Then we could wear our pretty earrings.

The day after the piercing, our earlobes were red and sore. A few more days, and they were seeping blood and pus. After a week we decided the straw wasn't working and put in the earrings. If taking them out was painful, putting them back in was agony. It was the only way to keep our piercings open, so we persisted, releasing our ponytails to hide what we'd done.

Kate did her best to talk sense to us, arguing that we should have had the doctor do it, if anyone, but at least we ought to see him now for antibiotics. We refused, fearing that the doctor – who didn't even want us to shave our legs – would insist we remove the earrings and let the ears heal. When Molly went for her German lesson with Dr Bauer, she put on a headband that covered her ears and the earrings, even though it made the pain worse. That's how much we wanted pierced ears.

Now, when I see men wearing an earring or teens with pierced bodies or tattoos, I understand, feeling again something of the same edginess our pierced ears gave us.

After we bought the earrings for Ana, I looked for something special for Father Bosque. I found a nice card but nothing else that I considered good enough. Finally, in Lee Wong's store, I came across a small leather-bound notebook, made in England. That gave me the idea of making a book of poems for him. I could write some down from memory and copy a few favourites from the remaining books in the school library. I decided to include a few I'd written myself. I went home, happy with my purchases but still not in the Christmas spirit.

Meanwhile, exams were underway at school. As soon as they ended, a whirl of school parties followed. Each class had its Christmas tea or social – all leading up to graduation exercises for the seniors. Graduation from St Monica's flouted US custom: not only did it occur in mid-December but also it took place in the evening: a ceremony of speeches and awards, followed by a play written and performed by the graduates and after that a dance (females only). It was prom night and graduation ceremonies rolled into one. A Pérez daughter was among the graduates, and after the official graduation ceremonies, almost everyone adjourned to the Pérez house in the valley for another of their famous parties.

Father Bosque took us, but we stayed too late for him. After a bit too much wine, we arrived home around one-thirty in the morning, only to discover that Molly had left her purse with the house key in it at the Pérezes'. Nothing to do but wake Father Bosque – never Father Peck, who had a spare key but would surely scold us for our carelessness.

We threw pebbles at Father Bosque's upstairs window until we woke him. Sleepy-eyed, he propped up a ladder against our house, climbed up to our kitchen window and pried it open. We were waiting at the top of the stairs when he opened the front door and stepped out onto the porch. Before we could enter, the wind blew the door shut in our faces. "Oh, no!" we cried out.

Dogs began barking and some of the neighbours came out to investigate. We were sure Father Bosque was going to have to climb the ladder again, but he opened the door with a flourish. He'd unlocked it from inside. We laughed so hard, couldn't help it, that Father Peck himself came outside to see what the ruckus was. To our surprise, when we explained what had happened, he merely said, "It can happen to anybody once in a while," and went back to bed.

In spite of his often distant manner, Father Peck had won the respect and affection of the townspeople of Angel Creek in a relatively short time. He was considered to be one of the "gud" priests. He didn't have any obvious vices, wasn't always preaching about money, nor did he cause or take much notice of gossip or scandal. He did his job quietly and effectively. Above all, he conducted himself with dignity and treated his parishioners with courtesy. As Father Bosque put it, "No unpleasant surprises with him. He's a fair man, a man of his word."

As time went by, Kate, Molly and I warmed to him and he to us. He was basically a loner whose only obvious passion was his ham radio. Seeing that we worked hard at our teaching, he shrugged off Mother Eugenie's criticism that all three of us were "gadabouts" who needed "reining in". He seldom invited us to the rectory himself, although he didn't seem to mind when Father Bosque did, and he rarely stopped by our house without some sort of business to transact.

Recently, though, he'd gone out of his way to be nice to us. When he heard that Molly and I were thinking about going to Mérida for Christmas, he told us that he always stayed at a tiny hotel, the Casa Lynch. He described the place as "charming" and offered to arrange a room for us with Doña Lynch, the proprietor. That settled the matter of where we would spend Christmas: Mérida it would be. He gave us a list of good, inexpensive restaurants. He even told us where in Belize City to catch the northern bus and went to the trouble of tracking down a bus schedule for us. When Kate heard our plans, she decided to travel with us to Mérida, stay a few days and fly on from there to Acapulco to meet her family.

Although Father Peck never once invited us to accompany him on a mission trip, he didn't object to our travelling with Father Bosque. In fact, he praised our zeal. Every now and then he went off into the bush, but more and more, he turned over almost all the mission trips to his young assistant. When they occurred over a free weekend, we usually went with Father Bosque.

That fall, we visited – sometimes more than once – most of the remote sea and mountain villages in our district. We ate whatever was served and usually slept outdoors under improvised tents or behind hastily constructed windbreaks on sandy beaches or hilltops. Sometimes we slept on the floor of the church, if there was one, and once, we fell asleep overlooking the sea, lying on a broad stone altar under a palm-leaf canopy, where a few hours earlier, Father Bosque had celebrated Mass.

The unfailing generosity of the villagers, their simple faith in God and the Church, and their unquestioning acceptance of us and unabashed curiosity and amazement about our lives in the States – as though it were some sort of wonderland – moved us and endeared them to us. It was a great privilege to sit beside a bedridden grandmother as she silently held our hand or to spend a morning or afternoon with the young children, preparing them to receive the sacraments and listening to them recite their lessons and prayers in adorable voices.

In the bush, we led a rugged existence that put the four of us entirely at ease in each other's presence. No pretence was possible when we regularly saw each other unwashed, dishevelled and grouchy. We knew each other by the scent of our sweat, and one sniff told me when Molly and Kate had their periods. Every trip, especially in the rainy season, tested our physical and emotional limits in one way or another. We might complain, but at the end of each trip, we couldn't wait for the next one.

Our last trip together into the bush was to the mountain we claimed and named – Father Bosque's parting gift to us.

Figure 13. Kate and Molly on Kamagacha. Photo courtesy of Malilee Zimmers.

Figure 14. Abby on "our" mountain. Photo courtesy of Malilee Zimmers.

A couple of weeks before Christmas, Larry Jarvis, the Peace Corps volunteer who taught at the agricultural college in the valley, dropped off a gift for us, a string of Christmas lights he'd bought in Belize City. We'd never seen anything like them. Each bulb was shaped like an animal. There were bears, birds, monkeys and tigers. David Lewis had brought us a fresh pine tree. We decorated it with construction-paper wreaths, but the electrical outlet near the tree didn't work, so we left the lights off the tree. Instead, we plugged the cord into the one working outlet in the living room, draping the lights over the back of a wooden chair. When we'd finished our work for the day, we turned off the overhead light and sat in the dark enjoying our glowing menagerie.

The effect of those lights on our collective mood was peculiar. They made us nostalgic for our northern homes, for snow and crackling fireplaces. At the same time, they put us in a festive mood – coloured lights lit most local celebrations, no matter what the season – so plugging them in, we felt like laughing and crying at the same time and didn't know whether to bless Larry or curse him.

Larry was another of Molly's conquests; he became hopelessly smitten with her. After Mrs Jefferson and Mrs Moss introduced him to us, he turned up at our house every time he was in town. With no encouragement from any of us, certainly not from Molly, he sometimes stayed for hours. One night, he dropped in when I was home alone, made casual conversation for the better part of an hour and then, to my relief, stood up as if to go. Just as I rose to see him to the door, he sat back down. Abruptly, he confessed to me that he was in love with Molly. He had to tell someone, he said. Did I see any hope for him?

I told him that Molly was "practically engaged" to someone back home. The news didn't seem to faze him.

"She's an all-American girl, the sort I've always dreamt of," he said. "I never believed I'd actually meet someone like her. Even if it's hopeless, that doesn't change my feelings for her."

Not long before our departure for the holidays, sitting alone in our living room, lit only by Larry's Christmas lights, I wondered if, in fact, my feelings for Father Bosque were all that different from Larry's for Molly. For weeks now, I'd been really happy only when I was with Father Bosque. In fact, my biggest regret about spending the holidays away from Angel Creek was being away from him. If anyone had told me that my feelings were "hopeless", it wouldn't have changed a thing. Nor did it change anything that, unlike Molly's clear indifference to Larry, every day I was more certain that Father Bosque cared about me just as much as I did for him.

For months, we'd been meeting most weekdays in the morning during my free period. As time went on, we stopped discussing my religion class and moved to other, more personal topics. He talked about his love for the poetry of Gerard Manley Hopkins, also a Jesuit priest, and John Milton, reciting favourite passages. In turn, I who had dozens of poems stored away in my memory retrieved some of them for him – sonnets by Shakespeare and John Donne, lyrics by Emily Dickinson.

I confessed that I had grown up substituting art for religion – my literature, art and music classes conveyed much more to me about the human spirit and the presence of God in the world than the religion classes and church services I'd sporadically attended. Only in college did I come to an appreciation of Catholicism through a study of its intellectual and artistic tradition. He spoke of an early and overwhelming sense of God's love for him and of a deep sense of empathy with others that drew him to the priesthood. As our time together wound down, we began to continue our conversations over afternoon tea and sometimes into the evenings.

A few times as a child, in addition to my girlfriends, I'd had a best friend who was male. We'd meet after school to talk about our classes and about favourite books, movies and TV shows. We'd debate things like whether Milk Duds or a Holloway's Slo-Poke Sucker was a better choice for the Saturday matinee. My friendship with Father Bosque brought back memories of those grade-school boys. Like theirs at the time, Father Bosque's interests and tastes perfectly matched mine. Yet, being male and female, we were distinctively different, like words in different languages that mean essentially the same thing. In contrast, Molly, Kate and I reminded me of homonyms, our many similarities masking deep differences in temperament, taste and personality.

It's almost impossible to chart the subtle changes in relationships as they occur. Like geological changes, when they're not explosive, they often begin too deep and move too slowly for easy observation and analysis. I'd had occasional warnings that my feelings for Father Bosque were stronger than I consciously admitted and a few signs that his for me were also more powerful than either of us acknowledged. Sometime that fall, the thought crossed my mind that my infatuation with Eduardo may have been a way of diverting my feelings for Father Bosque into something more manageable – and acceptable.

Ironically but predictably, our brief estrangement brought us back together with greater intensity than before. Not that we spoke of our feelings directly and explicitly, even then. A conversation we had in the weeks just before Christmas was typical. From the topic of that day's religion class, God's enduring love for humans, as exemplified by the Lord's Prayer, we'd moved to the subject of human love. Father Bosque said that his deepening sense of God's abundant and unchanging love for him and all creation filled him with a desire to share that love with others so that they could return it to God, generating an endless cycle of love and life.

That reminded me of Juliet's love for Romeo, as depicted by Shakespeare.

"'My bounty is as boundless as the sea, / My love as deep. The more I give to thee / The more I have, / For both are infinite'," I quoted. "It's like a mother breastfeeding her baby. The more she gives, the more she has to give."

"That's a beautiful image of love," he agreed. But he said that only God could give love so abundantly. Humans must "pass through" each other to reach God. And that was a wrenching experience because we naturally want to rest in the other, even though there is no lasting union except in God. In his view, the only way to true and lasting anything – beauty, goodness, joy, love itself – is in the self-giving love of Christ on the cross.

"There, our humanness reaches its summit," he said, "and from there and with Christ we must leap to God. We must not descend. To live this love, we must condition ourselves to make an offering of ourselves to God willingly and joyfully."

He went on to say that his life as a priest was a consequence of his desire to make such an offering. In His love for us, God brings humans together and fills their cups to overflowing, as He fills the mother's breast, so that others may drink of the joy, happiness and love that comes from such abundance. Each of us must pass through those we love and grasp God, lest selfishness hold us back from the source of all love.

His words moved me, even though I had no experience of the sort of love he described, and they would help me face his imminent departure.

Almost from his arrival, I'd known that Father Bosque would be leaving early in the new year. I regarded his departure as I did my own: far in the future, inevitable yet impossible to believe. Like death. But in early December, he'd received definite word that after the holidays he was being sent to a Jesuit seminary not far from Bogotá, Colombia, to finish his studies. He had at most a month left in British Honduras and only a couple of weeks in Angel Creek.

I thought back to the night he told Molly, Kate and me the news, in the very room where I now sat looking at the Christmas lights. He said he had something he wanted us to have, a memento of his country and of our time together. To each of us, he then presented a curved fang, the colour of an old piano key, from the tiger he'd shot; the fourth, he kept for himself.

The next afternoon, Father Bosque had called me over to the rectory. We listened to his new Leontyne Price album together, replaying *"Chi il bel sogno di Doretta"*, an aria from Puccini's *La Rondine*, time and again. The solo sound of the piano at the beginning of the piece was the sound of pure longing, and the song itself soared with desire. I had no idea what the words meant, but I knew they had to be about passion as youthful and strong as Leontyne's voice. Before I left, Father Bosque gave me a filigreed silver cross, which he fastened around my neck. He then told me he had a special gift for me.

From a back room, he brought out a box of thick cardboard, at least a foot deep, two feet wide and four feet long. He laid it on the floor, knelt down beside it and took off the lid. Carefully, he pulled away the tissue paper wrapping. "You're the one I want to have it," he said. It was the skin of the tiger, tanned and cured.

I sat for a long time, unable to say anything. It was a gift that meant everything to me, because I knew it was the most precious thing he had. But what was I to do with it? How could I explain it to Molly and Kate? To my family? To myself? I couldn't find words to thank him, but my tears seemed all the thanks he wanted.

"I'll bring the skin to you before I leave," he promised.

As I snapped shut the small suitcase I'd packed for our trip to Mérida, I heard Father Bosque's voice in the living room. Our boat for Belize City would leave around four in the morning, and I thought he'd come to wish us bon voyage.

"Father's taking the boat up to Belize City with us," Kate announced.

"I have to go up to get my visa and meet with my superior," he said. "So I thought, why not travel with the three of you? Gilly will drive us down to the pier."

Molly came out of her room. "I overheard. I'm so glad we don't have to say goodbye."

"No, not quite yet," he said. "We'll have many goodbyes before I leave for Colombia, but tonight won't be one of them."

After the blue Jeep, the mail boats were my favourite way to travel in British Honduras. They brought the metaphor of plowing the sea to life, the prow cutting into a sea that at this time of year was as gently rolling as a prairie, leaving a furrow of turned water behind. Because of the coming holiday, the *Heron H* was crowded with passengers and cargo headed north.

Molly and Kate fell asleep not long after we boarded, sitting on the deck out of the wind, heads on their knees. Father Bosque and I moved nearer the prow to stay awake, the sea spray misting our faces. We talked the entire trip.

He told me that he saw a life for me parallel to his own, fired by love of God and service to the Church.

"I do love God," I said. "And I want to serve God. But I don't want it to be an abstract love or a life that excludes other people. As you said, we can move to God through others."

"There's nothing abstract about loving God, whether we do it as a nun or priest, as a single or a married person."

Dawn came halfway up the coast. After sunrise, a couple of porpoises swam with the boat, arcing ahead of us. All on board regarded this vanguard as a sign of good luck, a gift from the sea.

Chapter 22

SLEEPLESS NIGHTS

MOLLY AND I RETURNED to Angel Creek two days after Christmas, out of money and exhausted. One of the priests from Corozal, where we'd arrived early that morning, took pity on us and offered to drive us home – a trip of about two hundred miles by road that took us most of the day. As we pulled up in front of the rectory around four in the afternoon, so did Father Bosque. He jumped out of the blue Jeep and came over to see who'd arrived in the unfamiliar Volkswagen.

"Where did you find these two, Father Arias?" he asked the priest, whom he recognized at once.

The story spilled out: how we'd spent a sleepless night on a jam-packed bus from Mérida to Chetumal, on the Mexican–British Honduran border; taken a taxi across the river to Corozal; and turned up just after sunrise at the convent there. The starched, German nun who answered the door took one look at us, at our uncombed hair and brown skin, our Mexican blouses and sandals, and thought we were gypsies. It took the priest to convince her we were PAVLA volunteers. She then let us shower and take a nap until mid-morning.

Father Arias came in while we were eating a late breakfast to say he'd been meaning to visit the priests in Angel Creek for a long time and, as he had a few days off, now was a good time.

Before we fell into bed around eight that night, we had supper with the priests at the rectory. Gilly served us red snapper, cooked by the nuns, and the five of us washed it down with a couple of bottles of unconsecrated altar wine that Father Peck supplied. He wanted to hear our impressions of Mérida, one of his favourite cities, and especially of Casa Lynch, the place he'd recommended.

We shared the highlights of the trip: the charm of riding horse-drawn cabs around the sixteenth-century city alive with fountains and parks; the surprise of encountering so many European tourists, many from Germany and France; the majesty of Chichén Itzá, where we'd spent the Saturday before Christmas. Casa Lynch had been perfect: within walking distance of the historic district, with a secluded inner garden and a spacious room overlooking it that Molly and I shared. We had plenty of room for Kate the two nights she spent with us. Molly had brought along our string of Christmas lights, and we plugged it in each night before we went to bed. Once Kate left, Molly and I hadn't been able to speak much beyond the basics with kind Doña Lynch, but her grandchildren, who studied English in school, translated for us. The breakfasts there were wonderful, especially the scrambled eggs served with refried beans, so filling we could save money on lunches.

The entire time we were away, the thought of Father Bosque's departure hung over both Molly and me like a sword. During our late-night exchanges at Casa Lynch, we talked about how much we dreaded his leaving; how life in Angel Creek could never be the same without him. When our money started running low, we decided to leave Mérida early and go home to Angel Creek for a few days, to spend them with Father Bosque. That would mean backtracking to Belize City for a three-day conference for the PAVLA volunteers that started the day after New Year's, but we decided it was worth the inconvenience.

After dinner the night of our return, Father Bosque walked us across the road. He held me back as Molly went up the stairs and handed me a little notebook. He told me it was an answer to the little book of poems I'd given him for Christmas. It was a journal of his thoughts over the Christmas holiday, written while we were gone. He'd written a few poems, too, he said, just for me.

I read the first entry, written the day after we left Belize City for Mérida, when he had returned alone to Angel Creek:

> *There is in me an emptiness only God can satiate. The thoughts and feelings passing through me at this holy season are part of my purification. They are a necessary part of self-abnegation. This fiercely burning fire has been consuming*

me in order to make God's love brighter in my soul! But, littlest sister, it hurts – hurts – hurts! Be assured that our conversations, like the one on the Heron H, are not dry acts of charity. They help us both, I believe, to love God better.

The words evoked in me the feeling of the songs Father Bosque played on his harmonica, all in a minor key, sad, lonely, passionate songs, and to me beautiful. I couldn't stop reading. Once I came to the end of the twenty-page, handwritten journal, I started over, reading until I fell asleep with the little book in my hand.

I recalled one of my college theology teachers saying that heaven is "everything all at once". In Angel Creek, I had found myself as close to that state as it is possible to come in a world of space and time. I had friendship, love, beauty and meaningful work. All of it confirmed the goodness of creation. It was a joyful existence. But even in Angel Creek, as Father Bosque's imminent departure made clear, that state, at least on earth, was temporary. Not only would Father Bosque leave us, but Molly, Kate and I would soon leave each other and this special place.

Only in memory could I come close to reclaiming what I was about to lose. But I knew from experience that memory is a pale existence, something like Plato's cave in the *Republic*, and a lonely one. I tried to preserve this time in the sun by writing each day, either in my little red diary, in letters to friends and family that I asked them to save for me, or in essays that I typed out for myself.

Everything he does is intense, I wrote. *When he laughs, it's as if his whole body would explode; when he's serious, one feels almost frightened of him. The three of us have been with him constantly, roaring along in the robin's-egg blue Jeep; sitting around a candle in our living room, having deep discussions; swimming or playing ball or beach picnicking. He sings at the top of his voice, plays the harmonica, quotes Milton and Hopkins, writes poetry, goes hunting. When I think of his leaving, it's almost like death.*

Much of my life had been defined by absence – disappearing parents, dying grandparents, taken-away siblings, long-distance boyfriends. Now I was in for that again, with all the feelings of deprivation that went with it. Such thoughts tore at me as I read Father Bosque's little Christmas journal. The only balm was that he dreaded leaving every bit as much as I dreaded his going.

And so our last days together in Angel Creek became a hectic dance. We clung to each other as time ran out.

That Saturday, Molly and I were to go with Father Bosque to one of the sea villages north of us, a place we'd never visited that sounded like someplace we *wanted* to visit. It was located at the mouth of Mullins River, an estuary with treacherous tides that had given the village its name. We'd been told that refugees from the Confederacy had settled the village during the US Civil War, although most had later returned to the States. The priests made the trip every couple of weeks, but until now, we'd never been able to go along. It was our last chance to travel with Father Bosque and probably our only chance to visit the Mullins River area. The village was about eight sea miles up the coast from Angel Creek, but the only road there was roundabout and unpaved once you left the highway. Even when conditions were good, it took a couple of hours to drive there, so we planned to stay overnight and return after Sunday Mass.

Molly woke up Saturday morning with a headache and cramps. "You know how horrible it is having your period in the bush, even without cramps," she said. "I'm so sorry, but I really can't go."

That meant I couldn't go either, no matter how desperately I wanted to, no matter how much I'd counted on spending that last weekend with Father Bosque. When I told him the bad news, he set his jaw and said I should go ahead and pack my bag. Molly encouraged me to go without her. Kate, I knew, would disapprove, but Kate wasn't here to voice her objections. Father Bosque was the priest, I told myself, and I trusted him to make the right decision. I decided to stop worrying and let events unfold as they would.

Not long after two in the afternoon, I heard the Jeep drive up, grabbed my bag with a change of clothes, said goodbye to Molly, who was curled up in bed with a hot water bottle on her stomach, and ran down the stairs. There was Father Bosque at the wheel and in the back seat his two nephews, James and Ian. The boys waved, bouncing up and down.

He told me he'd asked his nieces to come, but they had a party to go to.

"We're glad," Ian said. "Now we get to go with Uncle Charlie and his girlfriend."

"You mean, Uncle Charlie's friend who is a girl," James said.

"That's what I said," Ian objected. "Miss Abby is a girl, and she's a friend."

Uncle Charlie threw back his head and laughed, as much at my embarrassment as at Ian's words. He revved the motor, and we were off.

The day was lovely, warm in the sun but cool out of it. We made good time and reached the village a bit before four in the afternoon. While Father

Bosque set up for Mass and prepared to hear confessions, the boys and I went house to house, telling people the priest had come and Mass would be offered at five p.m. Usually, I would have had a catechism or Bible story session with the children, but there wasn't enough time on this trip. I finished knocking on doors with time to spare; the village had fewer than twenty-five houses clustered on a rise above the river, just before the river met the sea. When the church bell tolled, I climbed back up to the small but solid, white frame church, one of the best built in any of the villages or towns in the district.

After Mass, Father Bosque, the boys and I shared a simple supper. One of the village women brought us a main dish of rice and beans, simmered with coconut milk and spiced with peppers. We drank the warm, bottled lemonade – it wasn't safe to drink the water she supplied – and finished with oranges and biscuits we'd brought with us.

The two boys went off with some of the village children, and Father Bosque and I sat on the church steps talking until bedtime. He said his mother planned to have a family farewell dinner for him just after New Year's, and he wanted Molly, Kate and me to be there.

"I'll stay in Angel Creek through New Year's to help Father Peck out," he said, "and then I'll be in Belize City until just after Epiphany, when I leave for Colombia. When do you leave for your meetings?"

"We go early on Monday," I said. "By truck. Kate will meet us there. I believe she's flying from Acapulco into Chetumal and taking the bus down from there to save money. We'll probably be in Belize City for at least a week."

"Well," he said, "we'll make the most of that time. My brother-in-law has a motorboat, and he'll take us to the cayes. I want to be sure you see the coral reefs."

I'd heard about the beauty of the cayes, small islands off the coast famous for their fishing, sandy beaches and access to the coral reefs, second only to the Great Barrier Reef off Australia in size and beauty. Hattie had taken her toll, he said, and most of the vacation spots were closed. "We can still see the barrier reef, though, and spend an afternoon swimming off one of the islands."

He was full of plans. "Of course, you know the Quinlans, but I want you to get to know the rest of my family before I leave. They'll watch out for you after I go."

"You'll be gone so soon. A week isn't much time."

"Enough to create a world," he said.

Figure 15. Father Charles Bosque in the mountains near Mullins River. Photo courtesy of Charles Woods.

Figure 16. Abby holding a wild orchid. Photo courtesy of Charles Woods.

About ten that night, the boys curled up in a corner of the church on the bedrolls their mother had sent with them. Father Bosque had a bedroll for each of us. He set his up near the boys and put mine in an opposite corner of the church. But he and I didn't use them. We sat outside until all the lights in the village had gone out, and then, when it grew too damp and cold, we went inside.

"Shall we sit together here?" he whispered, pointing to the open space in front of the altar.

We sat in the darkness with blankets over our shoulders. Most of the time, we were silent. It was enough to be together, in this peaceful, prayerful place. Neither of us slept at all that night.

The next morning, after early Mass, we drove with the boys first to the sea and then to the mountains. Father Bosque had a camera with him and took pictures of me and the boys. I insisted on taking photos of him, too, even though I had to struggle for the camera. He found an orchid for me and took a photo of me holding it. I felt insubstantial from lack of sleep, as though I might drift away in the winds sweeping across the hills.

CHAPTER TWENTY-TWO

Early on the morning of New Year's Eve, Molly and I set out for Belize City. She still felt out of sorts. Even though I'd turned in early the night before, I felt out of sorts, too, as though I'd been drugged. She hadn't asked me for details about the trip to Mullins River, and I was glad not to have to put any of it into words. When I closed my eyes, instead of bumping around on a plank in a truck headed for Belize City, I was still in the darkness of the church in Mullins River, my senses filled with the shadow of Father Bosque's voice, his clean soap-smell, his warm breath close to my ear as he whispered, "I couldn't do this with anyone but you."

He said that if we'd met before he had taken final vows, he would have regarded it as a sign that he should take another path in life. His thought now was that I was meant to live a life like his, dedicated to serving God. He hoped for that with all his heart.

All I wanted, I swore to myself, was to go on as we had been. I'd never hoped for anything else. Even now, I had no desire for him not to be a priest. That was unimaginable. I believed in the sanctity and inviolability of vows and could sincerely say that I'd never allowed myself to imagine anything more than friendship with this man. Perhaps I couldn't think of myself as his "little sister", but I was content to be his "friend who was a girl".

As much as Edith Wharton's, ours was an age of innocence. From childhood on, my Catholic education had encouraged either repression or sublimation of sexual desire. For most of my life I'd been an apt pupil, looking to poetry, music, literature and art for sensual satisfaction as well as moral guidance. My capacity for restraint amazes me now as much as giving in to desire would have appalled me then. It was as much a part of me as keeping secrets had become. In many ways, the two went together. For me and for most of my generation, withholding had become a habit of being.

All the more surprising, then, that Father Bosque had with great tenderness in the dark church in Mullins River smoothed back my hair from my face with both hands and kissed me. And without any hesitation, I had put my arms around him and kissed him back – and not just once.

Molly and I walked the now-familiar route from the truck stop to PAVLA House, carrying our straw bags filled with a week's worth of clothes. As I unpacked them in the room set aside for the Angel Creek girls – Kate would join us in time for the teachers' meetings after New Year's – I noticed how faded everything was. All the coloured cottons were ghosts of their former selves, thanks to Josie's fierce laundering on the riverbank. My skin, on the other hand, was darker than it had ever been, a golden brown that I liked.

That night, I put on my best linen dress, once deep red but now raspberry pink except along the seams, and swept my hair up into a French twist. In spite of the pain, I pierced my throbbing earlobes with the gold earrings set with tiny rubies that I'd bought in Mérida with the Christmas money my grandmother had sent me. I loved them. They reminded me of her. She had pierced ears, and rubies were her birthstone. For the first time in months, I used lipstick. Our friend Julian Martin, the radio announcer, had invited all the volunteers to the Regency Club to welcome in 1963.

When the first dolled-up female volunteers came down the stairs, one of the guys whistled, and then they all did each time another of us appeared. Usually, we wore no makeup, our hair was wind-blown, our clothes drab. It was the first time we'd seen each other dressed up. Most of the males had on suit jackets and ties, some of them still wrinkled from months spent in their suitcases. Already celebrating, we walked in a noisy group north along the sea to the club. It was a balmy evening, like a fine June night at home.

I wasn't feeling festive until I saw the big, bright Christmas tree at one end of the dim hall, the only fir tree with electric lights and glass ornaments I'd seen all season. Julian had reserved a couple of long tables near the tree for his friends, away from the band so we could talk. Most of his crowd were already there when we arrived. The Belize City volunteers knew them all and introduced us. Molly and I had met a few on various trips to the city: suave Miles, animated Mimi Gregg, who wore a sprigged cotton dress. "Liberty of London," she said, when I admired it. There were also a dozen or so Peace Corps workers at the club, not in Julian's party, who soon came over and sat with us.

I hadn't expected to have a good time that night, but I did. Julian turned his considerable charm on me. He was a rare combination of great talker and excellent listener.

As we talked, he told me about his dream of eventually moving to the States and pursuing a career in journalism or the arts. Announcing was fine, he said, but all it amounted to was reading aloud on-air. He wanted more of a challenge in life.

"I envy you Americans. So much opportunity. You don't know how lucky you are. Britain is done for, or I'd move there. The future belongs to the

States. The problem is, everyone else wants to move there, too, and the waiting list is long."

"Well, then, you should get your name on the list as soon as possible!"

"Or marry an American!"

"Is that why you're being so nice to all of us?"

"If that were the reason, I'd have left the males off the guest list, my dear."

Thinking back, I guess I must have ended up flirting with Julian. Or at least encouraging his attention. All the champagne didn't help. I'm not sure who ordered it or who paid for it, but it started flowing just before the countdown to midnight and lasted through most of the night. Mostly, I remember feeling relieved that I could enjoy the company of someone, *anyone* male, other than Father Bosque. That must mean my feelings for him weren't exclusive, weren't romantic.

I knew he and I had crossed a boundary into dangerous territory at Mullins River, and part of me wanted to deny it. In any case, I told myself, he'd soon be gone and so would I, into separate lives. Yet I also knew I'd see him again in a matter of days, and I rode that excitement like a boat lifted by rough water.

At dawn, most of the PAVLA and Peace Corps volunteers were still at the club. We had a lot to celebrate. Future lives were taking shape around us. The Ritters, the couple assigned to Punta Gorda, had announced they were expecting a baby. Peg surprised all of us with the news that she and a Peace Corps volunteer we referred to as "The Cowboy" (he was from somewhere out west and usually wore a ten-gallon hat) had become engaged over Christmas. He was at least a head taller than she was, and the two made an imposing couple. After she made the announcement, she grabbed his hat and put it on her head. It suited her perfectly. They wouldn't be married until his two-year commitment was finished, she told us, but she was planning to sign up for a second year with PAVLA so they could be together. Bill, the St Ben's man who had the guitar – he played magnificently, we'd discovered over the course of the year – had also become engaged. He'd flown to Tulsa during Christmas break to give Maggie, his college sweetheart, a diamond ring.

Someone Molly met at the party dropped us off at the cathedral, where we went to early Mass. Afterward, we walked back to PAVLA House, where we slept until afternoon. As we were getting up, Kate arrived. Missed connections and a case of food poisoning had kept her from getting back for New Year's Eve, she said. Molly and I, like almost everyone else who'd been at the club, had raging headaches. One of the guys prescribed vodka and tomato juice, which he subsequently produced, but it only made matters worse for me.

The last thing any of us wanted to do was sit through two days of meetings. They turned out to be a hodgepodge of PAVLA business (the first day) and spiritual reflection on our experiences (the second). Father Weaver promised us a trip to the cayes once the meetings were over, but the weather turned wet and cold, and the trip, scheduled for Friday morning, had to be called off. Many of the volunteers set off for their towns and villages, but the Angels, as we were called, stayed on, waiting for Father Bosque's arrival.

Saturday afternoon, I was sitting in the PAVLA House parlour listening to an LP of Gershwin's *Concerto in F* when Father Bosque came in. He motioned for me to stay where I was and sat down across from me. We listened wordlessly to the music.

"Where did you get that record?" he asked, when the piece ended.

"Julian Martin lent it to me," I told him. "Isn't it beautiful?"

"It's not great music," he said. "Don't let him corrupt your taste."

I suddenly felt like Eliza Doolittle in *Pygmalion*. A couple of weeks earlier, I'd have accused Father Bosque of playing Henry Higgins. Now, I didn't have the heart to tease or talk back to him. Time was too short, too precious.

Before he left, he invited Molly, Kate and me for dinner that night at his mother's house. He said all his immediate family in Belize City would be there. "I want you to think of them as your second family," he said.

By this time, we knew the Quinlans well, and we'd also met other members of Father Bosque's family – I usually stopped by to see his mother and his Aunt Bitsy whenever I was in the city, and Molly and Kate had travelled to Mexico with some of the Chavezes the same weekend I went with the Zachariases to Half Moon Creek.

Dolly Chavez was one of Father Bosque's older sisters (there were two others we never met, one of whom we heard had a failed marriage to an Englishman). Dolly was in her early forties when we met her, had seven children and was still a beauty. Her husband, Louis, reminded us of Jeff Chandler, a famous actor at the time. Like his brother-in-law Al Quinlan, he impressed me as entirely devoted to his wife and family.

At the dinner, we met Ralph (pronounced "Rafe", as the British do), Father Bosque's only living brother. He was just a few years older than Father, married, with two small children. In his darker complexion, he resembled Lydie

Quinlan. Dolly and Father Bosque shared the same fair skin and bluish-green eyes.

The Bosques greeted us as though we were indeed part of the family. For dinner, we ate a spicy chicken *relleno* that Kate bravely took on, in spite of her still queasy stomach. Once again, I wore my raspberry linen dress and pinned up my hair. Mrs Bosque seated me next to Father Bosque at the long dinner table.

"You and Molly look French tonight," he said as he poured wine into our glasses.

He knew it was the highest compliment he could pay the two of us. Earlier, she and I had told him the story of our being mistaken for two French girls during our Christmas holiday in Mérida. We'd been enormously flattered and had tried to speak French to each other the rest of the afternoon. Kate, unmistakably Irish, smiled at our silliness when she heard the story, repeated for the benefit of everyone at the table.

Molly and I shared the fantasy (like some of the characters played by Audrey Hepburn in the films we'd adored growing up) of going off to Paris after our year in British Honduras. My other cultural Mecca was New York City, where I'd spent two summers working as a librarian's assistant by day and in my free time going to every museum in the city, lining up for every Broadway and Off-Broadway play I could afford, and never missing Shakespeare in the Park.

I pushed to the back of my mind the nagging suspicion that not even for Father Bosque could I manage life in a convent. He made his hopes for me uncomfortably clear in those last days I spent with him. He showed his affection for all three of us richly and variously, employing the resources of his entire family to offer us unmeasured hospitality and reveal to us the unique beauty of his people and his land. But I saw that his eyes were turned towards me, and the look of expectation in them was daunting.

One afternoon, he asked me to meet him alone at his mother's house. He took me to the upstairs sunroom where he'd studied as a boy and showed me his childhood toys, his books, notes and papers, and then pulled out an album of family photographs. We talked about our childhoods, our school days, our favourite books, films and music – whatever came to mind. It was as though before we parted we were reliving together our lives before we met.

He said that when he first saw me, he'd been touched by a certain sadness about me that convinced him I needed a friend. I told him about writing home that he was too handsome to be a priest – that made him laugh – but said it was his gusto that drew me to him.

Ours was a very special friendship, he told me, but it wasn't the sort of love that needed physical consummation to be complete. It wasn't platonic, either, he admitted. He was convinced that our feelings for each other were a way to connect to God.

Those feelings felt very human to me, as did my grief at our farewell after the early Mass he celebrated the day he flew to Colombia. That same day, Kate, Molly and I returned to Angel Creek and life there, without him.

Chapter 23

ABSENCE

MAYBE IT'S OBVIOUS, BUT taking roll in class one day, I realized that unless there is first presence, there can be no absence. Sherry was absent for the second time that week, and I once again promised myself I'd find out why. The first two terms, she'd missed class only a couple of times. Now, she was absent as often as she was present. Paradoxically, without her there, sitting in the back row, the first-year lit class seemed less than it would have been had she never enrolled at all. Even when she was physically there, her mind was elsewhere. When I called on her, she often asked me to repeat the question.

"Pay attention!" I would tell the class, looking directly at her.

"Lisnin' de bettah part ah learning, Miss!" Cassie volunteered, repeating Sister Veronica's constant refrain.

Sister Veronica, of course, had talked with Sherry about her absences and also contacted her father, who, she said, backed up Sherry's excuses: persistent headaches, an upset stomach, female problems, babysitting when her stepmother was ill. Sherry looked depressed to me; the light had gone out of her eyes. When I tried to talk to her, she wouldn't look at me – just kept repeating that everything was all right.

I finally stopped asking, more than a little depressed myself. Before Father Bosque came to Angel Creek, Molly and my students and a circle of others had filled my days. Now, even with Kate added into the mix, I felt an essential lack, as though a crucial ingredient had been left out of a favourite recipe. Maybe because of the complex richness of Father Bosque's presence, my life became somehow smaller and duller without him there.

Before he left, Father Bosque had asked me to keep a daily journal for him and said he'd do the same for me, so that we would know how time passed for us, away from each other. Wrapped in my Mexican shawl – I'd been wearing it a lot since he left – I often wept while I wrote, my spirit sodden with missing him. Unsure when we could exchange journals, we also wrote long letters to each other, but because his superiors could open those letters at will, he warned me that we had to censor every word. This disembodied relationship was worse than total absence, because it introduced me to a written persona so different from the Father Bosque I knew that it was as though an imposter had taken up his pen. Melancholy, abstract, his prose lacked the vigour and directness of the man himself. Most of all, it lacked the teasing and joking that made him such a vivacious companion.

Probably because he imagined the censors as he wrote, his letters were moralistic and filled with pious advice. They assured me of God's love – God never gives us more than we can bear, he wrote – and told me of his prayers for me in the form of masses and novenas. He called me his "Little Sister", and wrote of his dream that I, too, would find my true vocation, one that would allow me to serve God in a dedicated way. I, on the other hand, avoided such themes and wrote instead of the incidents of daily life in Angel Creek, details of my classes, stories of my students and of the small adventures Molly, Kate and I continued to have.

In one of my newsy letters to him, I described the biggest event of the new year, a visit to Angel Creek by Sargent Shriver, director of the Peace Corps and a brother-in-law of President Kennedy. Accompanied by four members of his staff, he spent an afternoon in Angel Creek, flying in and out on a small, chartered plane. All the volunteers, Papal as well as Peace Corps, were invited to afternoon tea with him at the convent.

We heard about the visit a few days in advance, and the dilemma was what to wear. Molly, Kate and I couldn't forget that this was Jackie's brother-in-law by marriage. We'd bought nothing new since we arrived aside from a few Mexican blouses, and we were tired of wearing the same things. There were a couple of dressmakers in Angel Creek, and they were a bargain by US standards, but they took a long time to produce a dress or skirt.

Before I left the States for British Honduras, I'd made a couple of simple dresses, sleeveless with a drawstring waist, by combining two of my mother's patterns from the 1940s. She was an excellent seamstress, and I'd picked up the basics from her. Now I managed to reproduce the pattern, and in only a couple of hours, the three of us sewed new cotton dresses by hand from fabric bought at Lee Wong's. Molly chose a discrete burgundy print, and Kate, neutral beige. I was torn between extremes: pale green cotton and hot pink poplin. I finally decided on the pink. The fabric had a sheen that intensified its brilliance. It was distinctively different, like nothing I'd ever seen anybody wear. When they were finished, Molly and Kate's dresses looked sweetly simple. Mine looked radioactive.

The tea party lasted no more than half an hour, just long enough for introductions, an exchange of pleasantries, and the consumption of a tinned biscuit or two with a cup of tepid tea. Surrounded by nuns and priests swathed in black and everyone else in muted colours, I sat noxiously radiant in the convent parlour, only an arm's length away from one of the Kennedy clan. Had he been there, Father Bosque would have teased me out of my self-consciousness. Without him, I was powerless to make fun of my vain certainty that everyone in the room was noticing me and would make fun of me later.

Sargent Shriver was just as I imagined Kennedy himself and his brother Bobby to be – tanned and handsome, with a strong jaw and a toothy smile, physically fit (surely he, too, played touch football at the Kennedy compound in Hyannis Port) and much younger-looking than his years (at the time, he must have been somewhere in his mid-forties). Though the word was not in common use at the time, Mr Shriver and the young men who accompanied him had a "preppy" look about them. They wore pale blue or white Oxford cloth shirts with tiny buttons at the tips of the collars that held down striped ties. To a man, they were clean-cut, classy but casual, offhandedly understated – definitely not hot pink.

The room was crowded and soon became stuffy. Mr Shriver had taken off his jacket. As he rose, he hooked it on a finger and slung it over his left shoulder, reaching out to shake Mother Eugenie's hand as he thanked her for her hospitality. When he stood up, everyone else did too, blocking the quick exit I'd planned out a side door. As I tried to slip through a knot of people, I bumped up against one of Mr Shriver's staff, a slender young man who, with his pale skin, looked freshly peeled. He apologized, even though our collision was my fault, and started a conversation.

I'd forgotten all about what I was wearing until he said, "You know, I really like your dress."

"You do?" Instantly, I loved my dress as passionately as I'd despised it not ten minutes before. Maybe Sargent Shriver had noticed too. "I made it myself," I boasted.

"Great colour! A lot of girls back home are wearing that colour too."

So much for my brief stint as an arbiter of fashion. Now, I wrote Father Bosque, whenever I wore my hot pink dress, it was with humiliation and a sense of shame at my own foolishness. He wrote back that he was pretty sure I was the first penitent whose sackcloth was hot pink.

I suspect my newsy letters frustrated him as much as his soulful epistles exasperated me. His went on, front and back, for pages in his characteristically vigorous penmanship, so physically forceful that it embossed the sheets of airmail paper, sometimes making both sides of the paper almost illegible. He repeatedly encouraged me to express my spiritual concerns as I had done so often face to face. I resisted, not sure why.

A few weeks after he left, Lydie Quinlan stopped by to deliver a thick manila envelope that Father Bosque had sent in a package to her. "He asked me to give you this," she said. She looked at me closely for a few seconds before she added, "You know, he isn't supposed to be writing to anybody except family."

After their house burned down, we'd seen far less of the Quinlans. They were still living with friends, two large families crowded into a place not much bigger than ours. Construction on their house was slow going; the foundation had been laid, but that was all. Lydie told me they were looking for a place to rent but nothing was available. She seemed weary, worn down.

"I'm sure Charlie misses all of us as much as we miss him," she said as she was leaving. "You go ahead and write him if you want."

By that time, of course, he and I had been writing each other for weeks.

The envelope, which I opened after she left, contained copies of the photographs we'd taken during the trip to Mullins Rivers, along with several of him at the seminary in Colombia, taken soon after his arrival. In them, he looked heartbreakingly handsome.

Seeing the photos, David Lewis commented – he hoped I wouldn't be offended – that in them I looked like a Creole girl. I couldn't have felt more flattered.

"These are great photos," Kate said. "When were they taken?"

I briefly told her about the trip to Mullins River.

"You went alone with him?"

"Molly couldn't go at the last minute. His nephews were there."

"There are so many photos of you."

"I didn't realize how many he was taking," I said.

Unlike his letters, those photos ignited all my longing for him. Weeks of restlessness followed. I was content with nothing, impatient with everything, yet I dreaded the passing of each day, carrying me farther away from the time we'd shared and the people we were in those photographs.

Independent of my will, my imagination fashioned scenes from fragmented memories, bringing new life to closed chapters. Certain episodes became set-pieces: me in the moonlight, lying under my mosquito netting, listening to Father Bosque play folk songs on his harmonica as he sat on the flat roof outside his bedroom window, all in the melancholy minor keys I loved. Father Bosque and the three of us, me in the seat next to him, speeding down the Hummingbird Highway in the fragrant night air, singing at the top of our voices. The piano introduction to Leontyne Price's rendition of an aria from Puccini's *La Rondine* echoing in the rectory study where we sat side by side, anticipating the song itself, full of loss and longing. And always, Mullins River – the dark church, redolent of incense, the physical closeness, the whispered words, the gentle, closed-lip kisses. So many of my memories of him involved music; even now, I hear those melodies with sweet sadness.

With renewed fervour, I wrote Father Bosque almost daily and continued to record my private thoughts in the thick notebook I kept for him. Although I tried to hide the extent of our correspondence, in part because he asked me to, Molly and Kate asked me repeatedly why I was spending so much time in my room.

"You don't seem very happy these days," Molly said. "Tell us what's wrong."

"I miss Father Bosque," I finally admitted.

"So do I," Kate said. "So much!"

"Every day I think of him," Molly said. "But you're acting like he died. Exactly what went on between the two of you?"

I assured her we hadn't done anything wrong and didn't plan to.

"Did you fall in love with him?" she asked me.

I didn't reply.

"Not with a priest!" she said after a moment of silence. "Priests are off-limits."

"I know that," I said.

"I never thought it was as serious as that," Kate said. "Even though I was always afraid the two of you spent too much time together."

There must have been ordained priests who left the priesthood in those days, but I certainly didn't know of any. Within a few years, priests and also nuns were leaving religious life in droves, but in 1963, the idea was shocking.

Kate's advice: stop thinking about him. Molly's: find someone else.

"Does there always have to be a love interest, Molly?" Kate asked.

"At our age, of course there does," Molly answered. "What about Eduardo? Have you given him up for good?"

"Yes," I said. "Thank heavens that's over." I told them I'd seen Eduardo and even talked to him a few times over the past several months, but my feelings for him had wilted like a plant without water.

"Ana must have been disappointed," Molly said.

"I told her I'd sworn off romance. She concluded I'd decided to become a nun."

"Is that what you're thinking of?" Kate asked.

"No. But I think that's what Father Bosque wants – for us to live parallel lives."

"It's a lot clearer now why he gave you the tiger skin," Molly said.

Not long after he'd presented each of us with a tiger tooth, Father Bosque had surprised me by telling Molly and Kate about his intention to give me the tiger skin. I probably would have kept it a secret, not sure how to explain it, but that was not his way. As we sat around our customary candle one December night just before Molly, Kate and I left for the Christmas holiday, he said that he wanted to tell us why he'd given each of us a tiger tooth and why he'd kept one for himself.

"It's to remind us of how close we've been to each other over these past six months and how very much being with you has meant to me," he said. He went on to explain that it was the first time in his life he'd been so close to any women except those in his family, and he was amazed that three wonderful women like us had become his dearest friends. "It's been almost too much crowded into too short a time. Like a chapter in a beautiful novel – like a dream. I want to thank you for that."

After a pause, he went on. "I also want you to know, Molly and Kate, that I've asked Abby to keep the tiger skin for me. I hope you'll understand. The last thing I want is for you to feel slighted."

"The two of you have always been especially close," Kate said. "If you've decided to make a gift of it to one of us, it's right that Abby should have it."

"You've given so many gifts to each of us," Molly said. "We couldn't ask for more."

Later that day, I had told Molly and Kate that I really didn't know exactly why he'd decided to give me the tiger skin, that I didn't know what I'd do with it or even how I'd get it back to the States. Kate commented that his extraordinary gift was yet another example of his impulsive and generous nature.

"True," Molly added. "And also, I think, of his fondness for you, Abby."

The tiger skin lay folded in the big box in which Father Bosque had first shown it to me and then brought it to me the evening we returned from Mullins River. With it was a note he'd written, titled *"Ave atque vale"*: "Hail and Farewell":

> *Jaguar – Symbol of the passion and violence that is in me, a human.*
> *Dead jaguar skin – Tangible evidence of this passion and violence – now somewhat under control – giving force to my endeavours – good ones only, pray God!*
> *Claws – Weapons of pain and injury – so often operative against myself and my God – now rendered harmless by God's overpowering love as I have found it in so many wonderful friends.*
> *Beauty of skin – The beauty God gave me – beauty in all aspects – beauty that is mine – be it ever so dull or ever so bright.*
> *Softness of fur – My tenderness and gentleness. The mighty jaguar – yet softened with such a delicate and gentle skin. My humanness!*
> *The whole gift – the Spirit of God. The Spirit of Love, making me pulse and hum. The Spirit that must make my life dynamic – and must keep it so for God's greater glory.*
> *The Spirit that makes me like you so much – the Spirit which makes me give you*
>   THIS BEAUTIFUL GIFT.

Clouding my already low spirits was my sense that Molly, Kate and I were going our separate ways more often. Molly was spending more time alone with David. Just before Christmas, she'd stopped writing Paul, sure for both of them that an engagement was not what either wanted. Meanwhile, Kate became involved in an epistolary romance with one of Paul's classmates at Harvard. She'd never met Jim O'Toole, but Paul's enthusiastic introduction and Jim's eloquent letters won her heart. He sent her his photograph, and the minute she saw it, she said, she fell in love. Soon she was spending as much of her free time in her room writing to Jim as I lavished on my correspondence with Father Bosque.

David had suddenly become religious, interested in everything Catholic. Molly wasn't sure whether it was because he thought he would have a better chance with her if he converted or whether his newfound faith had arrived the way it was supposed to, as a gift from God. Once or twice, he came to Mass with us, and he may have had a few private conversations with Father Peck. So far as I could tell, however, his exploration of Catholicism took the form of long discussions with Molly over gin and tonic about his doubts concerning not Jesus or even the Virgin Mary, but the Pope.

With Father Bosque's departure, our weekend mission trips had stopped abruptly, and we missed them. We volunteered to go with Father Peck or one of the priests who served as his assistant pastor (most of them filling in for a couple of weeks at a time, from other parts of the colony), but they showed no interest in taking us along. Consequently, we had more time for reading, although much of what we read was at cross purposes. From the nuns and priests, we borrowed religious and spiritual works that reinforced one world view, and from the Todds (whose baby boy looked just like Andrew) freethinking novels that challenged it.

The most unsettling books we read were written by women who had unconventional attitudes and lives. Pearl Buck exposed us to the idea of patriarchy through her novels set in traditional, male-dominated Chinese society. Isak Dinesen suggested that women could define themselves and construct their own lives even when married. Françoise Sagan's teenaged narrators introduced us to the emerging sexual revolution of the 1960s by showing us women who claimed their sexuality apart from marriage.

Some of our most heated discussions came from reading Sagan, a writer only a few years older than we were. Was the image of women in *Bonjour Tristesse* and *A Certain Smile* demeaning or liberating? Was our own innocence a virtue or an obstacle to knowledge and experience? Was the chastity we were taught to value an elevation of sexuality or a tool of male domination? Was the pursuit of pleasure frivolous or a worthy goal?

In particular, we debated whether a young woman like the narrator of *A Certain Smile* gains anything of real value by having an affair with an older, married man. Molly thought a young woman could learn a lot by being the protégé of an older man, even if there was no hope of marriage. He could shape your tastes and teach you about the world, she said. Having just been a protégé of Father Bosque, I had to agree, although our relationship and his teachings differed dramatically from those of Sagan's characters. Kate thought it would be fun – for a while, anyway, and especially in Paris – to live a hedonistic type of life, spoiled by an older man who doted on you. But, she asked, what if the pursuit of pleasure robbed you of joy in the simple pleasures of life? That would be the danger, she thought, and not worth the risk. My stance – and I couldn't decide if it was moralistic, pragmatic or cynical – was that such a relationship was unequal in too many important ways – age, experience, power – and would probably end in disappointment and disillusionment on one or both sides.

Our religious faith, closely allied with our moral framework, also caused heated debate. Had we been brainwashed like the *Manchurian Candidate* to accept a distorted view of reality? Were we in control of our choices or programmed to accept some sort of predestined plan engineered by the Vatican?

Molly came back from nights out alone with David with her face red and chafed from prolonged bouts of kissing. I found it hard to believe, but she told us that when David's emotions had become too intense while they were making out, she pulled out her rosary beads and knelt beside his bed to pray for chastity.

Extrapolating from the sexual advice the otherwise sophisticated nuns who'd taught me had offered, I speculated that some nun or other had suggested that manoeuvre.

"No, don't blame them," she said. "I thought it up myself. I didn't know how else to handle it. I have to say, it worked." So much for her participation in the sexual revolution.

But it began to dawn on all three of us that similar advice had been embedded in our consciences from an early age. At Corpus Christi grade school, as early as the second grade, I remembered being told never to touch myself "down there", not even in the bathtub. As puberty set in, my classmates and I were told that sexual fantasies were as sinful as the act of intercourse itself outside of marriage. Molly and Kate recalled similar warnings. We'd all repeatedly heard the story of Saint Maria Goretti, the twelve-year-old who suffered death defending her virginity. For years, I thought she was sainted for her sexual purity. In fact, as I learned only much later, it was because she forgave her attacker as she was dying. That was not the version I heard as a teenager.

Maintaining our virginity until marriage and our chastity until death was the moral imperative of the "good" girls of our generation, no matter what their religious faith. Sexuality, unlike other instincts and appetites, was a sacred thing, and the sexual act should be both an act of love and an expression of commitment – for females, anyway. We respected those who had taken vows of chastity out of devotion to God, assuming that the vows themselves would make keeping them possible. At the other extreme, we regarded casual sex, sex for the pleasure of it, as not only shameful but immoral.

The problem with these attitudes, as suggested by Sagan and some of the other authors we read, was the way society used them to keep women in line by condemning and casting out those who for one reason or another transgressed them. Could any work of literature make that point more poignantly than *Tess of the D'Urbervilles*? In our era, more than seventy years after that book was published, those who violated such moral strictures – even if in appearance only (tight sweaters, form-fitting jeans, too much makeup) – were pilloried as "fast, loose little hussies", the modern equivalent of "fallen women". That sort of ostracism, I began to see, served a moral agenda that kept not just nuns but all women veiled, and it vindicated institutions that gave men control over not only women's bodies but also our minds and souls.

I hated to admit it, but even Father Bosque served that oppressive system when he praised my innocence as a primary virtue. Part of the reason I balked at his letters was his constant admonition to preserve my "goodness".

Little One, he wrote to me – a twenty-two-year-old woman at the time – *don't take more than a little bit of wine when you go to parties or out somewhere. I don't want anything to happen to you. You'll always be able to control and handle yourself, won't you? You must be careful, for your likeableness could make others want to misuse you.*

Maybe I misinterpreted his words, but I resented such advice. *"I don't want anything to happen to you,"* he'd written. I wanted *everything* to happen to me! It seemed to me his notion of goodness was full of negatives: abstinence, denial, rejection. True, he'd always been protective towards Molly, Kate and me, and I'd thought of it as an endearing quality, a response to the often risky circumstances we got ourselves into, all of us pushing the limits. As the pile of his letters to me grew by inches, I longed for the uncensored words I remembered, words that revealed the unfettered man I knew and loved.

Meanwhile, Paul was appending plaintive notes to Jim's letters to Kate, asking her to send news of Molly and begging her to ask Molly to write. Paul wrote that he was to the point of hitchhiking down to British Honduras to see Molly, Harvard be damned.

Were my opening eyes making a cynic of me? In my sour moods, how opportunistic, arbitrary and self-involved attraction and love – in fact, all human emotion – seemed to me. If Molly hadn't come to British Honduras, would David now be courting me or Kate? And if Kate had come sooner, might Eduardo have pursued her? If Paul had given my name to Jim O'Toole instead of to Kate, would he and I now be writing letters to each other, planning to meet as soon as I returned to the States? And Father Bosque? If I'd been assigned to Belize City and Sue Ella of the earthy green eyes had taken my place, would she now be his "Little Sister"?

Chapter 24

REVELATIONS

WHAT HAPPENED TO THE Maya? The disappearance of Mayan culture fascinated the students in my IA history class no less than the question of the fall of Rome had intrigued me at their age. We had little information – certainly none in our textbook – about the people who had once flourished in their homeland, and with exams looming, very little time in class to discuss the topic, once it came up. Had nature – in the form of hurricanes, droughts, pestilences or earthquake – wiped out Mayan culture? Or had human nature – in the form of internecine wars between city-states, likely as virulent as those we'd studied between ancient Athens and Sparta – brought the cities to ruin? Having experienced Hattie, the students voted for the destructive power of nature. They would have starved, they said, without the food and clean water brought in by the British and Americans.

When David invited Molly, Kate and me to drive with him to the western region to explore the Maya ruins, we eagerly accepted. One Saturday in mid-February, we three folded ourselves into David's Simca and by early afternoon reached El Cayo, set in the hills near the Guatemala border. It was a stunning day: clear skies, low seventies without humidity. We stopped briefly to leave off our things at the house of a family who spoke only Spanish – David usually rented a room from them on trips west – before heading for Xunantunich, a partially excavated Mayan site about five miles west of the city. David told us that a few years earlier, a group from Cambridge University had done quite a bit of excavation. Theirs was the latest in a number of digs, most conducted by anthropologists and archaeologists from the United States. The site, he said, was now open to the public.

David said that wherever we saw a hill in the middle of otherwise flat land, a Mayan ruin was probably underneath. Odd bits of sculpted stone and shards of pottery were dug up all the time, he said. If David was right, the mounds that swelled in forests, on plantations and across the sides of mountains suggested that British Honduras had at one time supported a dense Mayan population. The image of ancient cities mounded in centuries of mud and overgrown by snarled, snaky vines both allured and appalled me. It made the ground we walked on at once a burial ground and a treasure trove.

The road we took from El Cayo followed the Mopan River, tree-shaded, glistening green in the filtered sunlight. Brown Indian women in dresses the colours of tropical fruit kneeled along the grassy edge, doing their wash. Had I been a painter, I would have set up my easel somewhere along that gently winding road.

To reach the ruins, we had to cross the river. A hand-cranked ferry bridged the two banks. David drove the Simca onboard, and as we ferried across, we sat on the side of the barge-like contraption with our sandals off, dangling our feet in the clear water. The other passengers, villagers toting baskets of leafy vegetables and cages alive with chickens and doves, watched us impassively. Red leaves floated in the stream, making it seem like the autumn we'd missed that year. The trip took about fifteen minutes, even though the river was neither broad nor swift. It was hard, slow work for the operator, who like most of the natives of this area was Mestizo. It seemed a safe guess that what happened to at least some of the Maya was intermarriage with the conquistadors.

We drove uphill a short distance from the ferry and found ourselves alone on a hilltop that overlooked the entire river valley. David pointed out distant villages hidden by canopies of trees, betrayed by smoke that rose from cooking fires. Breaks in the rain forest suggested scattered plantations. The ones to the west were in Guatemala.

It was my first experience of looking from one country into another, and it seemed strange not to see dotted lines, like those on a map. The Mayan city of Xunantunich, or whatever it was called in earlier times, had offered its inhabitants a panoramic view.

The ruins themselves were in various stages of excavation, most once again covered over with vegetation. Segments of stone foundations were exposed across the hilltop, but it was impossible to tell what sort of structures they had once supported, or how large they'd been. We wandered about the area for half an hour or so, climbing over the rubble, speculating on what life had been like a thousand years ago in this place. From our Christmas trip to Chichén Itzá, Molly and I knew there probably would have been a playing field for a ball game that required a stone hoop like the handle of a big teacup attached to one of the walls. The guidebook had told us that the loser of the game – or was it the winner? – had been offered as a sacrifice to the gods.

According to David, the biggest structure, partially excavated, was called "El Castillo". Nothing was labelled, and without his bits of information, we would have had no way to interpret what we were seeing. He didn't know much, and what he knew he'd picked up talking to natives as he went around the country on Forestry Service business. He told us that Xunantunich, given its location, was thought to have been a centre of some sort, governmental, maybe military, but most likely religious and ceremonial. If the latter, El Castillo probably hadn't been a castle at all but a temple.

Maybe that's where the rumours of a female ghost haunting the area had originated, in some bloody sacrifice of the past. She was said to appear frequently and disappear suddenly, often by walking through stone walls. What was she looking for? Life? Love? Revenge? Release? In modern times, we learned, the site had taken its name from her. "Xunantunich", David told us, translates into English as "the stone maiden".

If each mound represented a structure of some sort, this must have been a large settlement. As David pointed out, the mounds we could see suggested ten times as many extending far into the bush that surrounded the open area where the most extensive digs were. This place had once been home to tens of thousands, maybe hundreds of thousands of people. Their lives had no doubt been as ordinary seeming to them as our own everyday existences were to us.

Where and how, I wondered, did they experience the awareness of otherness that Xunantunich gave me? It was the same sort of feeling that came over me whenever I walked where I had walked with Father Bosque, or sat in a room where we had sat together, or drove in the robin's-egg blue Jeep, or kneeled in the church where he had said Mass.

Time had distanced me from those who once lived here, but the place itself preserved something of their spirit and allowed those who visited to resurrect it, or to try. At its source, the impulse to bring back, dig up, seemed to me in essence a religious one, evidence of faith in a reality that transcends time. But it was also a disturbing one. Isn't anything unearthed disturbing?

David suggested the three of us climb up on one of the stone walls so he could take our picture. We pulled ourselves up onto the highest wall from behind, where the earth had not been entirely cleared away, and followed his directions to where the light was best.

He called the photograph a group portrait of the "Three Virgins". This, he said, is what people in Angel Creek called us behind our backs. I suspected that the "people" he referred to were the Todds, but he insisted all sorts of people called us that, not only people from the valley and the Forestry Station but some of the shopkeepers and also the boys and young men in town.

In the photo, we are seen from below. Molly sits with legs crossed demurely at the ankle. She's at her softest and most wistful, melancholy almost, barely smiling (no dimples), off in her own world. Kate is in the middle, an insouciant smile on her face. She looks pert, a trifle flirtatious. One leg kicks out, as though longing to dance, her flip-flop dangling risquély from her toes. I stand on the right, a contrast to the two seated figures. It's me at my most austere, staring down with defiance into the eye of the camera, my feet planted squarely on the rock, as though I'd just emerged from it.

It seemed to me afterward that in that photo David captured our shadow selves, usually hidden from view. Though not a particularly good likeness of any of us, we treasure it.

It's one of the few pictures we have of just the three of us from that remarkable year.

Suddenly the hot weather was on us, with noonday temperatures climbing into the high eighties and nineties Fahrenheit, although the evenings could be cool. When we had a few days off at mid-term, Molly, Kate and I decided to go on our own to the place we'd visited in the Pine Ridge with David Lewis and the Todds. It was a trip of only sixty miles or so, but we had no easy way to get there. The cabin where we arranged to stay wasn't far from the isolated spot where director Francis Ford Coppola later built his mountain retreat.

We decided to take the truck as far as we could and hitchhike the rest of the way. Kate said young women hitchhiked all over Europe; she'd done it a couple of times while she was there. It proved so easy that we wondered why we hadn't always travelled that way. A couple of government workers picked us up first thing. We climbed in the back of their Land Rover, carrying our food and bedrolls with us. When they dropped us off at our cabin, they promised to help us find a ride back to the main road, where we could catch a truck to Angel Creek.

Figure 17. Molly, Kate and Abby, the "Three Virgins", on an excavated wall at Xunantunich, a Mayan archeological site in western Belize. Photo courtesy of Malilee Zimmers.

It was a lovely time, a mini-retreat before the rush of our final weeks in British Honduras. Each of the three days we were there, we walked five miles round trip to swim at the falls. There was a niche behind the biggest of them where we could sit behind a curtain of water. The sound alone was mesmerizing, and the glazed beauty of the forest and sky beyond was reminiscent of an Impressionist painting. We swam in the pool in front of the falls, so deep and cold our teeth hurt when we first jumped in, and then sunned on the rocks, sometimes falling asleep. We were so much a part of nature that birds would fly within our grasp, had we wanted to catch them. We carried picnic-style lunches with us and ate simple suppers, chili, beans or hash, served from tins heated in the stone fireplace in the cabin. We read, wrote letters and entries in our journals, took naps and talked late into the night.

I was glad to be there, even though, like a persistent toothache, missing Father Bosque dulled every pleasure. At twenty-two, I had begun to fear that the best of life was over. All I could see ahead was saying goodbye to Angel Creek and, just as painful, to Molly and Kate. We wanted to stay together and talked about volunteering for a Jesuit programme in Japan that Father Weaver had told us about. The problem was that we had no guarantee we'd be assigned to the same place. We spent hours fantasizing about sharing an apartment in a place yet to be decided – but first, we had to return to homes that were hundreds of miles apart and find jobs to earn money for whatever came next.

My mother had written to invite me to spend the summer with her and my stepfather while I looked for a job. I'd spent a couple of holidays with them, but I had mixed feelings about moving in with them for an entire summer. My mother and I had lived apart for almost seven years, counting the year just past. My stepfather went out of his way to be nice to me, and I adored my baby brother. I loved my mother much more than I was willing to admit, but I had trouble knowing how – or whether – to show it.

In the weeks before I had left for British Honduras, I would suddenly find myself in the middle of another senseless argument with her. I couldn't keep myself from criticizing the way that in my opinion she was spoiling my little brother, bringing him home a new toy every time she went shopping. I resisted her attempts to "buy me off" (as I thought of it at the time) by preparing the foods that I'd loved as a child: waffles for breakfast, banana cream pie for dessert.

"But they used to be your favourites," she'd say when I didn't show the enthusiasm she expected.

"I'm not ten years old any more, Mom," I'd tell her.

The same with the "little surprises" she lavished on me: a prepaid appointment with her hairdresser, a few dollars slipped inside my purse at the end of a visit, a bottle of perfume tucked into my overnight case. I was loath to let her know how much receiving them from her meant to me.

By volunteering for a year instead of looking for a job right out of college, I'd backed myself into a corner. Unless I enlisted in the military, as my two oldest brothers had done, or joined a convent, as Father Bosque wanted me to do, I had noplace else to go after I returned to the States. My ailing grandmother had sold her house and moved in with one of my uncles and his family. I hadn't heard at all from my father for over a year. I had only an airline ticket, supplied by PAVLA, and enough money to get myself home. Like it or not, I could see no alternative to accepting my mother's offer.

The plan I sketched out for myself during that long weekend was to treat my mother and stepfather with as much courtesy, as much kindness as I could muster, pay for my room and board in part by babysitting and helping around the house, work as many jobs and save as much money as possible, and leave Crystal City no later than the end of the summer.

Molly's plan was much the same: go back to Wisconsin, work and save money until she could get out of there, away from "small towns, small people, small talk", as she put it. She'd go to Japan or New York or Paris, with me and Kate if that worked out, but on her own if not. She no longer talked about marrying Paul, although she didn't rule it out.

Only Kate knew for sure what she would do – take summer courses at Marquette with money borrowed from her parents while she applied for a fellowship to grad school. She still wasn't quite sure what she intended to study. If grad school didn't work out, she'd join Molly and me wherever we ended up.

One night, I almost told them all that I'd left out of my family story. We were sitting before the fire. Molly was writing to Paul (she had recently resumed her correspondence with him as capriciously as she had dropped it). I was writing in my journal, and at my urging, Kate was reading *The Brothers Karamazov* for the first time. Dostoyevsky was my favourite author and *Brothers* my favourite of his novels, beating out even *The Idiot* for first place. I think it was because the world of the Karamazov family was, like my perception of my own, sordid yet at times flooded with mysterious grace and beauty that thwarted easy comprehension. With what words could I do justice to a childhood filled with misery but also the joy of the sticky green springtime leaves that had convinced even Ivan Karamazov of the wonder of life?

When the last big log in the fireplace fell, shattering and sparking into a universe of brilliant pieces, Kate looked up from her book and said something that almost convinced me that I could, after all, trust her with my family story in all its complexity and count on her to understand why I found it so difficult to talk about.

"This book is a masterpiece, Abby! All the variations of the human soul in this one family!" Kate said she wasn't sure she understood a fourth of the novel, but it brought her close to a new realm of experience. "Maybe my mind – or maybe it's my heart – isn't developed enough yet to comprehend it all," she said. "But seeing into the depths of human nature in this novel, I'm left with a desire to love more completely and fully, without judgement, like Alyosha."

Why not tell them, right here and now? I opened my mouth to speak. "Hey, Kate, hey Molly, you know how old Karamazov abandoned his kids? Well, both my father and my mother deserted us, and by the way, I have two brothers and two sisters I never told you about." Nothing except a little "uh-huh" eked out. After a moment or two of silence, Kate went back to her book, and I sat staring into the embers.

"To love more completely and fully, without judgement." That was the missing piece. I picked up my pen, and in my diary wrote: *If others knew how selfish I've been with my family, missing a million chances to forgive and love more deeply and show it. That's why I must stay with my mother this summer. If I can't love my own flesh and bones and blood, who can I ever give myself to?*

Dr Bauer had a new car, a big event in Angel Creek in those days. The few automobiles that had survived Hattie were made to last as long as possible. Dr Bauer's Austin sedan had been shipped to him from England. After so many trips in the blue Jeep and David's two-door Simca, it seemed like a limo to us. He often invited us for rides in the evening, especially if he was driving out to the valley on a hot night.

One evening in early April, not long before sunset, he stopped outside our house, honked three brief times in the pattern familiar to us and asked us to ride with him to call on a Ketchi Indian family that lived just off the Hummingbird Highway. As we drove, he told us that one of the children, a boy of eight, had died suddenly that afternoon from what he was sure, from the description, was dysentery. Now the sister was sick. He thought it might console the family to have the American teachers come to view the boy's body. I saw my own apprehension reflected in Kate's and Molly's faces. We hadn't been to a wake here, only a couple of funeral masses and burials, and we had no idea what to expect.

It was dark when we arrived, although a half-moon was rising in the night sky. The first thing we saw as we drove into the clearing around the house was a group of six men under a kerosene lantern hanging from a tree limb. The lantern swung in the wind, and in its erratic light the men worked with saws and planes, hammers and nails, making a small coffin. Parts of it leaned against the tree, the wood green and raw looking.

A man who introduced himself as the boy's father stepped forward to greet us and thank us for coming. The boy's mother soon joined us, and she too expressed her gratitude, with tears. The boy's sister was very sick, she told us, and she asked us to pray for the girl, and for her son who was now "with the angels".

The mother led Dr Bauer into a bedroom at the back of the house to examine the daughter while the father ushered Molly, Kate and me into the main room. Women of various ages, most likely relatives and neighbours, sat on benches and mismatched chairs against the walls, which were covered from floor to ceiling with sheets of old newspaper. A few nodded silent welcomes as the father led us to a table at the far end of the room. On it lay the boy, whose name we were told was Mario.

For eight years old Mario was small. His little hands lay at his sides. For some reason, his feet were bound together, and a folded handkerchief had been wrapped under his chin and knotted at the top of his head, its edges sticking up like the ears of a small animal. The boy was dressed all in white, in what must have been his first communion outfit. Six candles had been set around his body; they provided the only light in the room.

I'd never before seen a dead child – nor anyone newly dead. The sight affected me powerfully and strangely, in a way that sounded crazy when I later tried to describe it to Kate and Molly.

As I stood beside Mario's body, so very still, I became intensely aware of my own, a humming hive, breath rising and falling, blood pulsing, eyes glazing with tears, armpits and palms oozing sweat.

The thought came to me, *Of course! It was little ones like this that Jesus raised from the dead.* Then my rational mind switched off, and in an instant too brief to measure, as palpable as my own existence, I sensed Mario's spirit. Like fire. A small, inextinguishable flame.

For that briefest of moments, I *knew* that what the mystics and poets write and the gospels teach is true. Death has no sting and the grave no victory.

As I came back to myself and saw the corpse of that child stretched out before me, great sorrow along with human fear and doubt seized me. A little boy gone because he was poor and born in the bush.

Good Friday came ten days later, on 12 April, and on this evening, almost everyone in Angel Creek, Catholic or not, lined up outside the church as the sea turned from silver to ashen grey in the twilight. As night fell, we lit our candles one from another until, alight with sacred flame, we moved within the darkness. Father Peck led the way, carrying a wooden crucifix high in the air. We shuffled along the narrow village lanes, following the cross, singing and chanting prayers in unison.

The Stations of the Cross had been set up at fourteen houses along the route, and we stopped at each, meditating on the progress of Jesus of Nazareth towards seemingly certain death. Looking up at the sky, where storm clouds gathered, the priest cried out in a voice loud enough to be heard over the rising wind, "Lord, have mercy! Christ, have mercy!"

The journey culminated at the Angel Creek River. Father Peck stood in the middle of the bridge that marked the centre of town, surrounded by a crowd that filled the bridge and both banks of the river almost to the sea. He held the cross steady, even though the wind, stronger now, snatched at his vestments and slapped at our flames. Needing no amplification, he delivered his brief sermon.

"Christ used his freedom to save us from sin and death," he proclaimed. "Our lives are like this river. The river flows into the sea and never returns to being a river again. So, too, our lives flow into eternity, and we can never relive them." Thus, he concluded, we must make good use of our time here and now by freely accepting God's life-giving gifts of faith, hope and love.

At home later, Molly, Kate and I said little to each other. Kate wrote in her journal, but I didn't want words to distance me from the solemn ceremony we had participated in. Surely these Easter mysteries were deeply true, I told myself, and their promise of transformation trustworthy. In spite of its hardships – or maybe because of them – my life in Angel Creek had confirmed that forgiveness and love, unlike bitterness and blame, can renew and lift us up.

I took it as a sign of hope that this year Easter would be followed immediately, on Easter Monday, by my birthday. A few days earlier, I'd written to my mother:

Strange to be almost 23. I'm pretty old. But not very. There's still a lot of life left in me. I love the world and people and dreams and everything, everything, everything. It's God's greatest privilege, to be alive. I want to find work and go to school and probe for beauty and write and show the world that man is NOT an animal but noble, meaningful, exquisite – yet incomplete.

When I entered my bedroom that Good Friday night in 1963, I heard through the open window the sound of drumming in the distance. Garifuna danced in their tents on the edge of the village, continuing their prayer in a way that offered a powerful sequel to what we had just experienced. I wished I could dance out my sorrow and joy with them.

As I lay down under my mosquito net, my body pointed towards the sea, I imagined myself riding the river of time to wherever it would carry me.

Chapter 25

LEAVING ANGEL CREEK

SO MANY LASTS – OUR FINAL days and nights in British Honduras filled with them – some already memories, some still to come:

End-of-the-school-year parties with our students and the other teachers. A send-off organized by the nuns and Father Peck. Among the many guests, Josie and Gilly, the Quinlans, Ana, Marita and the little boys – but not Eduardo, who has moved to Half Moon Creek. Our last opera night (*La Bohème*) with Mrs Jefferson and Mrs Moss. One last, long swim with the Camelot Boys and another with the girls, who struggle to keep up with us in the petticoats and cotton dresses they wear as bathing suits.

A goodbye glass of schnapps with the doctor and a farewell cup of tea with Therese and Ugly Baby, now an adorable one-year-old mouthing his first words. A last dinner with David and the Todds, bookending our time in British Honduras.

David will come for a final visit. He bears a beautiful mahogany bowl. The local craftsman he commissioned months earlier to make three has managed to finish only one. I have the tiger skin and Molly has him, he says, so it's only fair that Kate get the bowl. (Molly confesses years later how keenly she regrets the loss of that magnificent bowl.)

A dilemma about how to get the tiger skin to the States. I finally pack and ship it COD by sea and rail to my mother's address. (It will take three months to arrive and push me once again to near penury.) I carefully wrap the filigreed silver cross, also a gift from Father Bosque, in my Mexican shawl and bury it among the clothes in my locked luggage. Along with the shawl, it disappears en route. The tiger tooth, I carry with me.

Before we leave, Jean Martinez will cry out, "I wish you had never come here, Miss, only to leave us now!" She runs away before I can answer. Three minutes later, she's back, in tears. "Miss Portah is so much myself that I never want to leave her."

I spend an hour at the river with Victoria Flores, one of the third-year Busy Bees. As I help her scrub the Flores family laundry, she tells me how much she'll miss me. "It's the only year we evah have a newspapah," she tells me. Then, in a matter-of-fact voice, she adds: "You won't remembah us, Miss. People be like dat. 'Dat poor place, dose silly girls,' you'll say. You won't remembah."

"I will remember, Victoria," I promise.

Sherry reappears for the last few weeks of classes and once again follows me home from school. She announces her intention to spend all the time she can with me "before the end". A farewell gift from her: a black and white photograph – lovely! – of her dressed in her school uniform, her hair, long at last, trailing over one shoulder, the sea as backdrop.

A year later, I hear that she's dropped out of school and has given birth to a stillborn son. Rumour has it that it's her father's child. At first, I'm incredulous and then depressed for days. How could I have ignored signs of serious trouble ahead? Her mood swings, those uncharacteristic sudden silences. The absences from class. Her crossed fingers as she described her relationship with her father: "We are close like this, Miss." Although I write her, I receive no answer. I curse the naïveté and self-absorption that blinded me to her plight.

A few more years go by and one of her classmates from Angel Creek writes that she's just seen Sherry in Belize City, working as a waitress. "I almost didn't recognize her, Miss," I read. "She cut off all her long hair!"

Sissy will ask for my address – "Write it down, Miss!" – so she'll know where to find me when she comes to the States. She sends me a few letters, but we eventually lose touch with each other. She does make it to the States, I hear, although we never manage to meet. She will work her way through three husbands, returning to Angel Creek to marry the third in a miniskirt that scandalizes the town.

A tearful goodbye from Ana, who wishes for a different ending: "No matter what you think, Eduardo cared for you," she tells me. We exchange a few letters before she stops answering. A decade later, Jean, who has become a Holy Family sister, writes that she's recently seen Ana Zacharias jogging down a New Orleans street outside the convent. Jean reports that Ana has settled in New Orleans with her husband, also from Angel Creek. I vaguely remember him, a pleasant Latino fellow about Ana's age. I hope it's a love match.

Long after the fact, I hear that in the years after I leave Angel Creek, Eduardo becomes involved with one of Lee Wong's daughters – her father forbids the relationship – and then with a young Garifuna girl, who bears his child. "He really loved her," Jean tells me, "but there was no hope of marriage." Eventually he does marry. No one from Angel Creek, according to Jean. His wife might be from El Salvador, she thinks, but she isn't sure.

By the time of Belize Independence in 1981, I learn from Charlie that Eduardo has become one of the richest men in the country. He's living in Belize City, but his dream of orange walks isn't entirely forgotten; he's heavily invested in the citrus industry. It's whispered, though, that he's earned his millions in the drug trade. Eduardo, a drug lord? I find it difficult but not entirely impossible to believe.

Molly, Kate and I delay our imminent parting. When we leave Angel Creek at the end of April 1963, we travel south by mail boat to Puerto Barrios in Guatemala. Together, we take a hectic, terrifying trip through Guatemala, where soldiers armed with rifles stop our bus. The three of us huddle together as they question and search the passengers and their belongings. Overhead, we hear the soldiers thrusting bayonets into the sacks and baggage on the roof.

We continue on narrow mountain roads to Antigua, the ancient capital, a pristine, flowery retreat in a war-ravaged country. Later, at the airport in Guatemala City, Molly clings to Kate and me as we prepare to board our flight back to the States. She sets off alone for Mexico City.

Chapter 26

THE RIVER OF TIME

NOT LONG AFTER OUR return from British Honduras, I drop a bombshell on Kate and Molly in the form of a long letter to each of them with details of my family situation and an apology for not having told them sooner, face to face. I half expect never to hear from them again. Both, however, respond immediately, their letters filled with affectionate concern.

Molly registers her surprise, spends a paragraph or two consoling me, assuring me there is nothing to forgive, and moves cheerfully on to other topics. Characteristically, Kate's carefully worded reply offers sympathy and understanding as well as a bit of analysis as to why I've acted as I have. It concludes with a gentle admonition urging me to try harder to stay in touch with reality. My challenge, as I see it, isn't so much staying in touch with reality as communicating it to others. A small difference to others, perhaps, but a big one to me.

The three of us meet again briefly in Chicago at the end of our first summer back in the States. It's August 1963, and I'm on my way to Michigan, where I've found a teaching job near Ann Arbor. Kate and Molly drive down together from Wisconsin to meet me at the apartment of a close friend of mine. Kate is in summer school at Marquette, trying out a few graduate classes, and Molly is temporarily living in Racine with her parents, working in an office. I've spent the summer with my mother and stepfather, more happily than I expected. My friend asks about my family, and I see the look Kate and Molly exchange. My letter is the proverbial elephant in the room. I don't say anything about it, and neither do they.

Within a few years of that meeting, all three of us are once again living abroad. Molly has settled in Paris and, after months struggling with the language, almost out of money (she survives by cashing in her return boat ticket), she at last finds a job in a bank. I'm in England with my new husband, Patrick Lucas, who has a post-doctoral fellowship at the University of London. Kate is in India with Jim O'Toole, her Harvard "pen pal", whom she's recently married. He's been awarded a Fulbright Fellowship to study Indian religions. Resurrecting her Creole, Molly writes me, *We spread out all over the world now, no true, Pet?*

A year or so before that, newly arrived in Paris, Molly had written to announce her engagement – not to Paul Herman, as I'd expected, but to David Lewis. She explained that on her way to France, she stopped off to see David, who'd just returned to England from British Honduras. On a trip through Wales, David asked her to marry him. She didn't say "yes" right away, worried by the religious differences between them, but she didn't say "no." He took her to meet his family, and she liked them very much, especially his mother. Not long after, David visited her in Paris, prepared to convert to Catholicism, and she accepted his proposal. *I love him very much and simply want to be with him always*, she wrote.

In the letter, Molly enclosed a signed, blank check and asked me to buy and send David several books to help him prepare for his conversion. I chose books by Thomas Merton and Frank Sheed, threw in Augustine's *Confessions*, and mailed the package to David with sincere congratulations.

By her next letter, Molly had broken the engagement. It had been a terrible mistake, she wrote, a thing of the moment. The worst part of the breakup was the letter she'd received from David's mother. Mrs Lewis had written that she hoped someone would break Molly's heart the way she'd broken David's.

When Pat and I visited Molly in Paris during our year abroad, she introduced us to the French lawyer she was dating. Harvard educated, cosmopolitan, several years older than she, Philippe was established in his own law firm. He reminded me immediately of Osmond in *Portrait of a Lady*, a man of refined taste who, I feared, would transform the vibrant, unaffected Molly I knew and loved into an effete, Europeanized stranger.

The marriage lasted five years, during which Molly remained very much herself, in spite of vastly improved French, a salon haircut and a stylish wardrobe. After the divorce, she found a position in international marketing at Printemps, one of the grand Paris department stores, and raised her two sons as a single mother. Meeting her former husband again after many years, I revised my opinion of him. He remains Molly's stalwart friend and a devoted father to her sons.

Just before they sailed for India, Kate and Jim O'Toole stopped in Ann Arbor to visit Pat and me on a trip east from Kate's small Minnesota town to Jim's family home outside Boston. In person, Jim struck me as even more handsome than his photographs. He was perhaps six feet tall, his eyes as blue as Kate's, though his hair was darker, and his good looks the epitome of the clean-cut ideal of our era. At age twenty-five, Jim was already very much a scholar and a gentleman. He was extremely serious and quite formal for so young a man, perfectly suited to genteel Kate, who obviously adored him.

I would see them again several years later in Boston, where I was living at the time. They and their infant daughter were on their way back from a second trip to India, visiting Jim's family before moving to the University of Toronto, where Jim had accepted a teaching position at St Michael's College.

With their daughter and the two sons who followed, Jim and Kate returned often, and for extended periods, to West Bengal to study and teach. Kate eventually completed a PhD in Indian Cultural Studies, published her dissertation on the educational philosophy of Rabindranath Tagore, and joined Jim part-time on the faculty of the University of Toronto.

First Molly and then my second husband, Daniel, and I visit Kate and Jim in Santiniketan in West Bengal, a tranquil village that surrounds a university founded by Tagore to preserve and celebrate Bengali culture. Vestiges of colonial influence remain, but the rituals of a vibrant local community flourish in the ruins of Empire. Comparing notes, Molly, Kate and I agree that the prevailing atmosphere takes us tangibly back to the British Honduras of our youth.

And what of Charlie Bosque?

The first meeting was the weekend after Thanksgiving 1963, at the end of his final year of studies in Colombia. He'd travelled to the States for knee surgery. At the time, I was teaching in Ann Arbor. I'd driven down to my mother's house with Pat Lucas, who was completing a PhD in psychology at the University of Michigan, to spend the holiday with my family. We announced our engagement during Thanksgiving dinner.

When I spoke with Charlie by phone, I told him Pat was with me and that we'd both drive up to meet him at the Jesuit Residence in St Louis, where he was staying. Throughout the fall, I'd written him about Pat and assumed he realized the relationship was serious. I decided to wait to tell him about the engagement face to face.

The weather that weekend was raw and windy, the dove-grey sky brooding snow. As we parked outside the residence, Charlie, who must have been waiting at the door, came out to meet us on the steps. His cassock whipped his legs. I was shocked at how woefully displaced he looked without the sea and bush as backdrops.

Afterward, Charlie wrote me that our meeting was one of the most painful experiences of his life, and I felt the same way. We both confronted the reality of our choices. As he wrote me later, *I have always wanted your happiness, and so my will helped me to see what was best for you. Love Pat with all your heart. I have no jealousies for that.*

The truth was I loved both men. I'd fallen in love with each of them at different times, in different circumstances. Both were extraordinary human beings. I'd chosen between them when I chose marriage over a committed religious life, but I hadn't fallen out of love with Charlie. Contrary to everything I'd ever read, one love didn't cancel out the other. They existed side by side, expressing themselves in different ways. I loved Charlie and expected to spend the rest of my life apart from him. I loved Pat and expected to spend the rest of my life with him in a way I had never conceived of spending it with Charlie.

In my letters to Charlie, I must have conveyed some of these thoughts. In any event, he thanked me *for writing in the way you did. You have poured reassurance on me. God brought us together – made you part of my life – and that is the way it will be.*

Not quite five years later, I saw Charlie again, once more in St Louis. He'd returned to the States, this time from Belize City, where he was teaching at the Jesuit high school, to see his doctors and talk with his superiors.

It was the summer of 1968, and Pat was dying of cancer. He'd been ill most of the previous year. When we returned from London, a medical team at Barnes Hospital oversaw his care, coming to our apartment to deliver the pain medication they trained me to administer. Charlie visited us one evening, asked me to clear off the top of the dresser, and celebrated Mass in our bedroom. A few weeks later, Pat died.

When I think of how robust he was when I first met him! Charlie wrote just after.

For a long time, Charlie and I stayed in touch. After he left the Jesuits in the early 1970s, he took on several part-time jobs before he accepted a full-time teaching position at St John's College, where he had been a student and then taught as a Jesuit. Occasionally, he mentioned various girlfriends and even sent me a photo of one of them. Two years after Pat's death, I met, fell in love with and married Dan.

It seems to have been clear to both Charlie and me that our time as possible lovers had passed. Perhaps he wouldn't put it this way, and maybe in fact he wouldn't agree, but I think we taught each other that while love transcends boundaries, passion exists in space and time.

After my second marriage, our correspondence slowed down. Months and then years went by between letters. The last I heard, Charlie was still single, still living with his mother and Aunt Bitsy in the old house where I'd visited the two women on trips to Belize City. Sometime in the mid-1980s, his letters stopped completely. Several of mine to him were returned, marked "address unknown". Around that time, I moved and had no way to send him my new address.

I thought of contacting the Quinlans for news of him, but by then twenty-five years had gone by since I'd last seen them. Was Lydie still alive? Would she remember who I was? Did she still live in Angel Creek? The only address I had was for the house that had burned down.

It's Sister Jean who tracked Charlie down for me. In the 1990s, she returned to Angel Creek as principal of the co-ed high school that replaced St Monica's. In one of my letters to her, I asked if she had any news of the former Father Bosque. In reply, she sent his address with the news that he had been very ill. Almost died, in fact. The doctors had given up hope.

Not long after, I receive a letter from him, the first in almost fifteen years. *You will think that this is a voice from the dead,* it begins. *I was almost dead – gave everything I owned away, what few possessions I had. But now I am doing better.*

He writes that he has never married. *Couldn't find anyone compatible,* he explains. He goes on to tell me that after first his aunt and then his mother died, the old house was sold, torn down, and a commercial building erected on the site. He then moved into an apartment with one of his nephews who needed a place to live. He has few family members left in Belize, he says. Over the years, most have moved away to Canada, the States, or Great Britain. His sisters Lydie and Dolly are in their eighties, both in poor health, and he doesn't see them as often as he'd like.

But he's not alone, he assures me. He's taken under his wing a young couple with a baby daughter who live near him. He's "Grandpa Charlie" to the little girl, and they've become like family.

Other promises in our long lives we won't keep; other vows will be broken. But I send news of Charlie's near-fatal illness to Molly in Paris and Kate in Toronto and with almost no discussion, we agree. It's time at last to keep the promise we made more than forty years ago, and return to Belize – and Charlie – together.

Epilogue

WHERE THE RIVER MEETS THE SEA

EARLY IN MARCH 2004, Molly, Kate and I find ourselves back in the town we still call "Angel Creek", though it was officially renamed Ahariduna in the mid-1970s by the Garifuna majority.

Molly has come from Paris and Kate from Toronto, both via Miami, travelling the last leg of the journey together. Kate has sacrificed her annual trip to India to join us; her husband Jim is there without her this year. I've come from Indiana with my husband, Daniel, where we've lived since our marriage in 1970. After earning PhDs from the University of Notre Dame, we both found careers at nearby St Mary's College. I teach literature in an interdisciplinary programme of cultural studies, and Dan oversees academic computing at the college.

The four of us meet Charlie in Belize City, where he has lived for the past three decades, and we travel together by bus to Angel Creek. The man we've remembered through the intervening years as a lithe and beautiful thirty-year-old is now in his seventies. His body is bent, his knees so ruined by arthritis that he can barely walk. But his hair, still dark as his mother's was at his age, has only traces of grey. His husky voice remains unchanged and unmistakable. His fierce energy and intense spirit are undiminished.

For our first few hours together, we can't keep our eyes off each other. We search each other's faces, study our gestures for signs of who we were and who we are now. Charlie tells us he'd recognize us anywhere, but I don't believe him. I see the look in his eye, as though he's viewing us through a lens that needs adjusting.

I feel that way myself, not only with Charlie but also with Kate and Molly.

I'd seen Molly as recently as the previous summer, but it took me a minute to recognize her as well as Kate when they arrived together in a taxi from the Belize airport. True, I was looking down from the third-floor balcony of our hotel, but when the taxi doors opened and they climbed out, I saw two attractive, middle-aged strangers.

At our guesthouse in Angel Creek, just as I'm about to step into the shower, my husband sees the announcement scrolling across the TV screen. "Listen to this!" he calls out and begins reading aloud: "The American teachers are back! Reunion tomorrow night at the Ahariduna Town Hall to welcome Miss Eliot, Miss Mannion and Miss Porter, who taught at St Monica's 1962 to 1963. Dinner seven o'clock sharp." There's a number to call for reservations, he tells me.

I wait in disbelief for the message to reappear. No one has mentioned a reunion dinner. Who'll remember us after so much time? As I stand there wrapped in my towel, the lights in the room flicker and go out, and the screen goes dark.

"Same old Angel Creek," I say. But within a few minutes, the electricity comes back on and stays on.

When we pick up Charlie at the home of James, his nephew – one of the Quinlan sons, now a man in his fifties – James's wife tells us that Sister Jean is the one who arranged the gathering at the town hall. It was supposed to be a surprise. No one, it seems, had anticipated our viewing the announcement on cable TV.

Because of confusion about the actual date of our arrival, we hear we've missed a welcoming parade, also arranged by Sister Jean. The Quinlans describe how, the previous afternoon, the uniformed high school students marched through the streets with banners flying, celebrating our return.

A few days before I left home, Sister Jean had telephoned me from Angel Creek, distraught. She'd been unexpectedly called away to a meeting at her motherhouse in New Orleans and would miss our arrival. Even though I assured her we'd still be in Belize when she returned and would see her then, she seemed inconsolable. Now I understand why. She's missing all the celebrations she planned.

"Do you recognize her?" Charlie asks in a low voice.

I turn, and there is the tiger skin – Charlie's tiger skin, and briefly, long ago, my tiger skin – hanging on the Quinlans' living room wall. Not long before my first marriage, I'd written that I wanted to return it to him. He

Figure 18. Charlie, Molly, Abby and Kate reunited, 2004. Photo courtesy of Daniel Mandell.

replied that he understood my feelings and if I insisted on sending it back, he'd keep it for James, who'd been with him when he shot her.

"I'm glad she's where she belongs," I say.

In the Riverside Café, on the south bank of the Angel Creek River (still called by its pre-Independence name), we sit long over our dinner of rice and beans and fried plantains, drinking bottles of Belikin, the excellent local beer, talking about all the changes. Paved roads, even a few three- and four-lane highways. Cars, trucks and buses everywhere. Well-built houses fanning out from the sea. Telephones. Internet cafés. Most astonishing of all, perhaps, the satellite dishes on most of the homes.

The next morning when we go back for breakfast, the proprietor of the Riverside Café says, "I saw you with that priest last night." She's the daughter of the Morrises, the couple who ran the pharmacy all those years ago.

"Do you mean Charlie?" I ask. "He's not a priest anymore. Hasn't been for years."

"Everybody still calls him that," she says. "He's a wild man. Always protesting for some cause, criticizing the government, writing letters to the newspapers, rabble-rousing. Knows how to take care of everybody but himself. He almost died, you know. The doctors gave up on him."

I think of the young family he's adopted in Belize City. We met the young mother and her little daughter while we were there, and she told us how much he'd done for them, seeing them through hard times financially and in other ways too, "like a priest would".

I'd heard a similar story from the taxi driver who drove us from the Belize airport to our hotel. He asked if we were visiting someone, and when I mentioned Charlie by name, he said, "Oh, Charlie Bosque. He dat radical Jesuit."

The period after he left the Jesuits, I realize, is the one I know least about. In one of his letters to me, he described his experience of the priesthood as one humiliation after another. The suspicion and prejudice he encountered daily finally drove him out, he said. He had been lifted up only to be brought low. After that, from what I've been able to piece together, he went through a dark time, drinking too much, not taking care of himself. I know little about the shape of that darkness, but I can now see for myself that he has found his way into the light again. I also see how much a priest he still is and always was – not in any institutional sense but in his deepest being.

Throughout the day, Molly, Kate and I run into people who assure us they'll be at the town hall that evening, even though none of us remembers who they are. We hope to see Josie and Gilly but find out Josie now lives in the States and – how can it be? – Gilly has passed away. So many others we knew have died: Mr Zacharias, Dr Bauer, and, most tragic of all, Sherry Cain, dead in her forties of cancer. Others like Josie, Julian Martin, Sissy Quinlan and Ana Zacharias now live in Canada or the United States. Eduardo has stayed in Belize and, we hear, lives in a mansion outside Belize City. "He's a big man now," people tell us. "Very rich – and also very fat, just like his father before him." Marita, mother to the youngest Zacharias children, is still alive, still living in the same apartment above the club. We wonder if we should visit her. "She wouldn't recognize you," Charlie says. "She doesn't recognize anyone now."

Our former neighbour Therese has left word at our guesthouse that she still lives in the same place and is counting on a visit. We go that morning. Over the years, her solid concrete house, built just after Hattie, has more than doubled in size with the addition of a large, modern kitchen, a family room and an entire second storey.

"Dis me hozbahn," she says, introducing a portly man with a greying goatee, not much taller than she. He asks us to call him "Papa Joe". Therese reminds us that Papa Joe was away the entire time we lived in Angel Creek. In fact, with only occasional visits home, he has spent most of his working life in the States. He says that many Belizeans who have lived abroad, even those who've become citizens of the United States or Canada, retire in Belize. He assures us that he missed his family and Belize terribly during all those years, but the money he earned bought the family the life they now enjoy. Not only do they own their house but also they've invested in a cooperative citrus plantation in the valley. He invites us to visit the plantation with him the following day.

After his return to Angel Creek, Papa Joe tells us, he was elected to consecutive terms as mayor. He worked to pave the roads and install the telephones, Internet, and cable television that have modernized Angel Creek.

In answer to our questions, Therese tells us their children and nieces and nephews are all grown and doing fine. She shows us family photographs, including several of the former "Ugly Baby", now a handsome, forty-two-year-old who owns his own business repairing electronics and renting out videos and DVDs in one of the stores on Market Street.

Even though Therese and Papa Joe have officially retired, they stay involved in community life, they tell us. As a team, they volunteer as marriage counsellors.

"Befoe, most Garifuna marry, but no longah," Therese says.

"De big challenge is getting de men involved in family life," Papa Joe agrees.

"Or work," Therese adds. "Mos men heah only lazy! Women do mos ahl de work." She blames what she refers to as "de tribal influence". We'd seen it in our time, too, but she insists it has grown much worse. Garifuna women need to join together to do something about it, she says. She's hopeful, because awareness of the problem seems to be growing.

Over tea and biscuits, Molly says, "Therese, do you know you were our first friend in Angel Creek?"

Therese turns to my husband. "Dese gals, dey difrant. Dey no stahnoffish. No lak some ah de nons an' priests dat no accep' Garifuna ways." She adds that the Charity sisters, who came after we left, were more open to Garifuna culture. They tried to speak the Garifuna language and even brought drums to church.

"But you," she says, turning back to the three of us. "You de fust wite people we evah grow close to. We don' fohget you, and now we know you don' fohget us!"

We spend the afternoon exploring Angel Creek. The town is, if not much larger, certainly more substantial than it was just after Hattie. Prosperous, even. Like Therese and Papa Joe's house, many of the buildings are concrete. Not only are the main roads paved but the bridges are wider. Automobiles, trucks, motorcycles and bikes crowd the length of Market Street. Replacing the old pier, a new, broad pier stretches far into the sea. At the small café on Market Street where we have lunch, the waitress tells us she is from Punta Gorda. She plans to return soon because she can't take the "fast pace" of Angel Creek.

Most of the old landmarks remain: the church, the convent, the post office and police station. But it seems symbolically appropriate that all the buildings that were the product and pride of the old order are visibly worn. Compared with the spacious, imposing houses that today line Front Street, the convent and the church, new when Hattie hit, now look like aged relatives. Cracks line the unpainted concrete facade of the church, the convent veranda and balcony sag, and some of the slats from the railings have gone missing. A rectory built after we left sits on the site of the old one, across from our former house. It is weathered but solid, an unquestionable improvement on the old "wrecktory". Although there are Jesuit missionaries from the States in other parts of Belize, the two priests in Angel Creek are Claretians from Ireland and Great Britain. They are probably the age of Fathers O'Dea and Peck when we knew them – a good twenty years younger than the three of us are now.

Dr Bauer's sturdy little house is unpainted, and when we peer in the windows we see it's empty. Our former house, too, is between tenants. For several years, we learn, it was used as a classroom for the youngest children. All the interior walls have been removed. The back end of the house that held the tiny kitchen and bathroom is gone. Father O'Dea's fancy stairway and porch railing are gone, too, replaced by raw, unpainted boards. Had ours really been one of the nicest houses in town?

In far worse shape is our old school, dilapidated, the upper stories boarded up. A Chinese family lives on the ground floor, we're told. Their laundry hangs under the first floor porch, lots of baby clothes in the mix. A vacant lot behind the building is littered with trash.

Decades ago, St Monica's merged with the boys' school and the smaller Anglican school. This co-ed, ecumenical high school, the best in town, offers college prep courses. We learn that the school where Sister Jean is principal was established only recently to serve students who want a more practical education.

When, a few days later, we visit its new facilities, we find writing and math classes tailored towards business. The school has a computer lab, even though the donated equipment is out of date, my husband tells me. There are also courses in industrial arts and home economics. Almost without exception, the four hundred students at Jean's school are Garifuna girls and boys.

I meet my counterpart, a young volunteer teacher from the Midwest. She teaches English, and her special project is building up the high school library with donated books from the States. She tells me that she shares a house with several other volunteers, males and females living together. Some are Peace Corps volunteers, others connected with the Jesuit Volunteers, who've replaced the Papal Volunteers of our day, phased out in the early 1970s. She says she's been in Angel Creek for almost a year, with one more year to go.

"They'll be two of the best years of your life," I tell her.

She looks unconvinced. "It's a very hard life here," she says.

Once I grow used to the obvious changes, I begin to feel at home. Roosters crow, chickens scratch in backyards, unleashed dogs ignore all boundaries, groups of schoolboys and young men gather in the late afternoon for pickup soccer and baseball games in the grassy field along the sea, just like long ago. In fact, as with Charlie and the three of us, the closer we look, the more familiar Angel Creek becomes. Past and present meld. In a few weeks we won't be able to remember, as Dylan Thomas wrote in an entirely different context, "whether it snowed for six days and six nights when I was twelve or whether it snowed for twelve days and twelve nights when I was six."

It's true that women no longer wash their clothes at the mouth of the river, nor do they carry tins of water home on their heads. Most houses have running water, and we discover several laundries in town where attendants wash and dry clothes in automatic machines for a few Belize dollars a load. In contrast to forty years ago, most of the young girls we pass on the street now wear shorts or tight jeans and tops that leave their belly buttons exposed. But most of the older women still wear the bright, full-skirted dresses of their youth, and the boys in their khaki shorts and the men in their dark pants and loose shirts look much as we remember.

As I walk along the lanes and across the field to the sea, space and time disappear in the salty sting of the sea breeze and its familiar fish-and-seaweed smell that I now label "spermy". My physical being reverberates with the insistent rhythm of water lapping the shore and wings flapping overhead as seabirds trace the ocean's edge. During the coming days, I find myself again exuberant in the overwhelming sensuality of Belize: the enveloping fragrance of citrus blossoms, the musky dankness of mangrove swamps, the sickish-sweet taste of papaya, the hazy violet-blue of distant mountains. In spite of all the changes, alive within me is the village of fifty years ago and the young woman who lives there still. A line from a poem by Wallace Stevens comes back to me: "Beauty is momentary in the mind – the fitful tracing of a portal; / But in the flesh it is immortal."

When we arrive at the "surprise" dinner that night, an attractive, middle-aged woman who reminds me of Lydie Quinlan meets us as the door. It's her daughter Alma. She leads us into the hall, decorated with crêpe paper and coloured lights. Molly, Kate, Dan and I are to be seated at the head table with the mayor of Ahariduna and his wife and a number of other local dignitaries. There's a podium to one side, with a microphone, a sign of speeches to come.

Alma takes us into a large kitchen off the main hall, where a cluster of women are preparing to serve the dinner they've cooked. Several of our former students are there. We're told who's who, who's missing, and who has moved where. Alma tells me that Sissy called from Tampa, where she now lives, to say she's sorry she can't be here.

"Only a handful of us remain in Belize," Alma says. "But all of us who still live in Angel Creek are here tonight."

"I remembah you, Miss, ahl dese years," a dignified Garifuna woman assures me. When she tells me her name, Olga Jean Diego, I recall that she was in my first-year composition class, along with Jean Martinez, Sherry Cain, Jessie Nunez and Sissy Quinlan. Her next remark takes me completely by surprise. "My first dahtah, she named aftah you, Miss."

"Are you telling me I have a namesake?" I ask, not sure I've understood.

"Yes, Miss. She carries your name."

Maybe it's silly, but I feel as though, without my knowing it, part of me has remained here all these years.

Charlie sits at a corner table with his nephew and his wife and Lydie and Al Quinlan, old now and a bit confused about who we are. With them is a woman Charlie introduces as Marie Sharp, the daughter-in-law of a prominent family from the district. She's famous all across Belize, we hear, because of her thriving business producing a wide variety of bottled sauces, some sweet, most hot and spicy. She invites us to come tour her factory in the valley when we visit Papa Joe's plantation. When we go, we find a small, well-organized plant that employs local workers, most of them female. On her four-hundred-acre farm she grows most of her own ingredients, harvested from fields of peppers, carrots, pineapples and papayas, and groves of mango, coconut, tamarind and annatto trees. After that, in every café and restaurant, no matter how small, we notice a bottle of her red and another of her green hot sauce on each table.

The reunion dinner begins with introductions by a master of ceremonies, hired for the occasion, followed by long, eloquent tributes by our former students. My doubts about their accuracy are confirmed when Dan is introduced first as my husband and fifteen minutes later, as Kate's. We hear that we've become legends in our years away, credited with inspiring our students to become poets, orators, dramatists and journalists. "They taught us to sing in French!" one of the speakers claims. (" 'Frére Jacques', 'Alouette' and 'Sur le Pont d'Avignon' were the extent of it," Molly whispers.)

When the encomiums are finished, we're asked for our memories. I mention the first thing that pops into my mind, a recollection of falling asleep on the beach and waking up, like Gulliver surrounded by Lilliputians, with village children leaning over me and staring at me intently. It's something I haven't thought of for forty years, didn't even know I remembered. I see the puzzled expressions on the faces before me – such an insignificant memory for so momentous an occasion. I don't try to explain, can't quite wrestle into words the significance of that awakening, with its unsettling feeling of boundaries crossed and reality redefined. For a fleeting instant back then and maybe for the first time in my life, I'd seen myself through the eyes of others, a stranger to myself as well as to them. They took me in, and I returned the favour.

Molly, Kate and I are presented with gifts that amaze and delight us: hand-painted seashells, hand-woven baskets, carved wooden fish and birds, all made by the students at Jean's school. A local author, Felicia Hernandez, gives each of us an inscribed copy of her autobiography, filled with family stories. When I open it later that night, I encounter a grandmother who has found her voice.

Figure 19. Garifuna dancers at the reunion dinner, 2004. Photo courtesy of Daniel Mandell.

She proudly claims her Garifuna heritage and passes it on through her storytelling.

The dinner is a Belizean feast: rice and beans cooked with coconut milk in the Creole way, chicken, fry fish (a Garifuna speciality), green beans, cassava bread with dipping sauce, ginger water (Jean later gives me the recipe: peeled ginger root boiled in water, put in a pitcher with lime juice and sugar, and refrigerated). For dessert, homemade cake and coconut ice cream. A DJ plays recorded music while we eat.

The amplified music stops as one of the local ministers steps up to the microphone to offer a prayer of thanksgiving. Just when I assume the event has come to an end, a troupe of dancers and drummers explodes out of a back room. These are the grandchildren of the Garifuna townspeople we watched years ago from the sidelines on high holidays. The young women, dressed in patterned skirts and white blouses, and men in tight pants and bright shirts immediately begin call-and-response to the beat of the drums. Sometimes the women dance out to meet the men, sometimes the men engage the women, and sometimes one or two dancers break free to dance either alone or together in intricate patterns. It's called "punta" dancing, and there's an entire genre of music called "punta rock", we learn. This district is its centre.

"And now, Teachahs, you dance wid us," one of the young women says, inviting us onto the dance floor.

As Molly, Kate, my husband and I rise, hands reach out to bring us into the circle. Before long, almost every able-bodied person in the room has joined in. Impossible to resist the rhythm of the drums. Our bodies recognize and follow a beat that calls and responds to our throbbing hearts. Like blood moving through our veins, a vital spirit surges through the dancers. I experience it as spiralling gyres of gratitude.

Dancing with the Garifuna that night in Angel Creek remains the purest form of prayer I've ever known. In retrospect, I connect that joyful motion to the worship of Shakers, filled with song and movement, the whirl of dervishes as they spiritually ascend to Allah and the postures of the Hindu god Shiva, who dances creation into and out of existence.

One of the women at the dinner, Phyllis Cayetano, a teacher at the local high school and a friend of Jean's, invites Kate, Molly, Dan and me to her home for breakfast the next morning. She says she wants us to meet her husband, Roy. He studied at the University of Toronto, where Kate teaches, and also the University of Michigan, where I earned a master's degree. Phyllis tells us that her husband loves Rabindranath Tagore, the subject of Kate's dissertation, and adores poetry, the subject of mine. He is an expert on Garifuna culture and has written a dictionary of the Garifuna language.

Molly declines because one of her sons, Alexander, and his fiancée, Sylvia, along with her brother, Ted, an emergency room doctor from Chicago, are due to arrive sometime the next morning from Belize City. Phyllis invites them, too, but Molly explains that she isn't exactly sure when they'll arrive. They come too late to join us.

"Such a pity to have missed it," she says when we tell her about it later that day. "I have so many questions, still, about Garifuna culture. It was so full of mystery when we were here. Most of it was behind closed doors."

Roy, we tell her, is as regal as his name, long and straight and thin as a spear, his leonine hair knotted into dreads. He sits at the head of the huge table in a high yellow house that overlooks the river and the sea. People come and go as we eat an elaborate breakfast of fry fish, johnnycakes, hard-boiled eggs, sausage, a spinach-onion pie and refried beans. Several young people who've already eaten, read or quietly converse in a corner. They are briefly introduced, but we're not sure if they are Roy's children or his disciples.

Phyllis, as intelligent as she is beautiful, is a lively talker, but even she becomes quiet when Roy speaks.

He tells us his story. He grew up in a small village south of Half Moon Creek, the schoolmaster's son. His father sent Roy's sisters, rather than his sons, off to high school – much the same story I'd heard from one of my students forty years before, told this time from the brother's point of view. To earn money for his education, Roy worked as a teacher's assistant for three years and then, without ever attending high school, passed the entrance exams for Belize Teachers College. He subsequently interrupted a career in education a few times to study in the United Kingdom, the United States and Canada.

In answer to our questions, Roy gives us what amounts to a short, fascinating course on Garifuna customs and culture. We talk about Garifuna spirituality, which he defines as a way of being that enables the human community (the "earth world", in his words) to stay in touch with the spirit world and its inhabitants, the spirits of the ancestors. The elders mediate such contact, he says, as does a spiritual leader called the *buyei*, a Garifuna word he translates as "the chosen one". Yes, this leader is a type of shaman or medicine man, he affirms, but make no mistake. The *buyei* can be either male or female.

When we ask about the dances and drumming, Roy talks at length about funeral and other ritual celebrations, called *dügüs* in the Garifuna language. Preparations for a traditional *dügü* can take a year or more. The villages plant cassava and raise piglets for the *dügü* itself, which when it occurs goes on for many days. It begins with a couple of dories going out over a weekend to gather fish. When they return there is a procession, drumming and dancing, followed by feasting. Most *dügüs* go on for as long as nine days, he says.

At the heart of the *dügü* is the *mali*, when people gather in a circle to affirm the community's continuous place in time and space. Three drums are at the centre of the circle and signify past, present and future. The central drum also symbolizes the heart. At the climax of the *mali*, everyone sings, "I for you, my grandmother, and you for me," and "I placate you my grandmother, my grandmother I placate you." He tells us that the grandmother is a key figure in Garifuna spirituality, the living link with the spirit world and a representative of continuity. Through the *dügü* the individual and the community achieve healing and "atonement" – quite literally, physical, social and spiritual "at-oneness".

That he speaks so openly and in such detail about Garifuna traditions amazes me. During my time in Belize, Roy's was a hidden culture, oppressed and in response concealed from public view. I find his revelations even more of a surprise than the public nature of the dancing and drumming the night before. What was once secret is now revealed. With what effect and to what end? I wonder.

As if in answer to my unspoken question, Roy explains that young people are no longer learning the Garifuna language, and few follow the old ways. He and those who work with him are committed to preserving the old language and documenting traditional ways. Otherwise, he fears, they will be lost forever. As he speaks, his pride in his heritage gives me my answer.

Before we leave, Roy asks one of the young men to bring him a drum. "I will recite for you one of my poems," he says. "I call it 'Drums of My Fathers'." As he beats out a slow rhythm, he chants in his thrillingly deep voice:

> Drums of my Fathers
> Rumbling in my bones
> > Organ music.
>
> Drums of my Fathers
> Beating in my mind
> > Jukebox blaring.
>
> Drums of my Fathers
> Capturing my soul
> > Sing a Hymn to Mary.
>
> Words of my Fathers
> Tumbling from my mouth
> > Speak the Queen's English.
>
> Drums of my Fathers
> of my grandfathers
> of my ancestors
> Drumming in my psyche
> Drums of my Fathers
> Drum! Beat!
> Beat on! Drum on!
> And on!

It's more than a poem, I think, the hair on my arms rising. It's a prayer, no less than the dancing last night.

Molly, Kate, Dan and I spend almost every spare minute with Charlie. We have discussions over meals and each evening, late into the night. His favourite subject (along with Notre Dame football and Chicago Cubs baseball) is US politics. He stays up-to-date, thanks to cable TV, and pelts us with questions, forgetting that Kate and Molly have lived outside the United States for most of their adult lives. What do we think of Bush's invasion of Iraq? Is the claim of Weapons of Mass Destruction in Iraq a mistake or a lie? He's inclined to think the latter. We all agree with him.

He bemoans corruption in Belize. The tourist trade has risen to a million visitors a year, he tells us, but only the top officials benefit from the docking and port fees paid by the huge cruise ships. The politicians sell public lands to private developers and keep the profits; inevitably, development and the so-called progress it brings come at the cost of the environment, destroying the rain forests and the wildlife they support. Add to that the drug trade, he tells us, which is big business in Belize, much of it occurring just offshore. Drugs and drug money have turned everything rotten, he says: the political system, the law enforcement agencies, and both public and private morality.

Charlie's temper flares as he talks. "There was so much hope for the future when we were all in Angel Creek," he says, "with the promise of independence and self-government, even though it didn't actually come for another twenty years." He would never want colonialism back, he quickly adds, but the current state of affairs in Belize is, in his opinion, close to chaos: a government deeply in debt, inflation on the rise with recession setting in, and an AIDS crisis, to boot.

"And what happened to Vatican II?" he asks. "Remember the optimism we had in those days, the changes we expected? Today, the Church is in chaos too." News of the sexual abuse scandals of the clergy and the resulting coverup at the highest levels has only recently emerged in the mainstream press. "You'll see, it's just the tip of the iceberg," he predicts.

"It's caused me like so many others to lose faith in the Church as a moral guide," Kate says.

"Ironic, isn't it," says Molly. "Almost everyone in Belize was Catholic then, like most of Mexico and Central and South America. It was the Church that brought the three of us to Belize so many years ago and made us friends. I'm sure we've all changed in many ways since then, but maybe most of all in our attitudes to Catholicism. I know that's true for me."

When she moved to Paris all those years ago, she tells us, it didn't take her long to realize that for most Europeans, Catholicism was dead, "killed by the wars." The churches were museums, not places of worship. If she stayed in Paris, she knew she'd lose her faith.

"I found it impossible to be a good Catholic there," she says, "with everyone living for the day, ridiculing the rules of religion. The greatest cathedrals of Europe are in France, but they are ancient historical monuments linked to a dead past." Being close to nature in Angel Creek, with its "golden, blinding sunsets," all of us believing together, enabled her to feel close to God. "But I couldn't be a Catholic alone," she says. "After a while, I stopped trying."

Charlie tells us that he still considers himself a Catholic, but he's realized that along with respect for certain of the Jesuits he knew as a boy, fear and ignorance were what brought him into the priesthood. "The freest act of my life was when I left. I've never regretted it. I couldn't be a priest in today's church, with a hierarchy that acts like Vatican II never happened. Or even worse, was a big mistake."

Kate cites Pope John Paul II's televized visit to the United States in 1979 as a turning point for her. Sister Theresa Kane, who was at the time the head of the Leadership Conference of Women Religious, publicly challenged the pope to include women in all ministries of the Church. He responded with silence. When he returned to Rome, he issued a condemnatory statement, obviously a response to what she had said. "I saw then that I couldn't reconcile my feminism with Catholicism," Kate says.

She tells us that living in India and Bangladesh exposed her to the patriarchal patterns in all religions. Eventually, she found herself moving away from organized religion towards a more Tagorean view of the world, one that was freer, more creatively intuitive, with an emphasis upon compassion rather than a monolithic code dictated by a hierarchy. "That being said," she concludes, "I continue to love the Catholic Mass and many of the Catholic rituals. And of all things, I still pray to Mary!"

When my turn comes to speak, I credit Saint Augustine's – my small, inner-city, integrated African-American parish – with keeping me in the Church. I'm aware of the contradictions and discrepancies between my own feminism and some of the pronouncements of the hierarchy, especially on women and sexuality, but St A's keeps me involved in one of the best things about

Catholicism, its commitment to social justice. And, I tell them, it makes me part of a diverse community like the one I first experienced in Angel Creek. "It's an essential part of my life," I say, "one I probably wouldn't even know I was missing without Belize."

Molly, Kate and I agree that perhaps the greatest benefit of the year in Belize was that it opened our eyes to the unexamined social and cultural biases we shared with most white Americans of our generation. Even though we couldn't name or analyse it until much later, we independently came to the realization that we were complicit in a system we came to deplore. By propping up the Eurocentric curriculum at St Monica's and abetting the imperialism of both Church and State, we played a part, no matter how unintentional or small, in prolonging the exploitation and denigration of the native people of developing countries like Belize. Our growing awareness prepared us to welcome the coming deluge.

"It's easy to look back now and see the beginnings of change all around us that year we were in Angel Creek," Kate says. "And inside us too. *The Feminine Mystique* was published while we were here, even though I wasn't aware of it till later. But all those books by and about women that we read and discussed primed me for the second wave of the women's movement."

Martin Luther King's *Letter from Birmingham Jail* was also published then, I recall. And the March on Washington and the "I Have a Dream" speech occurred within a few months of our return to the States. We left a segregated America and came home to the beginning of the Civil Rights Movement, with eyes opened wide and able to see what was in front of us.

At the University of Michigan, I'd joined a chapter of the Student Nonviolent Coordinating Committee (SNCC, pronounced "Snick", for short) and helped raise money in support of those travelling to participate in sit-ins and civil rights marches in the southern states. That eventually led me and my first husband to protests and teach-ins against the war in Vietnam.

Sitting on the veranda of Charlie's nephew's house, watching the moon climb from the sea as in the old days, we form a convivial circle. It's expansive enough to include Charlie's nephew and his family, my husband Dan and, once they arrive, Molly's brother and her son and his fiancée.

"This is what I remember best and miss most from our year in Angel Creek," Molly says. "The people, the conversation and camaraderie. It changed us. I realize now how rare and wonderful that time was."

"No matter how far away from each other the stream of life takes us or how long we're apart, our memories of that year tie us together," Charlie says. "And enrich us."

One of my friends has a theory about years. Some years are like that, she says, filled with people and places and events and joys and sorrows that change us forever. They transform us and determine who we are and who we will become. She calls a year like that "a necessary year". That's what Molly, Kate, Charlie and I shared in Angel Creek, each in our own way: a necessary year.

By the end of the week, Jean still isn't back from New Orleans. Molly's son and his fiancée, who have been travelling for several weeks in the Caribbean, go off to the cayes to scuba dive. After that, they'll return to Paris from Belize City. Molly, Kate and I plan to revisit and introduce Molly's brother Ted and my husband, Dan, to some of the places we loved forty years before, beginning with the Pine Ridge. We invite Charlie to come along, but he says with his bad knees, he's better off staying put. We leave word for Jean that we'll return to Angel Creek the following weekend, and I promise to call mid-week to work out details of when and where we'll meet.

In our rented van, we take the Hummingbird to the Western Highway, a quick trip compared to years ago. It's the biggest difference, I think, the effect of the improved roads on my sense of space and time. I'm reminded of my first trip back to my childhood neighbourhood as an adult. A landscape remembered as macrocosmically large appeared reduced to microscopic size. The walk to school that once seemed to take hours I accomplished in fifteen minutes. Here, just as unexpectedly, the microscopic suddenly looms large, in Alice-in-Wonderland mode. When we turn off the highway, we are back in a world where a fifteen-mile drive over unpaved, potholed back roads is reckoned in hours, not minutes.

I've heard that a pine bark beetle has pretty well destroyed the Pine Ridge, but it's worse than I feared. Most of the pines look charred, as if by fire. It's almost as bad as the blasted landscape just after Hattie. The once verdant forest has been ruined for generations to come. But, I console myself, if Angel Creek, now lushly green, is any indication, nature will heal itself in time.

We arrive at our eco-lodge in mid-afternoon. When I made the reservation for the group, I estimated it was within walking distance of the falls Molly, Kate and I remembered from earlier visits. After we settle in the thatched-roofed cottages, lit by battery-operated lanterns and equipped with solar-

Figure 20. Abby, Dan, Molly, Ted and Kate at one of the pools on the Rio On. Photo courtesy of Daniel Mandell.

heated showers, we go searching for "our" falls. The proprietor of the lodge, a crusty old guy from the States who loves Elmore Leonard novels and looks like he belongs in one, gives us directions to what he thinks we're looking for. We wear our bathing suits under our clothes, and when we find the place he's sent us, we pull off our khaki shorts and T-shirts and leap into the pool.

"Is this really the place?" I wonder aloud, looking around. There is a waterfall, but I remember something more dramatic.

"There's no little niche behind the fall," Kate says. "Don't you remember sitting behind the falling water? Abby, I remember your saying it was like being inside an Impressionist painting."

"All three of us fit in that niche," Molly says. "At least, that's what I remember."

But our confidence in our collective memory is shaky. "Maybe it just seems smaller," I say, factoring in the microscopic effect of time, and they agree. But we can't let it go.

"No, this isn't the place," Molly decides a few minutes later. "It's too tame."

She remembers a high ledge of rocks above the falls and along the river that flowed from the pool. "Don't you remember that the year after we left, one of the PAVLA volunteers slipped on the wet rocks and fell into the stream? They didn't find her body for weeks."

"Such a tragedy," Kate says.

We swim, dry off in the late-afternoon sun, and head back to the lodge. There's a small, screened-in pavilion outside our cottages.

"Let's meet there in fifteen minutes," Ted says. He's seven years younger than Molly, a compact, good-looking man whose grey hair belies his smooth, boyish face.

When we gather in the pavilion, Ted lifts an expensive-looking leather case onto the picnic table. Knowing Ted is an MD, I assume it's a medical bag of some sort. He snaps open the latches and pulls out not the stethoscope I expect but a big bottle of gin, another of vermouth, and a couple of smaller bottles of tonic water. The case also contains glasses, various openers and a carafe for mixing martinis.

"It was our dad's," Molly tells us.

"I didn't know he'd passed away," I say.

"Oh, he's very much alive at ninety," Ted says, "but I so obviously coveted it that he gave it to me as an advance on my inheritance."

Thus begins a nightly ritual of pre-dinner booze and conversation. "Just like our orgies of yore," Molly declares. "In fact, now that I think of it, they were the start of my lifelong love-affair with gin and tonics!"

Maybe it's the alcohol, but at supper that night – a fine meal prepared without electricity by our book-loving proprietor and his wife – Kate confronts me after I mention my youngest brother, the one who was born not long before I left for Belize and who now plays in a country rock band, The Bottle Rockets.

"I didn't know you had a younger brother," Kate says, an edge to her voice.

I regard her with disbelief. "I'm sure I told you about him," I say.

"I'm sure I thought you were an only child the entire time we were here," Kate insists.

Reverting to old ways, I remain silent until someone changes the subject. I realize that this time, while we're here together, I have to talk about my silence all those years ago. It may be anticlimactic, but I see it's necessary for me to explain and apologize face to face while we're once again together in Belize.

And I do a few days later, when Kate, Molly and I are alone. As I choke out the first words, the head of Medusa loses her frigid power. At last, I'm able to speak freely about my past, as though a spell has been broken. The last shards of shame, anger and fear melt away.

After our eco-lodge dinner, Ted suggests we go for a nightcap to Blancaneaux Lodge, only a mile or two up the road. That afternoon, we'd passed the entrance looking for our waterfall. It's film director Francis Ford Coppola's jungle retreat, now open to the public.

With its luxury hotel and deluxe cabañas, polished furniture, brilliant native textiles, terraced lawns, lush plantings, crystalline pools and waterfalls, it's a Hollywood version of our eco-lodge down the road. I feel like we've entered an elaborate set on the equivalent of a studio back lot. We hear that helicopters fly in the guests, undaunted by rates we consider exorbitant.

The Courvoisier Ted treats us to in the gleaming hotel bar brings with it a taste of the culture shock Kate and I experienced when we spent the night in New Orleans on our way home from Belize forty years before. "I don't belong here," I said then, walking down Bourbon Street, appalled by what I regarded as its decadent opulence. "This can't be my country!"

The next morning, we continue the search for our waterfall with new directions from the bartender at Blancaneaux Lodge. "Only two miles away. Can't miss it. Just look for the signs," he assured us. We drive around for an hour, stopping to explore a spacious cave along a fast-moving stream, once inhabited by the Maya. On its bank is a giant kapok tree, sacred to the Maya, a sign informs us. But no waterfall.

We give up the search and drive on to El Cayo and Xunantunich. When we stop for lunch at a roadside restaurant, Molly buys some postcards. And there it is, among them – a photo of our waterfall, cascading over a tall, rocky ledge into a wide and deep pool, just as we remember it. It's identified only as one of the falls on the Rio On.

"At least it really exists," Molly says.

"I guess we weren't meant to find it this trip," Kate sighs.

We find Xunantunich with no trouble at all. The same manually operated car ferry takes us across the river to the site of the ancient Maya ruins. There we find a parking lot, entrance fees and a concession stand, incontrovertible signs that modern civilization has also found its way here. Where there had once been grassy mounds, massive buildings now stand, some of them forty feet tall.

Old snapshot in hand, we search for the half-excavated wall where David Lewis took our photograph in 1963. We want another on the same spot. Nothing matches. At last, we settle on a wall with a ledge we can perch on, Molly and Kate sitting, me standing as in the original photo. Even before we see the developed photographs, we know we've failed to reproduce the original. Our shadow selves are nowhere to be seen.

There are, however, consolations in the place as it is now. We climb to the top of the reconstructed El Castillo with its panoramic views. To the north and east, we see Xunantunich unearthed and restored, acre upon acre of monumental buildings. To the east and south, the Mopan River Valley and the nearby city of San Ignacio (we still call it "El Cayo") expand before us. And to the west, we overlook the hills of Guatemala to the far horizon.

By mid-afternoon, we're ready to head towards the Placencia Peninsula. It's hard to believe we can arrive by nightfall, but that's what we've been told. Looking at the map, the distance is about a hundred miles, but we have to zigzag our way there. From the Western Highway we turn off onto the Hummingbird just before Belmopan, the capitol of Belize, built after Hattie, and follow the Hummingbird almost to the sea. We then follow the Southern Highway for about twenty-five miles before turning onto a thirty-mile road down the Placencia Peninsula. Before the Southern Highway was built, the trip would have taken not hours but days – if the weather permitted.

Until the turnoff from the Southern Highway, we make excellent time. But the last thirty miles are torture. The road is unpaved, a lunar strip of craters, and it's dark by the time we reach Placencia, the only town of any size on the peninsula that bears its name. The town itself is a few miles past Sand Bight, our actual destination, but with a larger choice of hotels and restaurants.

Dusty, exhausted, hungry, we're at the low point of our journey. We take the first rooms we find, tiny and (it turns out) airless, in a B&B next to a bar where (we discover) a band blares deep into the night. For what seems like hours, we stand in line for a table in a palm-roofed restaurant overlooking the Caribbean. The food is so-so, the prices inflated. For the first time since our return, we feel like tourists.

As he pays for our dinner with a credit card, Dan realizes his passport is missing. We hurry back to our room to search through our luggage. Not there. We finally think to look in the van, where after a frantic search we find it lodged in a crack between the seats.

The next morning, Kate tells us her new, expensive camera is missing. She's sure she had it at Xunantunich and thinks she remembers carrying it from the van to her hotel room along with her luggage. Someone has cleaned her room while we were at breakfast, she says. The camera is gone, but nothing else seems to be missing.

After we conduct without success an inch-by-inch search of her room and then the van, Kate reports the loss to the owner of the B&B, who assures her the staff is known to him, all quite trustworthy. As she leaves his office, she sees a village boy with a suspiciously similar camera and points him out to the owner of the B&B. He talks to the boy, calls his family and later assures Kate that it is indeed the boy's camera, a gift from an uncle in the States.

"I'd really like to leave this B&B," Kate says. "It isn't just the missing camera. The rooms are stifling, and it's very noisy here."

We find a quiet place on the edge of town with enough room for all of us, less expensive, with windows overlooking the sea and a large, open lounge where we can read the papers and order tea and coffee. The beach here, with its blindingly white sand and towering palm and coconut trees, reminds us of Sand Bight, all those years ago. After Angel Creek, Sand Bight is the place we most look forward to revisiting, though not without trepidation. Has it, once a simple fishing village, become like Placencia a resort town?

No. Definitely not a tourist spot. We find the beach littered with discarded plastic bags and bottles, empty cigarette packets and candy wrappers. Most of the houses near the water are dilapidated, the pier broken and the trees snapped off. We identify the hospital, once the pride of the village, abandoned. We see no resemblance to the Sand Bight of forty years ago.

An able-bodied, middle-aged man who stinks of liquor approaches us and asks where we're from. He tells us that Hurricane Iris hit the village hard two and a half years earlier, on 8 October 2001. He talks a bit longer, tagging along as we walk along the beach, before he asks for a handout. We see another man headed in our direction and walk quickly to the van, the two of them unsteadily following us.

"I need cheering up," Molly says.

We decide to stop at the Turtle Inn, a few miles farther on, for a drink. It's another Francis Ford Coppola fabrication, an imitation of a Balinese-style paradise: thatched roof, open-sided wood and glass structures that blur the distinction between inside and outside. We choose seats at an almost deserted bar that overlooks the sea, choppy in the rising wind. The barkeep asks where we're from and tells us he's from Punta Gorda but now lives in Placencia.

"Francis a regla guy," he tells us. "Wayah sarong, go bayahfut." He spends a couple of weeks a year in Belize, we hear, part of it in the Pine Ridge, the rest at Turtle Inn, taking an active interest in "ahl de detail".

"Always the director?" Dan asks.

The barkeep laughs and nods. "Yes, sir, mon, ahlwaz de dahrectah. A gud one!" The year after Francis built the Turtle Inn, he says, Iris destroyed it. But Coppola rebuilt within two years, even though aid from the government was not forthcoming.

When we ask why not, he answers, "Politics," and explains that this area of the country is "red", traditionally voting for the opposition party, the UDP (the United Democratic Party). The "blues", or PUP (People's United Party), are the majority party and control the government and its allocation of relief funds, which – according to our source – go to their supporters.

"Dis spot one ah de worse foh hurricanes an' strong wind," he says. As if to prove his point, the wind gusts and our paper napkins fly away. "Time to close op and move inside, mistahs and mizzhuhs," he announces.

The following day the wind is blowing too hard to go to Silk Grass Caye for snorkelling, as we've planned, so we travel across the lagoon to Monkey River by speedboat. It's a quick trip into the past. All around us are the mangrove swamps we once paddled through with Father Bosque, less mysterious now in the noonday sun. In Monkey River, we transfer to a smaller craft and head upriver into the rain forest, in search of the howler monkeys that have given the village its name.

Our guide introduces himself as "Percy, King of the Howlers". He tells us he's a mix of East Indian and Creole, a "medicine man" who knows all the flora and fauna of the bush because he grew up there. Anchoring our boat along the riverbank, he leads us on a long trek into the bush, demonstrating his knowledge by pointing out and identifying plants hidden in crevices, naming the bright birds flashing by, and just when we think there are no monkeys to be found, sighting a family of them high in the treetops. He then justifies his title with ear-piercing howls that cause a ruckus in the leaves above us. We suddenly see half a dozen monkeys performing acrobatic leaps from branch to branch.

Like it or not, we're in full tourist mode by the time we return to the peninsula. The beach at Sand Bight has been a bitter disappointment, but we search out others along the peninsula that astonish us with their beauty.

"See, we didn't make it up," we tell Dan and Ted, who more than once have wondered if we're romanticizing the past. "You can see it's really like what we remember!"

She's now in her late fifties, but the minute I see the small, solid woman dressed in the contemporary garb the Sisters of the Holy Family in Belize now wear (the traditional Garifuna blouse with a dark, full skirt), I recognize Jean Martinez, now Sister Jean. She stands on the balcony of the Angel Creek convent, waiting for us as we drive up in our rental van. Grizzled hair under her short veil, yes, but her face is the same smooth brown, her eyes brightly alert and alive, her smile dazzling. When she speaks, I hear the deep, rich voice I remember.

"Well, hello, Miss Portah," she says. "My Miss."

I wish I could say that I never lost contact with any of those who were so important to me during that year in Angel Creek, but the truth is, most of my correspondence with former students petered out after a letter or two. Even with Molly and Kate, sometimes a year would go by with only a Christmas card, if that. Jean is the only one who writes faithfully. On my birthday, I receive cards and, lately, telephone calls from her. She sings "Happy Birthday to You" to me in her lovely alto voice. Every now and then a gift arrives, one of them the beautiful gold earrings that I wear to our meeting.

Dan and I have driven up from Placencia to meet Jean. At week's end, we'll see her again with Kate, Molly and Ted, but I've promised her this one day alone together.

For several hours, we sit in an upstairs parlour in the nearly deserted convent. Only two sisters now live here, along with a few female students from the high school who've come from distant villages. We meet one of them when we go to the kitchen to make ginger tea. Jean tells us they help the sisters with the cooking and cleaning in return for room and board. She says the congregation is trying to sell the building to the diocese. She and her companion will then move to a smaller place.

"It's too big for us," she says, "built for an earlier time when we had many sisters. Now, as you can see, it's falling down around our ears." Even though it needs repair, the spacious, colonial-style structure, with its high-ceilinged

Figure 21. Kate, Sister Jean, Molly and Abby, where the river meets the sea. Photo courtesy of Daniel Mandell.

rooms, each tall window fitted with folding shutters against the subtropical sun and high winds off the sea, offers sanctuary in a restless world.

During our time together, Jean shows us her collection of favourite books and stacks of personal journals, written over many years. She fills us in on her research for her master's thesis, which argues for the integration of Garifuna healing rites into Catholic communal worship. She then reads to me from her poems. One of them has won a prize and several have been published.

"I have always written since our days together, Miss," she tells me. "Do you recall how you made me write each day at your dining table? When I couldn't think of anything, you would say, 'Just sit there till you do.'"

She adds that Jessie Nunez, another of my former students, is also a published poet and writer of folk tales. "You gave us that, Miss."

"Yours were the gifts, Jean."

We have lunch at a small restaurant on the river and spend most of the afternoon visiting classes at Jean's school. She takes me to an English class and asks me to give the students advice "like you used to give us, Miss."

"Use verbs," I say. "Active verbs."

Jean chuckles.

We finish the afternoon as we used to, so many years before, with a long walk together along the sea.

If I were writing a novel, this chapter would end with Molly, Kate, Charlie and me back on Kamagacha, our mountain. Past and future selves would meet in a glorious apotheosis as the full moon rose. Indeed, nature seems to be preparing the way for such a triumphal end. We are only a day or two shy of a full moon.

We tell Charlie that before we leave Angel Creek, we want to revisit Kamagacha. Will he go with us? He points out the obvious. He can't possibly climb Kamagacha. Even if he could, he's not sure he could find it after so many years. Too much has changed.

In answer to our questions, he recalls that the mountain is located about twenty miles southwest of Angel Creek, somewhere within the Cockscomb Basin Forest Reserve. He could be mistaken, but he thinks our mountain is near Cabbage Haul Gap. Since the 1980s the area around Cabbage Haul has been designated a wildlife sanctuary and jaguar preserve, he tells us. There's now a paved road into the sanctuary and some well-maintained hiking trails, or so he's heard, but the road he knew – the unpaved road we travelled in the robin's-egg blue Jeep – has most likely returned to jungle long ago. "And there must be scores of mountains just like ours in the Coxscomb Range," he warns.

Nevertheless, Molly, Kate and I decide to have a go at finding it. We make our way to the Forest Reserve and follow signs to a small Maya village with numerous shops that along with souvenirs and local crafts sell entrance tickets to the park. We're told that the actual visitors centre, with information about the park and trails, is another six miles into the Reserve. Unless we know the exact name and location of the mountain we're looking for, we're warned that the forest rangers probably won't be able to help us. Even if they can, we'll have a long hike ahead of us through fairly rough country. No vehicles are allowed beyond the visitors centre.

We know our mountain's name, Kamagacha, and also its precise location: forty years in the past. But we're no longer foolish enough to think our memories will take us back there, not after our fruitless search for our waterfall, the stone wall at Xunantunich and the pristine village of Sand Bight. Looking up from sea level, we conclude that it's enough to stand in Kamagacha's shadow as the sun slowly moves to the west.

Our last night together, we join Charlie for a farewell dinner at a restaurant overlooking the sea. It's a balmy evening, and we choose a table on the terrace. To accompany our red snapper – we remember it as our favourite dish forty years ago – we decide to order wine, an extravagance in Belize. Molly chooses a California chardonnay, which she judges excellent, even though, she says with a smile (and we all agree), it doesn't quite measure up to our shared memory of the unconsecrated altar wine the Angel Creek priests provided on special occasions.

"This is just like old times," Charlie says.

For hours, we sit around the table, eating and drinking together, telling stories, sharing our lives. And there it is, where the river meets the sea – a full moon rising.

AUTHOR'S NOTE

IN WRITING THIS MEMOIR, I have discovered that memory – anchored in personal experience – and imagination – impatient to fly free of the constraints of exactitude – are indispensable and at times contrary collaborators. Even though I base my work on copious letters, diaries, journals, photos and other material from the time, memoir is at best an art of approximation and this narrative in essence a recreation.

To preserve privacy and also to acknowledge and emphasize that what I write here is my interpretation of actual people, places and events, I've changed the names of some of the people and a few of the places central to the story, most notably those of the main characters, the town where we lived, and a few of the villages whose inhabitants I describe in detail.

To convey to the reader a sense of the lived experience of an earlier time and place, I have employed a literary approach that may seem unusual in a work of non-fiction. Perhaps the most obvious reconstruction is my use of dialogue throughout the memoir. All the conversations are based on exchanges that actually took place. Sometimes they are transcribed word-for-word from primary sources – in most cases, letters and diaries. (Of course, those sources themselves were not literal transcriptions but reconstructions from memory.) More often, the conversations in the memoir are based on memories shared by "Molly", "Kate", "Charlie" and me or on summaries and allusions in the primary sources available to me. They are, however, no less autobiographical than if I were writing a play or film script based on my experiences. That being said, everything I've written here is as "true" as memory and language allow.

ACKNOWLEDGEMENTS

WRITING THIS ACCOUNT TOOK more than ten years. I accomplished it only with the cooperation, collaboration and support of many. Foremost among them are "Molly", "Kate" and "Charlie". We talked and wrote extensively about the project, sharing memories and material. Fortuitously, my mother, the late Genevieve Foley Henneman, my grandmother, the late Augusta Donovan Foley, and my friends Vincent Massaro, Sally Hohn Cantwell and Sally's husband John saved and later returned to me the letters I had written to them during my year in Belize. "Kate" shared letters and a diary from that year. Although almost all the letters "Molly" wrote were lost along the way, she contributed an autobiographical statement that I used with her permission in writing the book. She also gave me permission to include copies of photographs she took in 1962 and 1963. Her son, Alexander Zimmers, scanned some of them for me. Her brother Tighe Zimmers and my husband, Dan, made available photographs they took of the return journey. Ken Jameson, our long-time friend, kindly allowed the use of one of his photographs, taken in Central America, for the cover. In addition, "Charlie" approved the use of photos he took in 1962 and gave me permission to quote freely from his letters and other writings. In the text, I use italics to distinguish excerpts quoted from letters and diaries written at the time from the memoir itself, which I composed over the past decade. The exception is student writing.

Particular thanks go to my former students Sr Jean Martinez, SSF, and Jessie Nunez for allowing me to quote excerpts from poems and essays they wrote as class assignments. Excerpts from the student newspaper are either paraphrased or quoted directly from the original. Some of the other student work is reconstructed from notes or from memory.

Thanks, too, to all those who read and responded to multiple drafts of the manuscript with constructive comments, criticisms and suggestions, chief among them Ann Kimble Loux, on whose gifts as an editor and critic I relied throughout the entire writing process; Charles Woods, my source on Creole culture and language; and Malilee Zimmers, Kathleen Fridgen O'Connell, and former students Cara Ford Cernak and Kirsten Kensinger, whose detailed critiques challenged me to rethink and revise even as their enthusiasm kept me writing. Others contributing to the project in indispensable ways include my technologically savvy and wonderfully patient, loving and wise husband, Daniel Neil Mandell, Penny Brooke Jameson, Kathleen Hohn Dahm, Dennis Porter, Colleen Stern, Lynn Tyas, Tighe Zimmers, Mary Skinner, Elli Haber, Patricia Cunningham, Margaret Moira O'Brien, and Maureen Cadley, who shared with me her idea of the "necessary year". The members of my multi-generational book group read and discussed the manuscript at a crucial stage: Mary Houser Hagan, Sara Hill Voth, Pat MacDonald, Lynn McDonald, Melissa Thatcher Pitt, Ellymay Wynia and Janet Kelley Barabasi. Thank you, ladies! Many Saint Mary's College colleagues, especially Professors Jerry McElroy, Marcia Rickard (a superb proofreader), Becky Stoddart, Philip Hicks and John Shinners, offered a listening ear as well as sage advice. Paula Lawton Bevington, Dana Greene and Gabrielle Robinson also generously shared their guidance and wisdom. Thanks, too, to the director and staff of the University of the West Indies Press. You were my first choice as publisher, and I'm grateful to Linda Speth, Shivaun Hearne and Allyson Latta, a brilliant editor, for seeing this memoir into print with great consideration as well as professional competence. You were a joy to work with.

Saint Mary's College, Notre Dame, Indiana, helped to fund this project with a faculty development research and travel grant and a year-long sabbatical, both essential to its completion.

Special thanks to Roy Cayetano, who shared some of his vast knowledge of Garifuna life and culture with me, read, corrected and commented on several chapters and kindly gave me permission to quote from his beautiful poem "Drums of My Fathers". Thanks, too, to his wife, Phyllis, who introduced us to her family and graciously welcomed us into their home. Juanita Joseph and her husband, "Papa Joe", also extended to us the warmest of welcomes as did many others, among them Anthony and Sylvia Kuylen and Anthony Chanona, who at the time served as mayor of Belmopan. They, along with all those who attended and contributed to our reunion dinner and the Garifuna dancing afterward, especially Sr Jean Martinez, Alva Kuylen and the late Olga Jean Diego, made our return visit to Belize a joyful homecoming.

Finally, and above all, my love and heartfelt thanks to "Charlie Bosque", "Molly Eliot", "Kate Mannion", the "Bosque", "Quinlan" and "Zacharias" families, and to all our "Angel Creek" students, neighbours and friends for making the year my compatriots and I lived among you an *annus mirabilis* – a miraculous, remarkable, necessary year. You know who you are.

www.ingramcontent.com/pod-product-compliance
Lightning Source LLC
Chambersburg PA
CBHW021339300426
44114CB00012B/1010